T5-ARZ-404

Money and Inflation

Money and Inflation

A New Macroeconomic Analysis

Sergio Rossi

University of Fribourg and Università della Svizzera italiana, Switzerland

Edward Elgar

Cheltenham, UK • Northampton, MA, USA

Published by
Edward Elgar Publishing Limited
Glensanda House
Montpellier Parade
Cheltenham
Glos GL50 1UA
UK

Edward Elgar Publishing, Inc.
136 West Street
Suite 202
Northampton
Massachusetts 01060
USA

A catalogue record for this book
is available from the British Library

Library of Congress Cataloguing in Publication Data
Rossi, Sergio.
Money and inflation : a new macroeconomic analysis / Sergio Rossi.
p.cm.
Includes bibliographical references and index.
1. Inflation (Finance) 2. Quantity theory of money. 3. Money. I. Title
HG229 .R67 2002
339.4--dc21 2001040972

ISBN 1-84064-857-0

Printed and bound in Great Britain by MPG Books Ltd, Bodmin, Cornwall

Contents

List of figures

List of tables

Foreword

by Mauro Baranzini and Alvaro Cencini[1]

> The classical theorists resemble Euclidean geometers in a non-Euclidean world who, discovering that in experience straight lines apparently parallel often meet, rebuke the lines for not keeping straight – as the only remedy for the unfortunate collisions which are occurring. Yet, in truth, there is no remedy except to throw over the axiom of parallels and to work out a non-Euclidean geometry. Something similar is required today in economics (Keynes, 1936/1973, p. 16).

THE QUANTUM THEORY OF MONEY AND PRODUCTION

This important volume by Sergio Rossi is a valuable contribution to what has been defined as the 'quantum theory of money', or the *École de Dijon et Fribourg*, a stream of economic thought headed by Bernard Schmitt which emerged in Switzerland and France in the late 1950s.[2] Linked with the analysis of Ricardo and Keynes, Schmitt's theory is anything but a simple reinterpretation of their works. On the contrary, starting from a new analysis of money, Schmitt undertakes to solve the main problem with which Ricardo was confronted: the determination of an invariable measure of value. The central point of this approach is represented by a concept of production and income that is radically different from the neoclassical or marginalist one. Income is no longer conceived of as a flow of expenditure through time, but as the result of a constantly renewed process of creation at each phase of production of goods and services. The traditional idea of income formation as a continuous or discontinuous function of time is rejected and replaced by what the new school calls a 'quantum theory of production'.

This school of thought claims that income is the instantaneous result of a production although it is necessarily related to a finite period of time. Every time a new production takes place, its measure is given instantaneously through the monetary payment of its cost. This payment is best defined as an emission where money and output define one and the same reality, that is, income. Thus, for Schmitt's school, another difficulty is overcome, the dichotomy between real and monetary phenomena being dissolved. Accordingly, rent, profit and interest represent a variable (endogenous) part of income from labour and, contrary to general opinion, they are not an irreducible component of national income.

After arguing that labour is the sole factor of production, Schmitt developed his theory using the concepts of creation and destruction. Hence, the Keynesian identities between income and the money cost of production on the one hand and between income and its final expenditure on the other hand, are integrated into a theory of 'emissions', production being a positive emission of income ('creation') and final purchase a negative emission ('destruction'). In other words, the payment of wages creates in each period a completely new income which is totally destroyed by its final expenditure, the two operations being logically instantaneous since expenditures become effective only at the very instant they take place.

Within this new approach to macroeconomics, Keynes's identities are firmly established and, for instance, it becomes impossible to explain inflation in terms of disequilibrium, either between saving and investment or between total demand and total supply. If an imbalance actually occurs – and the attentive reader will not miss the point that inflation is indeed defined as a macroeconomic imbalance between total demand and total supply – it must be explained within the necessary equality between the two terms. Identity and numerical imbalance are shown to co-exist, both being in fact required if inflation is to be rigorously defined. Total demand and total supply are thus seen as the two terms of an identity, which may nevertheless differ numerically in value. As is to be expected, new solutions relevant to macroeconomic analysis are presented; for instance, the main cause of inflation (and deflation) is attributed to the present structure of the banking system of payments, whose operations do not conform to the logical definition of money and to its conceptual distinction from income and capital.

It has been repeatedly voiced that this new approach represents a fundamental revolution in macroeconomics; in fact, it is high time for a change if, as maintained by Pasinetti back in 1981, it is true that,

> [o]ne might be tempted to say that the most remarkable feature of contemporary economic theory is its astonishing lack of new ideas. Indeed, with the exception of Keynes, all our economic theory, in its essential aspects, goes back to the nineteenth century. It is shocking: we have been able to refine and polish a great deal, but we have created nothing new (Pasinetti, 1981, p. 43; our translation).

The new analysis of money and production entails a fundamental revision of macroeconomic theory. In this section we introduce the most important contributions of the quantum-theoretical approach, which we shall briefly expound in the following section. Obviously this is not a comprehensive list of all the implications of this new line of thought, since many more issues have already been tackled and solved, and many others still await examination. The branching out of research lines in various directions bears witness to the strength of this new approach to the economic science.

We start by considering the four main issues at the national level: firstly, the determination of prices. As a matter of fact, in order to become economic magnitudes, real goods and services have to be measurable. Prices fulfil the task; yet the issue has long remained open as to whether absolute or relative prices are logically better suited for the task. In other words, is the determination of absolute prices (or values) logically prior to that of relative prices – as is claimed by classical economists – or can relative prices be determined independently of absolute prices, as claimed by marginalist or neoclassical economics?[3]

The solution put forward by the new school is based on the integration between money and output, obtained through monetary emission and gross domestic product. Once the measure of output is determined, the next step is to tackle the problem of capital accumulation, which plays a crucial role in the explanation of pathological states of our economic systems, such as inflation and unemployment.

The causal (sequential) relationships may be represented as follows:

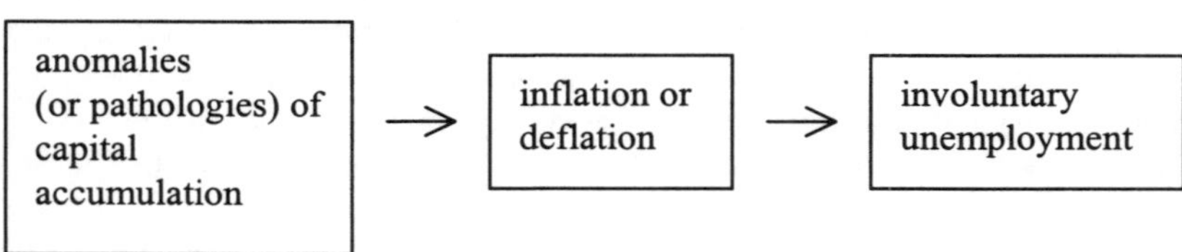

According to the quantum theory of money and production, capital accumulation is based on monetary and financial flows, that is, formation of wages and profits, and investment. While the concepts of wages and profits are straightforward, the analysis of investment necessitates a thorough investigation of the way profits are used by firms. The new approach to macroeconomics maintains that today's bookkeeping structure does not differentiate between redistributed and invested profits. Although profits shared out as interests and dividends are finally spent on goods and services, invested profits are an increase in fixed capital, where fixed capital defines macroeconomic saving, that is, that part of national income which is not consumed but invested in the production of capital goods (or more precisely 'means of production'). In particular, today's payments are entered into a single bookkeeping department, irrespective of whether they refer to distributed or to invested profits. This leads to a gross (normally overlooked) confusion between the formation of money income and capital formation. In order to separate consumption of goods and services from investment, a new bookkeeping technique has been devised. A carefully thought out reform is meant to prevent unwanted inflationary and deflationary phenomena. It should be noted that inflation is defined here as a loss of purchasing power suffered by each monetary unit, caused exclusively by a change in the numerical relationship between (domestic) money and current output of goods and services. As for unemployment, the relevant concept, within this framework, is that of Keynes's 'involuntary unemployment', associated with a lack of demand (deflation). It does not, however, include other forms of unemployment, such as frictional, structural or technological unemployment, which fit the category of 'voluntary unemployment'. We may anticipate the inference that while both imbalances[4] (inflation and unemployment) stem from the same cause (the pathological or abnormal process of capital accumulation), they co-exist only beyond a given stage of the process of accumulation. In the first phase of capital accumulation, inflation will appear first, a deficiency of global demand being the mark of an advanced level of accumulation.

Monetary phenomena, like real ones, have a macroeconomic dimension not only for nations, but for the whole world. In this context a number of issues stand out: firstly, the instability of exchange rates and financial markets; secondly, the charge of external debt servicing, and thirdly, the huge difficulties associated with the process of monetary unification. (The latter is of the utmost importance for the ongoing process of European monetary unification.) In the next section we deal in further detail with the various points mentioned so far.

A NEW WAY TO READ ECONOMIC FACTS

Price Determination

The very first problem every theory has to address is that of determining a unit of measure adequate to its object of inquiry. This is obviously true also in the case of economics. As the best known classical, neoclassical and Keynesian economists well knew, real goods and services must be measured in a common unit if they are to be made homogeneous. Now, things cannot be the same when value is considered as a substance or as a relationship between real goods or again as a relationship between goods and money. According to the idea advanced by the classics, value being a substance (materialised labour-time), the unit of measure applies to each single good, independently of its relationship with any other. There is a disadvantage, however, since labour units are not homogeneous. Different kinds of labour exist and there is no way to reduce them to the same denominator. Classical economists have searched in vain for a unique and invariable standard of value. Ricardo's unsuccessful attempts are there to prove that the search for such a unit was doomed to failure, for it was identified with a dimensional standard. No single or composite good can play this role, neither can labour-time, since time itself (our fourth or eleventh dimension) must be made homogeneous through an appropriate standard. On the whole, the very idea that value may be a substance incorporated into real goods and services is far-fetched. Value is not a metaphysical entity, and Walras had the great merit of introducing economic value as a pure number.

Unfortunately, however, Walras was convinced that value could be derived from the direct exchange between goods. As the new quantum theory shows, however, relative prices are logically undetermined, for relative exchange is unable to define a numerical relationship between goods. The problem is that numbers are not goods, while goods are not numbers. If they were, then the Walrasian general equilibrium system (GES) could provide a solution to the determination of relative prices. Yet, the assumption that goods may be seen as numbers (Debreu, 1959) has no logical foundation. It is as absurd to claim that a 'quantity of well-defined trucks is an integer' (Debreu, 1959, p. 30) as it is to maintain that the whole world is an integer. But, if goods are not numbers, Walras's GES is not a possible solution. The same conclusion is reached when GES is analysed on its own merits. A solution can only exist, in fact, if it is possible to establish an equality between the number of independent equations and that of the unknowns. For example, in the simplest case of a 'two agents–two goods' economy, the following three equations:

(1) demand for good *a* = supply of good *a*,
(2) demand for good *b* = supply of good *b*,
(3) demand for good *a* = demand for good *b*
(or supply of good *a* = supply of good *b*)

must be reduced to a single one in order for the single unknown (the relative price of *a* in terms of *b*, or, equivalently, of *b* in terms of *a*) to be determined. This is done by resorting to Walras's Law, which states that the sum of supplies necessarily equals the sum of demands. In our simple case, Walras's Law claims that the demand for *a* is necessarily equal to the supply of *b* and the demand for *b* to the supply of *a*. Now, while it is true that when equilibrium obtains the three equations are actually reduced to one, it is clearly wrong to assume that Walras's Law applies also during the search for equilibrium. During the phase of adjustment, before exchange actually takes place, supplies and demands cannot be taken to be equal, unless it is assumed that relative prices are given to the market. Free determination through competition can obviously not be reconciled with rigid pre-determination. When the system is meant to lead to equilibrium, equations (1) and (2) are both independent and so is equation (3), since at this stage the equilibrium price of *a* is not necessarily equal to the equilibrium price of *b*. The indeterminacy of relative prices is thus the logical consequence of the fact that, if limited to the point of equilibrium, the so-called Law of Walras is in reality a mere tautology. It is obviously true that in a relative exchange between two goods, *a* and *b*, the supply of *a* is a demand for *b* and the supply of *b* a demand for *a*. But this is the very definition of relative exchange and not a law leading to the determination of relative prices. To retain its significance, the neoclassical paradigm has to imply that good *a*, measured in physical units of *a*, is confronted with good *b*, measured in physical units of *b*. In this case, however, Walras's Law no longer applies, and the number of independent equations is bound to remain greater than that of the unknowns, which leads to the logical over-determinacy of the entire system.

Despite its failure to determine prices through direct exchange, neoclassical theory succeeds in switching emphasis from a dimensional to a numerical conception of value. Both Walras's concept of *numéraire* and Debreu's axiom as to the numerical nature of real goods and services are clear evidence of the neoclassical attempt to arrive at a purely numerical definition of prices. If this attempt fails it is only because numbers cannot be directly derived from goods. As maintained by Keynes, a satisfactory solution to the problem of value and prices requires the intervention of money. The contribution of the new quantum theory to this subject is particularly relevant as it pushes Keynes's analysis to its extreme consequences, showing that money is a purely numerical form, issued by banks and associated to output through the payment of wages. It also shows that, from an economic point of view, production is a creation and that it is through the absolute exchange between money and production that prices are determined. Starting from the analysis of double-entry bookkeeping, Schmitt (1984a) describes how money is issued by banks each time they carry out payments on behalf of their clients. Contrary to monetarist belief, money proper has no positive dimension in time. Its existence is confined to the exact instants when payments occur, so that it has neither mass nor velocity. Modern analysis shows that money as such is entirely immaterial, a unit of payment destroyed at the moment it is created. The instantaneous presence of money, however, is of prime importance for the existence of an economic system. Although it is an instantaneous event, a payment is sufficient to associate real goods and services to their numerical form. What remains after this instantaneous event and the destruction of nominal money (which, because of double-entry bookkeeping, flows immediately back to its point of origin) is a bank deposit, that is, a stock of money income whose object is the real stock of goods and services entered on the assets side of banks' balance sheets. Through the payment of wages, real goods and services are thus given a numerical form that makes them homogeneous. Production itself is thus an instantaneous event, a creation of output in the form of money.

Whereas in physical terms production is a process of transformation of matter and energy taking place through the continuum of time, from an economic viewpoint it is an instantaneous process, a creation giving rise to the economic form of produced output. Contrary to what is usually believed, production is not a (continuous or discontinuous) function of time, but an instantaneous event that *quantises* time. The finite and indivisible period of time issued as a *quantum* is that during which matter and energy are transformed. Hence, if a month is necessary to give matter and energy its final, physical form, the monthly output is issued as an indivisible whole at the instant the new physical object is given its economic, or numerical, form. The same quantum of time is again negatively issued when the product is purchased. This means that consumption – the final purchase of output – is an instantaneous event that, despite taking place at a different point in time with respect to production, coincides retroactively with it. This new 'time dimension' of economic events opens the way to a quantum-theoretical approach with far-reaching implications for economic analysis. In particular, the theories of profit, investment and capital accumulation are developed along new lines of research allowing to overcome the neoclassical dichotomy between real and monetary sectors. To illustrate this, let us say a few words about the way the process of capital accumulation is approached by quantum analysis.

The Process of Capital Accumulation

Thoroughly investigated by the classics and by the Austrians and neo-Austrians, the process of capital accumulation lies at the core of economic analysis. Like Ricardo (1817/1951), Böhm-Bawerk (1889/1959), Keynes (1936/1973), Hicks (1973), Bliss (1975) and some of their followers, Schmitt and his collaborators emphasise the role played by time in defining capital. In fact, the importance of time is evident from the start, the first form of capital being precisely that of capital-time. Because of the double-entry bookkeeping nature of bank money, on the balance sheet current income is necessarily entered as a liability, matched by an equivalent entry on the assets side. In fact, bank deposits define a debt (which banks incur towards the depositors) that is balanced by an equivalent credit (which banks hold vis-à-vis the public). Now, banks owe the owners of deposits the exact amount their clients owe to them; this is so precisely because they lend the sum which they borrow. In the familiar case of wage payments carried out by banks on behalf of firms, workers are credited with an amount of money income, which they immediately deposit. Wages are thus lent to banks as soon as they are formed. The technique of double-entry balancing, then, sees to it that banks cannot avoid lending to firms what they borrow from workers. Indeed, this is not surprising, since as a consequence of the payment of wages firms are indebted to banks, and banks are indebted to workers. Hence, the debt resulting from the payment of costs incurred by firms is actually covered by the income lent by workers. Between the moment it is formed and the moment when it is finally spent on the commodity market, income is saved by its owners and lent to firms, which thus cover their costs of production. Now, the income definitively spent by firms is not destroyed. On the contrary, its final expenditure will take place at a later moment, when the market for goods and services is actually cleared. Between the instant income is formed and lent, and the instant it is finally spent it is preserved in the form of capital (a capital-time whose task – paraphrasing Keynes – is to bridge the gap between present and future).

Another type of capital whose formation is explained by Schmitt's school along similar lines is what the classics already used to call *circulating capital*, that is, the fund out of which firms finance their investments. The whole of quantum analysis is developed in macroeconomic terms. Therefore, it would not be proper to interpret circulating capital from a microeconomic point of view. The problem is not to explain how a firm can raise sufficient funds to finance its investment, but rather how society as a whole can form a capital out of its current income and invest it in the production of means of production. In order to start a process of fixed capital accumulation, a society must save part of its current income and transform it into circulating capital. First firms have to realise a positive profit. It immediately appears that the set of firms may obtain a profit only at the expense of initial income holders, and that, by doing so, they momentarily accept to hold a stock of unsold goods. The monetary profit and the corresponding real stock of yet unsold goods are the two faces of a circulating capital that can subsequently be used to diverting some of the workers previously employed in producing consumption goods towards the production of capital goods. What is new in the analysis of capital accumulation propounded by the quantum theory of money and production is the role played by the structure of the monetary system of payments. According to this theory, capital accumulation may occur either in an orderly or in a disorderly (that is, pathological) way. Given the fundamental differences between money, income and capital, order requires banks to register payments in a double-entry bookkeeping structure in which capital transactions are distinguished from income flows. In other words, for their system of payments to be consistent with the very nature of money, income and capital, banks should be rearranged into three distinct departments dealing with monetary, financial and capital flows. Barring this, the process of capital accumulation – as is the case in today's banking systems – is bound to take place in a disorderly way, leading to such disastrous anomalies as inflation and deflation.

Referring to Schmitt's latest manuscript on capital accumulation, we may characterise this pathological process by the fact that, although invested by firms, profits are still available in the form of loanable bank deposits. Logically, the part of profits invested in the production of fixed capital goods should no longer be available on the financial market. Invested profits – which define a macroeconomic saving – are transformed into fixed capital, and it is in this form that they should be registered by banks. What is definitively saved by society as a whole should not be lent to anybody. Yet, contrary to logic, this is what happens today, since invested profits reappear as renewed income deposits. We are thus confronted with a *duplication*, the same income – the profit spent in the production of means of production – being still available to feed another expenditure on the commodity market. As is shown in Schmitt (1984a), Cencini and Baranzini (1996) and Rossi (this volume), this second expenditure is inflationary, since a given income should not exert a demand twice as big as the one defined by its purchasing power. The increase in demand resulting from the duplication characterising today's pathological process of capital accumulation is purely nominal and leads to a proportional decrease in the purchasing power of each single monetary unit.

Inflation and Unemployment

As we analyse inflation in relation to Rossi's work, we shall not discuss it in this short survey of the quantum-theoretical approach to monetary macroeconomics. A few remarks are in order, however, on the relation between inflation and unemployment. As we have already noted in the first section of our foreword, unemployment is considered in its most pathological form, that is, as the result of a lack of global demand. Also known as deflation, this state of affairs has nothing to do with microeconomic or behavioural mechanisms. Hoarding being logically impossible in a world where income is formed as a bank deposit, consumer behaviour is irrelevant to demand. In fact, contrary to what microeconomic considerations might suggest, global demand is not determined by the amount of income economic agents are willing to spend, but rather by the amount of income globally available. As financial intermediaries, banks lend what is lent to them. Moreover, respect of double-entry bookkeeping rules leaves them no other possibility than lending the exact amount deposited by their clients. The necessary balancing of assets and liabilities is evidence of this state of affairs. It thus follows that, whatever decision may be taken by individual economic agents, the totality of income formed is deposited with the banking system, and feeds an equivalent demand exercised either by its initial holders or by those who benefit from the loan granted by banks. No shortage in macroeconomic demand can thus ensue from microeconomic savings. This makes things conceptually more difficult, since it is no longer self-evident how current demand may fall short of current supply. If income is created by production and if the totality of income feeds global demand, how is it possible to find a positive numerical gap between total supply and total demand? And if a lack in global demand is the sign of pathological unemployment, how are we to explain stagflation? Inflation being defined as an excess of global demand over global supply, can global demand really be simultaneously greater and lesser than global supply? While no satisfactory answer has yet been provided by mainstream economics (whether neoclassical, monetarist or Keynesian), the new theory of monetary emissions points to a way out of the apparent dilemma. Both inflation and deflation, in fact, are shown to have a common origin – the pathological process of capital accumulation – which makes them mutually compatible. This does not mean, however, that the two imbalances are necessarily concomitant. Their common origin does not make them the twin effects of a unique cause.

Inflation is the first anomaly caused by our ill-functioning monetary systems. The duplication engendered by the renewed deposit of invested profits numerically increases global demand, thus entailing a loss of purchasing power for each monetary unit available in the system. Now, inflation is bound to remain the sole imbalance as long as investment remains profitable, that is, as long as the natural rate of interest (Wicksell, 1898/1965) is significantly higher than the market rate of interest. Yet, this situation is only a temporary one, all the more so that fixed capital amortisation brings about a process of over-accumulation. Thus, capital increases faster and faster, which inevitably leads to a decreasing ratio between profits and capital. When this ratio approaches the level of the market rate of interest, firms are discouraged from investing the totality of their profits in the production of instrumental goods. To avoid an excessive increase in capital (which would make its remuneration impossible) the set of firms invests part of its profit in the production of consumption goods. This increases the total supply of goods on the commodity market while leaving unaltered the income available to finance their purchase. Why is it so? Let us put it this way. Production creates the income necessary for the final purchase of output unless the payment of wages implies the expenditure of a pre-existent income. This is precisely what happens when wages are paid out of profits. In this case, the income spent for the payment of wages can no longer finance the purchase of consumption goods offered on the commodity market. In other words, when the banks' bookkeeping structure is such that financial and capital departments are not kept separate, investment leads to the replacement of a real income with a purely nominal one. When this occurs at a relatively early stage of the process of capital accumulation, the nominal increase entails inflation only. Yet, if it occurs at a later stage, when production of fixed capital goods is partially replaced by production of wage goods, the nominal increase is unable to match the rise in real supply. The purchase of new consumption goods requires a positive purchasing power, which a purely nominal income does not have. Deflation results therefore from the pathological process of capital accumulation having reached a level where fixed capital can no longer grow at the same pace as before. Capital over-accumulation (characterised by the phase of inflationary expansion of global demand) and diminishing capital accumulation (characterised by a deflationary increase in global supply) are both due to the fact that the logical distinction between income and capital is not mirrored by a similar distinction in the bookkeeping structure of banks. Surprising as this may seem, if the bookkeeping structure were perfect both imbalances would be impossible. Sceptics should bear in mind that economics is a science per se precisely because its proper object is *the product in the form of money*. Hence, because money is of a bookkeeping nature, it is perfectly understandable that logical shortcomings in the bookkeeping structure of our banking systems are bound to lead to serious anomalies such as inflation and deflation.

World Monetary Disorder

Today's world monetary system derives directly from the system set up at Bretton Woods in 1944. Despite subsequent modifications of the gold-exchange standard – particularly the decision to suspend convertibility in 1971 – transactions between countries are still settled in dollars or in some other key currencies. No true system of international clearing exists, and no international standard has yet replaced the US dollar. In such a context, it is legitimate to ask how and if monetary homogeneity can be achieved internationally. This amounts to asking whether or not exchange rates may be defined as the relative prices of national currencies and determined through the adjustment of their supplies and demands. Hence, we see how closely related international and national problems are. Actually, if it were possible to determine the relative prices of goods and services through their direct exchange on the commodity market, it would seem quite natural to look for the determination of exchange rates on the foreign exchange market. But, is it really so? Is it indeed correct to consider exchange rates as relative prices? Do currencies have a price? To answer in the affirmative would amount to claiming that, at the international level, national currencies are transformed from *means* into *objects* of exchange. A strange claim indeed, since money is the numerical standard in which prices are expressed and since, as such, it cannot logically have a price. Yet, this rather simple 'truth' seems to have been disregarded or at least played down by mainstream economics. The result is an incapacity to understand reality and provide a valid solution to the instability hampering our system of international payments.

Contrary to what is assumed in the majority of models purporting to explain exchange rate fluctuations, the new quantum theory of monetary economics shows that exchange rates are not exposed to national monetary disorders, interest rates, or commercial and financial imbalances. The fact is that, with the unique exception of external debt servicing, international transactions imply reciprocal transactions between countries, a condition necessary and sufficient to guarantee equilibrium on the foreign exchange market. For example, let us consider the case in which a given country, *A*, is a net commercial importer with respect to the rest of the world, *R*. Two situations are possible. If *A* is a key currency country, its net imports are paid by crediting the banking system of the rest of the world, *R*, with a bank deposit in money A. The net inflow of goods and services is thus balanced by an equivalent outflow of claims on *A*'s bank deposits. The demand for money R (MR) in terms of money A (MA), due to *A*'s net commercial imports, is matched by an equivalent demand for money A in terms of money R, which leaves the exchange rate unaltered. If MA is not a key currency, country *A* pays its net imports in money R. This it can do either by drawing on its official reserves or by obtaining a loan from *R*. Since official reserves are actually used for other purposes (mainly to reassure foreign investors), it is through a loan that *A* gets the amount of MR necessary to pay for its commercial imports. Now, the loan is obtained by exporting an equivalent amount of financial claims. Because of the net credit obtained from *R*, *A* incurs a debt, which is precisely the result of its net sale of financial claims. As in the previous case, the net purchase of real goods and services is balanced by a net sale of financial bonds, so that no variation in exchange rates occurs between MA and MR.

The payment of *A*'s net commercial and financial exports leads to the same result: the reciprocity of each transaction leaves exchange rates unaffected. This does not mean, however, that international payments are discharged in a purely logical way. The first case analysed above is clear evidence to the contrary. When paying for its net commercial imports, a key currency country subjects its money to a process of *duplication* that leads to the creation of an international, speculative capital. First developed by Rueff (1979), this analysis of the so-called euro- (or xeno-) currencies is a key element in the explanation of exchange rate erratic fluctuations. Let us briefly summarise the main logical steps of the analysis. The payment by a reserve currency country, *A*, of its net commercial imports implies the transfer to the exporting countries, *R*, of claims on *A*'s bank deposits. As shown by double-entry bookkeeping, not a single unit of the income formed in *A* is transferred to *R*. The credit entered on the assets side of *R*'s banking system means that a part of *A*'s bank deposits are now owned by *R*. The deposits themselves, however, are still entirely present in *A*'s banking system. Hence, what *R* earns is the ownership of a deposit that remains available in *A*. Now, the fact is that the amount of money A entered on *R*'s banking system becomes autonomous with respect to its corresponding deposit in *A*. As stressed by Rueff, money A is subjected to a duplication since it is simultaneously available in *A* and abroad. Yet, while the bank deposits in *A* define *A*'s current output, the duplicate invested abroad has no real content whatsoever. By allowing the duplication to occur and the duplicate to become autonomous with respect to the initial bank deposits, the present structure of international payments allows the formation of a capital whose nature is essentially speculative. With no link to real production, this capital feeds a speculative market in which national currencies become objects of trade and their exchange rates are directly dependent upon supply and demand. As it happens with real goods, xeno-currencies are sold and purchased for their own sake; yet, contrary to what happens with real goods, their price is not related to their cost of production. Moreover, being mere duplicates, xeno-currencies do not contain any real production either. Despite this lack of objective relationship with national outputs, xeno-currencies are autonomous objects of trade on the foreign exchange market. Therefore, what makes up the speculative character of this market is not the kind of transactions it deals with (some of which are not speculative at all), but the fact that its very existence is due to the pathological process of duplication that transforms currencies from means into objects of payment. Speculation is the effect and not the cause of speculative capital, which is the direct consequence of currency duplications. As soon as currencies are transformed into objects of trade, their exchange rates vary according to their sales and purchases, and speculation arises with a view to making capital gains from these variations. It is not surprising, thus, that this kind of speculation becomes the main cause of exchange rate fluctuations, which, in turn, become the main incentive to speculation.

Is there no way of escaping this vicious circle? Can order eventually be established at the international level? Quantum monetary theory provides the foundation for a reform leading to this result. Foreshadowed by Keynes's plan (Bretton Woods 1944), the reform proposed by Schmitt and his followers aims at transforming the present system of relative exchange rates into a system of absolute exchange rates. From a regime in which currencies are exchanged one against the other, we have to switch to a regime in which every currency is exchanged against itself, that is, a system where each time money A is exchanged against money R, MR is immediately exchanged back against MA. Far from being odd, this principle is the only one that is consistent with the bookkeeping nature of bank money and with its circular use. If explicitly applied to commercial and financial transactions between countries, it avoids duplication while it also guarantees exchange rate stability. Hence, the progress from disorder to order requires the creation of a structure allowing international transactions to take place through absolute exchanges. This may be done by following Keynes's suggestion to let a 'world bank' issue a new, international currency and act both as a monetary intermediary and as a clearing house.

For example, let us consider the way the payment of country *A*'s net commercial imports would have to be carried out. The principle of reciprocal exchange being fundamental to ensure the circular use of money, it must be applied also by the new world bank, which, according to the rules of clearing, could carry out *A*'s payment only if *A* is the recipient of an equivalent payment from the rest of the world, *R*. In our example, the new world bank would carry out the payment of *A*'s net commercial purchase only when *A* sells an equivalent amount of securities to *R*. The world currency issued by the new world bank would therefore be used simultaneously to convey real goods and services from *R* to *A*, and financial claims from *A* to *R*. The reciprocal exchange of commercial and financial assets would take place through the circular use of the new world currency, which, as any other bank money, would flow instantaneously back to its point of emission. By allowing the new world currency to be used in a closed circle, the new system would also guarantee exchange rate stability between MA and MR. Each national currency, in fact, would be exchanged against itself through the intermediary of the new world money. After being changed into the new world money and spent to pay for *A*'s commercial imports, money A would immediately recover its initial form, given the perfect reciprocity of exchange transactions. As a result, a substitution would take place between the real goods and services exported by *R* and the securities exported by *A*. Through absolute exchange, goods and services sold by *R* would become the content of money A, while the securities exported by *A* would take the form of money R. The new system of international settlements would thus guarantee the real payment of each transaction through the circular use of a currency – the new world money – which would never be transformed into a final good. By replacing today's regime of relative exchange rates with one of absolute exchange rates, it would also prevent the duplication of national currencies and ensure monetary stability.

European Monetary Unification

Not surprisingly, another problem tackled by the new quantum analysis of monetary economics is that of the European process of monetary unification. As is well known, according to the agreements subscribed by European Union countries (with the notable exceptions of Denmark and the United Kingdom) their national currencies are bound to be definitively replaced by the euro by mid 2002. By spontaneously giving up their monetary sovereignty, EU countries aim to achieve monetary stability, a result that has so far always escaped them as a consequence of erratic exchange rate fluctuations (in this respect, let us simply recall the dramatic collapse of the European Monetary System in 1992). Now, while it is obvious that if a single currency replaces a number of national currencies it also suppresses their exchange rates, it has still to be proved (a) that the negative effects of abandoning monetary sovereignty do not exceed the advantages of suppressing exchange rates; and (b) that exchange rate stability cannot be achieved without forcing countries to give up their national currencies. Let us consider these two points in that order.

Strongly supported by Germany and its neighbouring countries, the Maastricht criteria of convergence do not seem to have a decisive impact on the process of monetary unification. The Treaty plays down the possible negative consequences of the important differences still existing among EU countries, and the persistent devaluation of the euro is seen more as the result of a speculative onslaught on the European currency than as a sign of its fragility. An important point that seems to have been largely overlooked, if not altogether discarded, is the fact that monetary unification will bring about totally free capital flows. This may sound strange, of course, since free capital flows have been considered as one key goal of European integration long before any agreement on monetary unification. Yet, careful analysis shows that capital is indeed free to circulate only within the monetary 'space' of a single currency. In other words, monetary sovereignty allows capital to move freely within national boundaries, but prevents it from 'fleeing' from one country to another. This astonishing result is a direct consequence of double-entry bookkeeping. Issued by banks, money flows instantaneously back each time a payment is carried out. It thus follows that the entire amount of income created through production is necessarily deposited with the (domestic) banks that 'monetise' national outputs. Being derived from income, capital is therefore also a bank deposit. Now, it is impossible for the whole sum of bank deposits formed in a given country to be transferred to another country. Since scientific analysis is often hampered by misunderstandings, let us attempt to clarify the latter claim. Capital flight has always been considered as a transfer of capital between countries, since agents are obviously free to ask their banks to transfer their deposits abroad. Is it possible, then, to maintain – as we do – that not a single penny can leave the banking system from which it originates? The answer is based on the nature of bank money. If money income is defined as a bank deposit, it is logically impossible to retrieve it from a banking system and transfer it to another. What happens, then, when an agent asks his bank to transfer his capital abroad? Contrary to what is implied by the word 'transfer', no capital leaves its country of origin. The account of our agent is indeed debited by his bank, B_1, which gives him in exchange the ownership over a bank deposit formed in another country. His initial capital remains entirely deposited with bank B_1 and is exchanged against a claim upon a foreign capital deposited abroad. This is also what happens in the case of capital flight. Contrary to what the expression suggests, no national capital is lost by the country whose residents transfer their capitals to another country. This is not to say, of course, that no loss is incurred, for example by the fiscal authorities. If residents are successful in surreptitiously concealing their capitals from their taxman, they obviously cause damage to their country's domestic budget. However, their capitals do not leave the banking system in which they are deposited. Lost to the state, these capitals are still available within the national banking system.

The implications of this analysis of capital flight are far-reaching. In particular, it appears that national boundaries are an efficient barrier against capital movements only if they are based on monetary sovereignty. When monetary sovereignty is denied, a new monetary 'space' is created where capital can freely move from one region to another. European monetary union will bring about this result, with the undesired consequence that capitals will move massively from South to North, dramatically increasing the risk of unemployment in the South and social tension in the North. Put on the same footing as their northern competitors, southern firms will not be able to face the greater cost of their accumulated capitals, and might soon be forced to merge or shut down. Even such big firms as Fiat, Seat or Renault are likely to be taken over by their German competitors, with easily foreseeable consequences on unemployment. The fact is that, owing to important economic differences between national economies, in the last twenty years the process of capital accumulation has taken place at different costs within Europe. Now, the capital accumulated so far will bear fruit at different rates, according to the country in which it was formed. The decrease in the rate of profit that southern firms will incur after monetary unification will thus put them in jeopardy, forcing them to decrease their costs of production drastically. It is true that these problems should not arise in the newly unified Europe. However, monetary unification cannot cancel out the debts previously incurred by firms; neither will it redeem their interest debts. Differences in national processes of capital accumulation will have to be taken into account, and monetary unification does not seem to be the best way of doing it.

The case that can be made for maintaining monetary sovereignty is further strengthened by the observation that exchange rate stability may be reached without replacing national currencies with a unique European currency. Our comment on Keynes's plan of monetary reform finds fruitful application here. The same result that EU countries are aiming at through monetary unification can be reached in another way, averting the risk of any dramatic consequence on employment. To guarantee monetary stability it would be enough, in fact, to ask the European Central Bank (ECB) to use the euro between member countries and to act as the European Clearing House. Indeed, Europe has the great opportunity to implement a system that would substantially enhance economic exchanges between its member countries, allowing each of them to use the monetary and fiscal policies best suited to ensure economic convergence between them. The ECB already exists and it would be simple to organise it in such a way as to play the role Keynes envisaged for his International Clearing Union. The principles of clearing are well known, and the present system of gross settlements introduced nationally could be applied without difficulty in the context of TARGET (Trans-European Automated Real-time Gross-settlement Express Transfer system). Let us hope that reason will prevail, so that Europe can be saved a drastic increase in unemployment.

External Debt Servicing

Another line of research developed by the new quantum analysis of monetary economics deals with the servicing of foreign debt by non-reserve-currency countries. The main conclusion drawn in this respect by the theory is that indebted countries cannot help paying twice the amount of net interest due on their foreign debt. This is, admittedly, a rather unconventional assertion, and it cannot be explained in a few lines. Let us simply note here that the charge of interest payment would never double in a world in which national currencies were rendered homogeneous through a system akin to Keynes's *Plan for the Establishment of an International Clearing Union* (Keynes, 1980). The lack of a system of international payments conforming to the double-entry nature of bank money forces less developed countries (LDCs) to purchase the means of their external payments. The purchase of the mere means of payment has a net positive cost only when payments are unilateral, which is precisely the case with interest payments. By definition, interest payments are transfers that issue in a double charge since indebted countries have to face both a real and a monetary payment. In fact, they first transfer part of their national output to creditor countries. *Additionally*, they must give up an equivalent part of their reserves. Now, while the 'real' payment is perfectly legitimate (creditors being entitled to part of the income generated by their initial investment), the second payment is entirely superfetatory.

What is wrong with the present system of international payments is not the fact that indebted countries pay their creditors with a measure of net commercial exports, but the fact that they must also cover the cost generated by the unilateral transfer of a positive sum of national income. Being forced to pay with a foreign key currency, LDCs avoid the loss affecting their national income only by being subjected to an equivalent decrease of their official reserves or through an increase of their foreign debt. On the whole, the payment of x units of interest costs them $2x$ units, twice the amount due to (and obtained by) their creditors. Indeed, the second payment is not made in favour of the creditors, but of their countries, considered as a whole. This means that the payment of interest between countries can be properly understood only at a macroeconomic level. From a microeconomic point of view, the payment of interest defines a transfer of income from debtors to creditors. This is precisely what happens when interest is paid within a given country. Things change radically when the payments are across borders. The transfer of income between debtors and creditors can no longer take place without a monetary conversion of domestic into foreign currencies. In fact, this conversion is necessary to transform the payment of a domestic income into the payment of an equivalent amount of a foreign income. Put simply, the indebted country whose residents have to pay interests to foreign creditors gives up an equivalent amount of foreign exchange coming from its net commercial exports. Now, although it is true that part of the income generated within the indebted country, A, by the initial foreign investment is due to the creditor countries, R, it would be wrong to claim that A must pay R by giving away not only a part of its national output but also an equivalent amount of foreign currency. Having transferred to R a portion of its external gains derived from its exports, A should be quit. If this is not the case, it is because today's system of international payments does not allow the cost-free conversion of the payment made by the indebted residents of A into that carried out by their country. It is at the macroeconomic level that things go wrong. Indebted residents pay once, as required, and their country is forced to pay a second time because the unilateral transfer of interest creates a 'monetary hole' in A's economy. The consequence of A's unilateral transfer in favour of R is that an equivalent part of A's commercial exports is given free to R. Hence, the payment of interest by A's indebted residents entails a non-payment of A's commercial exports that must be matched by an equivalent decrease in A's official reserves. This second charge of external debt servicing immediately adds itself to the real payment of interest – the free transfer to *R* of part of *A*'s national output – thus doubling the total charge supported by country *A* and its residents. Once again, while the real payment prevents exports from increasing *A*'s official reserves, the monetary payment of interest requires a second measure of exports that are not paid by *R*, and which causes a monetary deficit. This deficit is then covered through a decrease in *A*'s official reserves.

If the indebted residents' payment were the only payment required by foreign debt servicing, country *A* would act as a simple intermediary. It would receive the domestic income spent by its residents and transfer an equivalent foreign income to foreign creditors. The conversion of domestic money into foreign currency would take place at zero cost, and the only charge of interest payments would be the amount of commercial exports necessary to pay country *R*'s creditors. Yet, barring a reform implemented by each single country, interest payments would imply a unique charge for *A* only if a system of international clearing allowed countries to benefit from a free conversion of their domestic currencies. In other words, the payment of interest would be normal if it were inserted into a system of reciprocal transactions between countries. As already suggested by Keynes in 1944, such a system is not intended to restrict transactions. On the contrary, it aims to provide a monetary structure allowing international payments to be carried out without causing any monetary disturbance, that is, without provoking exchange rate fluctuations and without forcing indebted countries to pay twice the interest accruing on their foreign debt. The new quantum monetary theory briefly presented here provides a detailed analysis of how the system of international payments should be structured in order to achieve this result. More important still, it offers a practical solution allowing each single country to protect itself from the second charge of external debt servicing. If adopted, this solution would reduce foreign debt servicing to a single payment, which would bring to the indebted countries a gain equivalent to the interest paid to their creditors. For example, in 1998, Mexico would have saved 12 589 millions dollars, Argentina 8976 millions dollars and Brazil 12 465 millions dollars. Each of these countries would thus have kept a disposable sum that has actually been lost in the 'black hole' of external debt servicing. The unjustified decrease in official reserves suffered by indebted countries under the present 'non-system' of international payments is equivalent to their interest payments, and measures the loss incurred by their Treasuries. The reform proposed by Bernard Schmitt and his school would prevent this from happening ever again.

THE ANALYSIS OF INFLATION

Traditional Approaches to Inflation

All traditional approaches to inflation stem from a research strategy grounded in the micro-foundations of macroeconomics. They all assume, in fact, that the loss in the purchasing power of money can be assessed with a micro-statistical apparatus which aggregates 'elementary transactions' into a so-called 'equation of exchanges'. Inflation is thus analysed by assuming that the loss in the purchasing power of money can be calculated by applying an index-number formula that is supposed to approximate the actual price level and its variations in time. 'Economists' perceptions of inflation rest on measurements of the "general price level" and on rates of change of price indexes' (Gale, 1981, p. 2). As there are many different ways of measuring prices and many different formulae for calculating a price level, there are also many different perceptions of inflation in the traditional approaches. The most commonly used measures of the rate of inflation are the percentage rate of change in a country's Consumer (or Retail) Price Index (CPI or RPI) or in its Gross Domestic Product (GDP) deflator. The symptom-based analysis of inflation is therefore grounded in a pragmatic definition.

Since the beginning of inflation analysis, theoretical debates have involved two mutually opposing strands of economic thought. Until the early 1960s, the analysis of inflation focused on cost-push and demand-pull mechanisms. Inflation was thus classified into two types according to whether price level increases originated in the factor market or in the market for produced goods. In both cases, inflation theories sought to determine the cause of the rise in commodity prices observed by means of price index analysis, and the possibility to curb inflation through monetary control. For a long time inflation theory has been set within a Phillips curve framework, implying a trade-off between inflation and unemployment both in the short and in the long run. This framework dominated the debate on inflation in the 1960s until Friedman's 1968 *American Economic Review* article, where the so-called 'natural rate of unemployment hypothesis' – to be developed later into the 'non-accelerating inflation rate of unemployment' (NAIRU) – was put forward.

In the 1970s the NAIRU hypothesis was challenged by the rational expectations school, which argued that economic agents use their information efficiently to anticipate future economic phenomena. The expected rate of inflation thus became an important variable in a number of macroeconomic models. Anticipated inflation is an idealised situation in which prices rise at the pace all agents expect them to rise and is said to be neutral with respect to monetary variables. Its effects on real variables depend on whether one considers money to be neutral or super-neutral; only in the latter case is a fully anticipated inflation thought to be neutral. On the contrary, unanticipated inflation may be analysed using the various kinds of probabilistic approaches to uncertainty. Because of the fundamental uncertainty accompanying this type of inflation and since it is not possible to analyse unanticipated inflation in isolation, its effects on the economic system are difficult to assess.

In the 1980s, further developments of the rational expectations hypothesis in inflation analysis brought to the fore the need to understand the policy-making process of those monetary authorities seeking to control inflation and secure price stability. The work done by Kydland and Prescott (1977) in the 'rules versus discretion' debate, developed later by authors such as Barro (1986), Fischer (1990) and Taylor (1993), added the element of central bank behaviour to the analysis of inflation. Towards the end of the 1980s, the policy goal of price stability became the ultimate (if not unique) objective of a number of monetary authorities in developed economies. Inflation analysis was thus linked to the problem of the dynamic inconsistency of monetary policy, in connection with the degree of a central bank's independence in setting its operational objectives. Emphasis was placed on the relationship that might exist between the inflation rate and the credibility of those monetary policies aimed at granting price stability.

Up to the 1990s, the analysis of inflation was thus conducted on the basis of the opposition between expected and unexpected inflation, a method which still occupies centre stage in the traditional approaches to the inflation problem. This echoes the perception of monetary policy and central banking as an art rather than a science, as Hawtrey put it back in 1932 (Hawtrey, 1932). The recently established European Central Bank and its monetary policy strategy epitomise this state of affairs (see European Central Bank, 1999; 2000).

Shortcomings of the Traditional Approaches to Inflation

In general, a major drawback is represented by the use of price indices both for technical and conceptual reasons. And Sergio Rossi shows this clearly in the first part of this book. There would be little point in repeating what Rossi has so circumstantially expounded. Let us merely stress that to assume inflation manifests itself through a rise in a price index may be highly misleading. There are in fact cases in which prices rise without there being any inflationary imbalance between total demand and total supply and, conversely, cases in which prices are stable or even decreasing despite the presence of inflation. We can grasp this easily if we bear in mind that inflation is best defined as a loss of purchasing power suffered by a country's monetary units, that is, as a discrepancy between the numerical form and its real content. Hence, for example, a rise in indirect taxation has nothing to do with inflation since it leads to a redistribution of income between citizens and state and not to a decrease in the purchasing power of the national currency. If the price of petrol rises because of indirect taxation, so does the CPI; yet, what is lost by consumers is earned by the state and, on the whole, national output is still the real object of the same monetary units. Conversely, a constant CPI cannot be taken to define a zero rate of inflation since, in the absence of inflation, technical progress would lead to a decrease in the CPI. If, despite the technological increase in physical output, the same goods are 'lodged' within the same number of monetary units, the purchase of total output requires an expenditure greater than its costs of production, which is the mark of an inflationary decrease in money's purchasing power.

Once it has been clearly established that inflation cannot be identified with an increase in prices, it becomes relatively easy to show that economic agents' behaviour cannot be the cause of this numerical discrepancy between money and output. In fact, while consumers, firms, government and commercial banks may influence market prices, nominal wages, monetary interest rates and credit policy, none of these factors can alter the relationship between national money and current output as determined by production. This becomes clearer if we bear in mind that payments are instantaneous flows, whose result is entered by banks as positive and negative deposits subjected to the principles of double-entry bookkeeping. Hence, for example, it can never happen that savings affect the money–output relationship, since the entire amount of money income saved by consumers defines a deposit that the bank necessarily and instantaneously lends to its debtors. It is clearly mistaken, therefore, to maintain that the behaviour of consumers may be behind a deflationary or an inflationary imbalance when they unexpectedly increase or decrease their savings. Hoarding is an ill-conceived process that has no right of citizenship in monetary economics. In the same way, it can easily be shown that neither can a government be held responsible for inflation. Every increase in global demand caused by a new investment financed by the government is, in fact, matched by an equivalent increase in global supply (the sole exception to this, which applies only to highly disorderly systems of payments, is the financing of budgetary deficits through monetary creation). Even the famous digging and filling of holes parable is not inflationary, since the government is bound to sell the filled up holes in order to cover their costs of production. What about commercial banks, then? Is it not true to say that they may be led to increase their credit unduly, thus triggering an inflationary growth of total demand? This is a question that Sergio Rossi deals with in detail and we shall not analyse it here. Let us simply observe that, when banks lend an amount greater than the one deposited with them by production, they are allowed to do so by a bookkeeping system whose structure is still imperfect. If a threefold distinction between monetary, financial and fixed capital departments were introduced, banks would know at each instant the exact amount of income they can lend to the public. The activity carried out by banks is not responsible for this imbalance; behind it is the lack of a proper structure of payments accounting for the factual and conceptual distinction between money, income and capital. It is at this level that the analysis of inflation must be developed. Indeed, the new quantum school carries out a 'structural' analysis of inflation by showing that the process of capital accumulation entails the creation of a sum of 'empty' money and that, despite being transformed into fixed capital, the income invested in this process remains available on the financial market. Rossi's book is about the need to move from a 'behavioural' to a 'structural' analysis of inflation, from a traditional to a quantum approach centred on the concept of money as purely numerical.

The role of central banks appears thus in a totally different light. Instead of analysing the way central banks may influence economic agents' behaviour by enhancing their credibility, it becomes essential to understand how they can improve the payment system. Whether correctly anticipated or not, inflation is a disorder that cannot be blamed on economic agents' behaviour, and that cannot be cured by forcing economic agents to behave rationally. The major task of central banks is not to work out the best monetary policy strategy given the rational expectations hypothesis, but to create a monetary structure allowing payments to be carried out in an orderly way. What central banks can and should provide is a system that guarantees the stability of the money–output relationship. Behaviour cannot be put under rigorous control neither should it. Not only is it hopeless to try to do so, but it is also pointless. Whatever decisions consumers, investors, firms or commercial banks take, they can never influence inflation. If nevertheless monetary units lose part of their initial purchasing power it is not because of the decisions taken, but because some payments are entered in the bookkeeping structure of today's banking systems incorrectly. Hence, the role of central banks is not to control decisions, but – let us say it once again – to provide commercial banks with a system of payments in line with the logical distinction between money, income and capital.

Before introducing Rossi's contribution in greater detail, let us once again emphasise that inflation occurs each time the monetary form of physical output is numerically increased. A rise in nominal wages increases numerically the monetary form of real output, yet it is not inflationary, since the new form is associated with a new output. Instead of a change of the previous relationship between money and output, we are confronted with a new relationship concerning an entirely new output. In order to understand inflation properly it is therefore necessary to comprehend the way money and output are associated as numerical form and real content. Thus, since a national currency can only be the *form* of the corresponding national output, it is inappropriate to look for an 'imported' inflation due to changes in the price of foreign goods or to a devaluation on the foreign exchange market. Whatever happens to foreign goods or currencies, the relationship between national money and national output remains unaffected. If the concept of 'imported' inflation has any meaning at all, it has to be related to a change in the domestic relationship between money and output induced by international transactions. As shown by Schmitt, an inflationary creation of domestic currency occurs each time exports are paid for in a foreign money which, because of its status of reserve currency, is entered as a positive asset in the exporting country's banking system. Here again it is because of the imperfect structure of the monetary system that inflation sets in. In particular, it is because currencies are erroneously taken to be positive assets that they are (again erroneously) assimilated to real goods, and that an amount of domestic money is created as their counterpart.

The drastic change in the analysis of inflation envisaged by Schmitt's quantum-theoretical approach is closely related to the role played by bank money and the structure of national and international payments. Instead of focusing on price indices, emphasis shifts to the way payments may alter the relationship between money and output. Structure rather than behaviour is pinpointed as the source of disorder, and a monetary reform is called for to get rid of inflationary and deflationary imbalances. It is in this context that Rossi's book may be seen as a valuable and timely contribution towards the foundation of a new, macroeconomic theory of monetary economics.

AN ASSESSMENT OF ROSSI'S CONTRIBUTION

As an active member of the new, quantum school, Sergio Rossi has been working for the last ten years on some of the most promising implications of

Schmitt's theory. In particular, before studying inflation he devoted a good deal of attention to the problem of European monetary unification, emphasising the role that the European Central Bank actually plays and the one it might play if EU member countries were allowed to retain their monetary sovereignty. The book we are introducing here is the result of research carried out mainly in London (both at the London School of Economics and at the University College London), where Rossi has had the opportunity to confront his ideas with those of economists of different schools. The number of qualified contributions he quotes testifies to his deep knowledge of the way inflation has been analysed by mainstream as well as by unorthodox economists. It is one of Rossi's merits that this book moves from a critical to a positive analysis of inflation by steps of increasing difficulty. The reader is thus taken on a stimulating journey where well-established 'truths' are challenged on logical and factual grounds; and a new interpretation is drawn, in which inflation is closely related to the process of capital accumulation.

Let us now introduce Rossi's contribution somewhat more in detail, following the summary of his book.

In Part One (Chapters 1 and 2) Sergio Rossi provides a methodological criticism of the concept of price level and its use for the measurement of inflation. He argues that price measurement issues are not merely a technical statistical problem, but are closely related to the theoretical choices of traditional inflation analysis.

In Chapter 1 he introduces the argument and develops the idea that the distinction between durable and non-durable goods is irrelevant for the construction of a price index (such as the CPI generally used to measure inflation). Having noted that consumption is an exchange and that, '[w]hen an individual buys durable goods, he or she may go on using them for his or her own satisfaction without implying that he or she goes on "consuming"' (Verdon, 1996, p. 162), Rossi argues that, from an economic point of view, consumption (exchange) is an instantaneous operation. In fact, consumption is an expenditure whose object is a pre-existent good; the physical properties of the good do not matter for price index analysis. In economic terms, any purchase on the product market consumes the exchange value of the good purchased, which then exists as a physical 'value-in-use' until it wears out. Therefore, Rossi argues, price index analysis should include the purchase prices of durable goods (for example cars, aircraft, computers), instead of converting them into a price of annual services – as is done nowadays in CPI analysis (see Advisory Commission to Study the Consumer Price Index, 1996, p. 82).

Chapter 2 takes a step further the critique of price index analysis applied to the measurement of inflation. In this chapter, the argument is based on the idea that a microeconomic approach (like aggregate price analysis) may not be adequate for the analysis of a macroeconomic problem such as inflation. Granting that the force of price index analysis is an adequate measure of the movement in aggregate prices for a given bundle of commodities, Rossi claims that this framework of inquiry does not provide a satisfactory measure of the purchasing power of money over domestic goods. The argument is developed in Chapter 2 at an intuitive level, and takes up the idea put forward in a classic paper on inflation that 'analysis of the inflationary process must involve the study of the whole economic system and not just of one or two markets in isolation' (Laidler and Parkin, 1975, p. 796). Rossi notes that measuring inflation by means of changes in a particular price level fails to consider the markets for produced goods as a whole, since the method based on 'representative baskets' cannot account for the sum total of aggregate output. Analogously, he points out that the representative-agent method on which consumer expenditure surveys are carried out cannot account for the sum total of aggregate demand. This criticism is developed in connection with the method of 'doing' macroeconomics by aggregation of microeconomic data. In fact the author aims to show that the methodological problems of inflation analysis encountered by price index construction may originate in the widespread idea that any macroeconomic problem can be fruitfully investigated by adopting a microeconomic stance. This enables Rossi to show that present inflation measurement problems are not technical, but essentially conceptual.

Part Two (Chapters 3 and 4) takes the analysis to a deeper level: it investigates the theoretical (neoclassical) foundations of price index analysis with respect to the inflation problem. The aim of Chapter 3 is to show that within the neoclassical framework of inquiry, neither the purchasing power of money nor the value of output can be determined; which leaves inflation unexplained and neoclassical economists unable to interpret variations in the money stock correctly. Rossi's attempt here is to put forward an internal criticism of neoclassical monetary economics. In Chapter 4 the author refines the argument, taking up the theory of monetary emissions developed by Bernard Schmitt and his school. Rossi's analysis of the confrontation between advocates of an exogenous money supply and supporters of the endogenous-money view shows that the *means* of payment and its *object* must be logically and factually distinguished. This distinction is presented and discussed at length in the second half of Chapter 4, where Rossi advocates a pure bookkeeping conception of bank money, opposing it to the neochartalist view of modern money recently revived by Wray (1998; 2000).

In Part Three (Chapters 5 and 6), having rejected neoclassical monetary economics on logical grounds, the author investigates an alternative approach to money and inflation, which he identifies in the post-Keynesian monetary tradition (see Fontana, 1999). In Chapter 5, Rossi criticises the two strands of post-Keynesian monetary thinking on inflation, namely (1) the idea that inflation may be defined – or measured – by the difference between the increase in money wages and the (average) increase in labour productivity, and (2) the idea that inflation may arise from a conflict regarding the distribution of income between firms and workers. On the first point, Rossi recalls Keynes's idea of measuring output in terms of wage-units, and shows that, in economic analysis, labour productivity cannot be measured without referring to workers' remuneration. He illustrates this criticism by stating that 'labour productivity and money wages are like the volume of a gas and the volume of the room in which the gas is released.' On the second point, Rossi argues that it is not a conflict about the functional distribution of income that causes inflation – which the author defines as a macroeconomic imbalance between total demand and total supply, and not merely as an increase in the targeted price index. As a matter of fact, since the distribution conflict between, and within, the various groups of agents cannot change the existing amount of income, the macroeconomic relationship between total demand and total supply of current output can never be affected by this conflict (which merely concerns the *distribution* of a given purchasing power).

Chapter 5 then goes on to consider the latest thinking of some leading post-Keynesian monetary economists on the question of inflation. In particular, it analyses the claim that credit facilities may be granted beyond the level that would ensure monetary equilibrium. In other words, Rossi wonders whether or not the relationship between money (that is, total demand) and output (total supply) might be affected by an excess of bank credit, which would thus contribute to the inflationary rise in goods and assets prices (Chick, 1986; 2000; Howells, 1995; 1996). Granting the effect of bank credit facilities on market prices, Rossi questions the macroeconomic impact of the banks' aggressive lending activity on credit markets. His conclusion is that excess credit facilities are not irrevocably inflationary for the economy as a whole, because their effect on the relationship between money and output is not enduring. In fact, bank loans have eventually to be repaid by their borrowers. Hence, the inflationary gap brought about by an excess of bank credit granted over any particular period is bound to be compensated for by an imbalance of the opposite algebraic sign when bank loans are reimbursed. This argument is illustrated with a simple, numerical example, where the author analyses second-hand transactions of housing assets in order to provide an explicit link with Howells's papers and to show the main differences between Howells's and his own approach.

Chapter 6 switches the analysis of inflation from the product market (which is the main focus of post-Keynesian analysis) to the factor market. The author maintains that inflationary pressures originate in the production process rather than in the circulation of already produced goods. Having noted that the formation of income is essentially an exchange of flows, he shows that the production of replacement goods (that is, the amortisation of fixed capital) may have a part to play in explaining inflation. His starting point is the contention that the value of replacement goods has to be added to the value of consumption and investment goods for the determination of national income, Y, since the production of replacement goods elicits a wage bill that logically enters the measurement of Y. Now, when workers' remuneration in the replacement goods sector is taken out of previously accumulated profits, firms purchase on the factor market the very output wage-earners are paid for. The bank deposits wage-earners are credited with are thus emptied of any newly produced goods, which opens up the way to an irreversible inflationary gap.

The last section of Chapter 6 presents an outline of the structural reform proposed by the Schmitt school in order to avoid inflationary imbalance. To illustrate the distinction between the three departments of banks (monetary, financial and fixed capital department), a numerical example is given that also integrates the discussion of second-hand transactions made in the previous chapter. This example enables the author to point out, in bookkeeping terms, the distinction between money and credit – two concepts often confused in post-Keynesian and circuit theories – and the mechanism that may control credit-led inflation.

Finally, in the Conclusion the author assesses his own work, answers the criticisms raised in the literature to the approach chosen and gives some perspectives for further research.

FURTHER LINES OF INQUIRY

As this introductory essay should have made clear, the new quantum-theoretical approach is bound to affect the whole body of macroeconomic analysis. As Lord Desai has put it,

> [t]he task of constructing a theory of a monetary economy is however still unfinished. A few economists are working away at this. . . . [T]he French–Swiss School of Bernard Schmitt . . . has been uncompromising in its determination to build a theory for a monetary economy. We do not as yet have such a theory, nor can one hope that it will come from an individual's effort alone, Keynes's own example notwithstanding. I welcome this work as a contribution to the collective social effort that must be undertaken if we are to construct such an alternative theory (Desai, 1984, p. xiv).

A new paradigm normally implies a thorough reassessment of the science or discipline under scrutiny; this obviously applies in the case of economics, too. It should come as no surprise, then, that the new monetary theory originally propounded by Bernard Schmitt and his school has far-reaching implications for the most important chapters of macroeconomics. In particular, as we have already discussed, the new theory has branched out to include the theory of value and prices, the process of capital accumulation and the anomalies of inflation, deflation and unemployment via a new analysis of money and production. The very existence of different national banking systems has urged a reassessment of a number of issues: exchange rates' and financial markets' erratic fluctuations, external debt servicing, and the processes of monetary unification.

A huge effort has been made since the mid-1950s, in reconstructing the whole body of monetary macroeconomics; but further refinement and extensions are needed. A unified analysis may be established and refined, in terms of value and prices, of the process of division of the productive economy into different sectors (those producing, respectively, wage goods, interest and capital goods, and replacement goods). Additionally, deeper insight may be gained into the mechanisms of the distribution of income among wages, (distributed or invested) profit and rent. A better understanding of the functional distribution of income may allow us to throw new light on the class- and personal share of income and wealth. Moreover, the process of personal wealth accumulation and inter-generational transmission may be fruitfully redefined.

The issues relating to the role played by the state (in particular: public expenditure, taxation and public debt) will also need to be reconsidered. Even as far as economic policy is concerned, as in the case of demand management, the new paradigm has profound implications: the absence of any fundamental relationship between successive production periods deeply affects the role and impact of the public expenditure multiplier. The 'earning through spending' theory of income is set aside, since the double-entry bookkeeping nature of money prevents the causal and automatic link between incomes of successive periods. According to the new, quantum monetary macroeconomics, the functional chain assumed by traditional analysis must be replaced by processes of creation–destruction (that is, production–consumption), every single process being logically separated from any other. By heeding this, future work will define what sort of non-functional links may exist between successive periods.

Further refinements may also be needed in the field of international economics. Although problems of great importance have already been thoroughly investigated,[5] such as the disorderly functioning of the international payment system, the plan for a reform of this system (which Bernard Schmitt has outlined) needs to be worked out in much greater detail. The same argument applies to the plan for the creation, in Europe and in the rest of the world, of homogeneous monetary areas compatible with the safeguard of monetary sovereignty.

Welcoming Rossi's book as a valuable contribution to this research programme, let us hope that others will follow soon, and that further progress will be made towards a complete, consistent and unified theory of economics.

NOTES

1. We would like to thank Simona Cain, academic secretary at the Economics Faculty, USI, Lugano (formerly of the Institute of Romance Studies, University of London) for precious editorial assistance in preparing this manuscript.
2. For an appraisal of main features of this school of thought see also Devillebichot (1969), Desai (1984; 1988) and Guitton (1984).
3. Should it be proved that relative prices cannot be determined on their own, neoclassical economics would be unable to measure real goods and services, and thus deprived of its proper object.
4. The term 'imbalance' is used in the sense of 'anomaly' or 'pathology'.
5. Schmitt (1973; 1975; 1984b), Cencini (1995; 2000).

REFERENCES

Advisory Commission to Study the Consumer Price Index (1996), *Toward a More Accurate Measure of the Cost of Living: Final Report to the Senate Finance Committee*, Washington (DC): Government Printing Office ('Boskin Report').

Baranzini, M. (ed.) (1982), *Advances in Economic Theory*, Oxford and New York: Basil Blackwell and St. Martin's Press.

Baranzini, M. and R. Scazzieri (eds) (1986), *Foundations of Economics: Structures of Inquiry and Economic Theory*, Oxford and New York: Basil Blackwell and St. Martin's Press.

Barro, R.J. (1986), 'Recent developments in the theory of rules versus discretion',

Economic Journal, **96** (conference supplement), 23–37.
Bliss, C.J. (1975), *Capital Theory and the Distribution of Income*, Amsterdam: North Holland / Elsevier.
Böhm-Bawerk, E. (1959), *Capital and Interest* (vol. II *Positive Theory of Capital*), South Holland: Libertarian Press (first published 1889).
Cencini, A. (1982), 'The logical indeterminacy of relative prices', in M. Baranzini (ed.), *Advances in Economic Theory*, Oxford and New York: Basil Blackwell and St. Martin's Press, 126–36.
Cencini, A. (1984), *Time and the Macroeconomic Analysis of Income*, London: Frances Pinter.
Cencini, A. (1988), *Money, Income and Time: A Quantum-Theoretical Approach*, London and New York: Pinter Publishers.
Cencini, A. (1995), *Monetary Theory, National and International*, London and New York: Routledge.
Cencini, A. (2000), 'World monetary disorders: exchange rate erratic fluctuations', Centre for Banking Studies / Research Laboratory of Monetary Economics, *Quaderni di ricerca*, 2.
Cencini, A. and M. Baranzini (eds) (1996), *Inflation and Unemployment: Contributions to a New Macroeconomic Approach*, ('Routledge Studies in the Modern World Economy', 4), London and New York: Routledge.
Chick, V. (1986), 'The evolution of the banking system and the theory of saving, investment and interest', *Économies et Sociétés*, ('Série Monnaie et Production', 3), **20** (8–9), 111–26.
Chick, V. (2000), 'Money and effective demand', in J. Smithin (ed.), *What is Money?*, ('Routledge International Studies in Money and Banking', 6), London and New York: Routledge, 124–38.
Debreu, G. (1959), *Theory of Value: An Axiomatic Analysis of Economic Equilibrium*, ('Cowles Foundation Monograph', 17), New York: John Wiley.
Desai, M. (1984), 'Foreword', in A. Cencini, *Time and the Macroeconomic Analysis of Income*, London: Frances Pinter, xi–xiv.
Desai, M. (1988), 'Foreword', in A. Cencini, *Money, Income and Time: A Quantum-Theoretical Approach*, London and New York: Pinter Publishers, xi–xiv.
Devillebichot, G. (1969), 'Note sur les travaux de Bernard Schmitt', *Revue d'économie politique*, **79** (3), 693–702.
European Central Bank (1999), 'The stability-oriented monetary policy strategy of the Eurosystem', *Monthly Bulletin*, **1** (1), 39–50.
European Central Bank (2000), 'Monetary policy transmission in the euro area', *Monthly Bulletin*, **2** (7), 43–58.
Fischer, S. (1990), 'Rules versus discretion in monetary policy', in B.M. Friedman and F.H. Hahn (eds), *Handbook of Monetary Economics*, ('Handbooks in Economics', 8), Amsterdam: Elsevier Science B.V., vol. II, 1155–84.
Fontana, G. (1999), *Essays on Money, Uncertainty and Time in the Post Keynesian Tradition*, unpublished PhD dissertation, University of Leeds.
Friedman, M. (1968), 'The role of monetary policy', *American Economic Review*, **58** (1), 1–17.
Gale, W.A. (1981), 'Introduction', in W.A. Gale (ed.), *Inflation: Causes, Consequents, and Control*, Cambridge (Massachusetts): Oelgeschlager, Gunn & Hain, 1–11.

Guitton, H. (1984), 'Préface', in B. Schmitt, *Inflation, chômage et malformations du capital*, Paris and Albeuve: Economica and Castella, 9–26.

Hawtrey, R.G. (1932), *The Art of Central Banking*, London: Longmans & Co.

Hicks, J.R. (1973), *Capital and Time*, Oxford: Clarendon Press.

Howells, P.G.A. (1995), 'The demand for endogenous money', *Journal of Post Keynesian Economics*, **18** (1), 89–106.

Howells, P.G.A. (1996), 'Endogenous money and the "state of trade"', in P. Arestis (ed.), *Keynes, Money and the Open Economy: Essays in Honour of Paul Davidson*, Cheltenham and Brookfield: Edward Elgar Publishing Ltd, vol. I, 105–22.

Keynes, J.M. (1930/1971), *A Treatise on Money* (vol. I *The Pure Theory of Money*), London: Macmillan. Reprinted in *The Collected Writings of John Maynard Keynes* (vol. V *A Treatise on Money: The Pure Theory of Money*), London and Basingstoke: Macmillan.

Keynes, J.M. (1936/1973), *The General Theory of Employment, Interest and Money*, London: Macmillan. Reprinted in *The Collected Writings of John Maynard Keynes* (vol. VII *The General Theory of Employment, Interest and Money*), London and Basingstoke: Macmillan.

Keynes, J.M. (1980), *The Collected Writings of John Maynard Keynes* (vol. XXV *Activities 1940–1944. Shaping the Post-War World: the Clearing Union*), London and Basingstoke: Macmillan.

Kydland, F.E. and E.C. Prescott (1977), 'Rules rather than discretion: the inconsistency of optimal plans', *Journal of Political Economy*, **85** (3), 473–91.

Laidler, D. and M. Parkin (1975), 'Inflation: a survey', *Economic Journal*, **85** (340), 741–809.

Pasinetti, L.L. (1981), 'Inflazione e sviluppo economico' in AA.VV., *L'inflazione oggi: distribuzione e crescita*, Atti della XX riunione scientifica della Società italiana degli economisti, Milano: Giuffrè, 41–73.

Ricardo, D. (1951), *On the Principles of Political Economy and Taxation*, Cambridge: Cambridge University Press (first published 1817).

Rueff, J. (1979), *Oeuvres complètes*, Paris: Plon.

Schmitt, B. (1960), *La formation du pouvoir d'achat*, Paris: Sirey.

Schmitt, B. (1966), *Monnaie, salaires et profits*, Paris: Presses Universitaires de France (also Albeuve: Castella, 1975).

Schmitt, B. (1971), *L'analyse macro-économique des revenus*, Paris: Dalloz.

Schmitt, B. (1972), *Macroeconomic Theory: A Fundamental Revision*, Albeuve: Castella.

Schmitt, B. (1973), *New Proposals for World Monetary Reform*, Albeuve: Castella.

Schmitt, B. (1975), *Théorie unitaire de la monnaie, nationale et internationale*, Albeuve: Castella.

Schmitt, B. (1982), 'Time as quantum', in M. Baranzini (ed.), *Advances in Economic Theory*, Oxford and New York: Basil Blackwell and St. Martin's Press, 115–25.

Schmitt, B. (1984a), *Inflation, chômage et malformations du capital*, Paris and Albeuve: Economica and Castella.

Schmitt, B. (1984b), *La France souveraine de sa monnaie*, Paris and Albeuve: Economica and Castella.

Schmitt, B. (1988), *L'ÉCU et les souverainetés nationales en Europe*, Paris: Dunod.

Schmitt, B. and A. Cencini (1982), 'Wages and profits in a theory of emissions', in M. Baranzini (ed.), *Advances in Economic Theory*, Oxford and New York: Basil

Blackwell and St. Martin's Press, 137–46.
Taylor, J.B. (1993), 'Discretion versus policy rules in practice', *Carnegie-Rochester Conference Series on Public Policy*, **39** (3), 195–214.
Verdon, M. (1996), *Keynes and the 'Classics': A Study in Language, Epistemology and Mistaken Identities*, ('Routledge Studies in the History of Economics', 7), London and New York: Routledge.
Walras, L. (1954), *Elements of Pure Economics or the Theory of Social Wealth*, translated by W. Jaffé, London: George Allen & Unwin (first French edition 1874).
Wicksell, K. (1965), *Interest and Prices*, New York: Kelley (first published 1898).
Wray, L.R. (1998), *Understanding Modern Money: The Key to Full Employment and Price Stability*, Cheltenham and Northampton: Edward Elgar Publishing Ltd.
Wray, L.R. (2000), 'Modern money', in J. Smithin (ed.), *What is Money?*, ('Routledge International Studies in Money and Banking', 6), London and New York: Routledge, 42–66.

Preface

This book investigates inflation from a new macroeconomic point of view. It originates in a critical appraisal of traditional inflation analysis, where the latter phenomenon is identified with an ongoing increase in the level of aggregate prices because ‘too much money is chasing too few goods’. It argues that the prevalent idea of money and output being two separate and autonomous objects can neither explain the purchasing power of money nor its variations over time. It also argues that output as a whole cannot be measured in this widely shared analytical framework. In fact, a new theory is called for. The analysis of inflation in the new framework developed in the book reveals its essentially macroeconomic nature. It is argued that to gain a thorough understanding of inflation it is necessary to focus analysis on the formation of national income and not on its distribution. Within the proposed new framework, the production process is investigated in terms of flows, rather than in terms of stocks changing hands in the process of output circulation; both money and banking are instrumental in generating, and measuring, macroeconomic magnitudes. Elaboration of the role of money and banking in this analytical framework provides a number of theoretical propositions that lead to the conclusion that the origin of inflation is ‘monetary’ and ‘structural’ rather than ‘real’ and ‘behavioural’. The monetary–structural element is the working of modern banking. When the payment system is designed to introduce the distinction between money, income and fixed capital into bank accounting, inflationary pressures are at least revealed and may be eliminated. This book seeks to contribute to such a conceptual design. However, readers with differing intellectual views may be puzzled, or annoyed, by the radical and unorthodox approach to money and inflation developed in it. Surely, it should come as no surprise that a prominent publisher like Edward Elgar had received conflicting advice on this book, because the conventionally educated reader might be reluctant to abandon those firmly held beliefs that this work deeply challenges, inviting to rethink monetary macroeconomics afresh.

Acknowledgements

It is the author's pleasure to acknowledge his intellectual debt to several people who have contributed to the development of this book in many important ways. In this regard, I would like to thank Victoria Chick and Lord Desai, the two supervisors of my PhD dissertation at University College London, for having discussed at length and commented upon the chapters of this work. I am also grateful to Mauro Baranzini, Heinrich Bortis, Alvaro Cencini, Bernard Dafflon, Claude Gnos, Augusto Graziani, Peter Howells, Alain Parguez, and Bernard Schmitt for their advice, encouragement and constructive criticism over the whole period I have spent in the United Kingdom since my first post-doctoral research year at the London School of Economics. I would also like to thank many people and institutions for the provision of scientific work that would have been otherwise impossible to obtain; in particular, the Bank of England, the Deutsche Bundesbank, the European Central Bank, and the Swiss Federal Statistical Office (especially Lorenzo Cascioni and Marcello Corti). Simona Cain made an important contribution in improving the style of the book. I am indebted to her as well as to the Swiss National Science Foundation, the *Commissione Culturale del Cantone Ticino*, the *Fondazione Lang* and the *Fondazione Leemann* for the financial support that led to the writing of this book. Although the author is the sole person responsible for the result, this work has also been possible thanks to a generous Overseas Research Students Award by the Committee of Vice-Chancellors and Principals of the United Kingdom, which is gratefully acknowledged. At a more personal level, I am most grateful to my mother for her constant, and multifaceted, support, particularly when stress and discouragement have put the completion of this research at risk. This book is dedicated to her. My warmest thanks go also to my uncle Sergio, who has managed to carry out with unequalled skill the heavy task of personal adviser in bad-weather times. Last, but not least, Maria-Theresia Brunner–Steinacher and Walter Zürcher are thanked for all their moral support during such a collective undertaking.

S.R.

Introduction

This book aims towards three goals.

The first is to discuss the methodological issues involved in the measurement of inflation, as established by reference to index number theory and its specific application, that is, the retail (or consumer) price index. As the influential Chairman of the Board of Governors of the US Federal Reserve System has recently observed, '[t]he remarkable progress that has been made by virtually all of the major industrial countries in achieving low rates of inflation in recent years has brought into sharper focus the issue of price measurement' (Greenspan, 1997b, p. 1). Granting this progress, a new set of issues is now emerging on the agenda of economic policy makers. 'As we move closer to price stability, the necessity of measuring prices accurately has become an especial challenge. Biases of a few tenths in annual inflation rates do not matter when inflation is high. They do matter when, as now, a debate has emerged over whether our economies are moving toward price deflation' (ibid., p. 1). Accurately measuring prices and the rate of change of aggregate price levels is indeed of central importance for current investigation into our market-based monetary economies of production. It is in particular necessary for analysing economic developments, including output growth, government spending, and poverty rates, as well as for conducting macroeconomic policy. In Greenspan's own words, '[i]f the general price level is estimated to be rising more rapidly than is in fact the case, then we are simultaneously understating growth in real GDP and productivity, and real incomes and living standards are rising faster than our published data suggest' (Greenspan, 1998, p. 1).[1] As a matter of fact, despite the advances in price measurement that have been made over the years, there remain unsettled technical and theoretical issues that are extremely complex and difficult to deal with in the field of 'measurement economics'. As one of the most distinguished experts of price index analysis recognises, '[d]ifficult technical issues inevitably arise in constructing price indexes, and such issues are often resolved by appealing to professional conventions' (Pollak, 1998, p. 74). In the case of the consumer price index (CPI), the most frequently used index to assess the movement in aggregate prices over a given span of time, recent work by the US Advisory Commission headed by Michael J. Boskin concluded that this index overstates the change in the cost of living by roughly one percentage point per year (Advisory Commission to Study the Consumer Price Index, 1996). Researchers in the United States and elsewhere have come up with similar point estimates, with a range of plausible values of 0.5 to 1.5 percentage points per annum (see for example Cunningham, 1996; Moulton, 1996; Shapiro and Wilcox, 1996; Greenlees, 1997; Bureau of Labor Statistics, 1997; Hoffmann, 1998; and the huge literature cited therein). 'Hence, the very first point the CPI Commission made in its report was that inflation is inherently difficult to measure in a complex dynamic market economy' (Boskin et al., 1998, p. 5). Further, while the CPI is the best measure currently available to gauge price movements, 'it is not a cost-of-living index and it suffers from a variety of conceptual and practical problems' (ibid., p. 23). In a nutshell, as Deaton has it, the CPI is 'a concept that is hard to define and harder to measure' (Deaton, 1998, p. 38).[2] It is precisely at the conceptual level that our investigation is situated, after an initial survey of the technical issues raised by the measurement of aggregate prices.[3]

The second goal of this book, in fact, is to show that the recorded technical difficulties in measuring inflation by price index analysis stem ultimately from a yet imperfect macro-theoretic appraisal of the working of modern monetary economies of production. To quote from *The New Palgrave* dictionary article on inflation, '[m]acroeconomics in general, and the theory of inflation in particular, is in a fluid state' (Parkin, 1987, p. 836). Based on the neoclassical analysis of money and inflation, the very concept of the price level seems indeed problematic. At the most fundamental level, it can be shown that any aggregate price index can logically be used to assess neither the purchasing power of money nor its variations over time. The principal argument is a compelling one, as we shall attempt to explain in detail. According to traditional analysis, monetarist as well as Keynesian, inflation is a situation in which too much money chases too few goods.[4] This amounts to saying that any inflationary state is characterised by an excessive money stock compared to the total stock of saleable output. So far, so good. Yet, how is this inflationary gap (to be) measured? Reference to the general price level and its variation over time would be a logically correct one if, and only if, the money stock and total output were autonomous and (at least in part) independent from one another. However, this cannot be so, neither in theory nor in practice. Besides the fact that the economic measure of output as a whole cannot be established independently of money (owing to the physical heterogeneity of the thousands of goods and services produced in any period), the aggregate level of prices is unable to measure objectively the two things on which it is based, namely money and output. Indeed, in the maintained method of economic analysis the measure of total output sold is determined via the aggregate price level, and the latter is arrived at by the confrontation on the market place between this very same output and the money stock. The argument is circular, as we shall see in the central part of this book.[5] Elaborating this point, it can then be shown that the theoretical problems of inflation analysis by means of price index computation may be ascribed to the underlying, and ill-grounded, neoclassical theory of money. As Lord Desai argues, one may confidently claim today that, in spite of two hundred years of monetary economics, there is still a manifest 'lack of a theory for a monetary economy' (Desai, 1996, p. 1). The need therefore arises to go so far as to reconsider the nature of money, in order to understand inflationary pressures[6] and, hopefully, to manage them accordingly.

The third, ambitious goal of this book is precisely to gain a deep understanding of inflationary disequilibria, grounding it on a sound theory of modern money. Assuredly, this is a challenging target. It might give rise to a number of fundamental questions which need further exploration, beyond the scope of this work. But it might also be far-reaching, inasmuch as it might provide us with a few macro-theoretic elements in order to elaborate an anti-inflation policy that can be successful. One of the most worrying conclusions arrived at by a number of inflation analysis surveys points indeed to the hazardous results of contemporary macroeconomic policies aimed at controlling inflation (Hudson, 1982, p. 55). Despite the low levels of measured price increases recorded in recent years, it can in fact hardly be denied that inflation, at present, still is a pathology of our money-using economic systems. The very practice of indexation is in itself the sign of a disorderly working of our monetary economies of production. It is the purpose of this book to give a fresh look at this disorder, that is, inflation, from a relatively new macro-theoretical vantage point that goes so far as to reconsider money and banking principles. As stated by Cencini and Baranzini in their 'Introduction' to *Inflation and Unemployment*, '[t]he concept of excess demand and the idea that inflation is provoked by an anomalous increase in the money supply have not been followed to their extreme implications and there is still a lot of confusion about the role played by banks in the process of money creation' (Cencini and Baranzini, 1996, p. 1). It is along these lines that our analysis has been conceived in an attempt to shed some light on a yet obscure topic, in order to forge ahead a research programme capable of achieving monetary order. Surely, much more work needs to be done in specifying the macro-theoretical elements put forward here, before our story can be made fully persuasive. But to the best of my knowledge, this is the only attempt to integrate the economics of inflation within a monetary investigation that goes to the roots of the phenomenon, by critically assessing the canonical research strategy of measuring, and seeking to control, inflation by means of price index analysis.

Such an approach quite naturally requires this book to be divided into three parts of equal importance. Following an order of increasing difficulty, this analytical structure is intended to isolate the crucial features of contemporary inflation analysis, in order to take the reader safely into a fruitful investigation of the political economy of inflation.

The first part is devoted to the methodological issues in the measurement of inflation, where emphasis is laid on both the perceived and unperceived weaknesses of the conventional analysis of price level changes. The problems already start with the need to define the object of inquiry, that is, inflation. As soon as the latter is defined as an ongoing increase in a somehow aggregate price level, the door is indeed opened for the introduction of the multifaceted price index analysis and the technical theoretical conundrum these indices inevitably raise. Whilst the age-long methodological debate in traditional analysis has focused on a number of technical issues, some important conceptual problems have probably been unnoticed so far and are still waiting to be brought forward in this framework. In particular, a principal point that seems to be either misunderstood or neglected altogether in the ongoing debate on price measurement issues concerns the heuristic status of a microeconomic investigation into what fundamentally is a macroeconomic pathology, that is, inflation. To put it briefly, the problems revolve around the paradigmatic approach to macroeconomics, linked to the search for microfoundations. By assuming that the functioning, as well as the malfunctioning, of the economic system as a whole can be apprehended, and perhaps cured, by modelling the representative agents' forms of behaviour and then aggregating the models' results over the entire set of economic units, mainstream investigation has been led into a dead end.[7] This is particularly evident in inflation analysis, where it is traditionally assumed that (the loss in) the purchasing power of money can be assessed with a micro-statistical apparatus grounded on the aggregation of 'elementary transactions' adequately fitted into a quantity-theoretical 'equation of exchanges'.

Although this book does not explicitly focus on the history of economic thought, the seeds of the main conceptual problems of contemporary inflation theory, and policy, can be found in the fundamentals of the quantity theory of money, which is indeed a quantity-of-money theory of the price level. Part Two is therefore aimed at a critical appraisal of this theory, in both its 'old' and 'new' portrayal. The idea of the existence of a price level, as well as that of the possibility to determine its magnitude by applying index number theory, were in fact laid down by the founding fathers of twentieth-century quantity theory, among whom Irving Fisher stands out for his influential book on *The Purchasing Power of Money* (1911/1931) and his related work on *The Making of Index Numbers* (1922). Hence, as we shall argue at length, the way out of the dead end in current inflation analysis seems to require a renewed critical appraisal of the quantity theory. In particular, one is led to ask if money and output really are two distinct, and (at least partly) autonomous, things, and whether money can be depicted as a veil – as suggested for instance by Professor Pigou (1949). Ultimately, the purpose of such an in-depth analysis of money is to provide some new insights into the hectic debate opposing the advocates of the exogeneity-of-money paradigm to the adherents to the endogenous money approach. In this connection, the still widely shared belief that money owes its existence to the definition by the State of the unit in which payments are made (see for example Wray, 1998b) does not go far enough to be able to distinguish analytically the logical nature of money from either its historical or jurisdictional origins (see Realfonzo, 1998, for an excellent discussion of these issues with respect to the 1900–40 money and banking debate).[8] A reconsideration of the means-of-payment function in adherence to a logical analysis of money is thus attempted in the central part of the book, since this analytical step may be instrumental to elaborate a realistic, useful, and policy-oriented theory of inflation.

The analysis carried out in the third, and last, part of this book should then be considered as a modest attempt to contribute to the construction of a modern paradigm for inflation analysis that fully complies with the logical nature of money as well as with the factual working of a monetary production economy. Based on the line of thought developed by Bernard Schmitt and his school since the early 1950s, such an investigation is centred on the banks' role in the monetisation of the national economy. In particular, a reconsideration of the essence of bank credit and its link to inflationary pressures may be pretty useful to re-appraise modern banking from a macroeconomic point of view. Starting from the intervention of the banking sector into what Davidson (1988) dubs the income-generating finance process, attention is drawn on the alleged monetisation by banks of agents' conflicting claims on available output. Known as the conflict inflation approach, this theory puts emphasis on the supposed behavioural causes of inflation, whose origin is ultimately ascribed to an ongoing struggle for inconsistent income shares between the different functional categories of economic agents (namely, capitalists and labourers, who may be stratified according to their relative labour skills). Now, since the struggle for the distribution of national income cannot really modify the amount of the latter, it is a matter of fact that the money–output relationship is never influenced by the former. So, the next step is to ascertain whether or not the behaviour of the banking sector can really generate inflationary pressures within the economic system. At this stage, care ought to be taken to assess the influence, both in space and in time, on the economy as a whole, of the banks' decision to grant credit to the public. Provided a distinction is made between the micro- and the macro-level of the economy, it can be noticed that bank credit and overdrafts are two forms of advances, and as such they can never be much troublesome for the relationship between money and output. In other words, at the macro-level monetary equilibrium cannot be definitively altered by what microeconomic theories of the banks' behaviour consider to be an excess of credit creation. A further analytical step is required to grasp the malignant nature of inflation and its irremediable alteration of the relationship between money and output, as depicted by the loss in the purchasing power of money. Referring to the analysis worked out by Schmitt (1984; 1996b) and Cencini (1995; 1996), and particularly to their conception of 'empty money', it can be shown that inflation is a pathology that arises within the production process, as opposed to the circulation of already produced goods. From this vantage point, the origin of the loss in the purchasing power of money is to be found in the process of fixed capital accumulation as recorded by the banks' bookkeeping. It is thus on the bookkeeping system of banks' transactions that research must be focused in order to see that the cause of inflation is 'structural' rather than 'behavioural'. As Cencini has pointed out, 'the relationship between money and output can be pathologically modified by a simple accounting mechanism that does not pay sufficient attention to the banking nature of money and to its functional link with production and circulation' (Cencini, 1995, p. 70). It is therefore towards the elaboration of a monetary structure of payment systems fully complying with the fundamental requirements of bank money that our efforts have to aim. The research presented here is only a tentative step in this direction. Other, and more important, contributions are to be made if an adequate theory of a monetary economy is to come into existence, to manage inflationary pressures in such a way that monetary order can eventually be achieved. We hope nevertheless to have shown, as Lord Desai indicates in the conclusion of his *Federico Caffè Memorial Lectures*, that 'it is possible to change old habits of thought and rethink the basic issues of monetary economics', to plant 'a seed that may bear fruit at some date in the not too distant future' (Desai, 1996, p. 21).

NOTES

1. See also Blow and Crawford (1999b, p. 1). The implications of overstating price increases for the general government budgetary policy are equally important. In the United States, for instance, it has been calculated that an overestimation of price increases of 1.1 percentage points per annum over the decade 1996–2006 would contribute about 150 billion dollars to the deficit in 2006 and 700 billion dollars to the national debt by then (Advisory Commission to Study the Consumer Price Index, 1996, p. iii). In 2008, 'the cumulative additional national debt from overindexing the budget would amount to more than $1 trillion' (Boskin et al., 1998, p. 3).
2. With a total budget of 25 000 dollars, the Boskin Commission has probably written the most influential measurement paper of the century in terms of its impact. As Diewert states, '[e]very statistical agency in the world is reevaluating its price measurement techniques as a direct result of [the Advisory Commission's] report and the widespread publicity it has received' (Diewert, 1998, p. 56). Yet, as a corollary of the 'Boskin Report', a growing number of professional economists are becoming unsatisfied with the research strategy of measuring inflation via CPI computation. Nordhaus goes as far as to maintain that '[t]he CPI is so complex an organism that, like a Star Wars computer code, few can understand its exact functioning' (Nordhaus, 1998, p. 67).
3. Issues of price measurement may be especially important for the European countries of the Economic and Monetary Union (EMU) area, and for their comparative performance according to the convergence criteria enshrined in the Maastricht Treaty (1992). This is why a Harmonised Index of Consumer Prices (HICP) has been developed by Eurostat (1997). HICP was first used to monitor performance against the convergence criterion for price stability, and from January 1999 it is used by the European Central Bank (ECB) as the target measure of inflation for the EMU area as a whole. Indeed, within a big and structurally heterogeneous single currency area such as 'Euroland', with a unique, one-size-fits-all monetary policy across all participating countries, a single, consistently measured, aggregate price level is necessary for policy making and to gauge the area-wide economic developments. Yet, as the ECB's President has been repeating since his appointment, the fact that the single monetary policy adopts a euro area-wide perspective means that it will not react to specific national shocks (Duisenberg, 1998, p. 4). Clearly, this amounts to saying that the single monetary policy – and thus the single, one-size-fits-all, short-term interest rate within the euro area, which is a necessary corollary of the European single currency – will not in the event prove to be appropriate to the domestic needs of each of the euro-member ('in') countries. No-one doubts that such a risk exists. It may result from cyclical divergence within the euro area, with some participating countries needing to stimulate domestic demand while others are already operating close to capacity (see D. White, 1999). It may arise from differences in budgetary positions even though these are to be constrained through the Stability and Growth Pact (see Rossi and Dafflon, 1999, on the loose definition of the latter). Or it may result from economic shocks of some sort that have a bigger impact on some countries than on others (for example the rise in oil prices in the 1970s, or the German reunification in the early 1990s). Eddie George, the Governor of the Bank of England, has recently been explicit on this point: 'the risk of divergent monetary policy needs within the euro area is real. And if there were a material divergence of monetary policy needs, that could lead to serious tensions, because alternative adjustment

mechanisms, such as labour migration or fiscal redistribution, that exist within individual countries, and which help to alleviate familiar regional disparities when they arise at the national level, are simply not well-developed at the pan-European level' (George, 1998, p. 2).

4. We shall examine the efficient causes of this phenomenon in due course.
5. This *petitio principii* notwithstanding, one must not overlook the fact that, by definition, each price level represents an equilibrium situation between money and output as a whole. So much so that by comparing the level of aggregate prices over time one can determine no inflationary disequilibrium at all.
6. As noted by De Vroey, '[b]efore examining the relationship of money to inflation, it is useful to dwell on the notion of money itself' (De Vroey, 1984, p. 382).
7. See Ormerod (1994, Part One) for a methodological critique of the present state of economics.
8. See also Bouvet (1996, p. 454) for a short discussion of the necessary distinction between the legal and the economic foundations of money and money's worth within the endogenous money approach. A critical appraisal of recent endogenous-money literature can be found in Rossi (1999). This topic will not be addressed here, since the objective of this book is to concentrate on a fundamental critique of traditional inflation analysis, grounded as it is on the concept of the price level and on the measurement of changes in the latter.

PART ONE

METHODOLOGICAL ISSUES IN THE MEASUREMENT OF INFLATION

1. The Methodological Debate in Traditional Inflation Analysis

SOME NOTES ON THE CONVENTIONAL MEASURES OF INFLATION

Defining Inflation

The problem of measuring inflation accurately starts with the attempt to define one of the distinguishing – though not essential – features which have been hampering the development of money-using economies from the antiquity through to modern times. As a number of surveys of inflation theory show,[1] neither a satisfactory nor an exact definition of inflation exists as yet in economic literature, despite the age-long theoretical debate on the purchasing power of money which followed the publication of Ricardo's *The High Price of Bullion* in 1810 (Ricardo, 1810/1951). From early on, much effort about analysing inflationary disequilibria has indeed focused on the most evident factual outcome of the whole process, giving rise to a widely accepted pragmatic definition. Thus, in its most basic terms, '[i]nflation is a process of continuously rising prices, or equivalently, of a continuously falling value of money' (Laidler and Parkin, 1975, p. 741).

Though commonly used as an undiscussed starting point for policy implementation, the symptom-based definition of inflation does not tell us anything about either the causes or the effects of the upward movement in prices. Following a pure empiricist perception, it simply underlines the fact that inflation manifests itself through a sustained increase in the general level of prices, that is, price increases have to be irreversible and concern a somehow weighted average of the prices of all goods and services sold in the marketplace, as we shall see later.

Yet, for those unwilling to accept the axiomatic equivalence between inflation and an ongoing rise in aggregate prices, the abundant literature offers more specialised definitions which bring out some particular characteristics of the phenomenon. In this framework, Bronfenbrenner and Holzman distinguish four alternative types of definitions:

1. Inflation is a condition of generalized excess demand, in which 'too much money chases too few goods.'
2. Inflation is a rise of the money stock or money income, either total or per capita.
3. Inflation is a rise in price levels with additional characteristics or conditions: it is incompletely anticipated; it leads (via cost increases) to further rises; it does not increase employment and real output; it is faster than some 'safe' rate; it arises 'from the side of money'; it is measured by prices net of indirect taxes and subsidies; and/or it is irreversible.
4. Inflation is a fall in the external value of money as measured by foreign exchange rates, by the price of gold, or indicated by excess demand for gold or foreign exchange at official rates (Bronfenbrenner and Holzman, 1963, p. 599).

The first two definitions put forward a causal explanation of inflationary disequilibria, echoing the famous monetarist proposition that '*inflation is always and everywhere a monetary phenomenon* in the sense that it is and can be produced only by a more rapid increase in the quantity of money than in output' (Friedman, 1987, p. 17).[2] According to both interpretations, the direction of causation goes from money supply growth to price increases ($\Delta M \Rightarrow \Delta P$), as was already claimed by the Bullionists at the time of the controversy between the Banking and the Currency schools.[3] In the first case inflation is traced back to demand-side factors, since the observed rise in prices is deemed to originate from excess aggregate demand in consumption, investment or government spending. In the second case a misleading behaviour of the monetary authorities is implicitly assumed to explain why an excessive growth of the money supply occurs in modern economies. As Friedman put it, '[m]onetary authorities have more frequently than not taken conditions in the credit market – rates of interest, availability of loans, and so on – as criteria of policy and have paid little or no attention to the quantity of money per se. The emphasis on credit as opposed to the quantity of money accounts . . . for many of the post-World War II inflations' (ibid., pp. 17–18).

The third definition quoted above is an elaborate version of the simple one laid down by Laidler and Parkin (1975). It suggests the existence of a kind of 'natural' rate of price increases, similar to the hypothesis introduced by Friedman (1968, p. 8) of an underlying natural rate of unemployment.[4] It also considers inflation as resulting mainly from a (real sector) shift in the aggregate supply function due to production costs increases, thus stressing the alleged cost-push causal explanation (as traditionally opposed to demand-pull inflation).[5] It finally introduces the analytical difference between anticipated and unanticipated inflation, which – according to Laidler and Parkin (1975), Frisch (1983, p. 12), Parkin (1987, pp. 833–5), and McCallum (1990, p. 964), among many others – is the key distinctive feature of contemporary inflation theory.

The last definition recorded in the survey paper by Bronfenbrenner and Holzman (1963) concentrates instead on the international effects of inflation, which arise in individual countries that are open economies. Yet, as recognised by Parkin, '[u]nderstanding the international generation and transmission of inflation in a flexible exchange rate world, such as that which had emerged by the mid-1970s, is still far from settled' (Parkin, 1987, p. 835). In this book we shall put this problem aside. The focus will be on the domestic aspects of inflation only.

Along with these 'empirical' definitions of inflation, it is possible to establish a threefold classification according to which criterion is used for that purpose (Table 1.1).

Table 1.1 A typology of inflationary phenomena

Criterion for classification	Attributes
1. Causes of inflation	a) Demand-pull inflation b) Cost-push inflation
2. Expectations of inflation	a) Perfectly anticipated inflation b) Imperfectly anticipated inflation
3. Rate of inflation	a) Creeping or moderate inflation b) Galloping inflation c) Hyperinflation

Source: adapted from Frisch (1983, p. 11).

Each of these criteria has given rise to an immense literature, which is extensively dealt with, for instance, by Bronfenbrenner and Holzman (1963), Laidler and Parkin (1975), Frisch (1977; 1983), Hudson (1982), and Parkin (1987). Their original common ground, as formulated at the outset of this section, can easily be traced back to the traditional (neoclassical) dichotomy, according to which the notion of price level is established by relating the stock of money with the stock of output (Figure 1.1).

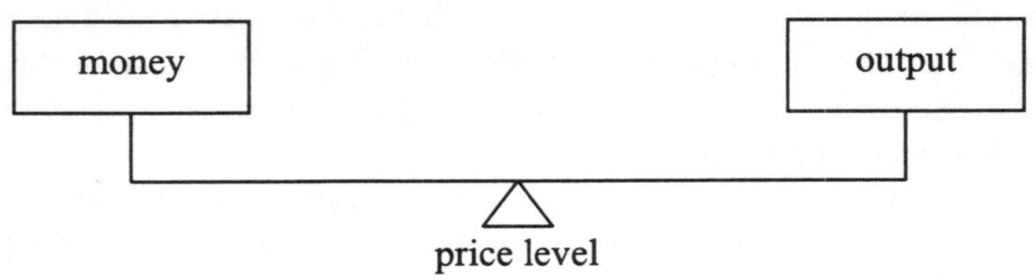

Figure 1.1 The concept of price level

In Figure 1.1 we put on a virtual 'numerical' scale the monetary stock, on one side, and the stock of domestic output (GDP), on the other side. The aggregate price level is arrived at by relating the two stocks. A short numerical example may be useful here. Consider period 1 (for instance, December 1999), where 2000 macro-units of money (M) exist alongside of 100 macro-units of output (Q) in any country whatsoever (C_w): the price level ($P = M/Q$) is then conventionally established at number ($P_1 =$) 20. Now, in order to know whether there is inflation or not and, in the affirmative, to measure the inflationary pressure in the period under examination, standard monetary analysis requires the comparison with some period taken as a reference. Suppose that period 0 (say, December 1998) is the base-period, and assume that price level P_0 is equal to 18 (as expressed by the same convention as above). In its simplest form, economic theory concludes that in the current period the observed national economy suffers from an inflationary gap whose measure (π) is extrapolated by the ratio of the two price levels, as in equation (1.1):

$$\pi \equiv (\frac{P_1}{P_0} - 1) \times 100 \tag{1.1}$$

'The inflation rate, of course, is simply the rate of change of the aggregate price level' (Gordon, 1992, p. 1). If the aggregate price ratio (that is, P_1/P_0) is greater (smaller) than unity, we are told that in period 1 there has been an inflationary (deflationary) gap whose magnitude (π) is customarily expressed in percentage points, as in equation (1.1). So, in our example, a ratio of 10/9 would mean that country C_w witnesses an inflation of 11.1 per cent over a twelve-month period, as calculated in December 1999.

Now, both the schematic representation in Figure 1.1 and equation (1.1) lead us directly to the problem of measuring the actual price level which ought to reveal the presence and the magnitude of any inflationary pressure. Let us begin with the canonical technical approach, which proves to be much more than a mathematical statistical conundrum. We will address the related conceptual issues in the second part of this book.

Introducing Price Index Analysis

The thousands of commodities produced in dynamic open economies such as those of OECD member countries make any price level measurement a formidable organisational and technical quandary. 'While it is conceptually easy to survey the prices of individual commodities at any given time, using these to produce a measure appropriate for monetary policy is far from straightforward. Gauging movements in aggregate prices is neither theoretically nor practically easy' (Cecchetti, 1996, p. 1). Moreover, as Greenspan (1998, p. 3) has argued so convincingly, the notion of general price level – and what one means by its change – is never unambiguously defined. As a matter of fact, each household buys a different basket of goods and services over any given period of time, and most firms produce various sorts of heterogeneous commodities. In the field of 'measurement economics', as Triplett (1975, p. 19) calls it, '[i]ndex numbers are used to reduce and summarize this overwhelming abundance of microeconomic information' (Diewert, 1987, p. 767).

Now, it is well known that the classical definition of index numbers can be traced back to Edgeworth, who proposed 'to define an index-number as a number adapted by its variations to indicate the increase or decrease of a magnitude not susceptible of accurate measurement' (Edgeworth, 1925, p. 379). Applied to the study of inflation, the clue of standard analysis as well as the origin of its methodological problems lies in this essential property of any price level. In particular, the crucial characteristic of index number analysis is that the number arrived at is only an index, not a measure, of the non-observable magnitude (Edgeworth, 1925, p. 382; Allen, 1975, p. 2). The calculation of the (general) price level is thus a mathematical statistical process which can give only a roughly estimated signal about the movement in prices occurring between two points in time. This severe limitation of traditional investigation has already raised many doubts about its validity in measuring inflation accurately. For instance, the 1975 *Report of the Inflation Accounting Committee* is entirely against such a methodology. It maintains in fact that changes in the aggregate price level are actually unquantifiable and that, therefore, the compilation of a general index of price changes is of little practical use (Sandilands Committee, 1975, p. 9). Moreover, as the joint winner of the 1975 Nobel prize for economics puts it in a classic paper on 'Measurement without theory', in this framework the choices of 'what measures to define and compute [for estimating price level changes] are made with a minimum of assistance from theoretical conceptions or hypotheses regarding the nature of the economic process by which the variables studied are generated' (Koopmans, 1947, p. 161).

Starting from the observed serious lack of satisfactory index numbers of the aggregate price level, Book Two of Keynes's *Treatise on Money* deals indeed with the problem of measuring the value of money from a theoretical point of view. Keynes firmly believes that,

> [a]n Index-Number of the Purchasing Power of Money should include, directly or indirectly, once and once only, all the items which enter into final consumption (as distinct from an intermediate productive process) weighted in proportion to the amount of their money-income which the consuming public devote to them (Keynes, 1930/1971, p. 57).

In his analytical attempt to distinguish among a series of secondary price levels, Keynes brought to the fore the still fundamental problems of (*a*) how to measure the value of money in any national economy and (*b*) how to compare it between two distinct points in time or according to the state of the economy.

> In the first place, we do *not* mean by Purchasing Power the command of money over quantities of utility. If two men both spend their incomes on bread and both pay the same price for it, the purchasing power of money is not greater to the one than to the other because the former is hungrier or poorer than the latter. . . . In short, comparisons of Purchasing Power mean comparisons of the command of money over two collections of commodities which are in some sense 'equivalent' to one another, and not over quantities of utility. The problem, therefore, is to find the criterion of 'equivalence' for this purpose (Keynes, 1930/1971, pp. 96–7).

Foreshadowing the modern conception of cost-of-living indices – which are based, as we shall see, on the theory of consumer demand and the implicitly related welfare approach[6] (see for example Braithwait, 1980; Pollak, 1989; Advisory Commission to Study the Consumer Price Index, 1996) – in his *Treatise* Keynes asserts that 'comparisons of the purchasing power of money are the same thing as comparisons of the amounts of money-incomes of similar persons' (Keynes, 1930/1971, p. 97). This framework of inquiry is basically of a microeconomic nature. Claiming that two sets of commodities are to be considered as 'equivalent' if the money-incomes spent for their purchase are the same for 'two persons of equal sensitiveness' (ibid., p. 97), it does not tell us anything on how to make such comparisons for the national economy as a whole.

We are in fact confronted with a double-sided approach to price level measurement, as neatly recognised by Allen (1975, pp. 5–6), which might also explain in part the still hectic debate over the best measure of price movements. On the one hand, many academic researchers aim at a broad objective – measuring the general price level or equivalently, so the argument goes, the purchasing power of money – without specifying the reference sample of consumers or the group of producers considered in this 'stochastic approach'. On the other hand, the majority of empirical analysts follow an 'aggregative approach' whose objective is usually to study the net income or standard of living of a selected group of individuals (for example unskilled workers, elderly or rent-earning consumers).

Now, in this framework it need not be emphasised that '[a]s each household has a slightly different pattern of expenditure, price changes will have varying effects and households will experience different rates of inflation' (House of Commons, 1988, p. 2). A voluminous literature has dealt with this problem, too large to be surveyed by a single researcher. In practice, if not in theory, a price index number is a somehow extrapolated average, a synthetic figure derived from a great variety of price movements. As we are going to see, there are countless ways of computing an average. There are also 'many different aggregate price measures, any of which could be used to measure the change in prices over time' (Beaton and Fisher, 1995, p. 5). The potential for arithmetical discrepancies between these different measures of inflation is indeed very high. How is it possible to choose among them the relevant price index for (monetary) policy implementation? Is there any 'exact' price index which can be used as an operational instrument to assess 'true' inflationary disequilibria from a macroeconomic point of view? Let us try to clarify the terms of the problem by referring to the technical path which has traditionally been followed to deal with it. In a further section we shall examine the usually associated methodological issues.

Selecting the Appropriate Formula

The calculation of the general price level and its related technical difficulties form part of the multifaceted index number problem (Samuelson and Swamy, 1974; Allen, 1975; Diewert, 1976; 1987). Its practical outcome is a series of different formulae put forward by various authors in an attempt to evaluate the change in prices occurring between two situations (usually defined as two distinct periods, that is, the base- or reference-period and the current- or end-period).

As is well known, the index number formulae most commonly used by contemporary statistical agencies to record the level of prices and the variations in that level are obtained from the original ones laid down respectively by Laspeyres (1871) and Paasche (1874). While attempting to improve the mathematical estimation of the average movement in prices in the national economy, Laspeyres was already aware 'that with these figures one cannot appraise the absolute loss in the purchasing power of money' (Laspeyres, 1871, p. 302; our translation).[7] Since the state of price statistics was not as reliable as it ought to be for that sort of extrapolation, Laspeyres maintained that price index analysis could only roughly estimate the decline in the purchasing power of money (ibid., p. 309).

Without dwelling on this technical issue from a historical perspective, the position of the Swiss Federal Statistical Office (SFSO) is particularly noteworthy for the case in point, inasmuch as the Swiss federal administration introduced in May 2000 its sixth totally revised consumer price index since its first computation in 1922. Consider the following quotation: 'A consumer price index may be defined and calculated in several ways. There is neither an ideal nor a unique index which is correct. Different conceptions are possible according to the use one is looking for' (Office fédéral de la statistique, 1993, p. 18; our translation).[8] Which functional form for a price index should then be adopted, if we are looking for an accurate measurement of inflation from a macroeconomic standpoint? The SFSO endorses the Laspeyres formula as the best solution for calculating national CPIs, more for the practical merits of its computation rather than for the theoretical qualities of the formula itself (ibid., p. 42). At a more sophisticated level, a large body of literature has grown up to work out the technical properties an index number formula should satisfy in order to justify its practical use. This 'axiomatic approach' brings to the fore a series of tests which seem to be reasonable and desirable for assessing the validity of economic index numbers (Diewert, 1987, pp. 768–9; Reserve Bank of New Zealand, 1997, p. 22). 'The test approach to index number theory . . . looks at an index number formula from the viewpoint of its mathematical properties' (Diewert, 1998, p. 48). By analogy with one-good-one-agent intertemporal equilibrium models, the criteria for finding well-behaved formulae say, for example, that,

> [i]f a single good's price doubles, the index should double; the index between any two dates will not be changed if the base period of the index is changed from one date to another; a dimensional change in the good (as from grams to pounds) should not change the index, nor should a dimensional change in money (as from pennies to dollars or dollars to pounds) (Samuelson and Swamy, 1974, p. 566).

Now, it is a well-established fact that '[t]he Laspeyres price index does not represent an ideal solution, neither from the viewpoint of both the axiomatic and the economic approaches, nor from the viewpoint of its use for deflating national accounts' (Office fédéral de la statistique, 1993, p. 42; our translation).[9] Indeed, '[the Laspeyres index] assumes no consumer substitution occurs in response to changes in relative prices, an assumption that is extreme, unrealistic and unnecessary' (Boskin et al., 1998, p. 7). On purely mathematical grounds, several alternative formulae have been put forward to give a better estimate of changes in aggregate prices than the one laid down by Laspeyres, which can be written as equation (1.2):

$$P_L \equiv \frac{\sum_{i=1}^{n} p_i^1 q_i^0}{\sum_{i=1}^{n} p_i^0 q_i^0} \times 100 \tag{1.2}$$

where:

P_L = Laspeyres price index
i = commodity i (for $i = 1, \ldots, n$)
p_i^1 = price of commodity i in (current-) period 1
p_i^0 = price of commodity i in (reference-) period 0
q_i^0 = quantity of commodity i purchased in (base-) period 0.

Addressing the choice of the relevant quantity vector (the q_i's) for price index analysis, Paasche argued that, to reflect actual inflation, this vector should capture the structure of expenditures in the current period (Paasche, 1874, pp. 171–3). The statistical approach suggested by Paasche associates therefore any price vector with the quantities pertaining to the end-period, as in equation (1.3):

$$P_P \equiv \frac{\sum_{i=1}^{n} p_i^1 q_i^1}{\sum_{i=1}^{n} p_i^0 q_i^1} \times 100 \tag{1.3}$$

where:

P_P = Paasche price index

q_i^1 = quantity of commodity i purchased in (current-) period 1.

Now, as a general rule, it is usually claimed that the Laspeyres index tends to overstate the upward movement in prices, while using the Paasche formula leads to underestimating price increases[10] (see for example Triplett, 1975, p. 22; Frisch, 1983, pp. 14–15; Gordon, 1992, p. 7; Cunningham, 1996, p. 13; Boskin et al., 1998, pp. 6–7; Diewert, 1998, p. 48). Further, according to one of the most prominent researchers of the US Bureau of Economic Analysis, 'the ratio of two different Paasche indexes has no standing in the theory of index numbers, and cannot be interpreted as an inflation measure' (Triplett, 1980, p. 569). In particular, calculating the change in a Paasche price index between two points in time (say, period t+1 in comparison with period t) has no clear meaning as a measure of inflation, because this ratio would have two distinct sets of weights (the q_i's in equation (1.3)), as in expression (1.3*):[11]

$$\frac{P_P^{t+1}}{P_P^t} = \frac{\sum_{i=1}^{n} p_i^{t+1} q_i^{t+1}}{\sum_{i=1}^{n} p_i^0 q_i^{t+1}} \times \frac{\sum_{i=1}^{n} p_i^0 q_i^t}{\sum_{i=1}^{n} p_i^t q_i^t} \tag{1.3*}$$

More recent theoretical work on index numbers has put forward different 'mixed-weight' formulae, in order to provide closer estimates of 'true' price movements in the aggregate (see especially Diewert, 1987, for a survey). As postulated by Pigou (1920, p. 84), Fisher (1922) and Bowley (1928, p. 217) in their contributions to the in-depth research activity on index numbers of the 1920s, a geometric average of P_L and P_P might represent a better approximation of the underlying aggregate price level, of which the Laspeyres and Paasche measures could be seen, respectively, as the upper and the lower estimated bounds. In its original form, what is now called the 'Fisher ideal price index' (P_F) is given by the square root of the product of P_L and P_P, as in equation (1.4):

$$P_F \equiv \sqrt{P_L \times P_P} \tag{1.4}$$

Further derivation from this 'superlative index number formula' – according to the terminology first proposed in a seminal paper by Diewert (1976, pp. 136–7) – led a number of mathematical statisticians to extrapolate price changes from a weighted geometric mean of the growth rates in prices,[12] by adopting the functional form advocated by Törnqvist (1936, p. 28) as in equation (1.5):[13]

$$P_T \equiv \prod_{i=1}^{n} \left(\frac{p_i^1}{p_i^0} \right)^{s_i} \times 100 \tag{1.5}$$

where:

$$s_i = (0.5) \frac{p_i^0 q_i^0}{\sum_{i=1}^{n} p_i^0 q_i^0} + (0.5) \frac{p_i^1 q_i^1}{\sum_{i=1}^{n} p_i^1 q_i^1}$$

represents the average expenditure share on good *i* over the two periods.

In fact, neither P_F nor P_T (the Törnqvist price index) has ever been widely used in the economic field, mainly because these formulae have no direct interpretation in practice (Allen, 1975, p. 2; Frisch, 1983, p. 15; Fortin, 1990, pp. 109–10). On the other hand, the continuous-time price index number due to Divisia (1925; 1926) – which also inspired the establishment of P_T as openly recognised by its proponent (Törnqvist, 1936, p. 28, n. 2) – is well known among econometricians for its many desirable properties (see for example Richter, 1966, pp. 749–53). However, as testified by econometrics literature, the basic difficulty with Divisia indices lies in what has been termed the path independence problem (Hulten, 1973, pp. 1023–4; Samuelson and Swamy, 1974, pp. 578–80; Diewert, 1976, pp. 124–9). Being obtained by a line integration over the path followed by the individual variables (in our case, prices and quantities entering the market basket over time interval [0, *t*]), the Divisia price index depends, as a general rule, on the trajectory over which the integration is taken. This means that 'a multiplicity of index values may be associated with any given point in the set of variables being indexed' (Hulten, 1973, p. 1017), depending on the particular path of integration which has been selected. Yet, to obtain the necessary and sufficient conditions for path independence, the Divisia index requires a set of very restrictive assumptions which threaten its analytical validity (Hulten, 1973, pp. 1018–19; Griliches, 1990, p. 188). In particular, to avoid indeterminacy, one has to assume that the vector-valued function is linearly homogeneous, and that, for empirical analysis, the continuous-time (shifting) weights can be approximated by some kind of either discrete (two-period) averages or chain indexing procedures (Hulten, 1987, p. 900).

All in all, without going further, we can conclude that the technical-statistical approach does not enable us to define any aggregate price measure as being better than the others. From a theoretical perspective, it is impossible to discriminate among P_L, P_P, P_F, P_T and whatever other price index formula the large literature may provide. Many contemporary leading professionals (econometricians, statisticians, and political economists) are indeed well aware of this failure, but do not seem to worry too much. Diewert is a case in point. According to him, 'it does not matter very much which of these formulae we choose to use in applications: they will all give the same answer to a reasonably high degree of approximation' (Diewert, 1987, p. 773). Yet, given the widespread use of price indices in current economic analysis – from monetary policy decisions to assessing national economic performance (and related cross-country comparisons) and escalating government spending and taxes – it can hardly be doubted that the exact measurement of inflation is a key problem which deserves a careful and thorough investigation, if we want to find an answer to the provocative assertion that 'the opinion of representative house-wives would be preferable to the formulae of mathematical statistics' (Edgeworth, 1925, p. 380).

DEBATED METHODOLOGICAL ISSUES IN TRADITIONAL INFLATION ANALYSIS

Since the publication of the so-called 'Stigler Report' (National Bureau of Economic Research, 1961), which represents the most comprehensive review of American price statistics in the twentieth century,[14] the official price indices compiled regularly by government statistical agencies have been subjected to a persistent barrage of methodological criticism (Blinder, 1980, p. 539; Gordon, 1990, p. 9). As a matter of fact, '[t]here has been increasing interest in recent years in the extent to which official consumer price indices may mismeasure the true rate of inflation' (Blow and Crawford, 1999b, p. vii). Although the vast empirical literature on this topic focuses mainly on three G7 countries (namely, the United States, Canada and the United Kingdom), the same set of issues apply, at least in part, to other official price indices as well (for example the newly revised Swiss CPI, which may be considered in the present context as representative of a heterogeneous, though small, country).[15] 'How to obtain information on who is buying what, where, when, why and how in an economy, and then to aggregate it into one or a few measures of price change raises a host of complex analytical and practical problems' (Boskin et al., 1998, p. 9).

With few exceptions, all aggregate price statistics are still constructed using fixed-weight Laspeyres indices, with reweighting every five to ten years (Diewert, 1987, p. 773; Turvey, 1989, p. 38). Table 1.2 shows the frequency of weighting revisions within the G7 (in comparison with a small, yet heterogeneous, country such as Switzerland), but it should be recalled that in some cases the process of revising weights does not abide by a strict temporal rule (Italy is a typical example).

Table 1.2 Frequency of weighting revisions of some official price indices

Country	Index name	Frequency of weighting revisions
United States	Consumer Price Index (CPI)	10 years
Japan	Consumer Price Index (CPI)	5 years
Germany	Consumer Price Index (CPI)	5 years
Canada	Consumer Price Index (CPI)	4 years
Italy	Consumer Price Index (CPI)	3 to 4 years[a]
France	Consumer Price Index (CPI)	5 years[b]
United Kingdom	Retail Price Index (RPI)	yearly
Switzerland	Consumer Price Index (CPI)	yearly

Notes

[a] The Italian weights are not revised following a temporal rule, but were revised in 1985, 1989, 1992, 1996 and 2000.

[b] From 2002 the revision will take place yearly.

Sources: Office fédéral de la statistique (1993, p. 43; 1999b, p. 8); Advisory Commission to Study the Consumer Price Index (1996, p. 16); Cunningham (1996, p. 42, Table 6).

Such an approach to price level measurement is necessarily backward looking (Heymann and Leijonhufvud, 1995, p. 99). Since aggregate price indices are compiled regularly but with a time lag and, moreover, with weights that fail to reflect truly contemporaneous consumption patterns,[16] they cannot be used to measure the movement in current prices. Further, although there already are many practical difficulties in gathering complete and accurate price data at the level of both representative items and elementary aggregates (Allen, 1975, p. 39; Turvey, 1989, pp. 53–83; Foss, 1993, pp. 277–8), a major methodological problem lies in the impossibility to obtain price information for the same bundle of commodities and services through time (Armknecht and Weyback, 1989, p. 107). As pointed out by the US Price Statistics Review Committee headed by George J. Stigler,

> [t]he data used in computing the value of a price index are ordinarily derived almost entirely from a highly complex network of samples – samples of goods and services, samples of localities in which prices are collected, samples of actual price reporters, and samples of points in time. It is therefore apparent that a value of an index depends upon the particular samples from which the basic data are obtained, and that different samples will lead to possibly different values of the index (National Bureau of Economic Research, 1961, p. 39).

On the whole, this state of the art is not altered but strengthened by the fact that commonly used price indices contain many sorts of biases, that are nevertheless to be kept conceptually distinct from the more easily avertible computational errors (which in practice have been eradicated since the introduction of both high-performing computers and well-tried software). For a caricatural picture of this latter aspect, let us follow Gordon's (1981) evocative tale and imagine that someone pushes the wrong button on a computer used for CPI calculation. If the resulting estimation of 'headline' inflation rate (that is, the twelve-month change in the overall CPI) is, say, 12.1 per cent instead of the 'true' rate of 11.1 per cent, as recorded by a competing government price measure such as the 'Gross Domestic Product deflator', then millions of households and firms may undergo a number of extra charges, or may benefit from windfall gains, which would also have important budgetary consequences for the general government sector. To cite an example taken from a recent US *Congressional Budget Office Paper*, '[i]f the CPI has an upward bias, some federal programs would overcompensate for the effect of price changes on living standards, and wealth would be transferred from younger and future generations to current recipients of indexed federal programs' (quoted by the Advisory Commission to Study the Consumer Price Index, 1996, p. 6).

No-one doubts that the construction of a measure for aggregate price movements still is a politically sensitive area (Gordon, 1992, p. 1; Silver and Ioannidis, 1994, p. 555; Shapiro and Wilcox, 1996, p. 3). The different distribution of income resulting from different price level estimates is perhaps the main obstacle to reach a broad political consensus on the extent to which money wages, social security expenditures and other disbursements (for example separate maintenance) ought to be escalated (by the annual percentage change in CPI) by law or by private contract. Any statistical extrapolation from official price series is likely to find both supporters and opponents, because, as we noted in the previous section, no single approach to index number construction yields the 'optimal' functional form (Allen, 1975, p. 3; Diewert, 1987, pp. 767–8). In the wake of the recent debate on inflation measurement issues, especially in the United Kingdom and in the United States,[17] this might be a good time to re-examine the problem of inflation from a relatively new macroeconomic perspective. Let us first address the methodological problems of traditional investigation and begin with the most debated issues. We shall turn to the deeper analytical questions in Parts Two and Three.

The Compositional Issue of the Representative Market Basket

Generally speaking, it is claimed that the CPI is the best measure currently available for measuring inflation (see the final report of the Advisory Commission to Study the Consumer Price Index, 1996, p. ii, as well as Cunningham, 1996, p. 9; Steindel, 1997). The theoretical framework for CPI construction is provided by the theory of consumer demand, as developed for instance by Lancaster (1971; 1991) and Deaton and Muellbauer (1980). Demand and hence the determinants of prices are based on the canonical utility function approach, first translated in indifference maps on a bidimensional (Cartesian) system by Edgeworth. Similarly, CPI compilation is grounded on a basket of consumption items (goods and services) sold in the marketplace, whose quantities (that is, the 'weights') are fixed according to the most recent nation-wide household expenditure survey.[18] To this approach, Keynes's main (involuntary?) contribution was to argue, in *A Treatise on Money*, that,

> [s]ince the Purchasing Power of Money in a given context depends on the quantity of goods and services which a unit of money will purchase, it follows that it can be measured by the price of a *composite commodity*, made up of the various individual goods and services in proportions corresponding to their importance as objects of expenditure (Keynes, 1930/1971, p. 53).

Now, in principle, an 'ideal' aggregate price measure would logically include all economic transactions recorded[19] over the chosen period (for example a calendar month). In practice, however, to make price index analysis manageable, government statistical agencies apply 'a simplified view of the marketplace and consumer behavior. This simplified view is reflected throughout the CPI approach' (Advisory Commission to Study the Consumer Price Index, 1996, p. 11). Thus, by definition, the selected sample of goods and services included in the CPI's market basket covers but a part of currently produced output and varies from a list of about 300 representative items (such as in the Swiss case)[20] to more than 70 000 commodities (as those subsumed in the American overall CPI).[21]

For instance, an important category of expenditures often omitted from CPI calculation, because of the 'almost insurmountable difficulties regarding existing methodology' (Balk, 1980, p. 68), concerns some goods and services of an exceptionally seasonal nature, such as fresh fruits and vegetables, Christmas trees or summer-rented flats.[22] As testified by empirical work of a number of both professional statisticians and econometricians, '[f]or food items, the price dispersion within an RPI item in a particular month, as measured by the coefficient of variation, is typically 5–15 per cent and for some foods such as fresh vegetables and some meat may be 25 per cent' (Carruthers et al., 1980, p. 20).

In a similar vein, the Bureau of Labor Statistics (BLS) – the government statistical agency responsible for CPI calculation in the United States – omits deliberately two categories of goods and services, namely 'out of scope' and 'truncated', from the overall consumer basket (Gale, 1981b, p. 60). Out-of-scope items (for example commuting expenses and life insurance) are not included in the Consumer Expenditure Surveys, mainly because the BLS has not been able to determine how to measure them for price index analysis. Truncated goods data, instead, are collected in these surveys but do not enter the actual sample of representative items forming the CPI's market basket.[23]

Yet, even accepting this framework of inquiry, the problem is, as already recognised in *A Treatise on Money* by Keynes himself, that 'the composite commodities representative of the actual expenditure of money incomes are not stable in their constitution as between different places, times or groups' (Keynes, 1930/1971, p. 95). By adopting the methodology of statistical sampling, the agencies responsible for official CPI computation are therefore constrained to accept, quite mechanically, an unrealistic set of restrictive (behavioural) assumptions,[24] which are reflected in the sampling techniques for selecting (*a*) the relevant geographic areas,[25] (*b*) the reporting outlets,[26] (*c*) the time of data collection,[27] and (*d*) the population surveyed.[28] As recognised by the authors of the so-called Boskin Report,

> one has to define the commodities and services the prices of which one wants to measure, how to measure them, how to collect data on them, over what span of time and at what interval, where and when to collect the data, and how to aggregate them into one or several overall summary statistics. At each of these levels, various judgments and assumptions must be made to make practical headway (Boskin et al., 1998, p. 6).

These judgements and assumptions are epitomised in the concept of the fixed-weight market basket, which necessarily becomes less and less representative over time as consumers buy different bundles of commodities. Indeed, the most striking example of the methodological problems inherent in the CPI approach probably relates to the failure to capture new sorts of goods in a timely manner.[29] This built-in deficiency reduces the ability of price index analysis to cover the actual consumption basket and, as we shall see later, to measure inflation accurately.

Now, a further difficulty in defining the appropriate market basket for inflation analysis arises with the category of 'durable goods'. As one of the most distinguished scholars in 'measurement economics' puts it, this is 'the segment of the economy where official price data are most vulnerable to inaccuracy, owing to the heterogeneity and changing specifications of durable goods' (Gordon, 1990, p. 9). For example, it is a well-known fact that, in developed market economies, by far the largest single weight in the overall CPI is given to the housing component (which is itself composed of several expenditure classes).[30] Without going into the details of this category, it is sufficient here to mention the twin major controversial points in the treatment of housing expenditure data, namely the treatment of homeownership costs and the related mortgage interest payments. In this respect, as reported for instance by Gordon, the American government statistical agency before 1983 had been making 'the fatal error of treating the whole population as if it were in the predicament of a newlywed couple buying its first house' (Gordon, 1981, p. 121). In effect, the BLS treated each homeowner as if he or she were buying a house outright, since it used price data of newly constructed home purchases for estimating the rate of change of the CPI's dwelling costs (Blinder, 1980, pp. 550–2; Gordon, 1992, pp. 40–1). In 1983, the housing component of the American CPI shifted to the so-called 'rental equivalence' approach, which simply assumes that homeownership costs move in proportion to market rents observed in the domestic private sector for similar properties.[31] The same treatment had been applied in the United Kingdom until 1975. In this country the costs of homeownership in terms of shelter prices have never been directly included in the monthly-calculated RPI. 'Before 1975 owner occupiers' housing costs (other than rates and maintenance) had been represented in the RPI by estimates of the rents which properties might have been let at on the open market' (Evans, 1989, p. 39). Yet, because of practical contingencies engendered by a marked slowdown in the British private-rented sector during the 1970s, since 1975, homeownership costs entering the monthly RPI have been measured by referring to annual mortgage interest payments, thus resorting to the well-known 'user cost' concept.[32] There were in fact many methodological objections to the standard rental-equivalence formulation, centred around the fact that most single-family homes are not rented and, therefore, the data collected in open markets cannot be used to estimate virtual rents of single-family houses (Blinder, 1980, p. 555; Gordon, 1981, p. 126; Wynne and Sigalla, 1996, p. 69). However, estimating housing expenditure data by adopting user cost formulae does not really improve the methodology of price index analysis. As far as mortgage interest disbursements are concerned, the calculation of the official homeownership index is indeed questionable, because 'the amount borrowed by a household for house purchase is largely determined not by house prices but by household income' (Evans, 1989, p. 41). Further, the user cost approach is too ambiguous to give a clear-cut shelter price proxy for the owned-accommodation index (Blinder, 1980, pp. 560–1; Evans, 1989, pp. 49–51; Fortin, 1990, pp. 125–7; Gordon, 1992, p. 41). There are in fact many ways to measure the user cost of housing, because various components might be included in (or excluded from) the relevant equation and, moreover, each ingredient (particularly, the mortgage interest rate) turns out to be inherently volatile.[33]

On the whole, although the rental equivalence approach might seem to fit the CPI's housing component better than the user cost approach, there are many serious problems of both a methodological and an empirical nature in its implementation. These problems are not specific to the housing component of aggregate price indices. An analogous set of issues may indeed apply to most durable goods (for example cars, aircraft, computers and other electrical appliances such as hi-fi equipment or microwave ovens – to quote only the main categories where empirical work is being carried out for price measurement purposes), for the problem at stake reverts to the daunting, and multifaceted, stock–flow analysis. In short, in the jargon of economics, the widely accepted definition of durability implies that one has to decide if, and how, to distribute the value-in-use of a durable good over its lifespan. The *locus classicus* of all such analyses is 'the fact that durable goods are consumed (and hence yield utility) only gradually over time' (Blinder, 1980, p. 549). Indeed, many influential economists maintain that we must price the service flow (say, over a year) of durable goods, instead of adopting their purchase price, when compiling price indices for scientific work.[34] Following this line of thought, the annual percentage change in CPIs ought to be based on a service-flow concept of durable goods, and not on 'a current acquisition price index that treats durable [good] purchases as instantaneous consumption' (ibid., p. 563).

Yet, it is important to underline at this juncture (as later chapters will show) that, despite appearances to the contrary, any purchase of durable goods is a consumption when considered from an economic perspective. As Verdon has it,

> [w]hen an individual buys durable goods, he or she may go on using them for his or her own satisfaction without implying that he or she goes on 'consuming'. If we want to endow consumption with any meaning at all in an experimental model of complete monetarization we must restrict it to the situation of exchange (Verdon, 1996, p. 162).

Now, as we shall see in Part Two, every consumption is an instantaneous action, since it takes an instant (that is, a zero duration in time) to record an exchange, or a payment, in its essential bookkeeping form. And it is necessary to proceed just one analytical step further in order to reach an important finding, whose theoretical consequences might be far-reaching. On reflection, it should indeed be clear that, from an economic standpoint, consumption is nothing more than an expenditure whose object is a pre-existent good. The physical properties of the good consumed need not concern us here, because we are confronted with the cancellation of a commodity from the economic field, not from the material world. This is not to say, of course, that a newly produced Boeing 777 ceases to exist at the very instant when the bank account of (say) British Airways is debited for its purchase price. What we claim is that this payment literally consumes the exchange value of the Boeing 777, whose existence will then be that of a physical value-in-use until it can serve its specific function properly.[35]

Overall, the distinction between durable and non-durable goods appears to be ill-founded in economics, because it pertains to the physical domain. It is indeed an arbitrary, or at least a subjective, distinction,[36] which gives a misleading view of the economic nature of output. The whole traditional analysis of inflation may consequently be weakened by it. Is a given price change in a good with longer physical durability any more inflationary than in a good with less? The question is ill-conceived (some would say it is nonsensical).

From Consumer Price Indices to Cost-Of-Living Indices

The methodological obstacles facing the calculation of the CPI as an accurate measure for the movement in current aggregate prices have led a number of prominent economists as well as various government agencies and private institutions (for example trade unions and consumer associations) to advocate the establishment of a Cost-Of-Living Index (COLI) as the objective in measuring consumer prices. Perhaps the crucial recommendation the Advisory Commission headed by Michael J. Boskin makes to the American official statistical agency concerns this specific point (Advisory Commission to Study the Consumer Price Index, 1996, p. iii).

It will help to start with two rigorous definitions:

- 'By the expression "cost of living" we mean the monetary value of those consumers' goods which are *in fact* consumed in the course of a certain period of time by an average family belonging to a given stratum of a population' (Konüs, 1939, p. 10).
- 'A cost of living index is a comparison of the minimum expenditure required to achieve the same level of well-being (also known as welfare, utility, standard-of-living) across two different sets of prices' (Advisory Commission to Study the Consumer Price Index, 1996, p. 20).

The COLI is the ratio of the minimum costs a representative household must support, in order to be on the same indifference curve under two price situations. This approach escapes the restrictive, and unrealistic, hypothesis of a fixed consumer basket, for any standard of living may formally be reached by various combinations of goods and services.[37] The underlying concept is thus based on equivalent baskets, rather than on identical baskets as for the CPI (Triplett, 1975, p. 21). So far so good.

Yet, there is no need to go any further into the study of the COLI approach to see that, in principle, a separate COLI could be developed for each and every household based on their actual consumption basket and prices paid (Advisory Commission to Study the Consumer Price Index, 1996, p. 2, n. 2; Pollak, 1998, p. 69). It is indeed widely recognised today, even among political economists and mathematical statisticians, that '[t]he whole of the theory of the cost-of-living index relates to an individual consumer' (Triplett, 1975, p. 65). Now, in practice, price index analysis never deals with the case of a single household. It may be symptomatic of the demise of price level measurement that two outstanding scholars at the Massachusetts Institute of Technology and at the National Bureau of Economic Research have recently admitted that '[w]hen it comes to dealing with groups of consumers, it is less clear what should be done, even in principle' (Fisher and Griliches, 1995, p. 230).

Neither the CPI nor the COLI is equipped to account for the specific expenditure patterns of different groups of consumers (Advisory Commission to Study the Consumer Price Index, 1996, p. 30). In both approaches, the compilation of aggregate price indices rests on expenditure data reflecting the preferences of some average, or representative, households rather than those of a heterogeneous population (Quah and Vahey, 1995, p. 1132; Advisory Commission to Study the Consumer Price Index, 1996, p. 71; Pollak, 1998, p. 75; Blow and Crawford, 1999b, pp. 5–6). Since consumption bundles vary across households, a long-standing controversial issue has been to depict, by a thorough empirical investigation, which types of households experience the largest price increases over a chosen period. As neatly summarised by Robert T. Michael in a famous paper on 'Variation across households in the rate of inflation',

> [t]he question of whether certain types of households experience *systematically* or *persistently* larger or smaller changes in the price of their market basket gets to the heart of the recently intensified social concern about the distributional impact of inflation on various groups in the economy – the elderly versus the young, the poor versus the wealthy, and so forth (Michael, 1979, p. 33).

It should be clear that a single, and somewhat synthetic, figure (be it obtained by adopting either a CPI or a COLI formula) cannot take into account, even approximately, the variability in households' consumption patterns inherent in modern dynamic economies. Hence the puzzling question (Prais, 1959, p. 126; Pollak, 1989, p. 119; 1998, pp. 70–3; Deaton, 1998, p. 44): whose cost of living should a price index represent?

Loosely speaking, it is assumed as a general rule that some average concerning a broadly defined group of households can be used as a roughly good estimator of 'the' national inflation rate. But this point is not corroborated by several empirical studies. On purely factual grounds, concern has indeed been expressed over the inability of a single aggregate price measure to be representative of different forms of consumers' behaviour (see for instance the report of the Sandilands Committee, 1975, p. 13, and Moore, 1990, p. 275). It has been alleged, for example, that '[t]he substantial differences in expenditure shares suggest that in a period of differences in rates of inflation among different commodities, the inflation rate for different age groups may differ' (Boskin and Hurd, 1985, p. 441). Accordingly, the escalation of a number of formal and informal contracts in proportion to the reference price index may be problematic. For instance, in the United States, '[e]ven though retirees are not members of the CPI-W population, the official CPI-W is the index which is used for determining changes in social security payments' (Hagemann, 1982, p. 495). Yet, using a specific subgroup price index, like CPI-W, for escalating (say) retirement pensions, might have an automatic, and unwanted, distributional impact across the whole population. The establishment of a separate price index for the elderly[38] has in fact been a matter of concern, at least in the United States, since the early 1980s (see Boskin and Hurd, 1985; Bureau of Labor Statistics, 1988, and the literature cited therein).

Now, it is very important to be clear on what any aggregate price index whatsoever is supposed to measure, and the purpose(s) for which it is put to practical use, especially considering the dispute on the choice of the commodities' weighting vector to compute a 'social' COLI.[39] When aggregating over a number of representative households, there are indeed two formal methods to calculate the weight of a particular commodity entering the index, as put forward in the classic (1959) paper by Prais. The conventional method consists in constructing a so-called 'plutocratic aggregate price index' (Prais, 1959, p. 127; Diewert, 1987, p. 774), which gives each household's consumption pattern 'an implicit weight proportional to its total expenditures' (Nicholson, 1975, p. 540). The plutocratic weights can be obtained by adopting equation (1.6):

$$\omega_i \equiv \frac{\sum_{h=1}^{m} p_i q_{h,i}}{\sum_{h=1}^{m} E_h} \tag{1.6}$$

where:[40]

ω_i = (plutocratic) weight of good i ($i = 1, \ldots, n$)
$q_{h,i}$ = quantity of good i purchased by household h ($h = 1, \ldots, m$)

and:

$$E_h \equiv \sum_{i=1}^{n} p_i q_{h,i} = \text{total expenditure of household } h.$$

As the functional form of its weights shows, the plutocratic aggregate price index 'gives a relatively greater weight to the richer households' (Prais, 1959, p. 127), that is, to households with relatively large actual expenditures.[41] Conversely, if one aims to give all households equal importance, regardless of their expenditure, then, according to the terminology introduced by Prais (1959), a 'democratic aggregate price index' ought to be established, whose weights would simply be obtained from equation (1.7):

$$\delta_i \equiv \frac{1}{m}\sum_{h=1}^{m} p_i q_{h,i} \tag{1.7}$$

where δ_i is the (democratic) weight of commodity i (for $i = 1, \ldots, n$).

Thus, in short, in the democratic price index each household counts equally, while in the plutocratic price index every pound of expenditure counts equally (Pollak, 1989, p. 123; Deaton, 1998, p. 42).

Yet, a question ultimately arises which goes right to the heart of the spurious 'social' cost-of-living indices: how to choose, in such an approach, the 'true' functional form for measuring inflation accurately over the economy as a whole, that is, across all sectors and all geographic areas; in short, across all economic agents? Once again, as noted above, there is no scientific way to deal with this problem, essentially rooted in a microeconomic research strategy. As far as democratic and plutocratic price indices are concerned, '[a]ny choice among them will depend on assessing the balance of political considerations' (Prais, 1959, p. 131). Perhaps, to conclude, the main point to be underlined here is the distributional issue involved in selecting one of the many aggregate price measures put forward in the vast economic literature. Indeed, households whose actual expenditure rises less than the percentage change estimated by the targeted price index, gain from both the indexed programmes of the general government sector and the escalated receipts they might benefit. The economic agents in the opposite situation lose, instead, part of their purchasing power in what may be termed a zero-sum game over the entire economy.

All in all, the main conclusion to be drawn from this methodological framework of inquiry is that estimating the movement in aggregate prices by means of a COLI cannot provide a more accurate measure of inflation than a CPI can do. Useful though they are, both approaches concentrate on the behavioural influence (mainly in redistributive terms) the process of ongoing rise in prices may have upon several subgroups of economic agents. The fundamental idea behind such a methodology rests indeed on an aggregative, microeconomic assumption, which admits that different sets of domestic income holders may experience different rates of inflation over the same period. Yet, as some macroeconomists like Quah and Vahey (1995, p. 1136) and Wynne (1999, pp. 1–3) have put it, the undeniable evidence that in each and every national economy a common monetary base exists across the entire set of economic units may suggest that there is a unique inflationary process (that is, a single inflation rate) in any given period. The importance of the preceding discussion of price index analysis for measuring inflation over a national economy needs, therefore, to be developed at a more fundamental level. This is the central theme of the next chapter, to which we now turn in an attempt to provide further analytical evidence in support of the line of argument we have been developing so far.

NOTES

1. Bronfenbrenner and Holzman (1963), Laidler and Parkin (1975), Frisch (1977; 1983), Hudson (1982), Parkin (1987) and McCallum (1990).
2. Unless otherwise indicated, italics are from the original quotation.
3. See Humphrey (1999, pp. 67–70) for a recent account of the Currency School–Banking school debate (1830–50).
4. Much discussion about the relationship between inflation and unemployment has given rise to the familiar acronym NAIRU (standing for Non-Accelerating Inflation Rate of Unemployment), which is but a modern reformulation of the basic idea supporting the (long-run) Phillips curve (Phillips, 1958). As neatly summarised by Gordon, '[i]f at any given time there exists a unique NAIRU, then the Phillips curve tradeoff is vertical at that unemployment rate' (Gordon, 1996, p. 1).
5. It has been suggested by Frisch that the dichotomy separating cost-push and demand-pull inflation has lost its meaning in recent literature on inflation, because it is actually impossible 'to identify empirically the two types of inflation' (Frisch, 1983, p. 12). Laidler and Parkin, following the same line of thought, go deeper and argue forcefully that '[s]ince inflation is a phenomenon affecting the whole economy, . . . the cost-push/demand-pull distinction [is] analytically unhelpful as a device for classifying those developments in inflation theory that are grounded in macro-economics' (Laidler and Parkin, 1975, p. 742). This is a point to which we shall return later.
6. 'How much would it cost in today's prices to make the consumer just as well off as he was yesterday? This question cannot be answered without resorting to an arbitrary intertemporal weighting of utilities' (Fisher and Shell, 1972, p. 1). To put the point sharply, Whittington – referring to the work of Amartya Sen – observes that 'utility is strictly a subjective concept, and there is no objective method of comparing the pleasure, or "standard of living", which different individuals derive from consuming even identical bundles of goods' (Whittington, 1983, p. 69). See also Keynes (1909/1983, p. 54).
7. The original (German) quotation sounds more peremptory: 'Dass mit diesen Zahlen über die absolute Grösse der Geldentwerthung nicht entschieden werden soll' (Laspeyres, 1871, p. 302).

8. No translation can properly render the emphatic tone of the original (French) version: 'Un indice des prix à la consommation peut être conçu et calculé de nombreuses manières. Il n'y a pas d'indice qui soit idéal ou le seul à être juste. Différentes conceptions seraient parfaitement justifiables suivant l'utilisation prévue' (Office fédéral de la statistique, 1993, p. 18).
9. 'L'indice des prix de Laspeyres ne constitue une solution idéale ni du point de vue des approches axiomatique et économique, ni du point de vue de son utilisation comme déflateur pour la comptabilité nationale' (Office fédéral de la statistique, 1993, p. 42).
10. The result that the Laspeyres price index always exceeds the Paasche price index is critically dependent on the functional assumption that consumers' preferences are homothetic (Blow and Crawford, 1999b, p. 11). 'In general, if homotheticity is violated, the Paasche price index may actually exceed the Laspeyres price index' (Anderson et al., 1997, p. 47). In practice, if not in theory, homotheticity implies unitary income elasticities of consumers' demand functions, that is, that individual preferences for different goods do not depend on the households' level of welfare (Samuelson and Swamy, 1974, p. 566; Deaton and Muellbauer, 1980, pp. 142–5; Whittington, 1983, p. 68; Barnett, 1987, pp. 145–9).
11. By contrast, the economic interpretation of the rate of change of a Laspeyres price index is straightforward, for this ratio is defined with a single (base-period) quantity vector (that is, q_i^0, as in equation (1.2)). Thus, after simplification, the Laspeyres version of expression (1.3*) would be written as follows:

$$\frac{P_L^{t+1}}{P_L^t} = \frac{\sum_{i=1}^{n} p_i^{t+1} q_i^0}{\sum_{i=1}^{n} p_i^t q_i^0}.$$

12. 'A superlative index requires the same information on prices and quantities as a fixed weight index, but involves interpolating between the two periods rather than treating one of them as the "base" period' (Advisory Commission to Study the Consumer Price Index, 1996, p. 23).
13. See Diewert (1987, p. 768).
14. This also according to the Advisory Commission to Study the Consumer Price Index (1996), which 'did not have the substantial resources that . . . the so-called Stigler Commission . . . had in 1961' (ibid., p. 88).
15. It is a fact that a representative 'Swiss consumer' does not exist, despite the limited size of the Swiss economy. Consumption is closely related to the culture, traditions, lifestyles, and development of the different regions forming the Swiss landscape. The same contention may be made, at a higher level, with respect to the European Union, since there is no identifiable 'European consumer' as such. The recently established Harmonised Index of Consumer Prices for EU countries participating (or wishing to participate) in the final stage of European Monetary Union – which is 'in the form of an index covering the euro area as a whole' (European Monetary Institute, 1997, p. 75) – is grounded in fact on a highly hypothetical consumption behaviour, based on a representative basket of consumers' goods averaged over many different, heterogeneous households. See Eurostat (1997) for both the methodological and the legal framework of HICP.
16. As Boskin et al. notice, 'the expenditure weights used in the Consumer Price Index are several years out of date even on the first day a revision is introduced. For example, [in the United States] the 1982–84 weights were implemented in the CPI program in 1987, and the 1998 revision will use weights from 1993–1995' (Boskin et al., 1998, p. 7).
17. See Bureau of Labor Statistics (1988; 1997), House of Commons (1988), Diewert (1990; 1998), Craven and Gausden (1991), Gordon (1992), Foss et al. (1993), Silver and Ioannidis

(1994), Beaton and Fisher (1995), Quah and Vahey (1995), Advisory Commission to Study the Consumer Price Index (1996), Boskin (1996), Cecchetti (1996), Cunningham (1996), Allen (1997), Greenspan (1997a; 1997b; 1998), Shapiro and Wilcox (1997), Steindel (1997), Abraham et al. (1998), Boskin et al. (1998), Deaton (1998), Nordhaus (1998), Pollak (1998), and Blow and Crawford (1999a; 1999b).

18. In the United States, the main source of information used to determine the specific items which comprise the overall market basket is the Consumer Expenditure Survey (CES). 'The Consumer Expenditure Survey provides a continuous and comprehensive flow of data on the buying habits of American consumers for use in a wide variety of economic research and analysis, and in support of revisions to the Consumer Price Index' (Mason and Butler, 1987, p. 22, n. 3). Since both the material and financial efforts of carrying out this review are very expensive, the federal government 'is only willing to allocate funds for such a survey every decade' (Gordon, 1981, pp. 116–17). Statistics Canada, the Canadian central statistical agency, conducts every four years a Family Expenditure Survey (FES), whose results provide the expenditure data for weighting the national CPI (Fortin, 1990, p. 116). In the United Kingdom, '[t]he FES is an annual random cross section survey of around 7,000 households (this represents a response rate of around 70%). [It] records data on household structure, employment, income and the spending over the course of a two week diary period' (Blow and Crawford, 1999a, pp. 16–17). See also Beaton and Fisher (1995, p. 6) and Cunningham (1996, p. 17).
19. It may be noted in passing that, by definition, this approach (stemming, basically, from a microeconomic research programme) cannot integrate the submerged (black) economy in the statistical model it rests upon (see for example Siesto, 1987, for an attempt to evaluate the submerged economy as a percentage of GDP). Failure to do so adds to the list of methodological drawbacks of price level measurement.
20. Ufficio federale di statistica (1993, p. 4). The British RPI is based upon 500–600 goods and services (see Craven and Gausden, 1991, p. 29; Beaton and Fisher, 1995, p. 7).
21. Actually, the price data for some 70 000 to 80 000 goods and services surveyed in the United States are used to form price indices for 207 item groups, which in turn are aggregated to form the overall CPI. See Advisory Commission to Study the Consumer Price Index (1996, pp. 24–5) and Hulten (1997, p. 92) for more details.
22. 'When making policy, central bankers would like to avoid responding to seasonal fluctuations in price data. While seasonality may be easy to understand in theory, it is extremely difficult to actually remove from most economic time-series' (Cecchetti, 1996, p. 16). For a recent methodological analysis of the seasonal component of aggregate price series in Italy, see Cubadda and Sabbatini (1997).
23. The category of 'truncated goods' is excluded from the consumer price index on account of its non-representativeness of households' consumption. It may comprise, for example, club subscriptions, primary and secondary private schooling, administrative charges for credit-card accounts, musical instruments, and some purchases of jewellery (Gale, 1981b, p. 60; Turvey, 1989, pp. 11–14; Ufficio federale di statistica, 1993, p. 13). Its exact content varies, of course, according to the country considered. It has also been alleged that '[n]onmarket items that heavily affect the quality of life are generally beyond the current scope of such indexes' (Boskin, 1996, p. 23). What is particularly noteworthy here is the difficulty of including public goods and services in CPI measurement, for, as a general rule, there are very few observable market prices in the public sector. Another related issue concerns the depletion of non-renewable resources and other unmeasured items such as environmental services. In fact, in the framework of 'green' national accounting, 'the value that consumers place on the current level of all nonmarket services provided by the environment, presents severe measurement difficulties' (Hamilton and Atkinson, 1996, p. 682). Yet, granting the importance of providing an all-inclusive socio-economic indicator for the actual level of human well-being as well as for sustainable development (see Pearce et al., 1996, and the environmental economics literature cited therein), the problem of

'greening' national accounting aggregates does not seem to be relevant to our investigation. Both environmental services (such as unpolluted air and water) and natural resources (for instance, oil and fuelwood availability) are not part of the economic field – unless they are monetised within a production process. To that extent, they logically do not have to be considered when enquiring into the (alteration of the) relationship between money and output (that is, money's purchasing power). A similar reflection also applies to unpaid work – for instance, a housewife's priceless contribution to the household's welfare or, at a more trivial level, do-it-yourself activities like gardening, decorating, plumbing etc. (see Robinson, 1956, p. 17, for a short list of important, but non-monetised, activities in modern societies). Although all these activities involve human effort (Jevons's disutility of labour), the fact that they actually do not generate money income excludes them from the field of inflation measurement. We should however not lose sight of the fact that all environmental as well as domestic services ought to be monetised, in order to measure resource depletion and pollution emissions in social terms, on the one hand, and to value yet unpaid work, on the other hand. Luxton (1997) provides a good survey of the problems involved in measuring and valuing unpaid work, although it would carry us too far afield to explore them in any further detail here.

24. As we shall begin to see in the next chapter, the resulting discrepancies with respect to macroeconomic reality are more fundamental than 'measurement biases'.
25. According to the 'Boskin Report', the BLS collects price data in 88 locations, called Primary Sampling Units (PSUs). In fact, only the price data of 44 geographic areas are aggregated for monthly CPI compilation (Advisory Commission to Study the Consumer Price Index, 1996, p. 13, n. 10). In a similar mood, with the fifth (1993) CPI reform the Swiss Federal Statistical Office has halved the number of municipalities ('communes') where price data are collected. There are at present (2001) 24 geographic areas which should represent the whole Swiss economy for price index analysis. Office fédéral de la statistique (1993, pp. 35–6, 79) and König (1995, pp. 37–9) give more details on this specific point.
26. 'Taking into account both the dispersion of price movements and the structures of distribution of particular goods, one needs as a general rule 2 to 6 price collection points per commune and for each type of goods' (Office fédéral de la statistique, 1993, p. 36; our translation). ['Compte tenu de la dispersion des variations de prix et des structures des canaux de distribution de certains produits, il faut en règle générale 2 à 6 points d'observation des prix par commune et par type de produits' (Office fédéral de la statistique, 1993, p. 36).] For its part, the American CPI rests upon expenditure data collected from 22 000 outlets sampled according to the so-called Point-Of-Purchase Survey (POPS) (Advisory Commission to Study the Consumer Price Index, 1996, pp. 12–13).
27. In the Swiss case, price data are collected during the first week of the calendar month to which the monthly CPI refers, in order to be as timely as possible (Office fédéral de la statistique, 1993, p. 40).
28. There are indeed as many possible CPI as there are different groups of consumers. In the United States, the two most commonly used measures are CPI-U and CPI-W. 'The former is for all urban consumers, roughly 80% of the population; the latter is for urban wage [earners] and clerical workers, about 32% of the population' (Advisory Commission to Study the Consumer Price Index, 1996, p. 2, n. 2). This is an important point to which we shall return.
29. One cannot be more explicit than this: 'The United States became a motorized society in the 1920's and 1930's, when there was an enormous improvement in the performance of automobiles along with a decline in their price – but the automobile was not included in the CPI until 1940' (Gordon, 1981, p. 130). As a more recent noteworthy example, in 1996 there were approximately forty million mobile phones in use in the United States, but the mobile phone was not included in the American CPI's representative basket at that time (Advisory Commission to Study the Consumer Price Index, 1996, p. 39).

30. In the United States, Canada, the United Kingdom and Switzerland, the housing component accounts for at least 25 per cent of the overall CPI.
31. A number of OECD countries, such as Germany, Spain, the Netherlands and New Zealand, rely upon similar properties' market rents for estimating the housing costs actually supported by owner-occupiers. See Evans (1989, p. 54, n. 6) for bibliographical references; Craven and Gausden (1991, pp. 32–7) and Reserve Bank of New Zealand (1997, pp. 7–10) for further details.
32. On measuring homeownership costs by user cost formulae, see Blinder (1980, pp. 557–65) and the literature he refers to.
33. The British government is indeed well aware of these failures, and tries to overcome them by targeting the annual growth rate of an index (known as RPIX) which excludes – attaches a zero weight to – mortgage interest payments (Bank of England, 1996, p. 5).
34. One of the many recommendations of the Advisory Commission to Study the Consumer Price Index (1996) focuses on this methodological issue: 'The price of durables, such as cars, should be converted to a price of annual services, along the same lines as the current treatment of the price of owner-occupied housing' (ibid., p. 82).
35. Notice the contrast between the economic and physical nature of the object consumed. For expositional convenience we abstract here from the case where the aircraft is resold in a second-hand market. Second-hand transactions will be dealt with later on.
36. In effect, to mention a rather extreme example, from a logical point of view a television set is not more 'durable' than an apple pie, which can be physically consumed over a week (provided that it is stored in the appropriate way) by eating a slice of it per day. Gordon seems to be aware that the distinction between 'durable' and 'non-durable' goods is ill-founded, for he claims that '[i]t is a sign of the times that many goods like sheets and draperies are officially classified as "nondurable" yet actually last longer than many "durable" goods' (Gordon, 1981, p. 131).
37. Within this theoretical framework, it should be recalled that the cost of maintaining a given standard of living can go down while the price of a fixed market basket can go up (Gordon, 1992, p. 7). Moreover, as Fisher and Griliches cogently note, 'there are [in reality] many true cost-of-living indices, each corresponding to a particular indifference curve' (Fisher and Griliches, 1995, p. 229, n. 1).
38. In the American context, Hagemann introduced the acronym CPI-R for the price index of retirees (Hagemann, 1982, p. 503). More recently, the BLS has created an experimental price index for elderly consumers (CPI-E) – defined as aged 62 or older – which is based upon different expenditure weights for the elderly than those for the rest of the population (Bureau of Labor Statistics, 1988, pp. 2–10; Berndt et al., 1997, p. 13). As a matter of fact, '[s]eniors get special discounts, for example, and their geographic distribution, and other factors might cause the prices they pay to differ slightly from those recorded in the CPI' (Advisory Commission to Study the Consumer Price Index, 1996, p. 71, n. 70).
39. On the concept of social COLIs and related technical issues, see Pollak (1989, pp. 128–52). Since the definition of a social COLI depends on the definition of a social welfare function, it seems unlikely that government statistical agencies will ever compute such an index (Pollak, 1998, p. 70).
40. Since it makes little difference in the present discussion, we ignore the superscripts concerning the two price situations (or the two points in time) entering the comparison, because it will ease the exposition to do so.
41. It may be of some help to recall that cost-of-living indices are obtained by the same mathematical technique as that used to compute consumer price indices. So, if a Laspeyres price index is the functional form selected, a plutocratic COLI would be arrived at by substituting the plutocratic weights (the ω_i's) for the standard (base-period) quantity vector (the q_i's) in equation (1.2).

2. From Technical Biases to Analytical Issues

In general, literature on price level measurement admits that CPI computation might be subject to a number of biases as a measure of the 'true' movement in aggregate prices. The analysis of biases in official inflation statistics is usually dealt with by referring to the objective of estimating the cost of maintaining a given standard of living,[1] which is assumed to be a better approach to the inflation problem than calculating the overall CPI. However, as we noted in Chapter 1, the COLI notion does not seem to perform better than actual inflation measurement, because it stems from the same conceptual framework and suffers therefore from the same analytical weaknesses. It is the purpose of this chapter to provide a critical assessment of the methodology used in aggregate price measures, moving from an essentially microeconomic insight, in the first section, towards a relatively new macro-theoretical paradigm that we shall introduce in the second section at an intuitive level. Although there exists a variety of aggregate price measures,[2] here reference will be made to consumer (or retail) price indices only, since these are the main, if not unique, empirical focus of contemporary inflation analysis.

MEASUREMENT PROBLEMS IN AGGREGATE PRICE INDICES

Broadly speaking, critics agree that among the various defects from which the CPI suffers, the most important ones are (*a*) failure to take full account of substitution between consumption items in households' expenditure patterns, and between shopping outlets, and (*b*) difficulty in capturing the change of quality of goods and services entering the market basket. The latter defect, together with (*c*) the difficulty in dealing with entirely new products, forms the so-called 'compositional' bias – according to the terminology propounded by Cunningham (1996, p. 12). Before addressing these and other related issues, it may nevertheless be useful to recall that the aggregation of price data into an overall index may also give rise to a formula bias in the CPI, since the functional forms used in price index analysis already differ on purely mathematical grounds (Triplett, 1975, p. 26; Griliches, 1990, p. 188; Advisory Commission to Study the Consumer Price Index, 1996, p. 4; Greenlees, 1997, p. 175). As we have already noted, the same set of disaggregated data may indeed produce several different estimates of aggregate price movements, according to which index-number formula is chosen for that purpose. Now, let alone the choice of the formula,[3] a series of imperfections still affect the CPI as an accurate measure of inflation, in spite of the undeniable evidence that '[t]he consumer price index is one of the most carefully researched and best executed statistical programs [in modern market economies]' (Shapiro and Wilcox, 1996, p. 2).

These imperfections in the measurement of aggregate prices and hence in that of the rate of variation of the latter, may be classified in two categories, according to whether their effect on the measured price level is a priori indeterminate or if they systematically overstate (understate) price increases. Generally speaking, errors resulting from consumers' substitution of goods and outlets over time have an indeterminate effect on the price level (and might thus to some extent offset each other at the aggregate level), because these substitutions may result from different forms of behaviour other than those elicited by the observed price differentials, and at the statistical level they may not be correctly captured by sampling techniques. On the other hand, failure to take full account of new goods entering the market as well as to measure accurately quality changes in existing goods, may impart a systematic, upward bias on measured price variations, because of the 'price cycle' followed by any new good and also because quality is generally increasing over time. Let us address these issues in turn.

The Substitution Bias

Historically, the substitution bias has been the first identified problem affecting the measurement of fixed-weight price indices. This bias can be separated into two distinct effects, namely item substitution and outlet substitution.

Item substitution

It is nowadays a well-established fact that,

> [s]ince consumers will substitute those goods whose prices rise less or fall more for those whose prices rise more or fall less – and within limits they can do this without reducing their levels of real consumption – the fixed-weight base CPI overestimates rises in the cost of equivalent market baskets (National Bureau of Economic Research, 1961, p. 52).

This statement is supported by some algebraic manipulations of a Laspeyres price index, as demonstrated for instance by Pollak (1989, pp. 11–13) and, at a less sophisticated level, by Cunningham (1996, pp. 20–1). In plain language, this is tantamount to saying that, by holding the base-period representative basket constant, the fixed-weight overall CPI puts too much weight on items that have become relatively more expensive and too little weight on items that have become relatively less expensive. The commodity substitution bias thus arises from the consumers' behavioural tendency to shift purchases away from goods and services whose prices increase relatively faster and towards products whose prices increase more slowly or fall.[4] 'Maintaining the basket constant for a number of years under these conditions implicitly gives too much weight to the first type of goods and too little to the second type, and therefore imparts an upward bias in the CPI inflation rate' (Fortin, 1990, p. 128).

The empirical magnitude of the item substitution bias depends ultimately on both the extent to which consumers buy a bundle of commodities different from the representative market basket and the extent to which relative prices move over the period in which weights are fixed.[5] There have been several careful estimates of item substitution bias in aggregate price indices, most of them relating to the American overall CPI. Some early empirical works 'suggest a discrepancy of less than one tenth of an index point per year' (Triplett, 1975, p. 26), which tended to increase in proportion to the increase in prices of individual goods (Braithwait, 1980, p. 73). More recently, using 1959–85 consumption data from the National Income and Product Accounts, Manser and McDonald's *Econometrica* (1988) paper gives an estimate of about 0.18 per cent per year for the item substitution bias affecting 101 commodity groups of the American CPI (Manser and McDonald, 1988, pp. 909–10). Using the same methodology, Shapiro and Wilcox predict an average item substitution bias of 0.2 percentage points per annum over the period 1996–2006, if no major changes in relative prices occur in this decade in the United States (Shapiro and Wilcox, 1996, pp. 17–18). This also seems to represent a plausible average figure for the Advisory Commission headed by Michael J. Boskin, whose estimated range lies between 0.15 and 0.25 percentage points per annum, even for the years following the benchmark revision of the national CPI in January 1998[6] (Advisory Commission to

Study the Consumer Price Index, 1996, pp. 64–70). Work by Cunningham on the British RPI suggests, instead, an upper bound of around 0.1 percentage points per annum, from which he advocates the sensitivity of the item substitution bias to the frequency of revisions. 'The more frequent the weighting revisions, the less the scope for the index to miss shifts in consumption patterns, and thus the less the scope for systematic [item] substitution bias' (Cunningham, 1996, p. 41).

Outlet substitution

It has been alleged by many applied economists that '[a] major trend in the twentieth-century marketplace has been the replacement of small independent "mom-and-pop"-style retailers with large retail establishments owned by chains' (Reinsdorf, 1993, p. 227). Since prices at the large self-service stores often appear to be lower than prices at the small points of purchase, consumers may shift their purchases from high-cost to low-cost outlets over time (Shapiro and Wilcox, 1996, pp. 33–4; Diewert, 1997, p. 429). Yet, the procedure for incorporating new stores into CPI outlet samples might cause a substantial long-term bias in the aggregate price index. In fact, because of the method used to rotate outlet samples, the periodic survey of the retail stores where agents purchase their goods and services[7] cannot keep track of actual outlet substitution, 'a process of gradual but steady replacement of higher-priced retail establishments by lower-priced entrants' (Reinsdorf, 1993, p. 235). Furthermore, '[s]ince price data are collected *within* outlets, the shift of consumers to purchases from discounters does not show up as a price decline even though consumers reveal by their purchases that the price decline more than compensates for the potential loss of personal services' (Boskin et al., 1998, p. 9). Yet, in contrast to the item substitution bias, 'which can continue forever as long as there is dispersion in relative prices, outlet substitution bias must end when low-cost retailers capture the entire market' (Diewert, 1998, p. 51).[8]

The empirical estimates of outlet substitution bias have been quite rare up to now, mainly because of the monumental data requirements to assess it. Building on the original, and highly detailed, work by Reinsdorf (1993) – who estimated outlet substitution bias to be 0.25 percentage points per annum for certain food and fuel items sold in the United States during the 1980s – some scholars have developed their own estimates of an average figure of this bias for the American CPI (Advisory Commission to Study the Consumer Price Index, 1996, pp. 67–8; Shapiro and Wilcox, 1996, p. 36), the British RPI (Cunningham, 1996, pp. 48–53) or other national aggregate price indices (see for example the work by Crawford on the Canadian CPI, reviewed by Cunningham, 1996, pp. 46–7). On the assumption that some 40 per cent of the overall CPI market basket would be affected by outlet substitution bias,[9] Reinsdorf's estimated magnitude has led the authors of the 1996 'Boskin Report' to figure out a new-outlets effect of (0.25 × 0.4 =) 0.1 percentage points per year for the official American price statistics (Advisory Commission to Study the Consumer Price Index, 1996, pp. 67–8). A similar empirical magnitude has been arrived at for the Canadian CPI,[10] whereas the results of the scenarios modelled by Cunningham (1996, pp. 50–3) range ultimately from 0.08 to 0.25 per cent per annum for the British RPI.

The New-Goods Bias

'The *new-goods bias* results from the inability of bilateral price indexes to take into account the fact that the number of commodities from which consumers can choose is growing rapidly over time' (Diewert, 1997, p. 430). In dynamic market economies where a large number of goods and services are introduced each year, failure to include, in a timely fashion, new items in the CPI basket may lead to a systematic overestimation of aggregate price increases. As argued by Boskin et al. (1998, p. 8) and Deaton (1998, pp. 38–9), the new-goods bias is in fact quantitatively important and very difficult to deal with, because there is no way to compute it on a routine basis. As a matter of fact, any newly introduced commodity usually undergoes a product cycle of falling price and rising sales;[11] later on in its 'life cycle', the good becomes 'mature' and ultimately its price grows more rapidly than the average price of its item category (because there is less opportunity for efficiency gains and the item is supplanted by other (new) products). 'The sequence is easily visualized as a "U"-shaped curve – the price of any given product relative to the consumer market basket starts high, then goes down, is flat for a while, and then goes back up' (Advisory Commission to Study the Consumer Price Index, 1996, p. 34).

To the extent that the government statistical agency's aggregate price measure delays the incorporation of new items into the index,[12] the overall CPI will tend to have an upward 'new-introductions bias' – as it has been termed by Triplett (1993, p. 200) – for it misses the price decline that typically happens in the initial stage of the product cycle. 'In addition, in a Laspeyres price index with a quantity weight that is fixed over several years, the increasing market significance of successful new goods is not taken fully into account, even if they are included – in small quantities – in the price index at a very early stage' (Deutsche Bundesbank, 1998, p. 56). As pointed out by Shapiro and Wilcox, earlier incorporation of new items into the aggregate price index cannot fix the problem within this framework of inquiry. In their own words,

> [e]arly incorporation of new items into the consumer price index will cause them to be underrepresented in the index because they will not have won a significant share of the market compared with the share that they may attain later in their lifecycle. On the other hand, late incorporation will cause the period of supernormal decline in relative price to be missed entirely. The only way out of this dilemma is to combine explicit modeling of the demand for new items with abandonment of the Laspeyres framework (Shapiro and Wilcox, 1996, pp. 27–8).

Given the abundance of new items becoming available each year, empirical assessment of this methodological bias is a very demanding task (primarily because of its voracious data requirements). Put simply, the magnitude of the new-goods bias depends upon the proportion of the households' expenditure on new items and the extent of any price cycle followed by the commodities newly introduced (Cunningham, 1996, p. 32). Trajtenberg (1990) attempts to measure this bias in the case of computed tomography scanners (a highly sophisticated diagnostic technology that produces cross-sectional images of the interior of the body), which have been considered as one of the most remarkable medical innovations of recent times. His findings focus on the initial stages of the life cycle of (these) new items and stress the fact that 'the biases stemming from overlooking the strict new goods case are in all likelihood nil, simply because the quantities of new goods sold at the time of their introduction (during, say, their first year), are usually very small' (Trajtenberg, 1990, p. 24). Using econometric techniques to appraise consumer preferences in the ready-to-eat cereal industry, Hausman concludes, by contrast, that the American price index for cereals 'may be too high by the order of 25% because it does not account for new cereal brands' (Hausman, 1994, p. 29). He maintains that a bias of this magnitude is worth worrying about, for in the period between 1980 and 1992 approximately 190 new brands of cereals were introduced into a pool of about 160 existing brands (ibid., p. 7). In the case of the British RPI, Cunningham assumes instead that a set of new electrical appliances as well as audio-visual products enter the marketplace in January 1987 but are not introduced into the domestic price index until 1991 (in fact, he adds, the date of their introduction can be delayed by several years without affecting the results significantly). By varying assumptions about both the change in the new-goods prices and the share of the item groups taken up, he derives a 'plausible range' for new-goods bias running from 0.02 to 0.16 percentage points per annum (Cunningham, 1996, pp. 38–9). On the whole, however, it is not yet clear whether these, and other,[13] specific new-goods bias estimates may be valid at a large aggregate level (such as the all-item CPI), because 'the scientific basis for making a judgment about the magnitude of the new-items effect is particularly thin' (Shapiro and Wilcox, 1996, p. 31).

The Quality-Change Bias

In many cases the introduction of a new item into the marketplace is in reality a mere change in (some of) the characteristics and features, that is, quality, of an existing product. The use of a fixed market basket fundamentally implies (the simplifying assumption) that the specification of the representative items does not change over time. Yet, '[i]f quality is seen as increasing over time (perhaps due to technological advance), a failure to deal with it will bias the RPI above a notional "true cost of living index", overstating inflation' (Cunningham, 1996, p. 15). As with the new-goods bias, this problem is rooted in the methodological apparatus supporting the research strategy of measuring inflation by means of aggregate price indices.

> Quality change poses severe problems for a statistical agency. It is non-mechanical in the sense that there is no way to determine quality change on a routine basis. It is heterogeneous in the sense that each quality change is *sui generis* and, like a child, requires individual attention. It is informationally demanding because it may require vast quantities of data that are expensive to obtain and often do not pass the test of a market transaction. Even though routine procedures are established to handle quality change, in the end quality decisions require the subjective judgment about the extent of quality change, and agencies are reluctant to make subjective judgments (Nordhaus, 1998, p. 61).

The main concern in current research is that overall consumer price indices may understate the extent of quality change associated with the introduction and diffusion of both improved production processes and better-quality products and might thus bias price measurement upward.[14] It is no exaggeration to claim, as suggested for instance by the Advisory Commission to Study the Consumer Price Index (1996, p. 31), that the difficult questions posed by quality change represent the 'house-to-house combat of price measurement'. There is no unique way to compute an average quality-change bias in aggregate price indices,[15] or to put it more picturesquely, 'there is no substitute for the equivalent of a ground war: an eclectic case-by-case assessment of individual products' (Shapiro and Wilcox, 1996, p. 40). There is indeed still much disagreement about the proper methods to use and the proper data to employ, in order to measure quality change for price index analysis (Greenstein, 1997, p. 331, n. 3). As pointed out by Blow and Crawford, '[n]one of these methods constitutes a rigorous, theoretically consistent approach to how quality affects prices' (Blow and Crawford, 1999b, p. 66).

Most academic research on quality changes can be traced back to Griliches's seminal work first published as a staff paper in the 'Stigler Report' (National Bureau of Economic Research, 1961, pp. 173–96). In his econometric analysis of quality change, Griliches applied the hedonic regression technique to provide a hedonic price index for automobiles, that is, a particular price index defined on the characteristics of cars.[16] Further studies for the automobile industry were then put forward, for instance by Triplett (1969) and Ohta and Griliches (1976), along the same lines. More recent leading research – such as Gordon's (1990) work on *The Measurement of Durable Goods Prices*, Berndt and Griliches (1993), Nordhaus (1997) and Raff and Trajtenberg (1997) – continued to investigate hedonic price indices for particular industries, but ultimately found that hedonic techniques are by no means a panacea. For instance, as the case is persuasively made by Alan Greenspan, '[t]he benefits of cellular telephones, and the value they provide in terms of making calls from any location, cannot be measured from an examination of the attributes of standard telephones' (Greenspan, 1997b, p. 3). Sometimes, there are in fact entirely new goods, with fundamentally different characteristics from their predecessors (albeit they both enter into the same statistical category). It thus appears that,

> [t]he best procedure for empirical price measurement is to combine the conventional and hedonic methods, taking advantage of the relative strengths of each. To the maximum extent possible, the conventional approach should be used to adjust the prices of different models for discrete options, accessories, and added features. Then the hedonic method should be employed to explain the remaining price difference as a function of basic dimensions or performance characteristics (Gordon, 1990, p. 101).[17]

Turning to the estimated magnitude of the quality-change effect, Gordon (1990, Table 1.2) claims that the American CPI for the alleged 'durable' goods was flawed by an upward bias of 1.54 percentage points per annum on average over the period 1947–83. However, since measurement problems appear to have declined over time, for the last decade of his price series (1973–83) he estimates an average bias of 1.05 percentage points per year. Yet, the methodological approach followed by Gordon is open to criticism. His data block, which he derives from mail order (Sears) catalogues and *Consumer Reports* (two sources independent of those used to compile official price indices), covers only about half of the weight of the 'durable' goods entering the CPI. He explicitly assumes that the rest of the overall CPI is not affected by quality-change bias. However, 'the evaluation that the rest of the CPI is unbiased represents an extreme one-sided answer to the question as to whether the components of the CPI subject to relatively little research are biased' (Advisory Commission to Study the Consumer Price Index, 1996, p. 32). So, by evaluating the American CPI component by component and extrapolating research on quality-change bias from one item group to another, when the groups appear to be related, the authors of the 'Boskin Report' (among whom was Robert J. Gordon himself) estimate an 'aggregate' quality-change effect of 0.61 percentage points per year for selected time intervals up to 1996 (Advisory Commission to Study the Consumer Price Index, 1996, pp. 31–60 and Table 2). This figure is considerably higher than the mean 0.25 percentage points per annum estimated by Shapiro and Wilcox (1996, pp. 40–1) in an analogous mood. In light of both the different methodological standpoints and the diverging factual results of current academic research, it seems thus reasonable to claim, as emphasised by Cunningham, that 'any estimates should be treated with considerable caution, given the uncertain theoretical base for the [quality-change] bias' (Cunningham, 1996, pp. 24–5).

All in all, although several recent studies address the issue of measurement biases in actual price indices by performing very careful calculations based on disaggregated price data, product specification and the like, it ought to be recalled that 'all of these estimates come from studies of product specific microeconomic data, and so lack the generality necessary to help gauge the overall bias in the aggregate index' (Cecchetti, 1996, pp. 2–3). As is the case with the calculation of the general price level itself, the assessment of the biases affecting any price index relies, in fact, on a series of simplifying assumptions that impinge on the pretended macroeconomic validity of the figure so calculated (Deutsche Bundesbank, 1998, p. 57). Such a conclusion is however disregarded by a number of influential researchers. The authors of the 'Boskin Report' are a recent example. They calculate a point estimate for the overall bias in the American CPI, by summing up the individual estimates computed for each of the specific imperfections described above (substitution bias, new-goods bias, and quality-change bias), and arrive at an average, upward total bias of 1.1 percentage points per annum,[18] with a range extending from 0.8 to 1.6 percentage points.[19] 'While 1.1 percentage point may seem to be a small amount in any given year, cumulatively year after year it adds up to a sizable difference, 14% over a dozen years' (Advisory Commission to Study the Consumer Price Index, 1996, p. 70)..

Now, it is certainly possible to pinpoint other methodological defects of actual price-level measurement, such as the 'aging bias' that might result from pricing, in successive periods, housing units that become progressively older (Randolph, 1988, pp. 359–62; Fortin, 1990, p. 124), or the use of sellers' price lists which do not reflect present market conditions (for example discounting)[20] (Gordon, 1971, pp. 123–31; Triplett, 1975, pp. 61–3). Similar problems stem from a microeconomic conceptual framework and are fairly straightforward to identify.[21] However, without anticipating, the main point to be underlined at this juncture pertains to macroeconomic policy – and its theoretical foundations – aiming to achieve economic stability. It is indeed well established that, for reasons that should become apparent later on, zero inflation does not fundamentally correspond to a zero rate of variation in any particular aggregate price index. For example, as recently stated by Mervyn King in a public lecture given at the London School of Economics to commemorate the fifth anniversary of the Bank of England *Inflation Report*, 'changes in indirect taxes or commodity prices often affect the domestic price level but do not in themselves change the underlying rate of inflation' (King, 1997, p. 8). As a matter of fact, an increase in indirect taxes is much likely to lead to an increase in the general level of prices, since the goods and services subjected to increased taxation become more expensive on the marketplace. This increase in retail prices and probably in the targeted price index has definitely a redistributive effect across the economy;[22] but it does not affect the purchasing power existing in the whole economy. In fact, if the purchasing power of a more or less broad group of consumers who make large use of the taxed goods (for example fuel, tobacco and alcohol) is affected negatively by the decision of the state to rise indirect taxes, the public sector obtains exactly that part of national income lost by the private sector. An analogous zero-sum process can also be observed within the private sector itself, when firms raise their mark-up in order to increase their share of total income (that is, profits). Certainly the resulting increase in retail prices enables firms to raise profits, *ceteris paribus*, but this does not have an inflationary impact on the purchasing power existing in the economy as a whole, because firms obtain a fraction of income previously held by other agents (that is, households). What is lost by one group of agents (households) is gained by another group of agents (firms), so that the overall process is a zero-sum game over the entire economy.

No variation in the targeted price index can therefore be ascribed to inflation without further investigation. Furthermore, there may be inflation even when price indices do not vary between two points in time. As pointed out by Chick (1978) with respect to post-war technical change and inflation data, both in the United Kingdom and in the United States, the stability of price indices combined with increasing productivity may hide the fact that inflationary processes are at work.[23] In fact, on the assumption that the mark-up does not vary, technical change leading to a reduction of unitary production costs will elicit a parallel decrease in prices.[24] If prices do not decrease and the targeted price index remains stable, this may be ascribed to inflation, which exerts its depressive effect on money's purchasing power.[25] Thus then, computing the variation in an aggregate price index cannot be deemed sufficient to assess the presence, and the magnitude, of inflation in any national economy. Ontologically speaking, a subtler analysis is required, even in the fictitious case where all measurement biases in aggregate price statistics were assumed away. On reflection it is in fact clear that '[t]here is a subtle distinction between targeting a fixed price level versus targeting a zero inflation rate' (Taylor, 1997, p. 8). However, it is fundamentally important to note that this distinction cannot be attributed only to the existence of measurement biases, as is generally done in current literature. In this respect, the following citations are quite telling of the fact that non-measurement issues have been unnoticed so far by a large number of observers.

- 'The existence of upward bias in the rate of growth of the CPI suggests that true price stability will correspond to positive *measured* CPI inflation' (Shapiro and Wilcox, 1996, p. 52).
- 'Price stability . . . may be defined as 1 or 2 percent measured inflation' (Taylor, 1997, p. 1).

Should monetary authorities and national policy makers be content with a rate of growth in the targeted aggregate price index of one to two per cent per annum, because the CPI measurement biases imply that this rate ultimately corresponds to effective price stability?[26] In Greenspan's words, 'policymakers must be cognizant of the shortcomings of our published price indexes to avoid actions based on inaccurate premises that will provoke undesired consequences' (Greenspan, 1998, p. 1). Indeed, inflation (mis)measurement also matters for the economy as a whole, because it has very important implications for both macroeconomic analysis and policy design. To take an oft-cited example, 'an overzealous pursuit of zero measured inflation may inflict unnecessary costs on society if the price indexes overstate the true rate of price increase' (Wynne and Sigalla, 1996, p. 56).

For the sake of exposition it is convenient to begin by addressing the main conceptual weaknesses of price index analysis in so far as the inflation problem is concerned. In Part Two we shall investigate more deeply the fundamental theoretical issues.

ANALYTICAL CAUSES OF INFLATION MEASUREMENT PROBLEMS

Back in 1930 Keynes was already aware that aggregate price analysis is an imperfect procedure to assess inflation, and his concern is worth quoting in its entirety.[27]

> Most of us were brought up to employ such index-numbers as Sauerbeck's or the *Economist's* much too light-heartedly, and without sufficient warning that, while there might be nothing better available, nevertheless the actual divergences between these indexes and the Purchasing Power of Money might prove to be, if we could calculate them, of very great significance both theoretical and practical (Keynes, 1930/1971, p. 67).

It would be naive to deny that since the publication of Keynes's *Treatise on Money* the aggregation of microeconomic price data has been considerably improved by several careful and thoughtful investigations. What we claim is that such methodological corrections cannot be sufficient to understand the problem of inflation. A fundamental analysis of both the nature of modern money and of the working of our monetary production economies is necessary for that purpose. In Keynes's own words, we must face those difficulties of our subject 'which depend rather upon reasoning than upon calculation' (Keynes, 1909/1983, p. 64). To begin with, let us attempt to develop a critical appraisal of price index analysis at an intuitively macroeconomic level. It is the purpose of the next two chapters to explore the theoretical framework in greater detail.

The Representative Market Basket and Total Current Supply

Besides all the methodological biases involved in traditional inflation measurement, there is unanimous agreement among economists that any aggregate price index weighs inadequately, or omits altogether, some important objects of expenditure such as several public goods[28] and personal services (see Keynes, 1930/1971, pp. 57–8; but also Desai, 1981, pp. 27–8; Fortin, 1990, p. 110, n. 3; Bryan and Cecchetti, 1994, pp. 195–6). Yet, the problem of the representativeness of selected items has been treated as a pure sampling problem in most academic research on aggregate price indices. In other words, because of the prevailing empirical approach to inflation measurement, economists have focused on microeconomic data requirements for (only) a certain number of varieties of particular products, instead of extending their analysis to the national economy as a whole. In particular, much discussion about aggregate price analysis has relied on the (often hidden) hypothesis that those varieties not selected for price index construction move together with those varieties which are included in the representative basket. Thus, the position of most scholars, best expressed by Triplett (1975), is to 'assume that price movements for Mercedes and Jaguar, or lobster and steaming clams (none of which is currently priced) can be approximated by price changes of Chevrolet and Volkswagen, or canned tuna and frozen haddock fillets (which are examples of product varieties priced for the CPI "automobile" and "fish" components)' (Triplett, 1975, p. 64).

Indeed, if one examines the index number problem in a heuristic manner, one infers that the validity of price index analysis is unavoidably restricted (to say the least) to a specific sample of goods and services, and that the selection of consumption items is purposively directed at not jeopardising the concept of aggregate price indices. Recently, Heymann and Leijonhufvud have achieved an elegant critique of the conventional analysis of inflation, which brings to the fore the fundamental weakness of both CPI and COLI compilation – as we have already noted in the previous section. In their own words, '"[t]he" inflation-rate itself is a construct of statisticians that may have little behavioural relevance to individuals all of whom are buying baskets of goods that differ from the CPI basket' (Heymann and Leijonhufvud, 1995, p. 41, n. 2). Stated somewhat differently, this means that there is no economic rationale for assuming that changes in prices of non-selected items are parallel to those of 'representative' products.[29] Neither is there any conceptual justification for eliminating certain varieties of a particular good from the inflation measurement procedure.

This worrying conclusion may be highlighted by a general consideration stemming from a macroeconomic line of thought. Granting the force of price index analysis as an adequate measure of the movement in aggregate prices for a given bundle of commodities, we may still maintain that this framework of inquiry does not provide a satisfactory measure of the purchasing power of money over domestic goods. As a matter of fact, an important, but too often neglected, point which emerges from a widely cited paper by Laidler and Parkin is that 'analysis of the inflationary process must involve the study of the whole economic system and not just of one or two markets in isolation' (Laidler and Parkin, 1975, p. 796). Yet, it seems almost trivial to note that measuring inflation by means of changes in a particular price level fails to consider the markets for produced goods as a whole; for this very methodology cannot account for the sum of aggregate output.

In *A Treatise on Money*, Keynes rightly pointed out (in a rather complex statement) that 'the Purchasing Power of Money [is] the power of money to buy the goods and services on the purchase of which for purposes of consumption a given community of individuals expend their money income' (Keynes, 1930/1971, p. 54). Now, as we shall see later on, money income is essentially defined by total domestic output, for it is the result of the monetisation of all costs of production.[30] 'In each period, say every month, the sum of all incomes formed by the employed "factors", contains the whole range of the new goods flowing from production' (Schmitt, 1996b, p. 86). When we get right to the heart of the matter, this amounts to saying that, in each period, the object of the global, or macroeconomic, expenditure of 'a given community of individuals' (that is, the whole set of economic units) is the total current supply of goods and services produced in the same economy. In inflation analysis, a main conceptual defect of price index application might thus be inferred from a simple representation in which money income is defined by the set of domestic output (Figure 2.1).

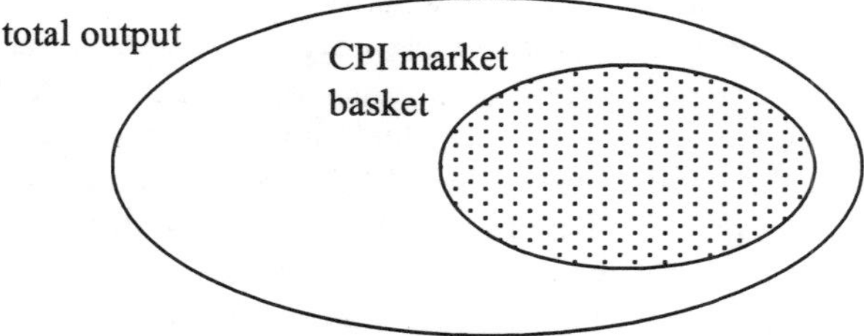

Figure 2.1 The macroeconomic inadequacy of the representative basket

Unless the CPI market basket really subsumes all currently produced goods and services – a task which is unanimously deemed impossible in any contemporary national economy[31] – its use for price index analysis cannot logically pretend to assess money's purchasing power (as lucidly noted by Keynes in the passage of his *Treatise* quoted at the beginning of this section).

Now, Fortin maintains that '[t]here are indeed two ways to measure the flow-value of goods and services: through consumption and through production. They are not the same, for two reasons. First, we do not consume all our production – in addition to consumer goods, we make investment goods, and goods for exports to foreign countries. Second, we do not produce everything we consume – we also import part from abroad' (Fortin, 1990, p.

110). Since they are closely intertwined in macroeconomic analysis, let us try to tackle these two issues together, although in the scope of this chapter we cannot take the matter at any depth.

From a macroeconomic stance, the measure of the newly produced output must logically be the same when it is taken in the flow of total production as when it is taken in the flow of total consumption.[32] Implicit in this viewpoint is the idea that money income can analytically be divided '(1) into the parts which have been *earned* by the production of consumption-goods and of investment-goods respectively, and (2) into the parts which are *expended* on consumption-goods and on savings respectively' (Keynes, 1930/1971, p. 134). Applied to the problem we are investigating, this means that from an economic standpoint it is unrealistic to assume that consumption refers to physical destruction (or transformation) only. In Chapter 1 we already pointed out that the purchase of a long-lived good (say, a car) cancels it from the economic field, at the very moment the payment is entered into its essential bookkeeping form. If indeed, as some economists seem to suggest (see Gordon, 1990), investment goods are but another name for durable items, then, conceptually, their purchase falls under the category of consumption.[33] If we define instead as investment, or capital, goods those goods bought by firms to contribute to production – stressing the fact that profits are comprised in the proceeds given in remuneration to the 'productive services' in the sense that they are an income that households transfer to firms on the product market (Cencini, 1995, pp. 52–3) – we understand without pushing the analysis any further that the money income spent in purchasing these investment goods has been saved by households (see Part Three for analytical elaboration). In summary, whatever their definition may be, investment goods are part of the newly-produced output.[34] Accordingly, their exclusion from the CPI market basket adds to the drawbacks of conventional inflation measurement, contrary to the assertion (see Steindel, 1997, p. 3) that including the acquisition prices of investment goods into the CPI compromises the price index's ability to track inflation accurately.

As suggested above, a further crucial point concerns international trade, and in particular the alleged phenomenon of imported inflation. What is particularly noteworthy here, is again the problematic performance of the CPI in measuring inflation over the whole national economy. As a matter of fact, by ignoring the changes in the prices of exported goods (since by definition only the domestically purchased items can enter the representative market basket), the CPI misses – time and again – an important part of the newly produced output. Further, it wrongly includes the prices of various imported goods (such as crude oil and other raw materials), which have nothing to do with measuring the purchasing power of domestic money over domestic output.[35] In this respect, the GDP deflator appears to be, in principle, a better estimator of the purchasing power of money, because it includes the prices of exported goods and excludes the prices of imported goods. Yet, from a methodological standpoint, the GDP price index is not really better than the CPI, because its compilation is based on the same price data for most of the items surveyed for aggregate price analysis (Moulton, 1996, p. 160). 'Hence, the GDP index shares many of the CPI's technical flaws' (Steindel, 1997, p. 3), and therefore cannot track true inflationary movements.[36] As we shall explore later on, a more fundamental analysis must be sought, one which takes up Keynes's breakthrough that,

> [h]uman effort and human consumption are the ultimate matters from which alone economic transactions are capable of deriving any significance; and all other forms of expenditure only acquire importance from their having some relationship, sooner or later, to the effort of producers or to the expenditure of consumers (Keynes, 1930/1971, p. 134).

The Sample of Population and Total Current Demand

It is well known that the bundle of commodities used for assessing aggregate price movements is made up following accurate statistical surveys of the goods and services purchased by a 'reference group' of households in some 'reference' year.[37] Indeed, it is hardly necessary to stress that '[d]ifferent people buy different commodities at different times' (Griliches, 1997, p. 171). Since the empirical results of CPI compilation are usually applied to different sets of consuming units (for example, wage-earners and unemployed; high-income and low-income families; pensioners and invalids), and for different purposes (for instance, indexing government spending or private contracts), a number of authors have been investigating what kind of measurement as well as methodological oddities this practice introduces in price index analysis.[38] In particular, as noted in Chapter 1, '[s]ome have suggested that different groups in the population are likely to experience faster or slower growth in their cost of living than recorded by changes in the CPI' (Advisory Commission to Study the Consumer Price Index, 1996, p. iii). Whilst this redistributive issue is still an open question,[39] it is unanimously agreed that any aggregate price index does not account for different expenditure patterns of specific groups of economic units (ibid., p. 30).

Now, analysis in this framework should go beyond the distributional impact of inflation on particular subgroups in the economy. In particular, at the conceptual level, one may ask if a representative sample of household budgets can logically be used for assessing the purchasing power of national money over domestic output. Let us try to clarify the basic line of the argument with a representation that now should be familiar to the reader (Figure 2.2).

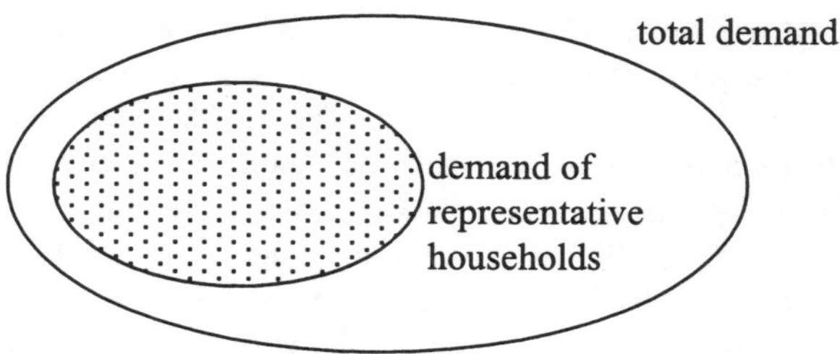

Figure 2.2 Total demand and representative demand

By analogy with earlier discussion, the essential feature of this approach is that the determining factor for assessing the validity of price index analysis as a proxy for inflation measurement has to rely on a macroeconomic line of thought. Put simply, the essence of the argument is to consider whether the sample of population surveyed can account for the total demand exerted over the whole economy. The answer is negative. Useful though they are, consumer expenditure surveys cannot keep track of total demand, because the method of sampling contrasts with a 'holistic' perception of the entire national economy. Intuitively, even the most accurately-built sample of economic units can reflect only part of current macroeconomic expenditure. By definition, any subgroup of income holders has indeed only a fraction of total money income.[40] Whilst one can certainly examine the effect of price changes across different consuming units, by estimating both aggregate demand and income elasticities for certain types of households and for given (categories of) products, it is impossible to say anything about the purchasing power of money (over domestic output) when dealing with the inflation problem at a sublevel of the entire economy. This point is fundamental, but it has been unnoticed so far by the economics profession. To investigate the extent to which inflation affects the relationship between money and output, that is, the relationship that defines the purchasing power of money, attention must be paid to the value of the newly produced output that can be purchased with the sum of money income currently available in the whole national economy. Before addressing this question from a strictly theoretical standpoint, let us bring to the fore a closely related important issue, which may be worth considering within the present context because of the methodology inherent in any aggregate price measure.

The Problem of Aggregating Microeconomic Data

Basically, the aetiology of defective analysis of total demand by means of any particular sample of population, as well as of total supply by means of any market basket whatsoever, might lie in the dominant paradigm's conceptualisation of macroeconomics as being the science of aggregating data over both agents and goods.[41] Current macroeconomic models suffer indeed from a serious problem, known as the aggregation problem. This issue is by no means novel (see Klein, 1946), and much has been written on it.[42] In its most basic terms, the aggregation problem has two facets. On the one side, by assuming that it is possible to construct a consistent macroeconomic system by aggregating data over both individuals and goods, the maintained method of economic analysis postulates that macroeconomic relations are a *replica* – on a larger scale – of observed microeconomic relations. Thus, statements that are valid for the individual are assumed to hold also at the aggregate level or for the economy as a whole. On the other side, according to this approach it is reasonable to analyse the economic behaviour of a population (that is, a group of individuals) by conceiving and modelling the behaviour of a typical or representative agent, and by transferring the results to the aggregate level. This is in fact one of the key assumptions made in perhaps the most widely used method of studying the macroeconomy, which models the structural relationships in a national economy by working out theories of individual behaviour and applying them to study aggregate behaviour. A recent expression of this approach has been summarised by Hartley in his critical work on *The Representative Agent in Macroeconomics* as follows: 'The first step is to write down the problem faced by the microeconomic agent in terms of fundamental parameters. This agent is assumed to be representative, and the solution to this problem is assumed to hold for the macroeconomy' (Hartley, 1997, p. 26).

So, when one investigates the problem of the measurement (and control) of inflation in the national economy, one might be tempted to derive from the aggregated results of a particular consumer expenditure survey – carried out with a specific sample of 'representative' agents – a kind of synthetic, and highly hypothetical, consumption behaviour that should hold for the whole economy under scrutiny. The factual relationship observed between a subset of income holders, on the one hand, and a subset of domestic goods and services, on the other hand, is thus assumed to be valid also for the entire economic system, with no misgivings about the very method of aggregation. Clearly, the national economy is considered, and modelled, 'as if' it were formed by a large number of agents, all of whom have exactly the same economic behaviour as the reference group of individuals surveyed by the nation-wide statistical agencies. The methodological biases occurring in the measurement of aggregate prices, described above, may therefore be ultimately the hallmark of the analytical weaknesses of a research strategy that reduces macroeconomic phenomena to the aggregation – over both agents and goods – of microeconomic magnitudes. Again, this point has been unperceived in the literature on price level measurement.

As a matter of fact, orthodox macroeconomic models often rely on the Marshallian legacy of codifying a representative agent's behaviour, to derive a corresponding behaviour for a large group of economic units, or, ultimately, for the economy as a whole. As has been emphasised by Kirman, '[t]he motivations for the extensive use of the representative agent are the desires to provide microfoundations for aggregate behavior, and also to provide a framework in which equilibria are unique and stable' (Kirman, 1992, p. 121). Hicks is a famous case in point. When considering the characteristics of the conventional method of economic analysis, he claims indeed that,

> it enables us to pass over, with scarcely any transition, from the little problems involved in detailed study of the behaviour of a single firm, or single individual, to the great issues of the prosperity or adversity, even life or death, of a whole economic system. The transition is made by using the simple principle, already familiar to us in statics, that the behaviour of a group of individuals, or group of firms, obeys the same laws as the behaviour of a single unit (Hicks, 1946, p. 245).

Now, if all 'singletons' were identical, one could quite easily admit that the behaviour of a single economic agent can appropriately represent the behaviour of the sum of economic units of the same type. Yet, in most cases, it is utterly misleading to identify the behaviour of the representative agent with the actual behaviour of the sum of agents acting in any national economy whatsoever. First of all, at the conceptual level, it might be very difficult to give a consistent, and operational, definition of what a representative agent is.

> The list of unanswered (and, possibly, unanswerable) questions is lengthy. What exactly is a representative agent? What does it mean to be 'representative'? Does 'representative' simply mean 'average', or does it mean something else? In a

> group of firms or agents with, say, 100 characteristics, how many of these characteristics must be well-reflected by a representative agent? And so on (Hartley, 1997, p. 16).

To take but an example in our specific field of investigation, it is worth pointing out that a number of empirical studies of aggregate price differentials between various categories of economic agents make, implicitly, the heroic assumption that the population within each subgroup of the economy is homogeneous (see Bureau of Labor Statistics, 1988, pp. 3–10; Berndt et al., 1997, pp. 34–7). Yet, as persuasively testified by Michael's (1979, pp. 45–6) and Hagemann's (1982, pp. 506–7) work, the observed price differences of market bundles purchased by different demographic groups in the same country are in fact smaller between these groups than within them. To this analysis one needs only add that, for each subgroup, the representativeness of collected data may also turn out to be highly unstable over time, as we have already noted.

Further, an even more important set of arguments has to be considered here, namely that representative-agent models give rise to a series of fundamental pitfalls when they are used to infer social economic behaviour from (the sum of) individual forms of behaviour (Martel, 1996, pp. 128–34; Hartley, 1997, p. 17; Dutt, 1998, pp. 313–16). We should indeed not lose sight of the fact that the foundations of representative-agent models are the so-called *homo œconomicus* and the marketplace. Individuals' (rational) behaviour is constitutive of the interactions between economic units, and methodological individualism[43] is assumed to be the ultimate factual underpinning of economic activity. Thus, probabilistic uncertainty and rational expectations play a crucial role in current macroeconomic analysis, for they are fundamental in constructing elaborate stochastic models of the economy. Such complex models might be of some help to grasp the (optimising) behaviour of (representative?) economic agents – consumers as well as producers – in an operational setting. However, granting their usefulness for a number of microeconomic investigations, we may still ask whether these analyses can appropriately deal with, and account for, the working of the national economy as a whole (Verdon, 1996, pp. 25–9, is rather critical on this point).

In the traditional method of modelling the economic process by means of a system of simultaneous equations, '[e]ach agent in the economy, whether a consumer or a producer, has at least one equation which describes his or her behaviour. The behaviour of the economy as a whole, at the aggregate, macro-level, is built up from the individual equations at the micro-level' (Ormerod, 1994, p. 78). Thus then, current economic analysis does not admit any solution of continuity between the micro- and the macro-level of the economy. In fact, several recent textbooks have made the (often implicit) assumption that micro- and macroeconomics have the same object of inquiry.[44] So much so that a large number of authors emphasise that the key distinction between micro- and macroeconomics concerns the level of aggregation of economic variables. 'In macroeconomics we are interested in the determinants of broad economic aggregates' (Schlicht, 1985, p. 8). One is thus led to ask when a microeconomic magnitude acquires a macroeconomic dimension. Analyses of phenomena concerning a single economic unit have in general been categorised as microeconomics. Analyses of the whole economic system have usually been attributed to macroeconomics. But how should one classify an investigation about, say, a particular industrial sector or a specific subgroup of income holders of a given country? Which number of economic units is (to be) considered as drawing the borderline between a micro- and a macroeconomic framework of inquiry?[45] A possible answer to these questions can be provided if one considers the conceptual distinction between macro- and microeconomic operations as being analogous to the logical distinction between a set and its elements.[46] This proposition amounts to saying that a single individual's action may prove to be of a macroeconomic nature, that is, it may concern the set of economic agents, whereas there may exist some situations which do not pertain to macroeconomics although they concern the sum of economic agents. Given the scope of this chapter, we cannot take the time to explore these startling facts thoroughly. However, to get the flavour, let us give two quick stylised examples.

Consider first the case where agent W is employed by firm F during period P to carry out some paid work. (Indeed, this is the hallmark of modern economic activity.) When W receives his or her remuneration for the 'productive services' he or she has provided F, a (new) net value has been formed for the economy as a whole. As a matter of fact, W obtains a claim on a bank deposit (+) corresponding to the debt (–) incurred by F towards the banking system which monetises the transaction; and the goods newly produced (+) are the macroeconomic value par excellence. All this will be elaborated later. For the present it might help the reader to sketch a numerical example, and suppose that the value of the newly produced output is measured by 100 units of money. Accordingly, the banking system's balance sheet would match W's deposit (+100) with F's debt (–100), and total current output would be increased (+) by 100. On the whole, (+100 –100 +100 =) 100 units of value would have been formed in the operation described above. The productive activity of a single agent (W) gives rise to a net value over the entire set of economic units indeed. Stated a little more fully the above argument amounts to saying that production is a macroeconomic phenomenon, and that its result cannot be thoroughly appraised if one merely considers it as an exchange between workers and firms (an issue we shall explore in Chapters 4 and 5).

By contrast, the sum of all fiscal disbursements paid by the private sector to the general government sector over, say, a fiscal year does not define any macroeconomic magnitude, irrespective of both the size of the given community and the amount of income involved. Fiscal transfers simply redistribute money income in a different way than originally allocated by the remuneration of the factors of production. Even if they involve the sum of economic agents existing in a national economy, these transfers do not have a macroeconomic dimension, because they ultimately depict a zero-sum process: income is neither created nor destroyed by them; only (part of) its 'property rights' are transferred across the economy.

On the whole, contrary to current economic theories, it should therefore become intuitively apparent that the nature of macroeconomic phenomena cannot be appraised through the aggregation of microeconomic magnitudes.[47] Another way of reaching the same conclusion is to note, in Kirman's words, that '[t]here is simply no direct relation between individual and collective behavior' (Kirman, 1992, p. 118), thus echoing Paul A. Samuelson's argument of the fallacy of composition.[48] Reducing the behaviour of a group of different economic units to the behaviour of a somehow representative standard utility, or profit, maximiser might lead to conclusions which can be either misleading or wrong (Kirman, 1992, p. 117; Janssen, 1993, pp. 84–93; Martel, 1996, pp. 140–1). 'It is a fact that the use of a representative consumer assumption in most macro work is an illegitimate method of ignoring valid aggregation concerns' (Lewbel, 1989, p. 631).

Now, there is no real need for us to explore all of these issues, although they ought to be carefully considered by anyone interested in modelling the decision-making process of a single agent and transferring it to the aggregate level. For our purposes, it is sufficient to note that both representative-agent models and microfoundational approaches that aim to bypass the consistency problem in aggregation[49] need the representative agent to portray the set of preferences of every single individual in the national economy. As this proves to be impossible in any economic system where millions of diverse agents have heterogeneous preferences as well as different forms of behaviour, representative-agent models are neither a proper method nor a particularly useful means of studying the economy as a whole (Hartley, 1997, p. 3). When we get right to the heart of the matter, we may thus claim that 'the representative agent methodology described above is a gross fallacy of composition which disqualifies *any* kind of microfoundation from being a logically consistent and complete foundation for macroeconomics' (Martel, 1996, p. 128).

To sum up, this methodology, widely shared as it is, hardly does justice to the nature of a macroeconomic problem such as the one which is dealt with in the present book, namely the alteration of the relationship between money and output. In so far as the analysis of inflation is concerned, doing macroeconomics by aggregation (of microeconomic magnitudes) entails a reductionist vision of the real world, for it fails to consider what Ingham (1996, p. 509) portrays as the 'social' structural conditions for the existence of money. To be more precise without anticipating, one has to ask whether the method of calculation, and the representativeness, of any price index can account for the variation in the purchasing power of money over total saleable output. As far as the choice of the functional form of the index number is concerned, we noted that the use of the Laspeyres formula has been strongly criticised by mathematical economists as well as by professional statisticians, without so far putting anything better in its place. Figures 2.1 and 2.2 offer two additional points, which no one has ever raised in the study of inflation by means of price index analysis. To this analysis we then have to add the above considerations stemming from the aggregation problem, which is but another way of looking at the same problems as those put to the fore in the two previous subsections.

Ormerod summarises this set of arguments by stating that the macroeconomic principles of a monetary production economy cannot be deduced from simple extrapolation from the behaviour of its individual components: 'The whole is different from the sum of the parts. There is such a thing as society' (Ormerod, 1994, p. 91). Hence, the need for an organic, fully-fledged macro-analysis arises ultimately from the observation that a fundamentally atomistic paradigm cannot appraise the working of the economic system as a whole.[50] 'Microeconomic questions require microeconomic theories although macro considerations might contribute to solve them. On the other hand, macroeconomic questions cannot typically be analyzed fruitfully in microeconomic terms' (Schlicht, 1985, p. 101). In fact, there can be no microeconomic foundations of macroeconomics.[51] The conceptual distinction between micro- and macroeconomics is both analytically clear-cut and operational, and may be supported by the argument according to which analogies between micro- and macroeconomic laws could prove to be seriously misleading, if not entirely wrong (Schlicht, 1985, pp. 63–4; Caballero, 1992, p. 1291). To put it yet another way, we might claim that a macroeconomic phenomenon is not the sum of the relevant microeconomic data. So, what is particularly noteworthy here is that no aggregate price measure can ever account for the underlying phenomenon of inflation, since any price index is fundamentally grounded on the (ill-founded) research strategy of doing macroeconomics by aggregation.

The kind of result we are looking for is ultimately similar to the demonstration that, to quote Schumpeter, 'it is possible, as we have put it, to introduce money on the ground floor of general economic analysis without adopting the aggregative view' (Schumpeter, 1954/1994, p. 278). To put it clearly, our aim is to show that a truly macroeconomic analysis of (the variation in) the purchasing power of money has to abandon any aggregative view of the national economy, to embrace a modern theory of money that successfully overcomes the dichotomic representation of the working of our monetary economies of production. Our next challenging task is therefore to attempt to appraise traditional inflation analysis in light of this alternative research programme, and to relay it with a monetary theory of production that conforms to the nature of modern money. It is indeed the purpose of the remainder of this book to examine the depth and breadth of the inflation problem from a purely theoretical standpoint.

NOTES

1. 'The assessment of biases in the CPI requires a cost of living index as a point of reference' (Advisory Commission to Study the Consumer Price Index, 1996, p. 63). See also Moulton (1996, p. 164) and Diewert (1997, pp. 427–8).
2. For instance: wholesale price indices, producer price indices and GDP price indices.
3. In what follows, a Laspeyres price index is the functional form adopted, since this is in fact the case in most OECD countries.
4. See the final report of the Advisory Commission to Study the Consumer Price Index (1996, pp. 21–4) for a hypothetical numerical example of commodity substitution bias.
5. It is pretty obvious 'that lengthening the period of time that the Laspeyres weights are held constant considerably increases the size of the bias' (Braithwait, 1980, p. 73).
6. For an overview of the 1998 revision of the American CPI, see Greenlees and Mason (1996, pp. 6–9).
7. In the United States, this is the task of the Point-of-Purchase Survey. 'Outlets are chosen and rotated every five years from a Point-of-Purchase Survey, asking consumers where they purchase goods and services, with probabilities of outlet selection proportional to expenditures' (Boskin et al., 1998, p. 6). See Armknecht et al. (1997, pp. 379–80) for more details.
8. Diewert notes however that, in the future, 'new outlet competition will come from discount selling of goods over the Internet' (Diewert, 1998, p. 51).
9. The item groups supposed to be open to bias include: food and beverages, housing maintenance, household fuels, housefurnishings, apparel commodities, motor fuel, medical

care commodities, entertainment commodities, tobacco, personal care (Cunningham, 1996, p. 46, n. 12).

10. See the work surveyed by Cunningham (1996, pp. 46–7).
11. Alfred Marshall was among the first to acknowledge the existence of such a product cycle, as the following passage indicates: 'A new commodity almost always appears at first at something like a scarcity price, and its gradual fall in price can be made to enter year by year into readjustments of the unit of purchasing power' (Marshall, 1887, p. 373). See Hicks (1940, p. 114), but also Diewert (1998, p. 53) and Wynne (1999, p. 11).
12. Robert J. Gordon forcefully notes that 'the [American] CPI did not introduce autos until 1940, more than two decades after Ford's "Model T" brought the automobile to the average family. Penicillin entered the CPI in 1951, after it had already experienced a 99 percent decline from its initial price. Air conditioning entered the CPI in 1964, more than a decade after the widespread sale of such products. The pocket calculator entered the CPI in 1978, after it had declined in price about 90 percent from early models introduced in 1970' (Gordon, 1992, p. 9). More recently, video-cassette recorders (VCRs), microwave ovens and personal computers (PCs) were included in the American CPI in 1987, 'a decade or more after they had penetrated the market and their price had fallen 80 percent or more. Cellular telephones won't be included in the U.S. CPI until 1998, despite the fact that there are 47 million U.S. cellular subscribers today' (Boskin et al., 1998, p. 10). In the United Kingdom, VCRs, compact-disc players and microwave ovens were not added to the all-items RPI until 1987 – 'by which time some 43.5% of households owned a video-recorder' (Cunningham, 1996, p. 37).
13. See the work reviewed by Shapiro and Wilcox (1996, pp. 30–2) and Wynne and Sigalla (1996, pp. 67–8). More recently, Blow and Crawford (1999b, pp. 45–56) have carried out research on the UK National Lottery – launched in November 1994 and not yet included in the RPI –, using revealed preference and non-parametric statistical methods to calculate the lower bound on the reservation price of new goods.
14. 'Obviously we do not want to count as true price increases those price increases that accompany the introduction of new models of existing products that are superior to the existing goods' (Wynne and Sigalla, 1996, p. 56). It should also be noted in passing that in a few cases quality seems to be deteriorating over time, 'such as the disappearance of full service gas stations, and the decline in the quality of in-flight service on some airlines' (ibid., p. 62). 'Other analysts have pointed to reduced convenience and comfort of air travel, deteriorating quality of higher education, increases in travel time and driver irritation resulting from growing traffic congestion, and widespread declines in the quality of customer service as examples of quality decreases that are not accounted for in the CPI' (Abraham et al., 1998, p. 33). Nordhaus points out further 'quality deterioration of existing products, which is the exact counterpart of the appearance of new products. The downside of the automobile and air-travel revolution is the deterioration in rail service; typewriters are perfectly adequate for many tasks but have largely disappeared from stores; as software programs are upgraded, they become so complicated that their use seems to require an advanced degree; many electronic devices have daunting instructions; the self-service revolution has led to the demise of many service-oriented retail businesses; the house calls of the family doctor are a fond memory; and so forth' (Nordhaus, 1998, p. 65).
15. On the conventional methods used to handle quality changes in existing products, see Gordon (1992, pp. 27–9), Advisory Commission to Study the Consumer Price Index (1996, pp. 36–7) and Nordhaus (1997, p. 42).
16. 'The "hedonic", or, using a less value-loaded word, characteristics approach to the construction of price indexes is based on the empirical hypothesis (or research strategy) which asserts that the multitude of models and varieties of a particular commodity can be comprehended in terms of a much smaller number of characteristics or basic attributes of a commodity such as "size", "power", "trim", and "accessories", and that viewing the

problem this way will reduce greatly the magnitude of the pure new commodity or "technical change" problem, since most (though not all) new "models" of commodities may be viewed as a new combination of "old" characteristics' (Griliches, 1971, p. 4). On hedonic functions and hedonic indices, see Triplett (1987). On hedonic regressions and quality change, see Gordon (1971, pp. 131–41).

17. 'Specifically, hedonic techniques are not able to deal with quality changes that are not easily quantified (such as the handling characteristics of a car, the multitasking ability of a personal computer, or whether an item of clothing is in or out of fashion)' (Wynne and Sigalla, 1996, p. 63).
18. A serious problem that must be addressed when trying to draw firm conclusions about the sign and magnitude of the overall bias concerns possible double-counting of some of the biases. In particular, as Wynne and Sigalla cogently observe, '[c]an we simply add together estimates of the quality adjustment bias and the new goods bias, given that the distinction between the two is elusive? Is it possible that traditional substitution bias and quality adjustment bias are aspects of the same phenomenon? The same question can be raised for outlet-substitution bias . . . : how do we disentangle this from other more traditional forms of quality and substitution bias?' (Wynne and Sigalla, 1996, p. 82). As recently stated by Blow and Crawford, 'the direction of bias in the RPI formula is unknown *a priori*. . . . [T]here is no theoretical presumption of an upward bias in the RPI formula' (Blow and Crawford, 1999a, pp. 2, 29). Yet, as empirical evidence shows, the overall CPI tends to overstate the increase in prices year by year. This means that over the years price measurement biases are compounded.
19. In a similar vein, Shapiro and Wilcox 'estimate that there is a 90 percent probability that the total bias in the CPI is greater than 0.6 percentage point per year, and a 90 percent probability that it is less than 1.5 percentage points per year' (Shapiro and Wilcox, 1996, p. 43). The mean estimate of their empirical analysis occurs at just 1 percentage point per annum, thus roughly endorsing the numerical evaluation made in the 'Boskin Report'. See also Moulton (1996, Table 1) and Greenspan (1997a, p. 1) for other recent estimates of the overall bias in the American CPI. Note that simulation and extrapolation from available data for the United Kingdom has led Cunningham to guesstimate a 'plausible range' for the overall bias in the actual RPI of 0.35 to 0.8 percentage points per year (Cunningham, 1996, pp. 57–8). This gives about half the average figure of the American case and may be ascribed to the more frequent weighting revision in the United Kingdom than in the United States (see Table 1.2).
20. 'It is well known that very few consumers ever pay the list, or "sticker", price for a car' (Wynne and Sigalla, 1996, p. 57).
21. This does not mean that they are easily solved, as a quick survey of the most recent literature clearly shows. In fact, as recently stated by a leading central bank, 'the methodological difficulties [in the measurement of aggregate prices] cannot be completely overcome' (Deutsche Bundesbank, 1998, p. 61).
22. The first form of income redistribution is from the private sector to the general government sector, in the case at hand, but a chain of other distributional effects may of course be observed both between these two sectors and within the private sector itself. To give only an example, consider the tobacco tax: if the retail price of a packet of cigarettes increases because of an increased indirect taxation, the present generation of smokers transfers a greater share of national income to the general government sector, which may then either redistribute it to particular groups of individuals (pensioners and disabled people, unemployed, political refugees) or invest it according to the current budgetary policy needs.
23. See also De Vroey (1984, p. 382), who refers to a 1980 *Cahier du CEPREMAP* by Lipietz and Hausmann.
24. According to Pasinetti (1993, pp. 79–81), it is necessary to break down the general

dynamics of prices into an inflationary component and a structural component, since the average rate of productivity growth of the entire economic system is usually very different from the rate of productivity growth in any specific sector of the economy. 'Both components have important and pervasive implications, but of a very different nature. The structural component is tied up with problems of attainment of efficiency in each single branch of production. The inflationary component concerns the economic system as a whole' (ibid., p. 81).

25. Note that inflation may occur even in a situation where the targeted price index indicates a reduction in prices. In this situation, the reduction in prices is smaller than it would have occurred if inflationary processes had not been at work.
26. To give an example, 'owing to statistical uncertainties, the Bundesbank considers the objective of price stability to be broadly achieved if the measured inflation rate is between 0% and 2%' (Deutsche Bundesbank, 1998, p. 58). For the same reason, the ECB's inflation target is to maintain HICP below 2 per cent (European Central Bank, 1999, p. 46).
27. Joan Robinson (1956, pp. 20–4) pointed out some related conceptual problems in measuring the purchasing power of money, but was silent on the link with inflation analysis.
28. It can indeed be very difficult to measure prices for the general government supply. '[F]or example, how does one price the protective services of the armed forces?' (Steindel, 1997, p. 3). See also Reserve Bank of New Zealand (1997, pp. 14–17).
29. It may be worth noting in passing that '[t]o the question, of what our representative commodity should be representative, there is no one answer. It will depend upon the object which we have in view' (Keynes, 1909/1983, p. 96).
30. At this stage, it may be useful to recall Keynes's proposal 'to mean identically the same thing by the three expressions: (1) *the community's money-income*; (2) *the earnings of the factors of production*; and (3) *the cost of production*' (Keynes, 1930/1971, p. 123). More on this later.
31. When considering the microeconomic foundations of inflation measurement, Fortin argues that the best measure of the aggregate price level 'is the average price level of *all* transactions carried out in the economy in a given period' (Fortin, 1990, p. 109). He immediately recognises, however, that this index 'is so broad and would be so costly to construct that it does not currently exist in any country' (ibid., p. 110). What he does not seem to consider is the analytical relevance of this ideal price index for measuring inflation (and not simply for evaluating aggregate price changes), an issue to which we shall return.
32. As far as (the depreciation of) the purchasing power of money is concerned, this claim might be supported by the evidence that each pound of expenditure on the factor market is essentially identical to any pound of expenditure on the market for produced goods. If money is affected by a pathology (whose origin will be investigated in the third part of this book) that reduces its purchasing power, it need not be added that each money unit ineluctably loses the same fraction of its original value, be it spent on the factor market or on the product market.
33. A fundamental criticism of the ill-founded idea of durability in economics can be found in Chapter 1. It will be recalled here that, '[e]ven in common parlance, we implicitly term a consumer, not so much someone who uses up commodities as someone who buys them, as a "big spender"' (Verdon, 1996, p. 107).
34. It is worth noting that sometimes the same item may be either a consumption or an investment good, depending on the functional classification of the purchaser (Chick, 1983, p. 45). As Verdon observes, '[w]hether or not we choose to call a commodity an "investment good" should have nothing to do with the intrinsic properties of this commodity, but with the uses the individual wishes to put it to' (Verdon, 1996, p. 160). For instance, a car bought for personal (or family) use is a consumption good; used to provide taximeter cab services, it is an investment good.

35. We do not deny that a rise in the prices of imported goods can lead to a generalised reduction in the purchasing power of consumers. To that extent, the CPI might offer an accurate reading of the level of households' satisfaction. But it must always be kept in mind that '[i]nflation is equivalent to a decline in the internal purchasing power of the pound' (House of Commons, 1988, p. 5). To be more precise, 'inflation is a disequilibrium affecting domestic money in its relationship with domestic output. A change in the price of foreign goods does not alter the purchasing power of domestic money, which can only be exerted over domestic output' (Cencini, 1996, p. 34). This is an important point to which we shall return.
36. Considering the contrasting behaviour of alternative price indices, Gordon has suggested that any monetary authority 'needs to decide which inflation index it is trying to stabilize, e.g., the GDP deflator, the deflator for Personal Consumption Expenditures (PCE), or the Consumer Price Index' (Gordon, 1996, p. 6). Indeed, the sometimes widely differing rates of change in these price indices may become a political issue, as testified by the following passage taken from a classic survey of inflation theory: 'The Ikeda Government in Japan . . . relied on wholesale price indexes to show that the rapid economic growth of 1960–62 was not inflationary, while the Opposition relied on consumer price indexes and national income deflators to show the reverse' (Bronfenbrenner and Holzman, 1963, p. 598, n. 8). Note that in the 1970s the wholesale price index was renamed the producer price index (PPI) (Gordon, 1990, p. 9, n. 5).
37. Generally speaking, the reference (or survey) year is not the same as the year when the specific price index is conventionally set equal to 100 (Fortin, 1990, p. 116). See Silver and Ioannidis (1994) for further discussion on this point.
38. See, for example, Sandilands Committee (1975, pp. 9–13), Triplett (1975, pp. 65–6), Michael (1979), Hagemann (1982, pp. 494–502), Boskin and Hurd (1985, pp. 439–46), Bureau of Labor Statistics (1988, pp. 12–18) and Fisher and Griliches (1995, pp. 230–2).
39. See Berndt et al. (1997), as well as other recent empirical studies cited therein.
40. In this respect, within the set of total demand represented in Figure 2.2, it would have been possible to distinguish the demand of firms from the demand of households. However, since to exert a demand it is necessary to have an income, and since original income holders are households (that is, wage-earners), the distinction would not affect our analysis at this stage (which, let us recall it, is intended to remain within simple, intuitive boundaries). In other words, since profits are formed on the market for produced goods and services, the demand exerted by firms is ultimately a surrogate of the households' one: it is namely exerted with the income transferred, via the mark-up price mechanism, from the latter to the former. The distinction between firms and households will be considered in Parts Two and Three, where analysis is refined and developed on macro-theoretical grounds.
41. As testified long ago by Schumpeter, 'many economists of our own day . . . divide up economic theory into a theory of the individual firm and a macroeconomic theory that is to take care of the relations between aggregate consumption, investment, employment, and so on' (Schumpeter, 1954/1994, p. 997). Most contemporary economists believe indeed that 'the distinguishing feature of macroeconomics is that it collects both individuals and goods together to aggregates and bundles, respectively' (Felderer and Homburg, 1992, p. 11).
42. See, for instance, Van Daal and Merkies (1984), Lewbel (1989), Stoker (1993) and Hartley (1997), as well as the abundant literature cited therein.
43. The concept of methodological individualism (first used by Schumpeter, 1954/1994, p. 889) portrays the working of the entire economic system by relating ultimately all social phenomena to individuals' behaviour. To quote Boland, '*[m]ethodological individualism* is the view that allows *only* individuals to be the decision-makers in any explanation of social phenomena' (Boland, 1982, p. 28). Game theory epitomises perhaps the most clear example of this research strategy, since it deals with the agents' optimising behaviour in a

general-equilibrium framework of inquiry. See Walliser and Prou (1988, pp. 109–14) for a fairly non-technical discussion of this topic.

44. As Boland would say, 'the basis of macroeconomics is the view that it is possible to keep the aggregated quantities in focus. But most important is the view that all of macroeconomic analysis is methodologically and perfectly analogous to microeconomic analysis. . . . We are saying that if microeconomic theory is true, then the nature of the macroview or the aggregated view of the economy cannot be inconsistent with the microview' (Boland, 1982, pp. 84–5).
45. It need not be emphasised that such an approach does not give entire satisfaction to those who adhere to an organic-cum-holistic view of a monetary production economy. See for example Vercelli (1991, pp. 234–7) and Bortis (1997, pp. 365–8).
46. Formal logic rejects the definition of a set as the sum of its elements. As a matter of fact, addition (that is, the operator '+') is not a logical operation on the elements of a set, but it applies to the domain of real numbers ($\mathfrak{R}$). This is not to deny, of course, that an addition of the elements of a set is possible when these elements are of a numerical nature. But this operation has nothing to do with the definition of the set.
47. As writers like Boland have often observed, '[d]emonstrating the dependence of all macroeconomics on microeconomic principles is essential for the fulfillment of the (methodological) individualist requirements of neoclassical economics' (Boland, 1982, p. 80). Moving away from the microeconomic foundations of macroeconomics then implies – to use Colander's (1996) metaphor – climbing down the Walrasian mountain and starting again up another mountain. It is the purpose of Parts Two and Three to explore a relatively new path.
48. 'A fallacy in which what is true of a part is, on that account alone, alleged to be true of the whole' (Samuelson, quoted in Hartley, 1997, p. 170).
49. As pointed out by Samuelson referring to the fallacy of composition, '[w]hat is true for each is not necessarily true for all; and conversely, what is true for all may be quite false for each individual' (quoted in Hartley, 1997, p. 174).
50. See Verdon (1996, pp. 13–14). In his rigorous attempt to work out a conceptual synthesis of classical and Keynesian political economy in modern terms, Bortis notes that 'the question of proportions, i.e. part–whole relations, is fundamental, and this implies that society is primary and is more than the sum of its parts' (Bortis, 1997, p. 8). In the language of this section we can rephrase this argument by quoting the 1980 Nobel prize winner for economics, who as long ago as 1946 pointed out that '[t]here is no reason to assume . . . that there is something sacred about a sum', when examining the economic significance of aggregates (Klein, 1946, p. 310).
51. Everyone familiar with even rudimentary economics should know that '[t]he goal of microfoundations is to explain aggregate relationships in terms of individual behavior' (Hartley, 1997, p. 132). It is sufficient to note here that this line of thought is deeply rooted in methodological individualism, as suggested previously, and that aggregation of microeconomic data is the hallmark of textbooks' macroeconomic models. As has been clearly perceived by Laidler, '[i]n the process of acquiring market-theoretic microfoundations, macroeconomics thus lost its separate identity' (Laidler, 1993, p. 28).

PART TWO

TOWARDS A MACROECONOMIC ANALYSIS OF INFLATION

3. The Neoclassical Analysis of Inflation: a Critical Appraisal

As writers like Gale have long and often observed, '[e]conomists' perceptions of inflation rest on measurements of the "general price level" and on rates of change of price indexes' (Gale, 1981a, p. 2). These indices have become an important part of economic investigation and are in fact considered as the operational counterparts of the (never unambiguously defined) concept of the general price level. In the first part of this book we set out to show that price index analysis suffers from important methodological weaknesses (more fundamental than technical defects), which make it theoretically inappropriate for measuring inflation over the entire set of economic units, that is, from a macroeconomic vantage point. The focus on price indices in current inflation analysis might indeed give rise to significant errors in monetary research, in theory as well as in policy making. As we shall argue, adhering to the price level idea implies adhering to the traditional dichotomy between money and output, a theoretical approach that appears to be in contrast with the principles of a monetary economy of production. By the same token, economic policy makers may be misguided in policy design if they rely on price level measurement, because the very measures they focus on in reality may not represent what they assume to be measuring (with a high degree of approximation, given the index number problem that we explored in Part One). We leave it to future research to determine to what extent these errors affect negatively the level of well-being of current and future generations of income holders, both taken as a whole and considered at the 'sublevel' of the entire population of a national economy. A line of argument that might be more relevant to our main theme relies in fact on the grounding of price indices (or aggregate price levels) in economic theory (see for example Fisher and Shell, 1972, p. ix; Triplett, 1975, p. 19). It is indeed no exaggeration to maintain, as Schumpeter so convincingly noted in his *History of Economic Analysis*, that

> index numbers pertain to the province of the statistical technician and their theory

> should accordingly be part of the theory of statistics, just as is, for example, the theory of sampling. A great part of the work on index numbers was in fact done by statisticians or by economists who cared little for 'economic theory.' For instance, the formula that of all displayed the most indestructible vitality is due to a man who cannot without qualification be called an economist at all, Laspeyres (Schumpeter, 1954/1994, pp. 1092–3).

Elaborating this point, one might argue that the index number approach to the inflation problem – so deeply rooted in current economic analysis – has failed to bring out a thorough understanding of the underlying causes of the ongoing rise in prices. To put the point sharply, one might claim that in established monetary economics there is a manifest lack of an adequate theory of inflation. As the case is forcefully stated by Hudson, '[t]he consequence of this is that we can offer no cure for inflation with the certainty that it will work' (Hudson, 1982, p. 55). This comment is as relevant today as when it was made nearly twenty years ago, although there has since been extensive writing on the subject (which remains highly controversial in current debate). Woodford (1997, p. 2) has depicted the current state of inflation theory by observing that the traditional approach to the problem of measuring (the movement in) aggregate prices – and, so the argument goes, inflation – takes as its starting point the neoclassical quantity theory of money,[1] which is ultimately a theory of the general price level (Laidler, 1991, p. 84).

Yet, before addressing neoclassical monetary economics from a critical point of view, a remark is in order. In the remainder of this book we will follow Patinkin's terminology, in so far as the term 'neoclassical' is used here 'as a shorthand designation for the once widely-accepted body of thought which organized monetary theory around a transactions or cash-balance type of equation, and which then used these equations to validate the classical quantity theory of money' (Patinkin, 1956, p. 96). Similarly, we will use the term 'monetarism' to characterise the 'contemporary incarnation' (Congdon, 1978, p. 3) of the (still) dominant theory, which considers the purchasing power of money as the reciprocal of the general level of prices (see for example Fisher, 1911/1931). While one might quarrel with the existence of a unique, and unambiguous, monetarist doctrine (Mayer et al., 1978, p. i), it is indeed a widely held view – also among those economists who define themselves as monetarists (without necessarily endorsing the term itself)[2] – that the basic idea which lies at the roots of monetarism (as an economic tenet) can be traced back to the quantity theory of money (see Mayer et al., 1978, pp. 1–5; Desai, 1981, p. 15; Kaldor and Trevithick, 1981, pp. 1–2; Laidler, 1981, pp. 1–5; Cagan, 1987, p. 493). In fact, according to two distinguished adherents to neoclassical monetary economics, '[t]hough it has been under persistent challenge, the quantity theory of money has, in one form or another, dominated the literature on inflation for the greater part of the last three hundred years' (Laidler and Parkin, 1975, p. 744). After an initial exploration and discussion of this theory in the different formulations it has received over the last hundred years, this chapter aims to put forward an internal critique of established monetary analysis, in order to call for an adequate theory of modern money and of the working of our monetary production economies.

THE OPTIMUM QUANTITY OF MONEY AND OTHER ISSUES

The neoclassical (quantity) theory of money receives a variety of treatments in economic analysis, owing to the fact that its advocates sometimes follow different lines of reasoning, although they always put forward the same conclusion as far as the relation between the stock of money (or its purchasing power) and the general level of prices is concerned. 'In its traditional format, the quantity theory of money is a body of doctrine concerned with the relationship between the money supply and the general price level' (Vane and Thompson, 1979, p. 25). Among the various, rather crude, formalisations that one could find in the vast literature, the two most general formulations of the quantity theory in monetary economics are the transactions form and the cash-balance form. Despite their common conceptual ground, these formulations stem from two different methodological lines of approach. It is to them that we now turn, so as to be able to explore their 'contemporary incarnation' critically.

The Fisherine Quantity Equation

As Hicks recognised in November 1934 before the London Economic Club, the most startling issue in monetary economics lies in the preoccupation of neoclassical theorists with the so-called quantity equation. 'This equation crops up again and again, and it has all sorts of ingenious little arithmetical tricks performed on it' (Hicks, 1935/1967, p. 62). In all its versions, though to various extents, the quantity equation rests on a rather simple conceptualisation of the circular flow of income, where the famous Clower's dictum ('*money buys goods and goods buy money; but goods do not buy goods*')[3] is portrayed as being the distinctive feature of any monetary economy. In this analytical framework, the goods and services sold are purported to move in the opposite direction to that of the flow of money. 'If the money flow is clockwise, the "real" flow is counter-clockwise' (Dean, 1965, p. xii). Thus, paraphrasing Patinkin's (1956, p. 1) open statement in *Money, Interest, and Prices*, the natural starting point to study the working of a monetary economy seems to be the commodity market, where (relative) exchanges are supposed to take place between two distinct things or stocks: money and output (Figure 3.1).

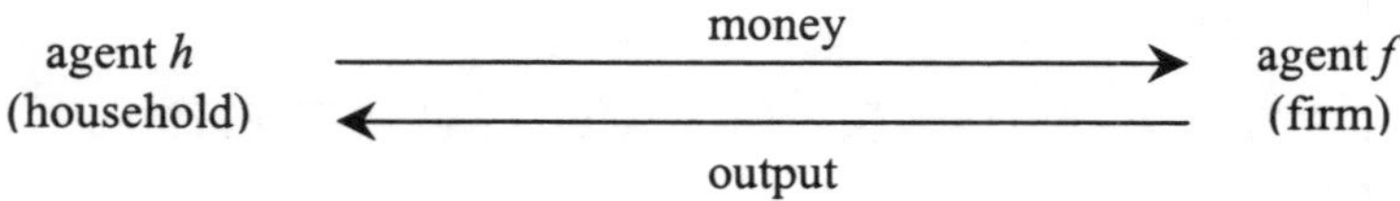

Figure 3.1 The concept of relative exchange

Now, moving from aggregation over many agents and multiple kinds of commodities sold in the marketplace – a conventional methodology in economic research, which, as we have already noted, is not free from analytical errors – the most popular formulation of the quantity theory of money says that the total sum of monetary transactions is related (as we are going to see) to the value of the goods and services sold. In its most basic terms, what has been called the equation of exchange may be written as equation (3.1):

$$MV \equiv \sum_{i=1}^{n} p_i q_i \tag{3.1}$$

where M is the quantity of money available in the economy, V is the average number of times that each unit of money is used in transactions, p_i is the price of commodity i (for $i = 1, \ldots, n$) entering into exchange, and q_i is the quantity of each commodity exchanged. As pointed out by Irving Fisher in his influential work on *The Purchasing Power of Money*, for aggregation purposes '[i]t is desired, then, in the equation of exchange, to convert the right side, Σpq, into a form PT where T measures the volume of trade, and P is an "index number" expressing the price level at which this trade is carried on' (Fisher, 1911/1931, p. 195). This is where, and how, the correspondence between the general level of prices and its alleged operational counterpart, the price index, enters established monetary analysis, as noted in Part One.

Since the canonical formulation put forward by Fisher, whose mathematical form goes back to the seventeenth century,[4] the fundamental equation of exchange has thus been written as equation (3.2):

$$MV \equiv PT \tag{3.2}$$

This formalisation[5] is known as the transactions form of the equation of exchange, because '[i]n this version [of the quantity equation] the elementary event is a transaction – an exchange in which one economic actor transfers goods or services or securities to another actor and receives a transfer of money in return' (Friedman, 1987, p. 5). As we have previously observed, this statement is the axiomatic definition of a monetary exchange, that is, a transaction where monetary assets exchange for non-money goods (Spindt, 1985, pp. 178–80). Indeed, probably the most recurrent, and undisputed, assertion in monetary economics literature is epitomised by the following theorem: 'By *monetary trade* I mean trade in which a single good plays a distinctive asymmetric role as one side of virtually all transactions' (Starr, 1980, p. 263).

Now, quite apart from a careful and thorough investigation into the economic nature of so-called 'monetary goods' (that is, the exact components of M, entering each and every form of the equation of exchange),[6] an age-long controversy has arisen on the heuristic character of what has since been known as the Fisherine quantity equation. On the one hand, authors like Friedman have often maintained that '[e]quations (3.1) and (3.2), like the other quantity equations we shall discuss, are intended to be identities – a special application of double-entry bookkeeping, with each transaction simultaneously recorded on both sides of the equation' (Friedman, 1987, p. 5). Because one agent's sale is another agent's purchase, the sums received for output sales, appearing on the right-hand side of the Fisherine equation, must necessarily equal the sums expended by domestic income holders, which – owing to the idea of relative exchanges (see Figure 3.1) – must again equal the existing money stock times the 'average' turnover of a unit of money (shown on the left-hand side of the equation) (see Fisher, 1911/1931, pp. 15–17; Dean, 1965, p. xiv; Frisch, 1983, p. 219; Bordo, 1987, pp. 175–6; Duck, 1993, p. 2). Harrod gives a clear illustration of the necessary truth of the equation of exchange, worth quoting in its entirety.

> The tautological nature of the equation, if this is the right term to use, springs from the fact that the price of a packet [of cigarettes] is *defined* as being the amount of money that is given for it. What is handed out in payment for the packet is the same as what is received for the packet. The necessary truth of the equation is

simply a generalisation of this for all transactions within given limits of time and space (Harrod, 1969, p. 154).[7]

Yet, by contrast, several other writers argue that the Fisherine equation is not an accounting identity but an equilibrium condition. Indeed, to quote Schumpeter, 'Fisher did not say that MV is the same thing as PT or that MV is equal to PT by definition: given values of M, V, T tend to *bring about* a determined value of P, but they do not simply *spell* a certain P' (Schumpeter, 1954/1994, p. 1096). Thus, in equations (3.1) and (3.2) one has to substitute the sign of identity (≡) with that of equality (=). As is well known, this argument centres on the probable causal relationships between the four variables characterising the quantity equation. As Patinkin (1956, p. 1) puts it, the equation of exchange (3.2) can be looked upon as a specific proposition about the causal relationships determining the equilibrium price level. In particular, the general level of prices may be seen as the resultant of forces represented by aggregate demand (MV) and aggregate supply (T) of current output. In Fisher's own words, '*[t]he price level is normally the one absolutely passive element in the equation of exchange.* It is controlled solely by the other elements and the causes antecedent to them, but exerts no control over them' (Fisher, 1911/1931, p. 172). This can be formalised by writing $P = f(M, V, T)$.

Along these lines, one might then assume, as most advocates of this approach do, that both the transactions volume of goods and the velocity of money are exogenously determined by technologies and institutions (for instance payment technologies, consumers' tastes and trade unions), which is tantamount to saying that both T and V may be taken as constant in the short run:[8]

$$T \equiv \overline{T}$$

$$V \equiv \overline{V}$$

where a bar over a variable denotes its supposed exogeneity. On these assumptions, the Fisherine quantity equation has in fact been converted into a theory of the determination of the general price level, that is to say, the quantity theory of money or, more properly, the quantity-of-money theory of aggregate prices. Indeed, manipulating Fisher's equation of exchange (3.2) yields the following equation (3.3):

$$P = \alpha M \qquad (3.3)$$

where α is a constant since it is the algebraic expression of $\overline{V}/\overline{T}$.

Equation (3.3) states the proportional relationship between the general level of prices and the quantity of money available in the economy, and represents the most common formulation of the quantity theory of money. 'To use the correct arithmetical term, given the conditions of demand for money, its value *varies inversely* as the quantity available, or in other words the "general level of prices" *varies directly* as the quantity of money available' (Robertson, 1922/1937, p. 32).[9] The main conclusion usually drawn from this analysis has been to derive a quantity equation in rate-of-growth form, that could explain the rate of increase in aggregate prices by the rate of change in the money supply. Indeed, differentiating equation (3.3) with regard to time and dividing both sides by P (= αM) gives the following equation (3.4):

$$\dot{P} = \dot{M} \tag{3.4}$$

where a dot over a variable represents a proportionate rate of change.

On the whole, in its strictest (some would say naive) form the quantity theory of money claims that the money supply is the main, if not unique, determinant of the price level,[10] and that the rate of growth of the stock of money determines the rate of inflation – as measured by the variation in the targeted price index – from which the given economy suffers over the period under examination. If the assumption of a constant volume of transactions ($T \equiv \overline{T}$) is relaxed, equation (3.4) becomes equation (3.5):

$$\dot{P} = \dot{M} - \dot{T} \tag{3.5}$$

thus giving rise to the famous Friedmanite proposition that '*inflation is always and everywhere a monetary phenomenon* in the sense that it is and can be produced only by a more rapid increase in the quantity of money than in output' (Friedman, 1987, p. 17).[11]

Yet, the transactions form underlying the quantity theory of money (as well as the theory of inflation, as we are told) has been strongly criticised by its opponents. In particular, Hegeland – echoing Hicks's contention quoted above – asserts again and again that '[t]he only thing the equation of exchange demonstrates is some arithmetic relations between the symbols included. Nothing can be said as to causal relationships between the different elements' (Hegeland, 1951, p. 39). As a matter of fact, 'the quantity theory is *no explanation* of changes in the value of money' (ibid., p. 59), for 'the equation of exchange does not determine the purchasing power of money, *i.e.*, *P*. As mentioned above, this *P* is merely a weighted average of all individual prices' (ibid., p. 93).[12] All this will be developed later. At this point, it is sufficient to emphasise the criticism voiced by the 1988 Nobel prize winner for economics, who as long ago as 1966 maintained that,

> [t]he link of proportionality at any given time between the quantity of money and the product of the price level and the level of activity (relation 3.3) is a relationship of interdependence, and from the dynamic standpoint of causality can obviously be interpreted in either of two ways. It may mean that the price level is proportional to the ratio of the quantity of money to the level of activity; or it may mean that the quantity of money is proportional to the product of the price level and the level of economic activity (Allais, 1966, p. 1153).

A similar treatment was also given by Dean (1965, pp. xiv–xv), when he observed incidentally that the value of money's velocity of circulation (*V*) has always been empirically defined, and calculated, so as to offset precisely the change in transactions volumes (*T*).[13] Thus, there is some reason to believe that the alleged causality among the four variables put forward by the Fisherine quantity equation might rely on a *petitio principii*, which, if demonstrated, might already raise some legitimate doubts about the validity of the traditional (neoclassical) analysis of inflation.

The Cambridge Quantity Equation

The Fisherine quantity equation moves from a desire to depict the macroeconomic relationship between the general price level and the money stock using an analysis in terms of circular flows. Yet, another strand of neoclassical (monetary) economists have been seeking to derive the demand for money following a microeconomic approach that considers money merely as a stock. The latter group of quantity theorists focus essentially on portfolio-choice analysis, for their main concern is with the individual's optimal relationship between his monetary (liquid) assets and his stock of other, non-monetary, goods (Friedman, 1969, pp. 73–4; Patinkin, 1972, pp. 107–8; Niehans, 1978, pp. 4–6; Herman, 1984, pp. 583–4; Bordo, 1987, p. 176). All sorts of money-in-the-utility-function models have thus been put forth (see for example Sidrauski, 1967; Grandmont, 1983, pp. 16–32; Poterba and Rotemberg, 1987; Woodford, 1990, pp. 1073–84; and the literature cited therein), trying to isolate the determinants of the amount of money a typical or representative agent may wish to hold for transactions purposes.

Ignoring the set of problems associated with the aggregation of microeconomic situations and with representative-agent models, that we already discussed in Chapter 2, the demand function for money (M^d) has usually been formally expressed as the demand to hold liquid assets (the so-called 'cash balances') in a certain proportion (k) of the value of total transactions (T) as determined by some index of the price level (P) (see Patinkin, 1956, p. 97; Vane and Thompson, 1979, p. 28; Frisch, 1983, p. 220; Friedman, 1987, p. 6). The optimum quantity of money that should exist in the national economy has then been derived by solving the following simple model, whose equilibrium condition is established in the familiar Marshallian way (money demand equals money supply, M^s):

$$M^d \equiv kPT \tag{3.6}$$

$$M^s \equiv \overline{M} \tag{3.7}$$

$$M^d = M^s \tag{3.8}$$

Now, whilst equations (3.2) and (3.6) stem from two different methodological approaches, which also make different use of stock–flow analysis in monetary economics, the cash-balance form of the equation of exchange – attributed primarily to the work of Pigou (1917) and Marshall (1923), and popularised by their Cambridge pupils[14] – may be viewed as a mere reformulation of the quantity theory of money derived from the Fisherine equation. The four terms in the Cambridge equation (3.6) have indeed the same economic meaning as those in the Fisherine equation (3.2), provided that k defines the average period of time over which households' cash balances can be used to purchase non-monetary goods and that it is numerically equal to the reciprocal of V (Harrod, 1969, p. 156; Macesich, 1983, pp. 26–7; Bordo, 1987, pp. 175–6; Friedman, 1987, pp. 4–6). In fact, Professor Pigou did not claim any essential difference to exist between his formulation and Fisher's. In his own words,

> [although] the machinery that I shall suggest in the following pages is quite different from that elaborated by Professor Irving Fisher in his admirable *Purchasing Power of Money*, and, as I think, more convenient, I am not in any sense an 'opponent' of the 'quantity theory' or a hostile critic of Professor Fisher's lucid analysis. He has painted his picture on one plan, and I paint mine on another. But the pictures that we both paint are of the same thing, and the witness of the two, as to what that thing in essentials is, substantially agrees (Pigou, 1917, p. 39).

Yet, the emphasis by the Cambridge school on the proportion of resources that economic agents choose to keep in monetary form (that is, liquid assets), instead of focusing on the circular flow of national income as Fisher's equation did, turned the attention of most contemporary monetary theorists to changes in the amount of the individuals' cash holding and their consequences in terms of price level changes (see Pigou, 1917, p. 54; Patinkin, 1956, p. 40). The portfolio-choice approach thus became the standard method for both theoretical and empirical investigation in monetary economics, and the determination of the equilibrium level of aggregate prices has since been viewed as a matter of simple equalisation of money supply and money demand, 'by help of merely arithmetic truisms, which largely reduced the economic significance of the argument' (Hegeland, 1951, p. 97). From then on, neoclassical (general-equilibrium) models of monetary economies experienced an unprecedented mushroom growth, in an attempt to integrate monetary theory and price theory[15] by modelling the interactions of multiple agents and commodities and by assuming money as a device for overcoming 'frictions' (also dubbed 'viscosities') in the commodity market.[16]

The Modern Quantity Equation and the Expected Inflation Rate

The modern version of the quantity theory of money emanates from an attempt to circumvent what his archpriest – to use Kaldor's (1970, p. 2) term – labelled 'the ambiguities of the concepts of "transactions" and the "general price level"', that, as he lucidly observed, 'have never been satisfactorily resolved' in received economic analysis (Friedman, 1987, p. 5). In fact, the large amount of research work carried out by quantity theorists over the last three hundred years has established neither a fully-fledged measure of transactions nor a comprehensive price index related to them (Bordo, 1987, pp. 175–6). As a result, a shift has occurred in monetary thought from the transactions version of the quantity theory of money to its income version.[17] Since the 'oral quantity theory tradition' developed at the University of Chicago throughout the 1930s and 1940s,[18] monetary economists have tended to make use of the quantity equation in its modern income form, which metamorphoses equations (3.2) and (3.6) into the following expression (equation 3.9) – viewed by Friedman (1987, p. 6) as a halfway house between the Cambridge version and Fisher's:

$$MV \equiv Y \tag{3.9}$$

where Y represents current national income (see Friedman, 1959 in Ball and Doyle, 1969, p. 139; Friedman, 1971, p. 329; Patinkin, 1972, p. 95; Bordo, 1987, p. 175). Hence, the necessary and sufficient condition for income growth (as well as for inflation, according to this postulate) has been written as equation (3.10):

$$\dot{Y} \Leftrightarrow \dot{M} \Leftrightarrow \dot{P} \tag{3.10}$$

so that the term in the middle is the sine qua non condition for the left- and right-hand terms (Stein, 1976, p. 254; Mayer et al., 1978, p. 5; Laidler, 1981, p. 1).

Now, it has been claimed that '[t]he modern quantity theory, and the monetarist school based on it, makes several fundamental departures from the neo-classical quantity theory' (Johnson, in Mayer et al., 1978, p. 131). In particular, whereas in the 'old' quantity theory the causal link ran from money to prices (see especially equations (3.3), (3.4) and (3.5)), in the 'new' quantity theory the direction of causation is from M to Y (on the assumption that V depends on a set of variables none of which is affected by (changes in) the money supply). The essence of monetarism is indeed that changes in the money supply cause proportional changes in national income, after a variable time lag.[19] The relevant passage in Friedman's dictionary article is worth quoting in its entirety: 'Today's income growth is not closely related to today's monetary growth; it depends on what has been happening to money in the past. What happens to money today affects what is going to happen to income in the future' (Friedman, 1987, p. 16).[20]

Yet, without going much further for the time being, on closer investigation the alleged explanatory power of the monetarist doctrine seems even more questionable than that of the 'old' quantity theory, in so far as the effect of monetary expansion on aggregate prices is concerned. Paul Davidson and Sidney Weintraub correctly note that, if national income is affected by money supply growth as monetarists claim, 'how much of the money increase runs in the form of price movements, and how much in output and employment, is left obscure' (Davidson and Weintraub, 1973, p. 1120). Indeed, the consolidation of P and T (see equation (3.2)) into a unique variable (Y) as in equation (3.9) entails *ipso facto* the annihilation of the distinction between price movements and transactions (that is, output) fluctuations, and the whole quantity-of-money theory of aggregate prices is consequently obscured by this fact.

To be true, Friedman himself explicitly acknowledged this problem of the modern quantity equation, when he observed that the latter 'has nothing to say directly about the division of changes in nominal income between prices and quantity' (Friedman, 1971, p. 337). He maintained nevertheless what might fairly be called the 'Friedman Rule' regarding the optimum quantity of money, which states that the best monetary policy to provide a Pareto-efficient allocation of resources, and thus maximise the level of well-being of (representative) agents, would be to maintain a rate of growth of the money supply so that 'the quantity of money per unit of output can be kept from increasing appreciably' (Friedman, 1987, p. 17). The idea behind such a quantity-theoretic proposition has been popularised by the policy-oriented assertion that the rate of money supply growth – minus the growth rate of output, as in equation (3.5) – should be kept constant over the long run, so as to produce a constant (that is, predictable) inflation rate, defined as the rate of growth of the targeted price index. As Frisch puts it, '[t]he recent reformulation of the quantity theory is the accelerations theorem. It implies that only an acceleration or a deceleration of the rate of money growth produces any real effects, i.e. employment and output effects, while a constant rate of growth of the quantity of money determines the rate of inflation' (Frisch, in Mayer et al., 1978, p. 114).[21]

So, granting the force of this conception, the 'rational-expectations revolution' of the 1970s shifted the attention from the causal link between money supply growth and price changes to the distinction between expected and unexpected inflation (Sargent, 1996, p. 539). In fact, the unpredictability of inflation, that is, uncertainty, has become one of the centrepieces of contemporary monetary economics, inasmuch as Friedman's 1976 Nobel lecture highlighted that 'what matters is not inflation per se but unanticipated inflation' (Friedman, 1977, p. 458). Indeed, the rational-expectations hypothesis claims that the individuals' economic rationality enables them to use both currently available information about the variables of concern to them and a correct theory of the interrelationships among these variables to anticipate future variables adopting optimal forecasting methods (Barro, 1976, pp. 15–25; Friedman, 1987, pp. 14–15). Hence, any anticipated growth of the money supply, like those ensuing from proclaimed governmental policies deemed credible by the private sector, would be immediately incorporated into inflationary expectations – via the monetarist 'transmission mechanism' – so that the resulting movement in aggregate prices would have ultimately no 'real' effect on national income (that is, Y, the consolidated variable in equation (3.9)). To quote Stanley Fischer on this point, 'any *anticipated* monetary policy action will not affect output. Rather, such actions are reflected in both the expected and the actual price levels, leading to no effect on output. The result . . . is that monetary policy actions affect output only if they are unanticipated – meaning not reflected in pricing decisions' (Fischer, 1987, p. 648).

A vast literature on this forward-looking approach to inflation[22] and its effects on output has then spawned neoclassical models of money-using economies.[23] So much so that, within monetary macroeconomics, Walrasian rational-expectations equilibrium models represent, today, the canonical way of dealing with individuals' maximisation problems in a consistently understood environment (Sargent, 1996, p. 545).[24] In particular, over the last twenty years or so, neoclassical monetary economists have been spending much time in order to build so-called 'overlapping-generations models', trying to cast new light on the existence of monetary (dis)equilibria in a framework revived by various sorts of game-theoretic approaches in the rules-versus-discretion debate. These models of money-using economies generally assume a two-period lifetime for each and every generation of agents,[25] in order to gauge inflation forecasts under the rational-expectation hypothesis of finitely-lived consumers. The *locus classicus* of all such analyses is Samuelson's 1958 *Journal of Political Economy* article, which put forth 'An exact consumption-loan model of interest with or without the social contrivance of money'. The approach suggested in this seminal paper stems from the research strategy according to which overlapping generations of consumers represent a sort of trading viscosity, something that inhibits the sacred Walrasian market clearing at each point in time. It has then been ambitiously claimed by one of the most outstanding proponents of this approach that 'models built on this [overlapping-generations] friction can be made to confront virtually every long-standing problem in monetary economics' (Wallace, 1980, p. 51).[26] To be true, advocates of this postulate mainly follow the cash-balance form of the quantity-theoretic analysis of monetary economies, because they consider money as a distinctive, intrinsically useless (if not worthless) asset that is known to be acceptable to all generations, whose utility functions always include its transaction-facilitating services[27] (see for example Lucas, 1972, pp. 104–9; Lucas, 1980, pp. 136–40; Wallace, 1980, pp. 52–60; Balasko and Shell, 1981, pp. 114–21; Sargent and Wallace, 1982, pp. 1215–27; McCallum, 1987, pp. 328–9; Woodford, 1987, pp. 53–63; but also Bernhardt and Engineer, 1994, pp. 495–9; Duffy, 1994, pp. 543–8; Bertocchi and Wang, 1995, pp. 208–10; Gottardi, 1996, pp. 78–80).[28] The following passage – by one of the most lucid critics of this method of monetary investigation – will serve to illustrate the crucial assumption made in all kinds of overlapping-generations models of monetary production economies. 'Workers can acquire [the monetary asset] by saving when young and then sell it for consumption goods when old. It is tempting to call this asset *money* and to exclaim, Eureka, here is the reason for the existence and value of money' (Tobin, 1980, p. 83). Put differently, in such a setting the mythical, and boldly mystified, double coincidence of wants feared by all neoclassical economists is reported to be ingeniously overcome by introducing a durable good called money, and further assuming that – in each market session – any purchase of (consumption) goods by the 'old' generation is a demand for labour (that is, output) to be provided by the 'young' generation.

There is no real need for us to explore in detail all of these models, whose common basic idea relies on the concept of relative exchange schematically represented in Figure 3.1 (and which will be taken up again in Chapter 4). The existing differences between rational-expectations, infinite-horizon models and overlapping-generations models with finitely-lived agents (the two most used contemporary approaches to study the working of monetary economies) are indeed more a matter of emphasis than substance.[29] They all share the belief – unanimously held by neoclassical economists – in a dichotomous world, where money is introduced in an Arrow–Debreu (general-equilibrium) framework of inquiry to accommodate some portrayed frictions in factor as well as in goods markets. To this analytical vision we now turn, in an attempt to mine from inside the fundamental pillar of both the traditional quantity theory of money and its contemporary incarnation(s).

THE DICHOTOMOUS REPRESENTATION OF MONETARY ECONOMIES

Over the years, as pointed out by Frank H. Hahn (1982, p. 21), the picture behind the now so-called 'cash-in-advance constraint'[30] has axiomatically postulated what neoclassical theorists have been seeking to account for in their research programme, namely both the existence and the value of money. A large amount of theoretical as well as empirical research along the lines of the most influential paradigm in (monetary) macroeconomics has thus developed and refined the dominant view of the workings of contemporary production economies, where the banking nature of money could no longer be denied.[31] Such an approach has long been trying to fit in an Arrow–Debreu fictional economy some kind of commodity- or fiat money, whose purported essential aim is to function as a means of exchange as lubricant as possible (see Hicks, 1966/1967, pp. 2–7; Hahn, 1973, pp. 230–4; Hahn, 1987, pp. 21–9; but also Rogers, 1989, pp. 58–67, for a thorough critical appraisal). Yet, an acute observer of the history of economic thought has recently noted that,

> the world of GET [standing for general-equilibrium theory] is in fact a dream world, a world which is not totally workable in the context of actual society. The number of actors on the stage in this GET world are far too few. . . . I will grant that such a retrogressive approach is an easy path if one wants to construct a model axiomatically, and it may also be of some use as a temporary means of facilitating

> the dichotomizing method, whereby entrepreneurs and bankers are put to sleep for a while (Morishima, 1992, pp. 198–9).

As a matter of fact, it is a widely-held view, even today, that our economic systems are characterised by two dichotomous spheres: the real sphere, where output and relative prices are determined, and the monetary sphere, whose unique function is to establish – via the best-fitted quantity equation – the general level of prices (and hence current national income) by means of the interaction between money supply and money demand. In this analytical framework, Harry G. Johnson maintains for example that,

> [t]he classical quantity theory, in its equation of exchange formulation, had the useful and necessary purpose of separating the theory of real equilibrium (relative prices and quantities) as determined by factor quantities, technology, and preferences, from the determination of money wages and prices – establishing what came to be known as 'the classical dichotomy' or 'the neutrality of money' or 'the homogeneity postulate' (Johnson, in Mayer et al., 1978, pp. 127–8).

This quotation has the merit of summarising in a single statement the threefold hallmark of received monetary theory, whose principal tenets are the neutrality of money and the homogeneity postulate, which are ultimately but a corollary of the traditional dichotomy referred to above. Though the depth and breadth of this familiar ground have already been well explored, a fresh look at it will serve us as a Trojan Horse to pinpoint some unfamiliar, and probably unpleasant, monetarist (or quantity-theoretic) pitfalls.

Money and Output as Two Distinct Objects

Let us reconsider the numerical example introduced in Chapter 1, where we assumed that in the given national economy a money stock of 2000 macro-units faces (or, as we are told, exchanges with) 100 macro-units of output, thus giving rise to a general price level of (P_1 =) 20. Analysed more closely, the paradigm underlying this theory raises serious doubts. There is in fact a fundamental oddity in the very definition of the general price level, as it so often appears in recent monetary economics literature. This problem arises out of the fact that the stock of goods cannot possibly be measured independently of money. Indeed, by relating the money stock with the stock of output the given quantity of money will buy, one does not explain where the measure of output comes from. In other words, if money and output really were two distinct things, whose asserted confrontation on the market ring would enable one to determine the current level of aggregate prices, how would it logically be possible to measure output without having recourse to the monetary sphere? How can output be valued – not to say exist – as an economic object, if it is abstracted from money (by considering the latter as a stock existing independently of the former, and vice versa)? And again, how can we posit in the above fictitious example that total output is equal to 100, without considering (in a way that shall be further investigated in Chapter 4) what neoclassical theorists call the 'dichotomous' monetary sector? At first glance, one might claim that output is measured in mere physical terms, so that in our economy there are, say, 100 tons of beef which encompass total national product of period (t =) 1. But it should take only a moment's reflection to see that this answer hardly does justice to the complexity of sophisticated market economies like those of the real world. It seems in fact almost trivial to note that any advanced economy currently produces multiple goods and services. In economic terms, their measure cannot be established unless they all have been homogenised by their monetary form, whose numerical magnitude measures national output objectively. Is it possible to add up, say, two tons of Scottish smoked salmon and five tons of Irish roast beef without resorting to their monetary measure (expressed by a number of pounds, or perhaps euros, as we shall see later)?

To concentrate attention on the problem we are investigating, it should be stressed that the attempt to explain inflation by observing the variation in the level of prices – by means of any index-number formula – openly contradicts logic, as soon as the intimately related requirement of measuring output objectively is brought to the fore. If, as they do, neoclassical economists define the general price level by the relation they virtually establish between the stock of money and the stock of output (and then consider any variation in that level as the reciprocal variation in money's purchasing power), their research programme on inflation is seriously weakened by the axiomatic dichotomy they establish between these two stocks. In fact, it is on this specific, but fundamental, point that neoclassical economics goes astray, as has been suggested by one of the most distinguished scholars of neoclassical thought. In his endeavour to provide *A New Formulation of General Equilibrium Theory*, as the subtitle of his 1992 book indicates, Morishima recognises indeed that 'the method of analysis dichotomizing economics into two specialized departments, real and monetary, is harmful and defective. We must deal with the economy as a whole uniting and interlinking the two subsystems' (Morishima, 1992, p. 184).

Now, without anticipating, one may still argue that central to all versions of the neoclassical (quantity) theory of money-using economies 'is a distinction between the *nominal* quantity of money and the *real* quantity of money' (Friedman, 1987, p. 3). It is in fact a well-known commonplace of received literature that '[t]he monetary analysis outlined [in it] differentiates explicitly between real magnitudes and nominal magnitudes' (Brunner, 1970, p. 24). The nominal quantity of money is a nominal magnitude in the sense that it is the number of money units which constitute what has been termed the money stock (*M*), as captured by the widely used statistical definitions adopted by central banks and international organisations around the world (M0, M1, M2, M3, M4 etc.). The real quantity of money is 'the volume of goods and services the money will purchase' (Friedman, 1987, p. 4); it is, in other words, the real object (or the purchasing power) of nominal money, and in this research strategy it is precisely obtained by dividing *M* by *P*.[32] In the light of the analysis put forth by the classics, particularly in Smith's *Wealth of Nations*, this line of reasoning could have been developed so as to firmly establish why its author claimed that 'the wealth or revenue . . . is equal only to one of the two values which are thus intimated somewhat ambiguously by the same word, . . . to the money's worth more properly than to the money' (Smith, 1776/1970, p. 386). In fact, an investigation into the nature of modern money might show that the distinction between money proper and money's worth, that is, the distinction between nominal and real money, might be considered as being analogous to the distinction between a numerical form and its real content (an issue we shall explore later on). However, since in neoclassical analysis the link between the nominal and the real quantity of money is provided by the price level, which is theorised as resulting from the confrontation of the stock of money with the stock of output, the investigation referred to above has simply been eschewed or, to borrow Morishima's phraseology, put to sleep for a (rather long) while.

The vicious circle inherent in received monetary analysis should by now be evident and may ultimately be formalised as follows:

$$\frac{M}{P} \Rightarrow m$$

and

$$\frac{M}{Q} \Rightarrow P$$

where the direction of the arrows indicates causality, and $m \equiv Q$ for the reason stated above. Thus then, the general level of prices is seen as determining and, at the same time, as being determined by the relationship existing between (nominal) money and (real) output. There is then some reason to believe that such crucial issues in monetary economics need re-examining. One might raise indeed two closely related questions, to which we now turn.

Money, a Veil?

Another argument often put forward by neoclassical theorists to provide analytical foundations to their dichotomous view of our economic systems refers to a romantic interpretation of the Pigovian idea of the veil of money.[33] For the sake of analysis it is worth quoting its original source at some length on this point.

> Take the real facts and happenings away, and the monetary facts and happenings necessarily vanish with them; but take money away and, whatever else might follow, economic life would *not* become meaningless: there is nothing absurd about the conception of a self-sufficing family, or village group, without any money at all. In this sense money clearly *is* a veil. It does not comprise any of the essentials of economic life (Pigou, 1949, pp. 24–5).

Stated in modern terms, this claim has been reformulated as to convey the idea of the neutrality of money on economic activity.[34] '[The property "money is neutral"] characterise[s] the claim that the set of equilibria of an economy is independent of the quantity of money (provided that the latter is always positive)' (Hahn, 1973, p. 230). As authors like Lucas (1972, pp. 113–14), Niehans (1978, p. 8) and Patinkin (1987, p. 639) have put it, even unanticipated variations in the money stock do not affect the equilibrium level of the variables resulting from supply and demand conditions in the real sector.

This issue is however rather controversial in so far as the expected growth rate of the quantity of money is concerned, and it has led neoclassical economists to distinguish between neutrality and superneutrality of money.[35] In the words of Douglas Fisher, '[b]y monetary *neutrality* we mean the (null) effect of a once-and-for-all change in the quantity of money on the real variables of the economic system. . . . *Superneutrality*, then, is generally taken to be the (null) effect of a once-and-for-all change in the *growth rate* of the quantity of money on the real variables of the economic system' (Fisher, 1989, p. 132). Yet, this distinction seems to contradict the crucial monetarist policy prescription of a constant (possibly low) rate of growth of the money supply, in order to keep inflation on its expected path and hence leave the 'real' economy unaffected. On the one hand, what Tobin (1981, p. 35) labels ideological monetarism promises to rescue our monetary production economies from (unexpected) inflationary pressures, by putting forward the previously mentioned 'Friedman Rule' as the specific remedy to the ongoing rise in aggregate prices. On the other hand, by the very idea of money being superneutral, theoretical monetarism claims that a (unique) change in the rate of money supply growth is harmless for economic performance, for it does not affect any of the real variables in the system. This contradiction has been unnoticed so far and might deserve further investigation. Although the issues involved in it are certainly more complicated than the above antithetical statements, within this paradigm the (super)neutrality of changes in the money supply has generally been treated as being equivalent to a mere change in the unit of account (Haliassos and Tobin, 1990, p. 909; Marty, 1994, p. 407).[36] What exactly a unit of account is, will be explored in Chapter 4. Here we must consider an even more important argument, which represents perhaps the most striking aspect of established monetary theory, and which is but another way to look critically at the alleged dichotomy.

When he put forth the neutrality-of-money idea in its embryonic form, Professor Pigou pointed out that 'the *number of units of money* . . . is, in general, of no significance. It is all one whether the garment, or the veil, is thick or thin. . . . I mean that if, other things being equal, over a series of months or years the stock of money contains successively mx_1, mx_2, mx_3 ... units, it makes no difference what the value of m is' (Pigou, 1949, p. 26). Let us refer to the same numerical example made earlier, when we supposed that 100 macro-units of output exist alongside of 2000 macro-units of money. According to the body of thought spearheaded by Pigou's quotation, the number of these money units may be multiplied by a scalar λ (where $\lambda \in \aleph^+$) without affecting what he calls the real happenings of economic life. Now, on further thought, one may observe that nothing enables him, or his sympathisers, to maintain that the expenditure of 2000λ macro-units of money on the product market elicits the power to purchase all the given 100 macro-units of output. So much so that the simple juxtaposition of the total stock of money (2000 macro-units) and the total stock of real goods (100 macro-units) – two distinct and independent magnitudes in neoclassical analysis – does not enable one to posit that the purchasing power of the money stock is defined by total output. In this theoretical framework, in fact, 'prices themselves are determined by relating money to product and, therefore, they cannot simultaneously be the necessary condition and the result of this relationship' (Cencini, 1988, p. 171). In other words, in this framework it may be the case that for the purchase of the whole national output a sum greater (less) than either 2000 or 2000λ macro-units of money is required. By positing a dichotomous economic system, in fact, the maintained method of analysis logically cannot establish the objective value of the existing money stock. 'The value of money remains unexplained because it is said to depend on a value [that is, the price level] that can only be determined once exchange has finally related real goods to one another' (ibid., pp. 123–4). Conceived in this way, the value of money is (left) indeterminate and, therefore, money cannot be said to be neutral. We simply do not know. As we shall see later, in order to determine the purchasing power of money, and to discover what money neutrality really means, one has to explain how money is associated with national output before transactions occur on the market for produced goods and services.

To sum up, although the modern version of the quantity theory of money has been strongly criticised by different contemporary authors (as will be further examined in Chapter 4), in this section it has been possible to raise two neglected points which go right to the heart of neoclassical economics. Firstly, monetarists and their most recent heirs, the partisans of cash-in-advance models and of overlapping-generations models, assume output without considering the fundamental problem of how to measure it.[37] Secondly, the same professional economists introduce an 'intermediary' good called money, while giving no logical explanation of its purchasing power. Put simply, established models of monetary production economies feature an unmeasured (unmeasurable) output as well as an unvalued (un-valuable) stock of money.[38] Both these fundamental problems come from the dichotomic vision of the economic system, and may be further highlighted by another argument centred on the conventional measure of inflation.

Homogeneity Postulate and Inflation

Granting the Pigovian (super)neutrality of money, it has been claimed that a change (say, an increase) in the money stock, no matter how distributed within the economy, will produce ultimately – once all adjustments have run their course – an equi-proportional variation (increase) in all prices, leaving real variables unchanged (Pigou, 1949, p. 26; Niehans, 1978, p. 2; Patinkin, 1987, pp. 639–40). This postulate can be ascribed to Hume (1752/1955, pp. 41–2). It was reformulated by Irving Fisher (1911/1931, pp. 29–32) and it has since been taught in macroeconomics courses by the now classic illustration which asserts that '[d]oubling the money supply doubles all nominal prices but leaves relative prices unaffected, therefore, the volumes of goods demanded and supplied remain constant' (Frisch, 1983, p. 226). Indeed, according to most adherents to neoclassical monetary economics, the fullest sense of the quantity theorem may be stated as follows. 'If, starting from a long-run equilibrium, the stock of money is doubled in the economy, then, regardless of how this money is initially distributed, the economy will not come to rest again until all prices have exactly doubled and every transactor's money holdings have exactly doubled' (Howitt, 1974, p. 143). In abstract formal terms, given two values of the money stock, M and M^*, this means that P and P^* are the corresponding (equilibrium) price levels and that $(M^*, P^*) = (\lambda M, \lambda P)$, where $\lambda = M^*/M$ for all $\lambda > 0$. This property has been termed the 'homogeneity postulate' (and it is said to denote the absence of 'money illusion' in agents' economic behaviour), because, in mathematical terms, demand functions are homogeneous of degree zero in money prices.[39]

Clearly, as Morishima observes, the homogeneity postulate is complementary to the quantity theory of money, in all its successive forms and varieties; without this property it would in fact be difficult to envisage neoclassical monetary economics (Morishima, 1992, p. 186). But this also implies that, '[o]nce the homogeneity [postulate] is rejected, it is evident that the quantity theory of money does not hold' (ibid., p. 187). Applied to our theme, this means that we need to consider carefully what the consequences in terms of inflation are if, say, the money stock is doubled according to the dominant paradigm.

Hence, let us return to our stylised example. Suppose that an imaginary helicopter tosses out another 2000 macro-units (m.u.) of money over the given national economy, where total output is fixed at the level of 100 macro-units as above. Abstracting from the final distribution of the new money stock among economic agents, how will this hypothetical operation affect the relationship between the stock of money and the stock of output, or, in short, inflation? To illustrate this point, let us write the two situations in parallel, before and after money injection.

Initial situation	*End situation*
Total output: $Q = 100$ m.u.	Total output: $Q = 100$ m.u.
Money stock: $M = 2000$ m.u.	Money stock: $M^* = 4000$ m.u.
Price level: $P = 20$	Price level: $P^* = 40$

It will not come as a surprise to the reader that the traditional answer to the above question hinges on the variation in the absolute price level. From this analysis one usually infers that the observed increase in the targeted index of aggregate prices represents the underlying measure of the current rate of inflation. Recalling equation (1.1), the actual inflation rate is thus said to be (π) equal to 100 per cent.

Yet, this view, widely shared as it is, does not contemplate the key problem inherent in the neoclassical dichotomy, as we have been trying to bring forward in this section. Indeed, in this framework, the fact that aggregate prices have doubled does not necessarily imply that the purchasing power of the money stock has been halved. Since the dichotomic account cannot establish the value of the existing money stock (neither does it allow to measure total output objectively), it has in fact nothing to say as to whether or not an increased money supply has an inflationary effect on the national economy. In a situation where the money stock has been augmented, by such bold fabrications as a 'gold rain', mainstream investigation cannot tell us if inflation will result. In such a situation, the only positive information actually conveyed by traditional monetary theory refers to the upward movement in the level of aggregate prices, as estimated by price index analysis, which is rather trivial indeed. This conclusion might surprise the reader, but it is in reality only a first, modest attempt to illustrate what Lord Desai in the 'Preface' to his selected essays in *Macroeconomics and Monetary Theory* portrays as 'the greatest obstacle to decent theorizing about a monetary economy' (Desai, 1995b, p. x). To put it clearly, the homogeneity postulate does not belong to modern (monetary) macroeconomics. Neither does the old-fashioned, quantity-theoretic paradigm based on a dichotomous analysis of our monetary economies of production. To quote Morishima again, '[t]he theory must be reformulated in a modified, more accurate form' (Morishima, 1992, p. 188). Only after this has been accomplished, along the lines we investigate in the next chapter, can we hope to reach a better understanding (of the causes) of inflation and thus propose the appropriate solution, which a correct analysis of the problem already contains.

NOTES

1. Keynes made a similar statement in his essay on 'The method of index numbers with special reference to the measurement of general exchange value'. He claimed in fact that '[t]he origin of the method is to be found in the doctrines of the quantity theory of money' (Keynes, 1909/1983, p. 105).
2. In 1968, Karl Brunner coined and first used the expression 'Monetarist approach' to characterise the body of contemporary monetary theory that emphasises the role of the quantity of money in economic activity (Brunner, 1968/1990, p. 391). In the First Wincott Memorial Lecture, delivered at Senate House, University of London, on 16 September 1970, Friedman expressed some dissatisfaction with the label 'monetarism' that had already been attached to the school of thought to which he made several important contributions (Friedman, 1970/1991, pp. 1–2).

3. See Clower (1967, p. 5). The Clower constraint – as it has been termed, although its author intends it as an axiom – serves to make money useful in general-equilibrium models of monetary economies. We shall examine its heuristic implications in due course.
4. See Bordo (1987, p. 176) and Milgate (1987) for the historical origin of the equation of exchange.
5. For the sake of argument we do not introduce here the longer form of the equation of exchange, which divides the stock of money into fiat money (M) and bank deposits (M'), and becomes: $MV + M'V' \equiv PT$. See Fisher (1911/1931, p. 48) for the exact meaning of the newly introduced symbols.
6. On the problems concerning the definition of M, see for example Schumpeter (1954/1994, pp. 1097–8). We shall address this important issue in Chapter 4.
7. See also Schmitt (1959, pp. 923–4).
8. In slightly more sophisticated versions of the quantity equation, the velocity of circulation of the money stock is assumed to be a function of the nominal interest rate. See Duck (1993, p. 2).
9. To be true, later developments of the Fisherine quantity equation questioned the fixity of the coefficient α. In particular, in his rather technical 'Restatement of the quantity theory of money', Maurice Allais claims that 'the coefficient of proportionality is not constant; its value at each moment depends on the past historical development of total outlay' (Allais, 1966, p. 1153).
10. Albeit considered as a constant in the short run, the velocity of circulation (V) of the money stock as well as the volume of output (T) may actually vary for several reasons, that are nevertheless portrayed as independent of the variation of the quantity of money available in the economy. Fisher (1911/1931, ch. 5), for example, affirms repeatedly that the causal relationship between M and P as explained by the quantity theory remains true, whatever happens to the other elements entering the equation of exchange.
11. In the symbology of Chapter 1 we would thus rewrite equation (3.5) as follows:

$$\pi \equiv \dot{M} - \dot{T} .$$

12. See also Hegeland (1951, pp. 164–6) for a restatement of the same criticisms.
13. This critique was already made by Joan Robinson (1956, pp. 403–4).
14. See Eshag (1963, pp. 18–25) on this point. Note that Marshall (1923) never employed any algebraic formula to render in mathematical terms his presentation of the quantity theory of money. In one of his most significant passages he claimed indeed that '*[t]he total value of a country's currency, multiplied into the average number of times of its changing hands for business purposes in a year, is of course equal to the total amount of business transacted in that country by direct payments of currency in that year. But this identical statement does not indicate the causes that govern the rapidity of circulation of currency: to discover them we must look to the amounts of purchasing power which the people of that country elect to keep in the form of currency*' (Marshall, 1923, p. 43).
15. As pointed out by the joint winner of the 1974 Nobel prize for economics, '[i]t is a peculiarity of all systematic treatises on orthodox economic theory that there is no inner connexion and integration of monetary theory with the central theory of prices. Usually the monetary theory is only a rather loose appendix to the theory of price formation. The central economic problems – according to the classical theory, those of production, of barter-exchange and of distribution – are treated, without exception, as problems of exchange value, or in other words as problems of relative prices. Obviously, by regarding the central economic problems in this way one entirely detaches their fundamental treatment from any monetary considerations' (Myrdal, 1939, p. 10).
16. See Hicks (1935/1967, pp. 64–8), Brunner and Meltzer (1971, pp. 800–4), Grandmont and Younès (1972, pp. 355–8), Clower (1977, pp. 210–11), Starr (1989, pp. 3–6), as well as a number of seminal contributions included in the latter volume.

17. See Howells (1996, pp. 107–11) for an interesting discussion of these two versions in connection also with the endogenous money approach. In Part Three we shall address non-income related transactions and their relevance to money emission.
18. Patinkin (1969) questions the existence of a distinctive Chicago tradition, as well as its analytical link to Friedman's monetary economics, which he depicts as an extension of Keynesian liquidity preference theory. With the publication of Patinkin's (1969) article, the notion that the Chicago oral quantity theory tradition was an invention spread rapidly and became widely accepted, as testified by a number of historians of economic thought quoted by Tavlas (1998, pp. 212–13). However, as argued extensively by Tavlas (1997; 1998), there really existed a Chicago oral tradition during the early 1930s, which was not to be found outside of Chicago and which contained important links to Friedman's monetary analysis, culminating in his restatement of the quantity theory. On the relationships between Friedman's thinking and Keynes's, see Dostaler (1998).
19. See Friedman's (1968) Presidential address delivered at the Eightieth Annual Meeting of the American Economic Association.
20. See also Hume (1752/1955, pp. 37–40).
21. See also Brunner and Meltzer (1976, pp. 154–5).
22. Contrast the backward-looking approach encompassed by price index analysis, as examined in Part One.
23. See Lucas (1972, pp. 119–22), Sargent and Wallace (1975, pp. 242, 246–9), Fischer (1980, pp. 211–20), McCallum (1980, pp. 717–18) and Taylor (1985, pp. 392–6, 403).
24. This approach is also known as the 'new classical macroeconomics' (see Fischer, 1987). Yet, one might object that '[t]he assumption of rational expectations which presupposes the correct understanding of the workings of the economy by all economic agents – the trade unionists, the ordinary employer, or even the ordinary housewife – to a degree which is beyond the grasp of professional economists is not science, nor even moral philosophy, but at best a branch of metaphysics' (Kaldor and Trevithick, 1981, p. 15). More recently, Laidler forcefully expressed the same concern in his 1988 Presidential address to the Canadian Economics Association, when he stressed that 'it is dangerous uncritically to model agents' behaviour on the assumption that they form their expectations using the same model of their economy as the economist who studies them. . . . [A]ttempts to model agents' learning processes "as if" they were econometricians seeking information about the economy by statistical induction seem to me to be of limited usefulness' (Laidler, 1988, pp. 702–3).
25. Woodford (1987) set forth an overlapping-generations model where all agents live for three periods.
26. It might help the reader to recall that the frictionless (non-monetary) Arrow–Debreu general-equilibrium model denies the existence of money as a means of payment or as a 'temporary abode of purchasing power', to use Friedman's consecrated phrase, 'basically because the Walrasian auctioneer obviates any need for a medium of exchange' (Fuerst, 1994, p. 582, n. 2). To account for the existence of money in neoclassical analysis one has therefore to assume *nolens volens* some kind of friction that hinders the clearing of all markets instantaneously and that money can help alleviate. See Starr (1989, pp. 3–6) for a concise discussion of the integration of money in general-equilibrium theory, and Geanakoplos (1987, pp. 771–7) for a summary presentation of the overlapping-generations method of monetary investigation.
27. Within modern neoclassical theory money is consequently treated like a perfectly durable good, since its service-flows enter wealth-holders' utility functions in exactly the same way as it is suggested be the case for other categories of durable commodities such as cars and owner-occupied housing. Yet, in Chapter 1 we already noted that the distinction between durable and non-durable goods is ill-founded in economics. This also raises the question of treating money as a peculiar good, an issue that we shall investigate in Chapter 4.

28. Surveys of overlapping-generations monetary models are provided by McCallum (1990, pp. 981–5) and Woodford (1990, pp. 1106–16). See also Geanakoplos's (1987) dictionary article.
29. Note, however, that overlapping-generations models can be an appropriate research strategy in some areas outside monetary macroeconomics. In particular, as has been suggested by Baranzini (1991, pp. 89–91) and Pasinetti (1993, p. 109, n. 6), the overlapping-generations analysis might be an appropriate framework for those theoretical investigations concerning individuals' decisions on how to distribute consumption and savings over their lifetime and with respect to inter-generational bequests.
30. See Lucas and Stokey (1983, pp. 78–82), whose model introduces the distinction between 'credit goods' and 'cash goods': the former can be purchased with current money-income but the latter only with (fiat) money previously accumulated. The first model to put forward such a constraint may easily be traced back to Clower's (1967) classic paper, where the author set to express analytically the requirement that money must be held before an exchange is to take place, for – as Clower's most famous phrase states – goods do not buy goods. See Fuerst (1994, pp. 582–5) and Huo (1995, p. 833) for more recent restatements of the cash-in-advance constraint along the lines put forward by Robert E. Lucas and Nancy L. Stokey.
31. Bank money has been analysed by post-Keynesian monetary economists, as I have shown elsewhere (see Rossi, 1998; 1999).
32. The real quantity of money (m) may thus be written as follows: $m = M/P$. Recalling that $P = M/Q$ (see Chapter 1) and rearranging the terms, this is tantamount to saying that $m \equiv Q$.
33. See Patinkin and Steiger (1989, pp. 138–41) for an interesting inquiry on the origin of this expression.
34. Hayek was among the first to claim that money should have a neutral effect on economic activity, so that, following Schumpeter (1954/1994, p. 277), his analytical picture may be classified as 'Real Analysis'. In his celebrated lectures at the London School of Economics, published in 1931 under the title *Prices and Production*, Hayek advocated that the first object of monetary theory ought to be an in-depth investigation of the conditions under which money-using economies behave 'as if' they were barter economies. Hence, his policy prescription concerned in principle the appropriate distribution of money balances (and credit) across the economy, rather than the stability of aggregate prices. See Desai (1981, pp. 33–5) and Patinkin and Steiger (1989, pp. 132–8), but also L.H. White (1999, pp. 110–15, 118).
35. See Fischer (1983, p. 8), McCallum (1987, p. 972), Parkin (1987, pp. 833–4) and Marty (1994) for a discussion of money's superneutrality.
36. Say, a decimalisation of the monetary unit (for example the changeover from 'old' to 'new' French francs in the 1930s, the British currency reform of the 1970s, the Brazilian decimalisations/renaming of the 1980s, or even more recently the introduction of the single European currency).
37. Let us stress that this measurement problem has a theoretical, not a statistical, origin. As Sraffa pointed out in connection with the definition of capital and its measure, there exist in fact two distinct types of measurement. 'First, there was the one in which the statisticians were mainly interested. Second there was measurement in theory. The statisticians' measures were only approximate and provided a suitable field for work in solving index number problems. The theoretical measures required absolute precision. Any imperfections in these theoretical measures were not merely upsetting, but knocked down the whole theoretical basis' (Sraffa, 1961, p. 305).
38. This argument might be rephrased by saying that a relative exchange cannot perform the task of measuring the (two) things exchanged, an issue that we shall explore in Chapter 4.
39. This property has also been expressed by saying that the demand function for money depicts a rectangular hyperbola in ($1/P$, M) space. This means that the product of M and

$1/P$ is constant when P (the absolute price level) changes. See Patinkin (1956, pp. 23–31, 39–45) and Niehans (1978, pp. 7–12).

4. The Argument Refined: Exogenous and Endogenous Money

As we have noted at the outset of this book, the characteristic of inflation is to be a condition of generalised excess demand, when 'too much money chases too few goods' according to the monetarists' jargon. The preceding discussion of the fundamental problems of neoclassical inflation analysis may thus be more convincingly elaborated by investigating now the essential origin (that is, the nature) of money. As a matter of fact, any demand – excessive or not – is expressed and exerted in money units. Hence, a rigorous study of the latter may be useful to cure inflation. To quote from a recent work, '[i]t is a truly well-documented empirical regularity that all persistent inflations are accompanied by a rising stock of nominal money (although recent advances in theory have deprived us of the understanding as to why this should necessarily be so)' (Heymann and Leijonhufvud, 1995, p. 12). To explain this phenomenon, and to determine the underlying mechanism provoking an excessive growth of the number of money units,[1] one cannot abstract from both the nature of modern money and its specific role in the economic process. This is a point still worth enquiring into (even after two hundred years of monetary economics), because still '[t]here is no generally accepted definition, among economists, as to what constitutes money' (Vane and Thompson, 1979, p. 49). As Schumpeter imaginatively put it no less than forty years ago, '[t]here is no denying that views on money are as difficult to describe as are shifting clouds' (Schumpeter, 1954/1994, p. 289). This comment is as relevant today as when it was made.[2] Too often the basic idea behind received monetary analysis relies a priori on the functionalist definition of money: 'money is what money does' (see Hicks, 1967, chs 1–3). And it need not be recalled here that the conventional representation of the generally-accepted-medium-of-exchange function (the most important quantity-theoretic function) of money[3] merely portrays it as the lubricant that can help alleviate trading frictions,[4] or as the wrapping paper which 'does not comprise any of the essentials of economic life' (Pigou, 1949, p. 25). In Hahn's terms, this raises the challenge of explaining money's positive exchange value in a framework where money is of no intrinsic worth and is generally accepted in exchange for goods and services (Hahn, 1973, pp. 230–6; Hahn, 1982, ch. 1). To this question we now turn, in an attempt to illustrate further the congenital defects of the established method of inflation analysis, which is founded, let us stress it, on the dichotomous view spearheaded by adherents to the quantity theory of money (see Chapter 4).

EXOGENOUS MONEY, OR THE DICHOTOMY REVISITED

As noted by Kaldor and Trevithick, '[o]ne problem which followers of the quantity theory of money had to face from the beginning is the basic question of how "money" is to be defined' (Kaldor and Trevithick, 1981, p. 11). This section intends to show that this conceptual problem is common to all recent advances within neoclassical monetary economics. So much so that for the purpose of our study we can refer to the exogenous-money view as a kind of portmanteau label unifying a number of established strands of thought. Let us start from the 'primary definitions' put forth by the father of the modern quantity theory of money, whose tenets are revived nowadays by various sorts of money-in-the-utility-function models as well as cash-in-advance models. 'Any commodity to be called "money" must be *generally acceptable in exchange*, and any commodity generally acceptable in exchange should be called money' (Fisher, 1911/1931, p. 2). These claims express a common-sense approach. Loosely speaking, money has in fact been considered up to now either as a (perfectly durable) commodity or as an asset, which 'enables the act of purchase to be separated from the act of sale' (Friedman, 1974, p. 8) – a vision stemming from the equation of exchange in its transactions form (see equation (3.2)). This is tantamount to saying that money separates barter trade into two chronologically distinct transactions. It behaves 'as if' it were an intermediary good in each of them (see for instance Clower, 1969, p. 14). The worrying double coincidence of wants is thus disposed of, as soon as there is something that every agent will accept in exchange as 'general purchasing power' and that can serve as 'a temporary abode of purchasing power' (Friedman, 1974, p. 9).[5]

Now, the very definition of M upon which the equation of exchange (and, ultimately, the whole neoclassical monetary theory) is based, appears problematic.[6] Even the most recent formal developments in monetary macroeconomics, such as the great variety of 'overlapping-generations' models, seem to be undermined by the same conceptual problem affecting their quantity-theoretic progenitors. Let us try to set out this problem. If the axiomatic starting point of received monetary analysis is a functional distinction between money and non-money goods (that is, the traditional dichotomy in its most elementary sense), then, as Clower pointed out, '[we have] to express analytically what is meant when we assert that a certain commodity serves as a medium of exchange' (Clower, 1967, p. 4).

The Medium of Exchange, a Monetary Asset?

In a 1985 *Journal of Political Economy* article significantly entitled 'Money is what money does', a member of the Board of Governors of the Federal Reserve System asserts that '[t]he view of money as means of payment on which the equation of exchange is based provides a relatively clear-cut criterion for which monetary assets to include as components of *M*. In particular, an asset is included if and only if it serves more or less generally as medium of exchange' (Spindt, 1985, p. 180). This statement deserves close attention, inasmuch as it represents the main axiom of any neoclassical monetary model put forth over the last hundred years. Wallace, for one, acknowledges that both money-in-the-utility-function models and cash-in-advance models are 'silent about the qualities an asset must possess in order that it yield utility or serve as a medium of exchange' (Wallace, 1988, p. 35). A conceptual investigation into the fundamentals of mainstream monetary macroeconomics could therefore shed some light on the nature of money, and specifically on its character of general equivalent of goods and services domestically produced. Although these issues cover a well-explored ground, their analysis may be helpful here, for it will serve us as a bridge to some relatively new theoretical insights.

In the most basic terms, according to the traditional postulate, monetary assets are those commodities possessing a means-of-payment attribute, in so far as they are generally accepted in exchange for other goods and services.[7] A simple picture might be useful here (Figure 4.1).

	money		money	
agent *p* (purchaser)	$\longrightarrow$ $\longleftarrow$	agent *s* = agent *p* (seller) (purchaser)	$\longrightarrow$ $\longleftarrow$	agent *s* (seller)
	good X		good Y	

Figure 4.1 The medium-of-exchange function of 'monetary assets'

The representation in Figure 4.1 is so familiar that it does not need any explanation, and the observation that two distinct exchanges are depicted in it might seem trivial. Yet, a number of analytical questions might be raised within this theoretical framework. In particular, where do the 'initial endowments' of both money and non-money goods come from? How can prices be formed on the commodity market? More generally, how can the value of the exchanged items be measured? These questions will be considered in the next section. For the time being, the reader's attention must be drawn to the fact that the exogeneity-of-money approach cannot provide a satisfactory answer.

Let us suppose that money enters the picture like 'manna from heaven', that is, it is dropped from the sky by the Friedmanian helicopter (Friedman, 1969, pp. 4–5). Assume also that the distribution of money across the economy is good enough to feature this (money) asset in each individual's portfolio. Similarly, assume that every trader has been allocated a set of real goods by, say, the invisible hand, and tries to maximise utility by exchanging (part of) them in separate, or simultaneous, market sessions. Although we accept all this uncritically here, a fundamental problem remains. What is the value of money? How much is a helicopter one-pound note worth?

It is well known that neoclassical (general-equilibrium) monetary economics often relies on the assumption that relative prices – for both money and non-money goods – are known to any agent through a kind of *deus ex machina*, that is, the Walrasian auctioneer.[8] This means that in the whole economy the price system is determined on the commodity market, when the relative exchange between money and output takes place (see for example Figure 3.1). However, the above fundamental question remains unanswered (not to say it has not even been addressed). In fact, neoclassical theory is unable to explain the value of money, because in this framework the latter 'is said to depend on a value that can only be determined once exchange has finally related real goods to one another' (Cencini, 1988, pp. 122–3). If an agent agrees to exchange part of his 'initial endowments' of goods for a number of money units (or for a number of units of the monetary asset), he does so because he knows the value of the received item, which he keeps as a temporary abode of purchasing power, since it will enable him to buy some other real goods in later transactions. 'But how can he assess the precise amount of purchasing power of the received sum if its value depends on the terms with which his commodity is finally exchanged with the other?' (ibid., p. 122). Clearly, this question cannot be answered. In neoclassical thinking, value is indeed a relative price. It is determined on the commodity market, where exchange is said to occur between two autonomous objects of trade. Hence, maintaining that the value of money is known when the (relative) value of the exchanged goods has been established, is tantamount to saying that money is inessential in Hahn's (1973) sense. So long as payments are conceived of as an exchange between two distinct and independent things – that is, an exchange involving money and non-money goods in a mutually opposing motion (as in Figure 4.1) – no theory can explain either the value or the existence of the alleged medium of exchange. How can the value of money be determined, if it is meant to depend on the purchasing power of money, which in the neoclassical 'cosmology' – to use Verdon's (1996) language – is established once relative exchanges between real goods and services have ultimately occurred? The question is clearly circular, as has been pointed out by Cencini (1982; 1988) with respect to the logical indetermination of relative prices.

Further, and closely related to the preceding discussion, one may also wonder how a good, albeit of a transitional or 'intermediary' character such as the socially selected monetary asset, can logically be, in one and the same operation, a medium of exchange and one of the objects of trade in every transaction whatsoever. On reflection, the traditional conception of money as the generally accepted medium of exchange appears ill-founded, and the confusion between means (that is, the instrument, or process, used in performing an action) and end (the object for which the action is performed) is not of a pure semantic order within this context.[9] In fact, as a quick look at Figure 4.1 shows, in the canonical modellisation of a monetary economy money does not play the role of a mere instrumental device – invented, as a social institution, to help overcome the daunting double coincidence of wants, and to alleviate the practical drawbacks (or frictions) of a non-monetary economy. Money enters every monetary exchange as the counterpart of non-money goods, and, as such, it is an object distinct from real goods and services, with its own 'mass' and velocity of circulation, in conformity to the dichotomic view (see Chapter 3). As such, money is not the instrument of payments but the thing which 'plays a distinctive asymmetric role as one side of virtually all transactions' (Starr, 1980, p. 263). Clearly, in this framework money is the object of supply and demand as are all non-money goods in the economy. Indeed, '[m]oney is treated as a stock, not as a flow or a mixture of a flow and a stock' (Friedman, 1987, p. 5). In this approach, money clearly is a store of value, 'a temporary abode of purchasing power' in Friedman's words. This issue is bound to raise with renewed concern the previously noted neoclassical problem of giving money a price, even though, ultimately, it is merely a worthless token used to circulate domestic output. To quote Balasko and Shell at some length on this long-standing puzzle of conventional monetary analysis,

> [m]oney does not in general serve as a proper store of value – i.e., money cannot have a positive price – in the finite-horizon economy in which the terminal date is known with certainty. The reason is obvious. Money is worthless at the end of the final period. Consequently, in the next-to-last period, individuals desire to dispose of money holdings in order to avoid capital losses. This drives the price of money to zero at the end of the next-to-last period. And so on. Individuals with foresight drive the price of money to zero in each period, i.e., the 'general price level' in equilibrium must be infinite. The natural way to permit money to be a proper store of value is to go beyond the finite-horizon model (Balasko and Shell, 1981, pp. 112–13).

This is perhaps the fundamental reason why so many money demand formalisations (cash-in-advance models, money-in-the-utility-function models and money-in-the-production-function models) have been developed over the last decades, along the lines of the portfolio-theoretic approach to asset diversification for finitely-lived 'representative' agents within an infinite-horizon framework.

To take the exploration of the nature of money further in our critical appraisal of neoclassical monetary theory, let us focus on probably the most fashionable form of economic analysis, namely the overlapping-generations method (OGM). As is well known, OG models investigate the working of contemporary payment systems assuming an intermediary commodity called money, to avert, or at least reduce, search and bargaining costs among the different generations of traders (usually ranged in two complementary classes, labelled 'young' and 'old'). These generations exist in any market period, since they overlap indefinitely as time goes by. On the standard OGM assumptions that (*a*) before the first-period exchange takes place (at time *t*) all monetary assets are in the old generation's portfolio, and that (*b*) the young generation produces, or is allocated, real goods for each market session (see Lucas, 1972, pp. 104–9; Wallace, 1980, pp. 49–60), and substituting agents *p* and *s* in Figure 4.1 with respectively the old and the young generation of traders, we get that '[t]he old at date *t* could sell their money to the young for commodities, who in turn sell their money when old to the next period's young' (Geanakoplos, 1987, p. 771). Yet, this method of monetary investigation, widely shared as it is, does no justice to the proper idea of the medium of exchange. The two preceding quotations clearly illustrate how the supposed means of payment is modelled as a saleable commodity, that is, as an asset with the highest degree of liquidity, whose existence would be like that of a perfectly durable good, handed down from one generation to the next. In his posthumous *A Market Theory of Money*, Sir John Hicks devoted an entire chapter to 'The nature of money', where he questioned this vision in the following terms.

> It will no doubt have been taken for granted that in the markets we have been discussing, the typical transaction was an exchange of some article (good or service) for something that was recognized as being money; and it may also have been taken [for granted] that the money was simply handed over, as one does when one buys a newspaper in a shop. A useful way of introducing the monetary theory, which will be the subject of the chapters which follow, is to begin by calling into question these two assumptions, asking how far they are justified (Hicks, 1989, p. 41).

As a matter of fact, following the traditional dichotomy, all neoclassical monetary models assume the use of the selected exchange intermediary to be adequately formalised by the excess-demand function for the money sector, as is the case with the excess-demand functions for goods and services in the real-sector subsystem (see Patinkin, 1956, ch. 8). In Fama's words, '[s]ince currency [that is, money] produces real services in allowing some exchanges to be carried out with lower transactions costs, currency has a demand function' (Fama, 1980, p. 50). So, although money is sometimes portrayed as 'the *means* to the acquisition of a subset of ordinary consumption goods' (Lucas and Stokey, 1983, p. 82), it nevertheless always enters neoclassical monetary models like a commodity of its own, that is, as a peculiar thing chosen (that is, demanded) – for its particular transactions services[10] – within the set of economic objects (goods or assets).

Now, Adam Smith saw it lucidly at the beginning of our science, the means of payment ought not to be considered as an object itself. Although in his time money was reified into a precious metal, which blurred the transcendent distinction between the instrument of payments and its material support (gold for example), in his *Wealth of Nations* Smith was already pointing out with admirable clarity the importance to distinguish money proper from money's worth, both analytically and in practice (Smith, 1776/1970, p. 386). In his own words, '[t]he great wheel of circulation is altogether different from the goods which are circulated by means of it. The revenue of the society consists altogether in those goods, and not in the wheel which circulates them' (ibid., p. 385). Yet, the idea of money as the instrument of output circulation has unfortunately been lost in more recent economic thought. As a quick example, let us consider the exchange between the whole national output of a given period (t) and the existing money stock. If we adopt, for instance, the overlapping-generations method of analysis, we can apply it either in time or in space, by simply substituting the old and the young generations of traders with, respectively, households and firms. To be sure, any neoclassical model of money-using economies can be represented as in Figure 4.2.

As is well known, neoclassical analysis portrays the sale (that is, consumption)[11] of national output as a relative exchange between two dichotomic stocks, money and real goods, which move in opposite directions between economic agents (see also Figure 3.1).

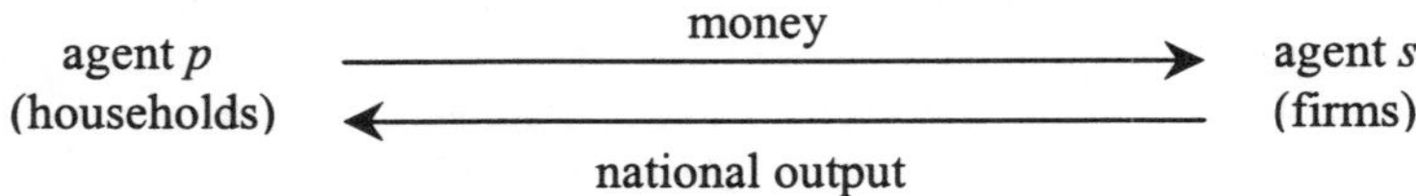

Figure 4.2 The sale of national output in neoclassical analysis

The saleable goods (and services, analytically included) leave the firms, where they were stocked, to be appropriated by households. Similarly, the existing money stock is transferred from purchasers to sellers, in a zero-sum process.[12] 'One man's spending is another man's receipts. One man can reduce his nominal money balances only by persuading someone else to increase his' (Friedman, 1987, p. 4). Stated differently, an offer to sell goods is a demand for money[13] – and vice versa – and both objects of trade are substantial, because they migrate across private endowments. Within such a framework, all that one can analyse is how money and non-money goods end up in individuals' portfolios, after total current output has been sold.[14] As Ingham forcefully observed, '[t]here is no attempt to account for the "concept" of money as a *measure of value* (or *unit of account*) – or even to recognize that this might constitute an intellectual problem' (Ingham, 1996, p. 515).

So, if one examines in a heuristic manner the concept of excess demand applied to money, one can notice that it is based on a setting where money can be either sold (that is, supplied) or purchased (demanded) 'as if' it were a good. This is essentially a restatement of the traditional dichotomic representation of money-using economies, which we began investigating in Chapter 3 and have been carrying on in this section. It can be rephrased by saying that there may exist a net supply of the nth commodity, conventionally labelled *numéraire*, which – according to Walras's Law – is in itself a positive excess demand for the other goods and services taken as a whole. Monetarists consider indeed this phenomenon to be the cause of inflation, so that (general) equilibrium can be restored – in a Marshallian sense – by a rise in the level of aggregate prices only.

However, recalling Smith's intuition, one could object that 'the great wheel of circulation' can logically be neither sold nor purchased; in other words, it is never the object of either supply or demand of its own. In fact, the means of payment must be conceptually distinguished from the things exchanged. To quote a famous opponent of the quantity theory of money, 'money as such is of no value and does not add to the output of real wealth' (Hegeland, 1951, p. 241). As testified by the non-addition of money and output in national accounts, the former is not really an element of the set of domestic goods, inasmuch as the value of money and the value of output are not added up to determine a country's total wealth. In the enigmatic words of De Vroey, which we hope to clarify later on, money is 'a non-commodity in a universe of commodities' (De Vroey, 1984, p. 383). Hence, the excess-demand method does not seem to be appropriate for money matters, and the whole analysis of inflation might thus be affected negatively by this approach. To be sure, what Niehans pointed out more than twenty years ago is still valid today. 'What we need is a theory that treats money not metaphorically *as if* it were a consumer or producer good, but as what it really is, namely a medium of exchange' (Niehans, 1978, p. 16). This observation is immediately reinforced in a footnote stressing that 'the real problem is not one of classification but of a better analytical understanding of the functions of a medium of exchange' (ibid., p. 16, n. 39). Thus, on the whole, we are still in quest of the nature of the means of payment, 'a topic for which monetarists have shown little inclination' (De Vroey, 1984, p. 381).[15]

The Cartalist Idea of Outside Money and the Inflation Tax

In parallel with the postulate identifying the medium of exchange with the 'matter' which carries out this function, it has been alleged that money is essentially an institutional symbol, that is, a 'creature of law' according to Knapp's *State Theory of Money* (Knapp, 1924, pp. 39–40).[16] Within the payment system, money should thus be viewed as exogenously given, because it would exist 'from outside' and independently of the set of real goods, as previously noted. Yet, 'helicopter money' is just a caricatural image of this phenomenon. A less imaginative approach considers money as the only legally valid means of payment (hence the expression of legal tender), for it alone has the *imprimatur* of the state (see for instance Wray, 1998b). So, while on one front there are those adhering to the view that the purchasing power of money is somehow linked to its physical representation (labelled Metallists for obvious reasons), on the other front there are those who deny 'the proposition that it is logically essential for money to consist of, say, gold, or to be promptly convertible into gold' (Schumpeter,

1954/1994, p. 288). Advocates of the latter view are labelled Cartalists (following Knapp's terminology),[17] and their number has increased with the development of modern payment technologies, since the latter are based on money's inconvertibility and make use of intrinsically worthless symbols. In the words of Goodhart, '[t]he substitution of fiat, paper money, for metallic coin as the main component of currency in the last 200 years provides strong support for the Cartalist view that the monetary essence of currency can rest upon the power of the issuer and not upon the intrinsic value of the object so used' (Goodhart, 1989b, p. 34).

So, let us imagine an economic system where the medium of exchange is 'a non-interest-bearing fiat currency produced monopolistically by the government' (Fama, 1980, p. 50). In this kind of model, money is not convertible into anything else (gold or wheat, for instance), and is never demanded for its own intrinsic value (which is zero, if one abstracts from the very little value of the paper on which it is printed). Several points can be raised.

First of all, at this stage of the analysis it seems almost trivial to emphasise that, contrary to the claim previously quoted, money is not produced, because otherwise it would logically pertain to the category of domestic goods defining national output. When we get right to the heart of the matter, including money among the set of commodities would raise the problem of measuring goods by means of goods, a problem that Ricardo had been trying to solve without success until his death. Whilst it is plain that paper money as such is the result of a production process (that is, the material result of the printing press) whose costs participate in the definition of national income, the paper is only the physical support (a representative sign) of the medium of exchange *proprio sensu*. Ontologically speaking, the means of payment is in fact the economic measure (or the monetary form) of domestic goods and services, because it does not have to be measured. In short, it is a unit of account with no dimension whatsoever, as we shall see in the following section.

But in the present discussion the main trouble is probably elsewhere. Provided that 'it is not legitimate to take fiat money to be an argument of anyone's utility function or of any engineering production function' (Wallace, 1980, p. 49), how can it enter, and circulate within, the 'real' economy? Fiat money has no intrinsic utility in consumption or production, and its own yield is zero (Haliassos and Tobin, 1990, p. 909). So, where does the value of fiat money come from? Why should economic agents willingly hold it as a temporary abode of purchasing power? Basically, a frequent assumption in modern neoclassical analysis has it that (outside) money is issued by the government – and distributed to the private sector via banks (hence the use of bank notes) – in order to collect lump-sum taxes from the individuals (Balasko and Shell, 1981, pp. 112, 115–16; Goodhart, 1989b, p. 36; 1997, pp. 17–21; Wray, 1998b, ch. 4).[18] Because of the economies of scale involved, the larger the taxes levied on households and firms, the more likely for the state-managed money to enter into private transactions as well. So much so that the 'sovereign power' may impose employing legal tender in such transactions, thus prohibiting the use of any other (private) medium of exchange. Accordingly, the exchange value of an intrinsically useless piece of paper – 'a ticket that admits the bearer to the great social store of all goods', in the phraseology of Schumpeter (1954/1994, p. 289) – would stem from the simple observation that 'one person gives up goods (objects that appear as arguments of utility functions, directly or indirectly) for fiat money only because the person believes that someone else will subsequently give up goods for fiat money at an acceptable rate of exchange' (Wallace, 1980, p. 49).[19]

To focus on the issues of immediate interest, one cannot but notice that this view of money is not different from the one investigated in the previous subsection. In spite of the intrinsic uselessness of fiat money, printed on almost costless paper, in this framework money is in fact considered, and modelled, as the counterpart of the real goods and services handed over the counter (Kocherlakota, 1998b, pp. 232–3, is a recent example). The neoclassical dichotomy is in the background, by definition, and variations (that is, increases) in the level of aggregate prices are the direct result of an overissue of bank notes, as the traditional interpretation of Ricardo's *The High Price of Bullion* has it (Ricardo, 1810/1951). Metallists and Cartalists share therefore the same conception of money-using economies on which the established method of monetary investigation is based. There is thus no need to redraw Figure 4.1 here, since no changes are necessary, to depict the exchange of paper money for real goods as neoclassical economists imagine. Hence, let us recall the conclusion already reached earlier on: since fiat money enters standard treatment of monetary production economies like an asset of its own, objectively distinct from (privately) produced goods and services, it cannot logically serve as a means of payment within this framework. It merely represents the historical evolution of the matter on which money is stamped (or marked), and the study of present e-money products along these lines would provide no further insight into the problems investigated here. Since this is an issue lying outside the scope of this book, we shall not pursue it further here.[20]

However, some important related points should be mentioned at this juncture, for they have often been raised within received inflation analysis. Traditionally, the idea of outside money has been associated with the power of the state to run the printing press, in order to obtain goods and services from the rest of the economy (see Gurley and Shaw, 1960, pp. 68–73, but also Wray, 1998b; 2000). As Keynes maintained at the beginning of Chapter 2 of *A Tract on Monetary Reform*, '[a] government can live for a long time, even the German government or the Russian government, by printing paper money. That is to say, it can by this means secure the command over real resources, resources just as real as those obtained by taxation' (Keynes, 1923/1971, p. 37).[21] According to this view, the state-issued money enters the economy as the counterpart of domestic output, since it is supplied to the private sector in exchange for real goods and services. Stated slightly differently, this proposition asserts that the monetary authorities never play the role of a deus ex machina in the monetisation of the economy,[22] but exert instead the 'sovereign power' sanctioned by law to collect what is known under the term 'seigniorage' (Black, 1987).[23] 'Seignorage is a kind of tax, alternative to explicit taxation' (Haliassos and Tobin, 1990, p. 895). '[It] is defined as the amount of real resources that a government acquires in a period simply by virtue of the fact that private agents will hold the currency it prints' (ibid., p. 951). This definition may be inferred from the allegation that the government sector has the monopoly on the emission of fiat (outside) money.[24] It implies that the public sector can undertake expenditure and partly finance the planned fiscal policies simply by a stroke of the pen (that is, the Treasury printing press).[25] Inflation would thus be the inevitable result of excessive government spending.[26] As Goodhart puts it, '[t]he key relationship in the C [standing for Cartalist] team model is the centrality of the link between political sovereignty and fiscal authority on the one hand and money creation, the mint and the central bank, on the other' (Goodhart, 1997, pp. 3–4).

Now, analysis must go further, and deeper, than the mere allegation that '[f]iat money is a form of credit where the issuing party is the state' (Shubik, 1987, p. 317). The inflation tax (or seigniorage) pertains to economic history, when debasement of minted coins was a source of funds for the local ruler.[27] A fundamental investigation into the matter should go beyond appearances, to dismiss the yet common belief that seigniorage is still part (albeit a small one) of government revenues. Let us start from the pretended emission of fiat money through the government account in stylised form (Table 4.1). As mentioned previously, leading professional economists maintain that outside fiat money is the private sector's claim on the issuing government (see Goodhart, 1989b, p. 287).

Table 4.1 The inflation tax: real goods versus nominal money

State			
liabilities			assets
Private sector (fiat money)	£x	Private sector (real goods)	£x

Now, since in this view the state-issued money is emitted to acquire real goods (and services) from the private sector, recorded on the assets side of the government's balance sheet, two crucial questions need to be addressed. Does the double entry in Table 4.1 have any meaning at all? In the affirmative, how can we measure the value of the goods (including any financial asset) recorded within the general government sector? Let us try to make sense of these points.

From a quick glance at Table 4.1, one might infer that the result of the operation would be nil, because the same agent, that is, the private sector considered here as a whole, is entered on both sides of the government's balance sheet simultaneously and for the same amount (for instance x money units).[28] However, as suggested above, it may still be argued that fiat money is the counterpart of real goods. In other words, the state-issued liability – which circulates as a means of payment among the public and may be returned ultimately to the issuer in payment of taxes – certifies the deposit of part of domestic output into the Treasury vaults.[29] The entry in Table 4.1 would thus not be pointless, for it would record the result of an exchange between equivalents that might be represented as in Figure 4.3.

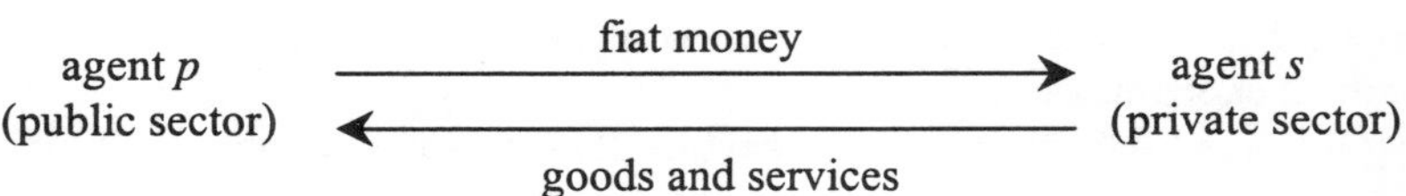

Figure 4.3 The exchange of fiat money for goods and services

According to this interpretation, the state issues IOUs (that is, promises to pay to the bearer the amount of, say, x pounds) in exchange for goods and services of the same worth. This view stems however from an oversimplified conception of a monetary economy. It depicts the emission of the alleged means of payment as a purchase for the issuer, an operation that is moreover not synallagmatic, because in the present case the issuing body cannot be sued. Since 'the recourse of an individual creditor is negligible against the state, but by the law of the state the fiat money must be accepted in payment to extinguish other debts' (Shubik, 1987, p. 317), this question has been on the agenda of those economists, such as Hayek and the adepts of the Free Banking school, that advocate the 'denationalisation of money' as a more efficient, that is, inflation-proof, form of organising a (privatised) payment system (Hayek, 1976/1978). Indeed, if our payment systems were built on the foundations depicted in Figure 4.3 (and in Table 4.1), free banking would be a legitimate, though radical, pretension by the private sector economy. In effect, why should the state have the privilege of obtaining goods and services by simply getting its own IOUs circulating within the national economy, that is, without ever really paying at all? Fortunately, the workings of modern payment systems do not abide by this supposed *lex monetae*. As a matter of fact, if the money-issuing mechanism described above were put to practical use, it would be affected by the same fundamental problems as those encountered by the monetarist approach to inflation (see Chapter 3). In particular, were fiat money the dichotomic counterpart of goods and services, no objective measure of the value of current national output would ever exist. As a brief reminder of Chapter 3, consider how commodities newly produced by the private sector could be valued on their own, in economic terms, without resorting to the monetary measure from the very moment of their production. No solution can be provided, because the exchange on the commodity market can only reveal the value resulting from the production process. In a similar vein, one might wonder how the value of a one-pound bank note is to be established in terms of the commodities existing in the natural state, so that the above illustrated exchange between the state and the administered 'populace' would be carried out on an egalitarian basis. It is impossible to answer this question objectively, as long as one does not get rid of the dichotomic view.[30]

Of course, we do not deny that the things produced on behalf of the general government sector, that is, public goods and services, can, and in fact do, have an economic measure in terms of money. Yet, this measure exists as a result of the monetisation of the production process by the banking system,[31] rather than as a result of an exchange of the kind epitomised by the above depicted swap between (fiat) money and output. Neither on the factor market nor on the product market does such an exchange between national money and domestic output ever occur. To claim the contrary would mean misunderstanding the very concept of the medium of exchange (an issue which we hope to have clarified by now), founding it on the false, dichotomic image of the real world.

Before passing on, and as a gambit, to the next section, which attempts to introduce organically into the economy both entrepreneurs and bankers (who, to borrow an image from Morishima, have been put to sleep in the monetarist edifice), let us try to elucidate briefly the credit granted by the private sector to the state, and to contrast it with the emission of fiat money. Contrary to the above quoted allegation that '[it] is a form of credit where the issuing party is the state' (Shubik, 1987, p. 317), paper money is not generated by law. As Menger would say, '[s]anction by the authority of the state is a notion alien to it' (Menger, 1892, p. 255). Indeed, the state may declare the legal tender by a political decision, but cannot determine its purchasing power, which is the result of economic activity, as we shall see later. This implies that, to understand the nature of money, one has to go beyond both the material and the chartal representations of the means of payment. As the present stage in the evolution of both domestic and cross-border payment systems shows, money is entirely of a banking nature. Current account deposits and bank notes are not fundamentally different, so much so that they can be used indifferently in any monetary transaction (Cencini, 1995, p. 37). When the central bank issues fiat money, it replaces in fact a deposit of the public with commercial banks (also dubbed deposit banks) with a certificate of deposit in central bank money – represented by bank notes and/or coins. 'Taking the place of [commercial] bank deposits, bank notes are one of the possible representations of a drawing right over national output' (ibid., p. 94), a transformation – literally, a change of form – which does not affect its object, that is, the purchasing power of money.[32] By the same token, when the central bank acts as the state's bank (although this is neither its essential nor its specific function),[33] it does so without modifying the existing relationship between national money and domestic output. In real-world economies, seigniorage is an optical illusion. If the general government sector is seeking the necessary funds to finance its current public policies, it must do so in strict compliance with the fundamental rules governing bank money, which stem from double-entry bookkeeping. In particular, all the state can do (and does indeed) to cover the primary deficit of its current account is to issue government bonds on the financial market. As Haliassos and Tobin have it, '[g]overnment bonds are simply a means whereby the current generation can undertake expenditure for which future generations will have to pay through increased taxes' (Haliassos and Tobin, 1990, p. 915). As a matter of fact, through the intervention of the central bank, the public sector can advance a purchasing power that will originate in a future production (of either the public or the private sector), by selling bonds to capture current private savings. In practice, this means that Table 4.1 has to be replaced by Table 4.2, which depicts the stylised result of any fund-raising operation carried out by the state on the domestic financial market.

Table 4.2 The financing of public sector deficits

Commercial banks

liabilities		assets	
Central bank	£x	Private sector	£x

Central bank

liabilities		assets	
State	£x	Commercial banks	£x

State

liabilities		assets	
Government bonds	£x	Central bank	£x

Through the sale of (say) treasury bills, the government acquires the savings formed within the private sector, thus financing its current account imbalance with the intermediation of the national banking system.

All in all, the reality of government finance is fundamentally different from the conventional interpretation put forth by advocates of the exogenous-money view. The private sector buys the newly issued government bonds, that is, it lends purchasing power to the public sector, through an exchange where the possible use of fiat money is just a particular form of transferring ownership over yet unsold output between the two complementary sectors of the national economy. No discrepancy of an inflationary nature can ever exist in such an exchange, because the purchasing power of money is unaltered by the sale of government bonds. Ultimately, what the private sector gives up is the drawing right over a given sum of bank deposits, represented by the number written on paper money (but a cheque would do as well), in exchange for the right to withdraw in the future an equivalent amount of deposits. 'The check [or the bank note] is merely the evidence of this right and of the transfer of this right from one person to another' (Fisher, 1911/1931, p. 35). It becomes therefore visible that the idea of outside (fiat) money as the state-issued acknowledgement of debt is ill-founded, because it is grounded on a theoretical framework where the emission of (paper) money and the financing of deficit-spending units are mixed up in a highly dangerous way for the socio-political cohesion of any national economy.

We put here aside the theoretical determination of the optimal degree of government fiscal imbalance, since this issue would carry us too far afield, without providing any analytical insight into the theory of inflation.[34] What is needed here, as Morishima (1992) has argued so convincingly, is to account for the functional existence of both banks and firms[35] in real-world economic systems, where the depression of the purchasing power of money still is a main problem for modern production economies. Only after this has been accomplished, along the lines we investigate next, can we probably begin to understand the underlying issues inherent in inflationary pressures.

ENDOGENOUS MONEY, OR THE ASSOCIATION OF MONEY AND OUTPUT

Money, a *Numéraire*?

Since the pioneering work of Léon Walras, mainstream economic analysis has been portraying money as the *numéraire*. To be more precise, two fundamentally distinct, and opposite, conceptions of the *numéraire* exist in the history of monetary thought, namely a physical and a numerical conception.[36] As neoclassical authors model it (see previous section), the *numéraire* is conceived of in physical terms, that is, as a commodity (or an asset) taken as standard in an economic system which remains essentially a barter trade system. However, the *numéraire* may also be conceived of as a purely numerical entity with no dimension whatsoever, that is, as a number that measures all the goods and services exchanged in an economy. According to Walras himself, in fact, money as such is a unit of account, that is, a numerical unit used to satisfy the 'needs of trade' without being itself an object of trade. In his own terms, 'the word *franc* . . . is the name of a thing which does not exist' (Walras, 1874/1954, p. 188). Indeed, the idea of money as a non-commodity has long existed in the history of monetary thought. Professor Pigou claimed that '[a] pound sterling is not a thing at all. It is a name handed down in history' (Pigou, 1949, p. 3). Joan Robinson argued basically along the same lines, when she stated that the pound sterling, 'in itself, is just a word' (Robinson, 1956, p. 28). All this conforms to the Smithian intuition that money is essentially a means of payment, or the wheel of output circulation, 'which, in point of principle, does not add to the amount of riches of a given economy' (Hegeland, 1951, p. 1).

Yet, despite Walras's perception that money is nothing but a numerical unit, neoclassical monetary theory has never succeeded in satisfactorily explaining the association of money (numbers) and output. As pointed out by Cencini, '[t]he mathematical device of taking a given commodity as standard by making it equal to number one is tantamount to being an illusory trick of arbitrarily associating real output and numbers' (Cencini, 1988, p. 112). Clearly, '*numbers* enter into the [neoclassical] picture only *axiomatically* and for one precise purpose, namely to pave the way for the implementation of mathematical techniques' (Schmitt, 1996a, p. 105).[37] By applying Walras's Law to general-equilibrium models of money-using economies, one could indeed always eliminate the money equation from any neoclassical system of simultaneous exchanges (Cencini, 1982, pp. 131–2; 1988, pp. 133–6). In fact, as we have observed in the previous section, 'although Walras does take one of his *n* commodities as numéraire (or unit of account) it is an essential part of his theory that the numéraire does not enter into the exchange in any different way from any other of the commodities' (Hicks, 1966/1967, p. 3). So much so that, in Walrasian economics, '[t]he numéraire is not money; it is not even a partial money; it is not even assumed that it is used by the traders themselves as a unit of account. It is not more than a unit of account which the observing economist is using for his own purpose of explaining to himself what the traders are doing' (ibid., p. 3).[38] In short, within general-equilibrium analysis money is inessential in the sense of Hahn (1973, p. 231). The medium-of-exchange function of so-called monetary assets is not necessary to determine the models' solution (Rogers, 1989, p. 63). As we have been trying to illustrate above, the alleged medium of exchange is theorised, and modelled, as the general equivalent of non-money goods. It moves, let us say, clockwise in any relative exchange where non-money goods move anticlockwise. To be sure, in such a framework any of the *n* commodities will do. As Hicks has it, '[a]ny of the other *n*–1 commodities might have been taken as numéraire' (Hicks, 1966/1967, p. 3). Overall, neoclassical monetary models are therefore essentially barter models, since '"money" may always be added [to them] without altering any of the perfect barter results' (Rogers, 1989, p. 46).

Now, the fundamental reason behind the unsuccessful attempts to account for the existence of money by means of received macroeconomic models can perhaps also be explained by the lack of analytical distinction between the functionally different economic agents participating in the production–consumption process. As previously noted, Morishima points to the fact that general-equilibrium theory usually deals with 'representative' consumers only, struggling for utility maximisation under some kind of intertemporal budgetary constraint. It neglects both the firms' and the banks' role in the macroeconomy, thus being a mathematical analysis of a dream-world, 'a world which is not totally workable in the context of actual society' (Morishima, 1992, p. 198). As a matter of fact, '[e]very transaction involves three parties, buyer, seller, and banker' (Hicks, 1966/1967, p. 11). If we analyse the factor market, where the newly produced goods are formed, we can observe that the payment of the 'productive services' involves three poles, that is, firms, workers, and the banking system taken as a whole. The same applies to the product market, because any transaction on produced goods and services requires a seller (usually a firm), a purchaser (usually a household) and a bank as its three constitutive poles. One has in fact always to remember that paper money is just the representation of a bank deposit, and that the transmission of bank notes between agents implies the transfer of the corresponding drawing right (purchasing power) over current production, recorded within the banking system. As stated by Cencini, 'every bank-note corresponds to a book-entry of which it is the mere "image"' (Cencini, 1988, p. 58). And it need not be added that the workings of our sophisticated financial markets obey essentially the same monetary structure, because any payment within the national economy is tautologically a monetary transaction carried out through the bookkeeping records of the domestic banking system.

However, if money and non-money goods were to be exchanged as claimed by adherents to the neoclassical cosmology, the banking system would be nothing but a go-between apt to smooth so-called market frictions. Like the *numéraire* featuring in any neoclassical model, its role would be inessential ultimately for a money-using economy, since it would originate in a profit-seeking behaviour of a particular type of entrepreneur, dubbed banker.[39] This is indeed the traditional treatment of money and banking in neoclassical macroeconomics. According for instance to Ball, '[t]he banking system is an intermediary in the sense that it *facilitates* the transfer of real resources from surplus to deficit spending units' (Ball, 1964, p. 168; italics added). Reference to the 'banking firm' would hence serve to distinguish a particular service provider among the set of domestic enterprises. Nothing else. Yet, the crucial question – generally neglected in monetary analysis – is to explain how the banking firm, or the banking sector as a whole, can (and does) provide an accounting system of exchange among economic units. This is the essence of modern banking. All the rest is ancillary to that.

The Means of Payment, a Double-Entry Integer

In his widely-cited *Journal of Monetary Economics* paper, Fama sets out to explain that 'the main function of banks in the transactions industry' is 'the maintenance of a system of accounts in which transfers of wealth are carried out with bookkeeping entries' (Fama, 1980, p. 39). He repeatedly observes that, in principle, providing an accounting system of exchange does not require any physical medium or a temporary abode of purchasing power, because the transactions aspect of banking is based on the double-entry mechanism of debits and credits (ibid., pp. 39–43).[40] Whilst paper money can be used to represent general purchasing power as well as to transfer its drawing rights among currency holders, the essence of the transactions services provided by the banking system is to rely on purely numerical units – integers having a concrete economic meaning, as we shall see later on – to carry out any exchange within the economy. As recognised indeed by Hicks in a 1975 Institute of Economic Affairs *Occasional Paper* quoted by Laidler and Parkin, 'money is now a mere counter, which is supplied by the banking system (or by the government through the banking system) just as it is required' (Hicks, quoted in Laidler and Parkin, 1975, p. 742).[41] Though embedded in the improper context of outside money, which we have already dismissed as ill-founded, the idea of (bank) money being nothing but a number issued on demand needs to be further investigated. As a matter of fact, '[t]his number is created by the banking system and this creation takes different forms depending on the technological and institutional context' (Bradley et al., 1996, p. 112). Since numbers have no economic value as such, the banking system can always issue the exact amount of money units the public is asking for (Cencini, 1995, p. 21). In fact, when providing transactions services to the public, banks make payments as demanded by their clients (hence the endogenous nature of modern money), debiting and crediting them through 'bookkeeping entries [that] are used to allow economic units to exchange one form of wealth for another' (Fama, 1980, p. 43).[42]

Now, the last quotation deserves close attention, for it might represent the crux of monetary analysis. Indeed, taking up Hicks's idea of money as a purely numerical unit (which might be viewed as a restatement in modern terms of the concept of the 'great wheel of circulation' put forth by Smith), one may note that book-entry money is not an asset (nor is it a commodity), because no single economic agent would ever give up real goods and services to obtain a sum of numbers (Schmitt, 1996b, p. 97). This is fundamentally the same point raised in the previous section: money is not the general counterpart of non-money goods; it does not exchange with them. On purely conceptual grounds, it makes sense to argue that any exchange concerns a single object, which, as perceived by Fama, is literally transformed by this peculiar operation on the marketplace involving necessarily the issue of the numerical 'counter' by the banking system. Though difficult to grasp, the analytical importance of what may be called, following Schmitt's terminology, an absolute exchange – to distinguish it from a relative exchange, where two distinct, and presumably equivalent, objects are traded in the imaginary world of neoclassical economists – cannot be underestimated. The principle of double-entry bookkeeping imposes in fact that for each single payment the same thing is recorded on both sides of a bank's balance sheet, because what the debtor owes the bank is, ultimately, the object of the bank's debt to its creditor. In other words, the bank's double entry is the numerical measure of the transaction, because the number of money units issued by the bank literally counts the value of the object (ex)changed.[43]

Let us try to clarify this difficult point by referring to a payment of x money units on the factor market, between a firm and its workers (Table 4.3). In fact, as Lavoie notes, '[m]oney is introduced into the economy through the productive activities of the firms, as these activities generate income. There can be no money without production' (Lavoie, 1984, p. 774). It is thus on the factor market that our analysis must be situated, to understand the essence of money in a production–consumption system (a conceptual step necessary to grasp inflation and its causes).

Table 4.3 The result of an absolute exchange on the factor market

Bank

liabilities			assets
Workers	£x	Firm	£x

To avoid the temptation to explain a deposit formation by having recourse to a pre-existent deposit (whose origin would remain unexplained), let us make tabula rasa of any existing bank deposit. In the period under examination, the payment of the wage bill is carried out without using a pre-existent deposit. It is precisely because such a payment is made from the tabula rasa that its result is a net income for the economy as a whole. In fact, as anticipated in Chapter 2, what is gained by workers is an income which is not lost by firms, the latter having no positive income to transfer to the former.[44] Now, as Table 4.3 shows, money exists as an asset–liability in any payment, because – being the numerical form in which both the debit and the credit are recorded – it appears on each side of a bank's balance sheet simultaneously and necessarily (Schmitt, 1975, pp. 13–18). In the words of Wray, '[o]nly if money were dropped from helicopters (or otherwise injected into the system) would it represent an asset without a corresponding liability' (Wray, 1990, p. 13).

This analysis has puzzled, stimulated, infuriated, or annoyed a number of economists (Desai, 1984, p. xi). As we shall stress again later on, the asset–liability nature of bank money does not conform to the statistical definition of modern money used by central banks and international organisations (Chick, 2000, p. 130). At a more fundamental level, it appears to some critics as being 'nothing more than the fact that when a bank creates money it simultaneously creates an asset and a liability' (Watkins, 1985, p. 596). Yet, when one goes beyond appearances, one can notice in this framework the fundamental link between money and production: the substance of the workers' deposit is the newly produced good(s) physically stored with the firm, which is indebted to the banking system for the payment of production costs, as recorded in Table 4.3. As a matter of fact, to make a payment, the bank has to record the object of the transaction both positively and negatively, in one and the same motion, for otherwise the basic rule of double entry would not be satisfied (the whole operation would be aborted and nullified). In other words, the entry on the assets side testifies that the firm has a financial debt whose real object is current output in physical terms, while the entry on the liabilities side records the same good(s) in the monetary form of a bank deposit owned by the factors of production. Both the debt of the firm and the deposit of the workers result from the exchange monetised by the bank, 'so that the deposit created by the bank is balanced by a debt *of the same sort*' (Cencini, 1988, p. 61). The payment entered in Table 4.3 is thus an absolute exchange, because the same thing – a given set of real goods and services – is the object of both the firm's debt and the workers' deposit recorded simultaneously in the bank's account. Whilst workers give up the newly produced commodities in their physical form when the wage bill is paid, they simultaneously obtain the same items in the numerical form of (x) money units as their remuneration. This change of form is testified by the workers' ownership of a claim over a sum of bank deposits resulting from the monetisation of current production.[45] So much so that workers can spend on the commodity market the newly formed bank deposit they own, to obtain the very object of it, that is, physical values-in-use.[46] Considering the absolute exchange of current national output as a whole, and contrasting it with the relative exchange imagined by neoclassical authors and depicted in Figure 4.2, would thus give the following representations (Figure 4.4).

a) On the factor market (instant t*)*

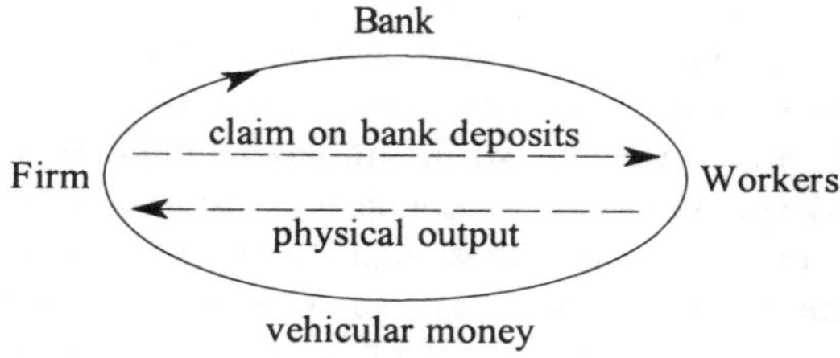

b) On the product market (instant t**)*

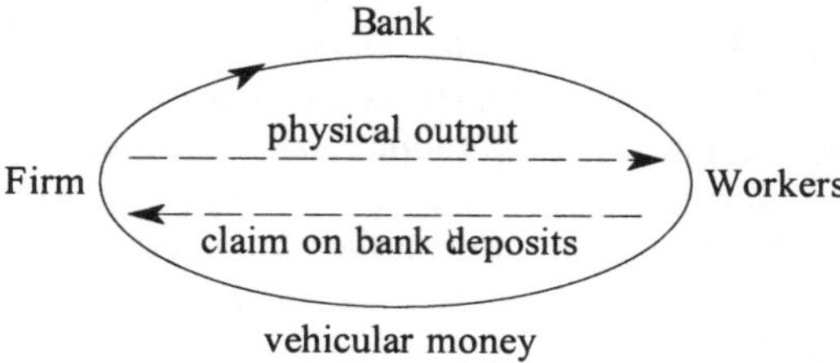

Figure 4.4 The two absolute exchanges of national output

The absolute exchange on the labour market gives rise to national income, since it associates current physical output with the numerical form issued by the banking system at instant *t*, that is, when the wage bill is paid. Workers are thus paid in an operation that grants them the right to withdraw the result of their own activity in the form of a claim over a sum of bank deposits. Thus then, the latter are not exchanged with the newly produced goods, but are these very goods themselves, moulded into their monetary form (issued by banks – hence the triangular nature of the payment). In the payment of the wage bill 'workers receive *their own product* in money. This transaction does not merely define an equivalence but an identity: every worker gets a sum of money which, because of its being issued through the payment of the wage bill, identifies itself with the real output of this same worker' (Schmitt, 1984, p. 347; our translation).[47] The reverse exchange taking place on the market for produced goods and services shows that until final consumption occurs (say, at instant t^*, after t) workers – or, more generally, income holders, if we allow for income redistribution – hold current output in its monetary form. At t^*, when they exert their drawing rights on the product market, income holders obtain in fact, in physical terms, what they previously have been holding in monetary terms:[48] an absolute exchange of the opposite algebraic sign than the previous one leaves them with a collection of values-in-use (that is, physical things), released from the monetary form in which the latter are subsumed through the banks' instrumental intervention.

So, to focus on the crucial point at issue, one can notice in this framework that money and output are not two distinct, and independent, things (as depicted, for instance, in Figure 1.1), with separate and opposing 'masses' that would require one to determine their contingent equilibrium via the general level of prices. Precisely – let us repeat it once more, since it will be a central argument for the analysis of inflation developed in Part Three – money as such is the numerical 'container' whose freight is given by the newly produced output. In this framework, therefore, money and output move in the same direction, as is always the case for a vehicle transporting its load.[49] Contrary to Clower's axiomatic image that 'money buys goods and goods buy money', by which traditional economic theory tries to give money an essential role within the dichotomic vision, money and output are respectively the numerical and the real aspect of one and the same thing, called income. In the remuneration of the production factors, 'money takes the place of the physical product and becomes its numerical form, so that the exchange between money and output defines their integration: money and output become the two complementary faces of a unique object' (Cencini, 1995, p. 16).

Now, one might still maintain that a unique object cannot be owned by two distinct agents, namely by a firm and its workers. True. In fact, current output belongs only to its production factors, that is, workers, from the very moment it is formed by the payment of the wage bill until its possible redistribution through income transfers (mark-up price mechanisms, direct and indirect taxation, and so on) within the economy.[50] Income holders, whether workers or other economic agents who take their place in the banking system's balance sheet, are the sole owners of yet unsold national output, although the latter is physically stored with firms and recorded within the banking system. Firms owe it precisely because it is the object of their debt to the banking sector (see Table 4.3), and the latter simply matches its credits and its debits so that deposit (that is, income) holders are the owners of total saleable output at any point in time.

At this juncture, one then has only to recall the clue of present-day monetarism (already investigated in Chapter 3, albeit on different grounds), to show how the maintained method of macroeconomic analysis fails to seize the (endogenous) nature of money and why, consequently, it is unable to tackle the inflation problem in accordance with the fundamental rules of bank money. Let us quote Friedman's dictionary article once again: 'Today's income growth is not closely related to today's monetary growth; it depends on what has been happening to money in the past. What happens to money today affects what is going to happen to income in the future' (Friedman, 1987, p. 16). There is no need to repeat here the analysis developed above, to emphasise that the paradigm underlying this view cannot provide an analytical framework for the elaboration of policy guidelines aiming to fight inflation successfully. In so far as money and output are considered, and modelled, as two different things (and not as, respectively, money proper and money's worth), the relation between them (that is, income) will never appear as distinct and crucial as it is, both in theory and in practice. Hence, the analysis of inflation as well as its cure will not be adequate to solve the problem for good. Our next task, therefore, is to explore an alternative paradigm for inflation analysis.

NOTES

1. In his *New Palgrave* dictionary article, Friedman himself acknowledges that within the analysis of inflation '[t]he deeper question is why excessive monetary growth occurs' (Friedman, 1987, p. 17).
2. In a similar mood, one may go back to Karl Menger's (1892) *Economic Journal* article 'On the origin of money', to find out that 'the enigmatic phenomenon of money' is an issue present in the whole history of monetary thought. As Lord Desai elegantly puts it, '[d]ebates over the last two hundred years have used the word money to cover a variety of situations' (Desai, 1987, p. 137). See also Sargent and Wallace (1982, p. 1212).
3. As noticed by Hegeland, '[t]he very name of Fisher's well-known formula, the equation of *exchange*, is a direct indication that money is dealt with only in its function as a medium of exchange' (Hegeland, 1951, p. 198).
4. Niehans cogently underlines that '[e]ach concept of friction . . . implies a corresponding concept of "marketability" or "liquidity" of different goods, measuring their ability to

overcome the frictions' (Niehans, 1978, p. 16).

5. It need not be emphasised that every single individual is bound to accept the exchange intermediary in use, for it is known to be acceptable to others by virtue of a tacit social contract. See Hicks (1967, p. 5), Clower (1969, pp. 14–15) and Hahn (1982, pp. 21–2).
6. In a different context, Stigum noted the divorce between form and content of mathematical symbols in both economics and economic modelling. 'To wit: Mathematics is created out of the empty set, and its assertions concern properties of symbols. . . . "[M]oney" and "capital" are symbols just as much as *x* and *y* are symbols' (Stigum, quoted in Chick, 1998, p. 1861).
7. Note that 'medium of exchange' and 'means of payment' are synonymous expressions here (see the Spindt quote). Every payment is in fact an exchange, as is unanimously agreed within the economics profession, though not on the same analytical grounds. This issue is taken up in the next section.
8. Kocherlakota and Wallace (1998) have recently recast this assumption in the idea that a regularly updated public record of all transactions can inform the optimal allocation of goods and services within a monetary production economy. A closely related paper by Kocherlakota (1998b) aims in fact at formally proving that any allocation which is achievable using an exchange intermediary (the monetary asset) could also be achieved by allowing agents costless access to a historical record (dubbed 'memory') of all past transactions. 'Hence, from a technological point of view, money is equivalent to a primitive form of memory' (Kocherlakota, 1998b, p. 232). Kocherlakota basically restates the same view when he concludes that '[m]oney does not reduce the cost of transferring resources from one person to another. There [is] no immediate technological reason why money should be a better numeraire than other goods' (ibid., p. 250). See also Kocherlakota (1998a) for a less technical presentation of the same argument.
9. On less sophisticated grounds, and from a conceptually different vantage point, Verdon (1996, pp. 21–2) raises an analogous criticism. Considering money as a commodity (ibid., p. 206, n. 9), he claims that 'money cannot be both a commodity and a measure of utility because it could not concurrently be something produced and exchanged (a commodity) and a simple medium of exchange and gauge of utility' (ibid., p. 22). Although Verdon seems to point out here the conceptual opposition between objects and means of payments, in his critique of the neoclassical paradigm he does not seem to understand the proper function of the medium of exchange (or of the means of payment). He maintains in fact that 'there is nothing neoclassical in acknowledging that money is both purchased and [sold], and therefore a commodity, since the money they [neoclassical economists] deal with is only the illusion of a commodity' (ibid., p. 106). See also Verdon (1996, pp. 38–44).
10. As a central bank officer puts it, '[i]n addition to general acceptability as means of payment . . . monetary services may consist in many other things, such as liquidity, portability, divisibility, and surety of nominal value' (Spindt, 1985, p. 177, n. 4). See also Laidler (1969, p. 511).
11. Recall that the economic definition of consumption must be distinguished from the physical one.
12. To use a famous image, 'money is like the "hot potato" of a children's game: one individual may pass it to another, but the group as a whole cannot get rid of it' (Tobin, 1987, p. 273).
13. Since in this framework money is considered as a temporary abode of purchasing power, acceptance of money by a seller of non-money goods is analytically a demand for money (as a demand for an 'intermediary' good).
14. Recall that 'invisible goods' such as personal services (for example haircuts) can be included in the broader set of real goods, without affecting analysis, because services too must be produced in order to be an object of economic investigation.
15. More recently, the same claim has also been made by Ingham, who maintains that 'as an

object of study in its own right, it [money] is neglected by the dominant or mainstream traditions not only in modern economics but also in sociology' (Ingham, 1996, p. 508).

16. Along Knapp's line, Wray (1998b; 2000) has recently recast this view in connection with Abba Lerner's functional finance approach.
17. To be true, Knapp (1924, p. 32) used the Latin word *charta* to mean ticket or token, and derived the adjective Chartal to describe the nature of the modern means of payment. 'Money always signifies a Chartal means of payment. Every Chartal means of payment we call money. The definition of money is therefore "a Chartal means of payment"' (Knapp, 1924, p. 38). More recent literature adopts the term Cartalism (dropping the etymological 'h') to indicate this view (see Goodhart, 1997).
18. In some hypothetical environments '[n]o inheritance is possible, so that unspent cash balances revert, at the death of the holder, to the monetary authority' (Lucas, 1972, p. 105).
19. See also Lerner (1947, p. 313).
20. For a modern theoretical approach to e-money, see Piffaretti (2000).
21. It should be recalled that in 1923 Keynes still adhered to the quantity theory of money. 'This theory is fundamental. Its correspondence with fact is not open to question' (Keynes, 1923/1971, p. 61).
22. The role of a deus ex machina means that the monetary authorities issue money without asking for any counterpart, a case put by Friedman in terms of 'helicopter money'.
23. Originally, seigniorage was an amount collected by the *seigneur* minting the currency out of precious metals. It was equal to the difference between the face value of the currency and the value of its metallic content.
24. In this context it may be noted that many influential economists claim that the central bank is simply an agency of the state. In particular, when the central bank issues bank notes and coins, it would act on behalf of the state: the general government sector would thus acquire a conspicuous amount of resources to finance public works.
25. In recent times, this has indeed been the case on a few exceptional occasions, such as a war or a major natural disaster (an earthquake, for example).
26. The convergence criteria put forth in the Maastricht Treaty are a recent example of policy guidelines for macroeconomic stability based on this theoretical framework. According to this view, excessive deficits of the general government sector ought to be avoided, in order to reduce the threat of inflationary pressures within the euro area. The required independence of national central banks as well as the compulsory introduction of the 'no bail out' clause are clear signs of this approach. See Parguez (1999) for a radical critique of the EMU agenda.
27. Even in these anachronistic cases, the expression 'inflation tax' is inappropriate and may lead one astray, for the collected amounts (by the *seigneur*) neither did nor could modify money's purchasing power. Only the distribution of the latter among economic agents was changed by the former, as is always the case when a tax is levied.
28. To simplify Table 4.1, we abstract here from the central bank, which in the present framework is considered merely as an agency of the state.
29. This deposit may be either provisional or definite. In the former case, the private sector will ultimately return fiat money to its issuer, to obtain the corresponding goods provisionally deposited into the treasury vaults. In the latter case, instead, the state acquires the ownership over the goods deposited – a legal right epitomised by the famous Latin expression *usus, fructus et abusus*.
30. As Wallace recently conceded, '[t]he challenge we face is to formulate models and policies that are consistent with the essentiality of money and that resemble both actual economies and actual policies' (Wallace, 1998, p. 230).
31. See next section.
32. As Joan Robinson noticed, '[t]he notes now circulating came into existence as the results of loans from the banks to entrepreneurs, who pay out wages in advance of receiving the proceeds of selling the goods which the workers produce' (Robinson, 1956, p. 226). Bank

notes are in fact recorded as a deposit in the central bank's balance sheet (Eichner, 1991, pp. 845–6; Lavoie, 1992, p. 164, Table 4.8). There is therefore identity between the stock of money and the sum total of bank deposits existing, at any point in time, in the economy as a whole. The statistical definition of money (M0, M1, M2, M3, M4 etc.) focuses indeed on these stock-magnitudes.

33. The specificity of central banking is to clear outstanding balances in the interbank market and thus guarantee the smooth functioning of national payment systems. See Rossi (1998, pp. 44–50).
34. One may remember that no particular figure or ratio has ever proved to be grounded on economic theory, as the controversy over the Maastricht budgetary convergence criteria has well emphasised recently. See Rossi and Dafflon (1996) on this issue.
35. Note that defining banks as a particular 'manufacturing' sector is an improper way to set this problem. As we are going to see, banks and firms perform two very different, and peculiar, functions in a monetary production economy.
36. Pasinetti (1993) has recently used the distinction between physical *numéraires* and nominal *numéraires* for the analysis of the structural dynamics of prices. Investigating the stability of the general price level, he namely pointed out that there exists 'an important asymmetry between monetary regimes in which the numéraire of the price system is physical, and monetary regimes in which the numéraire of the price system is a purely nominal unit of account, not linked to any quantitative specification of any particular physical commodity' (Pasinetti, 1993, pp. 63–4).
37. Notice the implicit reference to Debreu's (1959) axiomatic analysis lying behind his *Theory of Value*.
38. See Schmitt (1996a, pp. 110–19) for a development of this criticism.
39. Hence the conflation of firms and banks into the same functional category in mainstream analysis.
40. Note however both the difficulties and the hesitations of the author – Professor of Finance at the University of Chicago – to refuse conventional monetary analysis. In the abstract of his potentially path-breaking contribution, which remains ultimately on neoclassical grounds, he indicates that his paper examines the nature of 'a pure nominal commodity or unit of account [that] is made to play the role of numeraire in a monetary system . . . and how, through reserve requirements, banks get involved in making it a real economic good' (Fama, 1980, p. 39).
41. J.R. Hicks (1975), 'The permissive economy', in *Crisis '75...?*, IEA *Occasional Paper* Special, no. 43, London: Institute of Economic Affairs (reference taken from Laidler and Parkin, 1975).
42. On less developed analytical grounds, King and Plosser stress in an analogous vein the role of money and banking in reducing the so-called 'shoe leather costs' of individual transactions: 'The financial industry provides accounting services that facilitate the exchange of goods by reducing the amount of time and other resources that otherwise would be devoted to market transactions' (King and Plosser, 1984, p. 365).
43. It is worthwhile emphasising that a relative exchange cannot do such a thing, because it is impossible to measure the value of two commodities in a single operation. The principle of equivalence of the exchange-value of two traded objects acquires a heuristic status when allowance is made into the analysis for the concept of absolute exchange. See Schmitt (1966) for development on this topic.
44. See Rossi (1998, pp. 28–43) for an analytical elaboration of this point. The case when a firm spends a pre-existent deposit on the factor market will be investigated in Part Three.
45. This can be crudely formalised by writing the identity between domestic output and national income, that is, the sum total of the bank deposits newly formed – an issue that we shall explore in Chapter 5.
46. Using the common-sense notion of money, that is, bank deposits (inclusive of central bank liabilities, as we have pointed out in note 32), we might illustrate this absolute exchange by

an everyday example. When one gets a cup of coffee, say, by introducing a £1 coin in a vending machine, one changes the form of the object one owns: before introducing the coin in the machine, one owns the cup of coffee (or any other equivalent 'real thing', owing to money homogeneity) in its monetary form; after, one has it in its physical form (value-in-use). Note that we abstract from profits here, since this issue is not germane to the present discussion. See Part Three for inclusion of profits into the analysis.

47. '[Dans le paiement des salaires] les travailleurs perçoivent *leur propre produit*, en monnaie. Il ne s'agit pas simplement d'une équivalence mais d'une identité: chaque travailleur obtient une monnaie qui, du fait de son émission dans les salaires, s'identifie au produit réel de ce même travailleur' (Schmitt, 1984, p. 347). See also Cencini (1988, pp. 83–4).
48. Let us stress again that we abstract here from the firms' profits. In the last part of this book we shall introduce profits into the analysis.
49. The expression 'vehicular money' (see Figure 4.4) is meant to recall precisely this effect.
50. Let us underline that once output is sold, it does not constitute an object of economic investigation any more (for the sake of argument we abstract here from second-hand sales and purchases). Values-in-use are not objects of economic analysis.

PART THREE

A MODERN PARADIGM FOR INFLATION ANALYSIS

5. Wage Setting, Credit Policy and Inflation

In Chapter 4 we have noted that viewing money as exogenously given raises the two related questions of measuring output in economic terms and of determining the purchasing power of money objectively. These are two fundamental problems which the traditional dichotomy between output and money cannot resolve, as we have been seeking to explain since the second section of Chapter 3. Now, one might also be interested in investigating whether the supporters of the endogeneity-of-money approach have been able to fare better in this respect. Since this question lies outside the scope of this book, a constructive answer to it will have to wait further research. However, to focus on the object of this work, it might be worth investigating here whether the analysis of inflation, propounded by the adherents to the endogenous money view, provides a better framework in order to design and implement an anti-inflation policy that can be successful. Generally speaking, the endogenous money view has been identified with the post-Keynesian school of thought, which is the alternative to the neoclassical code[1] that we have critically examined in Part Two. It is therefore to post-Keynesian monetary literature that we shall refer hereafter.

Several authors within the post-Keynesian tradition consider that inflation has its source in the difference between the growth rate of money wages and the growth rate of (average) labour productivity (see for instance Moore, 1979, p. 57; Davidson, 1988, p. 167; Arestis, 1997, p. 101; Smithin, 1997, p. 403). In light of the methodological antagonism between Keynesians and monetarists in the history of economic analysis, what is most surprising is that this widely-shared idea of comparing labour productivity with money wages can be closely linked, as lucidly observed by Moore (1983, p. 542), to the well-known tenet of the neoclassical (quantity) theory of money. In fact, according to the contemporary incarnation of the latter, to wit, monetarism, inflation occurs, let us recall it, when the quantity of money per unit of output is 'excessive' (Friedman, 1987, p. 17). Now, besides the multifaceted conundrum (explored in Part Two) of measuring output independently of money,[2] which is perhaps the most fundamental expression of the cul-de-sac where the traditional dichotomy imprisons neoclassical monetary investigation, one must also consider how it would be possible to concede wage increases 'outnumbering' the wage-earners' product. To put it in simple terms, is it ontologically possible to measure labour productivity independently of the money wages distributed in remuneration to the workers whose productivity is the object of our measurement? Let us try to investigate this question more closely.

THE MACROECONOMICS OF THE WAGE BARGAIN

Labour Productivity, Effective Demand and Money Wages

In *The General Theory* (hereinafter also *GT*) Keynes set out to develop a monetary theory of production[3] with no reference whatsoever to either the general price level or its technical alter ego, the aggregate price index. Let us quote at length a crucial passage from Keynes's most studied book.

> The division of Economics between the Theory of Value and Distribution on the one hand and the Theory of Money on the other hand is, I think, a false division. The right dichotomy is, I suggest, between the Theory of the Individual Industry or Firm and of the rewards and the distribution between different uses of a *given* quantity of resources on the one hand, and the Theory of Output and Employment *as a whole* on the other hand. So long as we limit ourselves to the study of the individual industry or firm on the assumption that the aggregate quantity of employed resources is constant, and, provisionally, that the conditions of other industries or firms are unchanged, it is true that we are not concerned with the significant characteristics of money. But as soon as we pass to the problem of what determines output and employment as a whole, we require the complete theory of a Monetary Economy (Keynes, 1936/1973, p. 293).

It is precisely in order to study the economic system as a whole (its functioning as well as its malfunctioning) that Keynes dealt with 'The choice of units' in Chapter 4 of his *GT*. As a matter of fact, as noted by Bradford and Harcourt in their recent contribution to *A 'Second Edition' of The General Theory*, the first step required for the elaboration of the complete theory of a monetary economy is to find the appropriate units of measurement for the whole economy (Bradford and Harcourt, 1997, pp. 107–9).[4] In particular, Keynes was concerned with finding a measure of production that should be exact and precise for the purposes of a causal analysis (Keynes, 1936/1973, p. 39).[5] In short, since 'the community's output of goods and services is a non-homogeneous complex which cannot be measured' (ibid., p. 38) – because it is an incommensurable collection of miscellaneous things having a multitude of different physical attributes –[6] Keynes was led, and rightly so, to resort to money as the only means to obtain a homogeneous measure of national output (see Keynes, 1936/1973, p. 41; but also Carabelli, 1992, pp. 22–3; Bradley et al., 1996, p. 124). Indeed, '[t]he money value of output in a given period is a perfectly precise and determinate quantity, as money values are at all times strictly homogeneous' (Bradford and Harcourt, 1997, p. 116).

Now, if it is clear that money units are homogeneous when one understands their numerical nature (see Chapter 4),[7] one still needs to resist the temptation to make use of index numbers to measure the value of current aggregate output or the purchasing power of money (Carabelli, 1992, p. 24). As a matter of fact, both in the *Treatise* and in the *GT* Keynes was well aware that the concept of the general price level is vague and imprecise for the monetary theory of production (see Bradley and Gnos, 1991). So much so that this abstraction cannot be used to deflate the money-value of output, as conventional macroeconomics does with no analytical misgivings. In Keynes's own provocative words, to be echoed more persuasively by Schumpeter (1954/1994, pp. 1092–3) two decades later,

> the proper place for such things as net real output and the general level of prices lies within the field of historical and statistical description, and their purpose should be to satisfy historical or social curiosity, a purpose for which perfect precision – such as our causal analysis requires, whether or not our knowledge of the actual values of the relevant quantities is complete or exact – is neither usual nor necessary (Keynes, 1936/1973, p. 40).

In spite of the standard practice of determining the purchasing power of money by calculating the general price level and its variation over a given time span, this method in fact can only lead to 'mock precision' (ibid., p. 40) in the field of macroeconomic investigation, as we have been trying to show in Part One.

Having set himself the task to construct the complete theory of a monetary production economy using neither price index analysis nor the concept of aggregate price level, in the *GT* Keynes proposes 'to make use of only two fundamental units of quantity, namely, quantities of money-value and quantities of employment. The first of these is strictly homogeneous, and the second can be made so' (Keynes, 1936/1973, p. 41). Keynes believes indeed that the economic system as a whole can be positively analysed by focusing on money and labour only (ibid., p. 43).[8] In particular, the heterogeneity of labour can be overcome by reverting to the monetary measure of its result, in the sense that skilled labour can be weighted in proportion to its remuneration compared to the remuneration of unskilled labour.[9] In the words of Keynes,

> [w]e shall call the unit in which the quantity of employment is measured the labour-unit; and the money-wage of a labour-unit we shall call the wage-unit. [If X stands for any quantity measured in terms of money, it will often be convenient to write X_w for the same quantity measured in terms of the wage-unit.] Thus, if E is the wages (and salaries) bill, W the wage-unit, and N the quantity of employment, $E = N \cdot W$ (Keynes, 1936/1973, p. 41).

This passage is crucial. It might suggest that money and output are associated on the factor market, when the wage bill is paid out by firms to workers with the intermediation of the banking system. In fact, as Cencini points out, '[w]ithout this association, money would remain empty and output would only be a jumble of heterogeneous physical objects' (Cencini, 1988, p. 85). This means also that the monetisation of the production process is essentially a triangular operation (see Table 4.3 and Figure 4.4, panel a): it associates the numerical form issued by the banking system and the real goods resulting from the productive services employed by firms. The result of this association is money income (recorded in the form of bank deposits), and it is elicited by the wage bill paid for current production. Thus then, 'money gives its numerical homogeneity to physical output, and output becomes the content of money income' (ibid., p. 85). This process is the objective measure of economic activity and all inflationary phenomena must be explained by referring to it, as we shall attempt to show later on.

Yet, before turning attention to this alternative analysis of inflation, a further point should be emphasised, for it can help substantiating the present argument on purely conceptual grounds. As Bradford and Harcourt do, one might question the nature of the wage-unit within the money-cum-labour theory of value put forth in Keynes's *GT*. 'What is the nature of the wage for Keynes?' (Bradford and Harcourt, 1997, p. 118). If the wage bill results from the association of money and output on the factor market, and considering that labour is the sole true factor of production (Keynes, 1936/1973, pp. 213–14), one might still wonder whether wages are the price of labour, as Carabelli (1992, pp. 19, 25) seems to maintain. In the affirmative, a kind of weighted wage index must ultimately be found, in order to account for the great variety of wages paid for different types (or skills) of labour – a solution arrived at by Keynes himself in *A Treatise on Money*.[10]

> If so, then would not the attempt to measure average wages be subject to the same pitfalls associated with attempts to measure average prices? If this were the case, then the measurement of the quantity of employment in terms of labour-units would no longer be precise. . . . In short, Keynes's argument for his choice of units appears to fail (Bradford and Harcourt, 1997, p. 118).

From an exegetical standpoint Keynes's idea of the wage-unit can in fact be interpreted as tantamount to saying that the wage is the price of labour. As a matter of fact, in Chapter 21 of the *GT*, where Keynes deals with 'The theory of prices', he moves from the case of an individual industry to industry as a whole in the following terms. 'In a single industry its particular price level depends partly on the rate of remuneration of the factors of production which enter into its marginal cost, and partly on the scale of output. There is no reason to modify this conclusion when we pass to industry as a whole' (Keynes, 1936/1973, p. 294). Together with his acceptance of the neoclassical postulate that the wage is equal to the marginal product of labour (ibid., p. 5), this might indeed corroborate the interpretation that Keynes did consider the wage as a price (Carabelli, 1992, p. 25; Bradford and Harcourt, 1997, p. 118). According to this view, the wage-unit is essentially a price. So much so that money would be its standard of measure, and we are back to the method used to determine the aggregate price level. Labour, considered here as a particular commodity – a productive service in the sense of the Marxian labour force – would be traded against money according to the relative-exchange paradigm on which the neoclassical dichotomy is founded. As Davidson points out, in fact, 'on occasion, Keynes deflates nominal output by the wage unit (the money wage)' (Davidson, 1998, p. 36, n. 5), a method which bears a close relationship with the too familiar one used to determine the purchasing power of money by means of price index analysis. On this basis, it would be quite straightforward to conclude that Keynes considered the wage as the price of labour.

However, as Bradford and Harcourt mention, theoretically there also exists the possibility that Keynes did not view the wage as the price of labour, although this route has not (yet) been explored by the post-Keynesian tradition, to which both authors belong. 'The alternative possibility is that Keynes did not view the wage as a kind of price' (Bradford and Harcourt, 1997, p. 118). Indeed, a fresh look at the concept of the wage-unit put forth in the *GT* might indicate that Keynes was proposing an entirely different conceptual approach, which, when further developed, could lead one to a path-breaking conclusion. It is this alternative approach that we wish to explore here. Indeed, the crucial point is not to dwell on what Keynes was really thinking when he put forward the idea of measuring macroeconomic magnitudes in terms of wage-units. This question, quite rhetorical if considered from the vantage point of an exegetic approach, acquires a heuristic status when allowance is made for a theoretical investigation into the working of a monetary production economy. In fact, what counts here is whether an interpretation of Keynes's intuition different from those based on purely exegetical grounds can lead us to a better understanding of the working of modern monetary economies of production.

In simple terms, the idea behind such a proposition is that, moving from the definition of bank money as a mere number, it makes sense to argue that the exchange between money and output on the labour market is a complex operation,[11] namely an absolute exchange which defines their integration in the wage-units thus born as the sole precise and objective measure of economic activity taken as a whole. This line of reasoning has been put forward by Schmitt, who argues that, '[u]ltimately, the *number* of wage-units issued is the *measure* of the product of the economy' (Schmitt, 1984, p. 458; our translation).[12] According to this alternative line of argument, the wage-unit is not simply a unit of money paid out to current production factors. Nor is it a quantity of physical goods produced by any 'marginal', or unskilled, labourer. It is both, in the exact sense that the unit of measurement of macroeconomic magnitudes is output moulded into its numerical form by the payment of the wage bill, an operation confirming in practice Keynes's theory of labour as the sole factor of production.[13] In short, one cannot be more explicit than this: '[t]he unit of measurement is the wage unit, because monetary wages define the equivalence of form and substance, that is, of the product and the number of units of money paid out in wages' (Schmitt, 1986, p. 118).[14]

In this alternative framework it is then possible to maintain that each newly produced commodity is measured, as an object of economic analysis, by the number of wage-units recorded in the banking system's balance sheet when banks monetise its production costs. In simple terms, the wage bill paid for the production of any good whatsoever is the economic measure of the latter, since the former is defined by the association of a sum of mere numbers with a 'real thing' produced by labour. For example, good *a* is worth (say) x pounds and the value of good *b* is measured by y pounds, because their productive services elicit a wage bill of, respectively, x and y pounds.[15] This may explain why, in the end, '[t]he theory of value and the theory of money are strongly interconnected' (Carabelli, 1992, p. 26). Yet, on further thought, how are relative values determined? Granted that the workers producing (say) good *a* are paid with x units of money, why is it that the workers producing good *b* obtain y units of money in remuneration of their activity (with $x \neq y$)? Once again, the answer can be found in Keynes's work, namely in what he called 'The principle of effective demand' (Keynes, 1936/1973, ch. 3). This principle, though expressed by Keynes in a rather complex form, is worth considering, for it lies at the heart of modern macroeconomic analysis.[16]

> Let Z be the aggregate supply price of the output from employing N men, the relationship between Z and N being written $Z = \phi(N)$, which can be called the *Aggregate Supply Function*. Similarly, let D be the proceeds which entrepreneurs expect to receive from the employment of N men, the relationship between D and N being written $D = f(N)$, which can be called the *Aggregate Demand Function*. . . . The value of D at the point of the aggregate demand function, where it is intersected by the aggregate supply function, will be called *the effective demand* (Keynes, 1936/1973, p. 25).

Stated differently, this principle means that 'the effective demand is the point on the aggregate demand function which becomes effective because, taken in conjunction with the conditions of supply, it corresponds to the level of employment which maximises the entrepreneur's expectation of profit' (ibid., p. 55). To put it yet another way, 'the effective demand is simply the aggregate income (or proceeds) which the entrepreneurs expect to receive . . . from the amount of current employment which they decide to give' (ibid., p. 55). In short, '[i]t is supply–demand' (Schmitt, 1972, p. 117), for it is the point where the aggregate supply curve intersects the expected aggregate demand curve, 'in a given situation of technique, resources and factor cost per unit of employment' (Keynes, 1936/1973, p. 24).[17]

For the sake of argument let us reconsider a two-sector model such as the one where goods *a* and *b* make up total current output. Sector I produces consumption goods (*a*) and sector II produces investment goods (*b*). As Keynes has it, '[t]he amount of labour N which the entrepreneurs decide to employ depends on the sum (D) of *two* quantities, namely D_1, the amount which the community is expected to spend on consumption, and D_2, the amount which it is expected to devote to new investment. D is what we have called above the *effective demand*' (Keynes, 1936/1973, p. 29). The point at issue is thus the formation and final expenditure of national income as it is created by the productive activity of all firms taken as a whole, that is, in the consumption-goods as well as in the investment-goods sector. Precisely, according to Schmitt (1995–96, vol. I, pp. 78–9), the principle of effective demand means that sector-II firm pays a wage bill of y pounds (supply) to its productive services if, and only if, the expected sales of the corresponding output (that is, good *b*) – bought with the newly formed income (demand) – are equal to y pounds. If the expected proceeds were higher than y, the firm in fact would not yet maximise its profit by remunerating its productive services by that amount (on the assumption that other firms' expectations are absolutely fulfilled). As a matter of fact, the sum total of income available in the whole economy would not enable the firm to capture more than y, that is, more than what the latter pays out for the wage bill. Similarly, the same firm would encounter a loss if the expected proceeds from the sale of its output were less than y, that is, lower than the sum paid to the factors of this production. By the same token, the firm in sector I remunerates its factors of production with a wage bill of x pounds (supply) if, and only if, it expects a demand for good *a* equal to x pounds. Hence, according to the Schmitt interpretation of the principle of effective demand, the newly formed national income (x + y) will be spent for the purchase of good *a* in the proportion of [x/(x + y)] and for the purchase of good *b* for the rest (that is, [y/(x + y)]).

Overall, production is organised according to an effective demand which is merely virtual,[18] so much so that firms' expectations may turn out to be wrong. Indeed, as has been so often emphasised by Paul Davidson, 'Keynes argued that the economic future was uncertain in the sense that it cannot be either foreknown or statistically predicted by analysing past and current market price signals' (Davidson, 1998, p. 29). Clearly, what Keynes (1936/1973, p. 161) called 'animal spirits' can influence entrepreneurs' decisions of production. 'Once production takes place, however, effective demand becomes truly effective, and its value can no longer be distinguished from that of income' (Cencini, 1984, p. 177), because it is on that basis that the wage bill is really paid out. The value of output (or the measure of income, see Keynes, 1936/1973, p. 63; but also Gnos, 1998) cannot exist independently of the macroeconomic equivalence that money income establishes between the two opposite flows of its formation (on the factor market) and of its expenditure (on the market for produced goods and services), whereby income is produced and, respectively, consumed through a set of absolute exchanges of the opposite algebraic sign. As noticed by Verdon (1996, p. 112), the national income received by industry as a whole from the sale of the newly produced goods and services is the very same income which nourishes households' earnings within the production process. To put it in his own words, 'entrepreneurs in the short term produce through hiring labour and services and thereby distribute the very incomes from which emanates the demand for their goods' (ibid., p. 112). In a nutshell, effective demand is 'the amount entrepreneurs will settle to produce' (ibid., p. 112). More precisely, 'effective demand is defined as a two-way flux, firms "giving" and "receiving" the same product' (Schmitt, 1986, p. 117). In other words, income formation (that is, total supply, Y) and income final expenditure (total demand, $C + I$) are two identical magnitudes,[19] because otherwise they could not be measured at all in this framework.[20]

The above argument amounts to saying that any effective demand entails the exact measure of the corresponding output. Any increase in effective demand entails by definition an equally identical increase in output, for, let us repeat, the measure of the latter is precisely given by the wage bill paid out to its factors according to the circular flow of income depicted by actual effective demand.[21] Ultimately, this interpretation of Keynes's analysis of 'the choice of the units of quantity appropriate to the problems of the economic system as a whole' (Keynes, 1936/1973, p. 37) paves the way for the elaboration of an entirely new approach to the theory of inflation. It suggests, as we shall explore in Chapter 6, that inflation might be explained as a macroeconomic disequilibrium between total supply and total demand, in spite of their fundamental identity ($Y \equiv C + I$) as measured in the production–consumption process.[22]

Now, by formalising his conception of true inflation in relation to the expression 'MV=D where M is the quantity of money, V its income-velocity (this definition differing in the minor respects indicated above from the usual definition) and D the effective demand' (Keynes, 1936/1973, p. 304), Keynes was led to infer a theory of inflation pretty similar to the neoclassical (monetarist) one. Far away from the potentially path-breaking idea of what in his *Treatise on Money* he labelled 'profit inflation' (Keynes, 1930/1971, p. 155), which we shall consider later on, in *The General Theory* he focused on inflation in terms of the stability or instability of (aggregate?) prices as depending 'on the strength of the upward trend of the wage-unit (or, more precisely, of the cost-unit) compared with the rate of increase in the efficiency of the productive system' (Keynes, 1936/1973, p. 309).

Several post-Keynesian scholars have given the inflation problem the same treatment (or a very similar one). Kaldor and Trevithick, for instance, claim that, '[i]n contrast to the pre-first world war period or the inter-war period, [in the post-war period] average wages have invariably increased faster than average productivity, giving rise to an upward drift in labour costs per unit of output' (Kaldor and Trevithick, 1981, p. 17). Surely, increases in the physical productivity of labour may be compared to increases in money wages for any given set of wage-earners. However, similar comparisons stem from a yet imperfect consideration of the macroeconomic relationship between money and effective demand. The principle that authors like Kaldor and Trevithick do not consider is that labour productivity cannot but be measured in strictly monetary terms for economic analysis. More picturesquely, labour productivity and money wages are like the volume of a gas and the volume of the room in which the gas is released.

Let us explain this important point by means of a simple numerical example. Consider a manufacture of shirts. Suppose that, owing to technical change, a given worker, W, increases his physical productivity by factor 3: in period 1, before the innovation was introduced into the manufacture, W's labour productivity was (say) 10 shirts per working day on average; after, in period 2, it is 30 shirts per day. Are we going to infer that W's output is three times what it used to be? An economist's answer cannot abstract from the worker's remuneration. If it is plain, in fact, that the number of shirts has been multiplied by 3, it must also be noted that this increase in W's productivity concerns the physical objects only. What about W's money wage? To simplify, let us assume that the money wage has not changed from period 1 to period 2, that is, it is of (say) 100 pounds a day in both periods. With the benefit of Keynes's insight into the units of economic measurement, we can see that the measure of W's output has not changed over time either. As pointed out by Schmitt, who refers indeed to Keynes's choice of units,

> [i]t is no doubt true that technical progress enables the national economy to introduce more and more commodities into the form-utility; but output takes on the measure of the form and not the other way round; it follows that technical progress and accumulation of the means of production cannot multiply *output* in its exact sense: a greater diversity and a greater number of commodities are subsumed under an unchanged output. . . . [O]utput is measured by the wage bill; multiplication and perfection of the means of production are neutral actions as far as the payment of the wage bill is concerned (Schmitt, 1984, p. 495; our translation).[23]

In the case at hand, the wage bill generated in the remuneration of W's effort is equal to 100 pounds, even after the increase in W's physical productivity has taken place. So, since 30 shirts produced in period 2 are associated with the same number of money units as are 10 shirts in period 1, W's output is measured in economic terms by 100 units of money after as well as before the given innovation is introduced into the manufacture. Strictly speaking, and as astonishing as it might appear, W's output has not been increased over time.[24]

Consider now the much likely situation where W, arguing from the observed increase in physical productivity, asks the employer for a rise in his money wage. Supposing that this increase is granted, is it (or could it be, depending on the amount) of an inflationary nature? The answer should be straightforward by now. As Cencini states, '[e]very change in the sum paid to workers simply leads to a change in the way production is measured' (Cencini, 1995, p. 66). Output being measured by the corresponding wage bill, a variation in the amount of the latter is only a variation in the measuring scale of current production (Bradley et al., 1996, p. 131). For instance, if the wage bargain between W and his employer determines a period-2 money wage of 110 pounds per day for W, the corresponding output in the new situation is measured by this number of money units, no matter of the number of shirts he really produces per unit of effort.[25]

The above argument amounts to the proposition that a change in the money wage paid for a same worker's effort (say, an eight-hour day by W) does not modify the relation between the output newly produced and money (that is, the relation defining money's purchasing power). Although the shirts produced in the two periods, in the case at hand, might have exactly the same physical characteristics (that is, quality), a period-1 shirt is fundamentally different from a period-2 shirt in strictly economic terms. So much so that these two shirts could be measured by two different wage bills, as in our previous example, without such a difference being of an inflationary nature.

Yet, no one doubts that the increase in money wages per unit of effort may be ascribed to the workers' attempt at protecting their purchasing power from inflation, whose origin we shall begin to explore in the next section. Indeed, it is a fact that the purchasing power of wage-earners suffers from any loss in the purchasing power of money. Besides the attempt to gain a bigger share of total income in the distribution between real wages and profits, wage increases are actually claimed by trade unions in an attempt to limit the loss in their members' standard of living (in relative and/or in absolute terms). This probably is what led a large number of post-Keynesian scholars to embrace the so-called conflict inflation approach, a theory to which we now turn in an attempt to point out its inadequacies for the analysis of inflationary pressures. On account of the wide currency of this conflict theory, both in academic quarters and in public opinion, a critical appraisal of it may in fact be an important step towards understanding the inflation problem and its causes. In particular, the analysis we undertake next may be pretty helpful to underline the fact that observing the evolution of aggregate prices cannot be deemed sufficient to grasp the phenomenon of inflation.

The Conflict Inflation Approach: a Critical Appraisal

Since Rowthorn's (1977) influential *Cambridge Journal of Economics* paper on 'Conflict, inflation and money' was published, an expanding volume of literature attempting to explain inflationary pressures in terms of the conflicting claims on income by different functional classes of agents in the national economy has emerged (see Kaldor and Trevithick, 1981, pp. 16–19; Dalziel, 1990; Dawson, 1992, ch. 3; Dutt, 1992; Lavoie, 1992, ch. 7; Burdekin and Burkett, 1996; Palley, 1996, ch. 11, and the references cited therein). Although the contributions to this literature do not stem all from the same analytical view of the working of a money-using (production) economy and follow different political economy traditions (mainly the neo-Marxian and the post-Keynesian ones (see Skott, 1989), with fringes such as the French regulationists and, most importantly, the neo-Kaleckians), they all share an important number of essential points as far as the aetiology of inflation is concerned. In particular, they all share the belief that '[a]t the heart of the inflationary process is the question of relative income distribution' (Eichner and Kregel, 1975, p. 1308). This is why, for our present purposes, we can subsume them under the unanimously agreed conflict theory label.

As Burdekin and Burkett pointed out in their theoretical work on *Distributional Conflict and Inflation*, the Conflict Inflation Approach (CIA for short) has to be seen as 'a methodological *approach* to conceptualizing, modeling and econometrically testing hypotheses concerning inflation processes in different historical-institutional contexts, *not* as a particular model of inflation' (Burdekin and Burkett, 1996, p. 15). Accordingly, our analysis will centre on the CIA hypothetical framework of inquiry, focusing on the concepts of money, income and inflation it is based upon. We shall thus not attempt to survey the models built along these lines over the last twenty years or so, since this would be too large a task to undertake here, which moreover would not affect our critical appraisal of the underlying CIA's fundamental hypotheses.

To concentrate on the latter, it is fair to maintain that the CIA 'may be viewed as the lineal descendant of the theory of cost-push inflation developed in the 1950s' (Palley, 1996, p. 182).[26] As a matter of fact, among the possible sources of cost-push inflation suggested by adherents to this theory, by far the best ranked one is that arising from the assumed 'inconsistent claims on income that emerge from the income distribution struggle between workers and firms' (ibid., p. 182). In this view, the two parties' claims on income may exceed available output at the aggregate level. So, the excess of income claims over national output would be a fundamental causal factor of the observed rise in prices on the market for produced goods and services. Wage-earners try to counteract this upward pressure by bidding for higher wages, thus setting forth an alleged inflationary spiral in which each party seeks to achieve, or to maintain, its targeted income share.

Without entering here into either irrelevant details or mere technicalities uninfluential for our conceptual analysis, the CIA encompasses two types of distributional conflicts among the different categories of agents. The first is the well-known conflict between firms and wage-earners, dubbed, respectively, capitalists and labourers by those willing to stress the Marxian 'class struggle' in the distribution of national income (see Kalecki, 1971). The second arises within the working class itself, when each group of wage-earners attempts to re-establish what the latter 'consider to be their rightful place in the social hierarchy' (Lavoie, 1992, p. 414). In short, the two identified types of inflation-generating conflicts are referred to by the price dynamics they set forth, and are thus known respectively under the terms of price–wage spiral and wage–wage spiral. Our aim is to show that they both have the same conceptual problems, which in the end undermine their heuristic status for inflation analysis.

When we get right to the heart of the matter, we can notice that at the core of the CIA lie value judgements about income distribution among functional classes of economic agents. In this approach, in fact, 'inflation is explained by normative values, that is pay norms, customs, equity and justice. These norms have an impact on the perception of what is a fair relative wage, a fair real wage, and a fair profit share. They do have an impact on both the wage–price spiral and the wage–wage spiral' (Lavoie, 1992, p. 379). Indeed, a crucial concept introduced by Rowthorn (1977, pp. 216–17) is the so-called 'aspiration gap'. It indicates that what the parties to the wage bargain think to be just or right – on account of the set of value judgements referred to earlier on – does not always correspond to the wage structure actually obtained (see also Hicks, 1955, p. 390; Chowdhury, 1983, pp. 649–51; Lavoie, 1992, pp. 378–85, for similar restatements of the same idea). Overall, the share of national income that workers obtain in the wage bargain may be inconsistent with the targeted mark-up set by the firms' pricing policy on the product market. 'It is in this sense that inflation is produced by conflict over income distribution' (Palley, 1996, p. 186). More precisely, as stated by Burdekin and Burkett, 'implicit or explicit conflict over distributive shares is the fundamental basis of a rising price level, which in turn "resolves" the distributional conflict (albeit only artificially and momentarily) *via* the nominal inflation of the income available' (Burdekin and Burkett, 1996, p. 1). This is tantamount to saying that inflation, here traditionally perceived as an ongoing increase in the general price level, is the escape valve for inconsistent claims over social income (Dawson, 1992, p. 29). Or, using Davidson's phraseology, '[i]nflation is always and everywhere a symptom of the struggle over the distribution of income' (Davidson, 1991, p. 92).[27]

Similar ideas stem from the Kalecki–Weintraub analysis of income distribution within the national economy (Kalecki, 1971; Weintraub, 1978). This analytical framework has the merit to put forward a plausible explanation of income distribution in the aggregate, as it has some relevance to a causal analysis of price formation in the retail sectors (where firms' mark-up policies can determine the profit share realised on the product market). However, as Skott notes with cogency, the (Kaleckian) conflict theory of distribution – which lies behind the CIA – 'is based on microeconomic reasoning which cannot be extended to the macroeconomic level' (Skott, 1989, p. 40). In fact, a change in the functional distribution of income, as the one resulting from a modified bargaining power between firms and workers, does not modify the amount of national income existing in the period under examination. If it is likely that the real wage and profit shares claimed, respectively, by workers and capitalists are inconsistent, and that current income distribution is the outcome of the relative strength of each class on the factor market as well as on the product market, this 'class struggle' can modify, even marginally, neither total available income nor the money–output relationship established by the monetisation of current production. In other words, it is undeniable that there exists a close relationship between retail prices and income distribution, and that this relation can affect both the level and the 'organic composition' of future production. But this does not imply that a change in the functional distribution of income can lead to the formation of an inflationary gap, that is, a disequilibrium between total demand (that is, national income) and total supply (national output). 'A change in the distribution of national income only gives rise to zero-sum transfers: what some agents gain is lost by others' (Bradley and Gnos, 1991, p. 177; our translation).[28]

To take but a stylised example, let us refer to the situation described by Rowthorn (1977, p. 219), which may be illustrated as follows. Imagine a well-organised working class, WC, with strong trade unions capable of bargaining for very big wage increases.[29] We already know that reference to labour productivity cannot provide a theoretical benchmark in order to assess whether or not the wage-push is of an inflationary nature: the product being measured by the wage bill, an increase in the amount of the latter does not alter the relationship between money and output and therefore it must never be confused with inflation (since in the case at hand no disequilibrium between total demand and total supply can ever be observed in reality). As seen above, the increase in money wages merely is a change in the measurement scale of national output, which identically affects national income at one and the same time. Next suppose, always following

Rowthorn's example, that successful oligopolies, SO, dominate the product market. Owing to the SO's position of dominance, capitalists may pursue an aggressive mark-up policy designed to gain a very high share of profit on the market for the goods produced by the WC they employ. Rowthorn's conclusion epitomises the CIA's one and is worth quoting in its entirety.

> Thus, on the one hand workers are strong in the labour market, whilst on the other capitalists are strong in the product market, and as a result there is a major inconsistency between the two levels of decision-making: workers use their power to obtain big wage increases, whilst capitalists respond with price increases. The aspiration gap is in consequence very large and there is a high rate of unanticipated inflation (Rowthorn, 1977, p. 219).[30]

This last conclusion turns out not to be correct, if we define inflation as a macroeconomic disequilibrium between total demand and total supply (and not simply as an increase in the targeted price index). Surely, any decision by firms to rise prices on the product market may shift income distribution in favour of capitalists – *ceteris paribus*. Yet, the decrease in the wage-earners' income share (with respect to the outcome of the wage bargain) cannot be considered as signalling the presence of an inflationary gap, anticipated or not by the various categories of economic agents. As we recalled several times already, total demand exerted by income holders (whether households or firms)[31] cannot be modified by income redistribution; neither can the total supply of current national output. Any increase in money wages is in fact a numerical redefinition (via the wage bill) of the wage-earners' output newly produced, and any increase in the selling price of the latter does not affect the relationship between money and output, although it may of course give rise to a higher profit share for the firm(s) (see Gnos, 1998, pp. 44–5). 'Defined as that part of income that consumers [wage-earners in the present context] transfer . . . to firms, profit does not bite into the purchasing power of money at all' (Cencini, 1995, p. 52).

Unfortunately, a number of post-Keynesian authors seem not to consider this important fact yet. They set aside the analysis of money and output – and of their macroeconomic relation established by effective demand –[32] and seek to explain inflation by the conflict over the functional distribution of income. Dalziel (1990) is explicit on this point: 'The model [he proposes] is stripped of all unnecessary detail (for example, . . . money) to highlight the underlying mechanism that allows inflation to resolve income distribution conflict' (Dalziel, 1990, p. 426). Palley (1996) is another typical example. In line with Sidney Weintraub (1978), he 'suggests that incomes policy, which is designed to reconcile the conflicting claims of workers and firms, is a superior policy [in respect of traditional monetary and fiscal policy measures designed to curb inflation]' (Palley, 1996, p. 199).

Now, the incomes policy called forth by the CIA stresses incidentally that monetarism not only is an anachronistic theoretical construct; it is also bound to lead domestic policy makers into a dead end, because controlling the money supply cannot limit agents' claims for a higher share of national income. From the CIA's standpoint, the more the money supply is restrained (to try to counter demand-side inflationary pressures), the more the individuals' income claims on available output may be inconsistent in the aggregate. Both in relative and in absolute terms, the struggle for each unit of income would, in fact, become sharper the fewer money units are in existence. Yet, by emphasising functional income distribution and especially conflicting claims on total saleable output, the post-Keynesian approach seems to be grounded ultimately on the same fundamental, quantity-theoretic hypothesis on which monetarists have built their theory. More precisely, the theory of conflict inflation embodies the neoclassical dichotomy between the stock of money and the stock of output – as overtly embraced by Rowthorn (1977, pp. 235–6), who starts in fact from the basic quantity equation when discussing the role of money within the CIA (ibid., p. 230). Indeed, it cannot be denied that in any CIA-based model 'the inflationary gap is still fundamentally considered as an excess in the quantity of money over the physical volume of goods and services' (Bradley et al., 1996, p. 128). In this framework, using the CIA's own language, inflation involves an excess of money-income claims on available output, and 'must be conceptualized as the difference between *aggregate* real income claims (expressed in monetary terms as the total nominal value of contracts comprising the income side of GNP) and real income' (Burdekin and Burkett, 1996, pp. 13–14).

On the whole, one may therefore conclude that all those theoretical approaches seeking to explain inflation by social conflicts over the distribution of income among functionally distinct (classes of) economic agents suffer from the same conceptual problems of their monetarist alter egos (see Part Two). The alternative offered by the CIA's theoretical framework lies indeed between (1) a theory of inflation *à la* Dalziel (1990), where money plays such a passive role that it is (or can be) abstracted from when measuring macroeconomic magnitudes (like total output), and (2) a theory of inflation *à la* Burdekin and Burkett (1996), where money plays a more active role because it can exist independently of national income (see Rowthorn, 1977, pp. 229–30). The first point of view suffers from totally neglecting the essential role that banks play in a monetary production economy.[33] The second theoretical standpoint relies instead on a partial – if not superficial – understanding of this role, which to the best of our knowledge has never been dealt with (not even in passing) in the voluminous conflict inflation literature. Both urge on a deeper money and banking theory to inform the analysis of inflation. As we shall see in the next section, the bank credit mechanism could have in fact a part to play in the explanation of the formation of an inflationary gap, that is, a disequilibrium between total demand and total supply of current output.

Before turning our attention to this important topic, on which much research is needed (particularly at a time when speculation activities in financial markets represent an increasing share of total transactions),[34] let us attempt to consider the problem of income distribution and inflation within the theoretical framework used in this book. It will be seen that an increase in retail prices induced by inflation (on the assumption that an inflationary disequilibrium has been created by some yet unexplained mechanism) shifts income distribution in favour of capitalists, since it increases the profit share. It will also be seen that no price–wage spiral can actually be considered as a cause of inflation. The conclusion will be a restatement of the fact that price–wage spirals can in no case modify the relationship between money and output.

Let us consider a very stylised macroeconomic model and assume that the class of workers as a whole, WC, faces the class of capitalists as a whole, CC. Suppose that, as a result of the wage bargain, WC is remunerated with 120 macro-units of money for the total production of the current period. We already know that output as a whole is measured by the total wage bill paid out by firms for its production. So, the 120 macro-units of money have the necessary and sufficient power to purchase total current output. Two points need to be addressed at this stage, the first with respect to the conflict approach briefly investigated above, and the second in connection with the problem of inflation that we shall explore in the remainder of this book.

Let us imagine that CC seeks to obtain 25 per cent of total income as monetary profit of the period. To this end, CC sets retail prices on the product market higher than the corresponding factor costs, marking them up by the targeted profit rate (25 per cent). For instance, an item whose production cost is 20 pounds has a selling price of 25 pounds. Overall, on the assumption that each and every good is put on sale at a retail price 25 per cent higher than its factor cost, the expenditure of the whole amount of nominal wages (recorded in the form of a sum of bank deposits) enables WC to obtain only 75 per cent of total current output, since to buy the latter altogether an amount equal to 150 macro-units of money would have been necessary (in the case at hand no other deposits exist apart from those formed in the remuneration of the current production factors). If we analyse WC's expenditure of 120 on the product market, we can observe that 75 per cent of it covers the production costs of output sold,[35] the remaining 25 per cent being a transfer of income in favour of CC. By marking-up the selling prices of current output, CC is able to capture a monetary profit (24 macro-units of money) whose purchasing power is exactly defined by the stock of yet unsold output. On the whole, the income created on the factor market (120) is partly destroyed on the market for produced goods and services (96) and the rest is captured by firms as their monetary profit (24).[36]

Now, suppose that, owing to inflation, there is a general increase in prices (ultimately, this is the symptom-based definition of inflation). Applied to the stylised example investigated above, this means that output is sold at a higher price than in the previous case. Assume therefore that the very same output as above (worth 120, since 120 is the sum total of the wage bill paid for its production) is now put on sale at a price of 180 (instead of 150). Assuming that workers decide to spend their whole remuneration (120) on the product market, we can observe that this expenditure enables them to obtain a lower share of total output than before. To wit, WC gives up a sum of bank deposits equal to 120 to obtain in exchange goods and services whose production costs amount to 80 only. In fact, the share of real wages with respect to total income (120) is reduced by the inflationary rise in retail prices, to the benefit of the profit share captured by CC on the market for produced goods and services. In the case at hand, 40 units out of the 120 spent by WC are captured by CC as monetary profit, the rest (80) covering the production costs of sold output. Although this result is identical to the one arrived at by conflict theorists in terms of functional income distribution, it differs from the latters' result in so far as the causal link between income distribution and inflation is concerned. Conflict theorists would probably argue that the struggle for the distribution of national income elicits an inflationary rise in prices (setting forth a price–wage spiral), because the functionally distinct categories of agents cannot agree on the relative shares of total output. The approach adopted in this book suggests instead that an inflationary rise in prices (whose origin has yet to be explained) shifts the current functional distribution of income in favour of capitalists, CC, thus reversing the causality between income distribution and inflation put to the fore by the CIA. It need not be underlined here that this reversed causality also challenges the symptom-based definition of inflation introduced in Chapter 1, and adopted by conflict theorists, because at the analytical level it is no more sufficient to define inflation by its effect on prices.

It is particularly in an attempt to study an alternative paradigm for inflation analysis that we shall devote the remainder of this book to investigating the monetary macroeconomics of inflationary disequilibria. Given the importance of this problem, we hope that our attempt will arouse the interest of the academic as well as the policy maker, and prompt further research in monetary analysis for an inflation-proof economic system.

BANK CREDIT AND INFLATION

As some very rare 'Monetary Keynesians'[37] such as Victoria Chick, Hyman Minsky and Paul Davidson have pointed out, the credit facilities provided by commercial banks to the economy may be granted beyond the level that would ensure monetary equilibrium. In other words, the relationship between money and output might be affected by an excess of bank credit, which would thus contribute to the inflationary rise in goods and assets prices in actual markets. Linking the conflict inflation approach to the real bills doctrine,[38] Davidson (1988, pp. 166–8) maintains that the banking system can theoretically provide support to, if not generate, inconsistent claims on available output. More precisely, when he states that wage increases might be granted beyond changes in (average) labour productivity, Davidson holds the banking sector as co-responsible for the issue of so-called 'inflation bills'. As he puts it, '[a]ny healthy banking system apparatus which meets the needs of trade can be subverted to create an elastic currency of "inflation bills" rather than "real bills"' (Davidson, 1988, p. 167). So much so, that, in the view of Burdekin and Burkett, 'Post Keynesian models of the endogeneity of the stock and velocity of credit-money with respect to firms' money wage bills are really particular specifications of the monetary accommodation of excess income claims' (Burdekin and Burkett, 1996, p. 33).[39]

The monetary accommodation (by banks) of excess, or inconsistent, income claims is thus considered an inborn feature of endogenous-money systems, and must therefore be pursued further here in order to assess its macroeconomic character in respect of inflationary pressures.

Excess Credit Facilities and Inflation: a Reconsideration

In the face of 'endogenously changing financial practices' (Palley, 1996, p. 219), microeconomic theories of bank behaviour have been continuously revised, and improved, to account for those phenomena related to the bank intermediation process.[40] As a matter of fact, since the rapid development of liability management,[41] banks in general have been inclined to lend, following a policy of aggressive expansion of their balance sheets, each time the new credit facility is deemed profitable for their business strategy (Chick, 1986, pp. 115–18). Recently, in a series of papers, Howells (1995; 1996; 1997; 1999) has depicted this state of the art very clearly. He namely points out with cogency that what Davidson describes as 'needs of trade' (see above) are not the exclusive causal factor of bank lending.[42] 'Certainly the idea that new bank lending originates solely with firms and reflects their production plans now seems very naive' (Howells, 1996, p. 113). The relative increase in speculation, and hence in total spending, with respect to the value of current output is indeed a reality of modern capitalist economies which can no longer be denied.[43] Howells's conclusion 'is that bank lending results in a monetary expansion that may be quickly accommodated by multiplier-assisted increases in income, or it may not' (Howells, 1995, p. 96). In simple terms, if the new loans granted by banks are not associated with goods and services newly produced, the question Howells forcefully raises is to determine whether or not the 'deposits created by essentially speculative activity have any impact on the economy, different from the impact of deposits created in the wake of production' (Howells, 1996, p. 113).

In order to explore carefully the macroeconomic significance of this concern, let us analyse a stylised example of excess credit. As in Howells's work, let us focus on agents' borrowing to purchase second-hand housing assets, although any kind of speculative (that is, purely financial) demand for loans will do here. For the sake of exposition we shall assume that a single deposit bank represents the whole network of commercial banks, and that the bank-accommodated demand for loans exceeds by 10 per cent the deposits corresponding to, and resulting from, the monetisation of current production. There are no pre-existent deposits. So, if a worker (or any income holder, IH, if we allow for income redistribution within the economy) asks for, and obtains, a bank loan in order to purchase a second-hand housing asset whose price exceeds the worker's (or the income holder's) deposit, in bookkeeping terms the situation may be represented as in Table 5.1.

As explained in Chapter 4 (see, for instance, Table 4.3), the first double entry (1) is the result of the monetisation of the worker's current output, which occurs at the level of, say, 100 money units according to Keynes's principle of effective demand illustrated earlier on. Current income holders, IH, thus have a purchasing power of 100, saved in the form of a bank deposit until consumption takes place.[44] Now, if the bank were to grant a credit of 10 to current income holders (for instance, to our worker) for, say, a house purchase (see Howells, 1997, pp. 431–2), entry (2) would be recorded in the bank's bookkeeping as soon as the purchase is made.[45]

Table 5.1 A speculation-led excess of bank credit

Bank			
liabilities			assets
(1) Worker (IH)	100	Firm	100
(2) Seller	110	Worker (IH)	100
		Borrower	10

Yet, maintaining that for any bank loan there is a corresponding deposit is only saying the obvious fact that any double entry affects identically, at one and the same time, the assets side and the liabilities side of a balance sheet. As a result of the payment, in fact, the 10 units of money borrowed by the bank's client are instantaneously deposited by the seller of the house, who will have to choose the form in which he prefers to hold his wealth (expressed by a sum total of deposits equal to 110).[46] If he decides to buy existing and/or newly issued financial assets, the corresponding deposit is transferred to some other unspecified agents, who will then face a similar choice. Be that as it may, the 'last holder' of the deposit will spend it on the market for produced goods and services, so that, in our stylised example, 110 units of money will be used to purchase the very same output the production of which gave rise to a (wage-earners') deposit of 100 – in this example, no other output is available for purchase.

Assuming, to simplify what does not affect analysis, that total current output (worth 100) is sold at a price of 110 to the 'last holder' of the deposit which results from the credit granted to the borrower, the corresponding transactions are recorded as in Table 5.2. Entry (3) records the purely financial transaction between the seller of the house and another client of the bank, C (the 'households buy from households' case in the words of Howells, 1997, p. 431). It depicts the fact that the seller's liquidity preference leads him to buy some kind of financial assets from another household. Entry (4) records instead the result of the 'households buy from firms' case (ibid., p. 431), and epitomises the consumption of current output (sold at a mark-up over its production costs).[47] The overall result is that the firm makes a profit (10) because of the presence of a net borrower within the economy; this might lead one to infer that an inflationary pressure has been generated by the bank's excessive lending. In other words, there is an excess of aggregate demand, caused by too much money chasing too few goods.

Table 5.2 The macroeconomic result of excess credit facilities

Bank			
liabilities			assets
(1) Worker (IH)	100	Firm	100
(2) Seller	110	Worker (IH) Borrower	100 10
(3) Client C	110	Seller	110
(4) Firm	110	Client C	110
Firm	10	Borrower	10

The observed increase in output prices (and hence the firm's 'windfall' profit) should be sufficient proof of the likely consequences of the 'passing around' of 'extra-money', using De Vroey's (1984, pp. 384–9) language which we shall consider later on. To quote Howells again, '[u]nless *everyone* has an overdraft, unwanted deposits may continue to circulate. It is precisely this that gives rise to those repercussions on prices, quantities, of goods, assets or whatever' (Howells, 1995, p. 94).

The worries raised by Howells are legitimate, and certainly deserve careful attention by all those concerned with income distribution among economic agents. We indeed already noted in passing that the functional distribution of income has a close link with economic growth, too.[48] We may even claim that the latter is probably path-dependent on the former. Surely, purely financial transactions cannot generate economic growth, that is, additional income, but only transfer existing income among the parties (both in space and time). Only production can give rise to a net income within the national economy as a whole. This book, however, does not focus on economic growth. Nor does it focus on the distribution of income. It aims in fact at investigating the origin and cure of inflation, as well as at evaluating (as a by-product) recent monetary research, theory and policy.

So, to focus on inflation, we have to concentrate attention on 'the inflationary potential of a banking system on which there appear to be few constraints' (Chick, 1986, p. 122). As pointed out by Chick, '[t]he banks' aggressive lending activity may contribute to inflation' (ibid., p. 123), because the balance between assets and liabilities in the banks' accounts is not sufficient to prevent excessive credit to be granted.[49] Moreover, the widespread use of liability management and the pursuance of credit policies inspired by this business strategy have further enhanced the lending power of commercial banks, which have no innate structural device to prevent the financial bias towards inflation (ibid., p. 124).[50] All this, indeed, should be worrying enough to consider attentively the nature of credit-induced deposits with only a remote link to production. In short, is this superfetation of bank credit definitively inflationary for the national economy? Is the firm's profit (equal to 10 in the above example) irremediably inflationary, because it is due to an over-emission of money? Are income holders alienated, because their deposits are allegedly spoiled by the banks' sales- or profit-maximisation policies beyond a kind of notional threshold determined by the income-generating finance process *à la* Davidson (1988)?

Certainly these concerns are justified, in so far as they highlight the fact that the relationship between money and current output could be altered by excess bank credit. However, from a fundamentally macroeconomic point of view, using the Schmitt terminology[51] their object may be assigned the label of 'benign inflation', in the precise sense that this kind of alteration of the money–output relationship is not irreparably inflationary. In other words, the inflationary effect of excess bank lending is not cumulative in time. Let us attempt to explain why, referring to the stylised example made above.

When a borrower is granted credit, he actually engages himself to repay the loan back at the due date (inclusive of any interest payment agreed upon). The bank's recording of this loan in the assets side of its balance sheet testifies that the borrower relinquishes simultaneously a financial claim, perhaps by simply acknowledging his debt, that is, by endorsing the loan agreement in front of the banker. Now, what is the final object of the claim disposed of by the borrower and recorded within the bank's assets? This claim is a title to a future income that the borrower will earn and pay back into the lending bank. Indeed, as Cencini argues, 'the working of our banking systems is such that overdrafts of private banks are reduced to an advance' (Cencini, 1995, p. 62). As such, the monetisation by banks of borrowers' claims, as in entry (2) in Tables 5.1 and 5.2, does not irremediably modify the relationship between money and output. The increase in existing bank deposits entailed by the advance of a borrower's future income will be matched, in fact, by a correspondingly identical reduction of money income when the borrower reimburses the bank.

The importance of this argument is likely to impel us to prove our conclusion further, or more firmly. Consider the consequence of the loan repayment for the macroeconomy. When the excess of bank credit (which we know to be an advance of future income) over the value of current real goods falls due (say, in period n), the borrower has to surrender an equivalent part of his period-n income.[52] Clearly, if the loan granted in period 1 must be repaid in period 2, a period-2 income has to be transferred from the (period-1) borrower to the bank.[53] And when the reimbursement of an outstanding bank loan occurs, an equivalent deposit is simultaneously extinguished; a destruction also noticed by Howells, when he claims that '[o]nly actions that cause *repayment* of loans cause a reduction in deposits' (Howells, 1995, p. 100). Now, there is no real need to illustrate this destruction in bookkeeping terms, to infer that the reduction in (for instance) period-2 deposits amounts to an identical decrease in total demand. In fact, since any demand can only be exerted through an expenditure of bank deposits,[54] destruction of the latter *ipso facto* reduces current demand by the same amount. So, whilst in period-1-like cases total demand may be increased by excess bank credit such as to create an inflationary gap, in period-2-like situations this gap is compensated by a disequilibrium of the opposite algebraic sign, total demand falling short of the level established by the monetisation of current (that is, period-2) production. 'Hence, even if we claimed that private bank overdrafts are a cause of inflation since they modify the relationship between money and current output, we would have to add that the discrepancy between demand and supply which it causes is not seriously worrying, for it is bound to be compensated for in the following periods' (Cencini, 1995, p. 63).

This conclusion may be strengthened by three different arguments, each of them stressing the benign character of 'credit-led' inflation. Firstly, '[a]t any particular time, existing loans are being repaid while new loans are being demanded' (Howells, 1995, p. 90). Today's monetary production economies are indeed so complex that in any period of time new credit facilities are provided simultaneously with the repayment of outstanding loans,[55] 'so that the positive gap between demand and supply caused by bank overdrafts is normally balanced in each single period by an equivalent gap of the opposite sign' (Cencini, 1995, p. 63). The very large number of commercial banks operating within modern domestic economies is further guarantee that no serious inflationary threat can come from the bank credit mechanism: whilst some banks might grant an excess of credit in respect of the same banks' deposits, some others may lie behind or even encounter excess reserves.[56] Secondly, '[m]ost of the time the excess of credit granted by a bank leads to it becoming indebted to another bank, a situation which banks try to avoid as much as they can' (Cencini, 1996, p. 29). The ongoing multilateral clearing of interbank debts in the central bank's accounts is indeed a very efficient, and highly developed, mechanism aimed at minimising any excess of credit a single bank may grant over any particular period of time. Referring the reader interested in a macroeconomic analysis of modern interbank settlement systems to the work of Cencini (1995, pp. 31–46), let us very concisely note here that even the alleged lender-of-last-resort function taken on by the central bank has no inflationary bias when properly understood (Rossi, 1998, pp. 44–50). Inasmuch as commercial banks foster the distribution of income among the non-bank public without modifying the money–output relation, the central bank has no way to act but as a mere go-between in the interbank market. Being analogous to chemical catalyses, central bank's interventions within the national banking system neither do nor can affect domestic monetary equilibrium. Carried out on behalf of the reporting deposit banks, these interventions never really lead to inflation, because at worst they serve to advance a future income which will be destroyed when the corresponding output is formed. Thirdly, advances of income via the banking system (that is, commercial banks and the central bank taken as a whole) are beneficial to economic growth. They accelerate in fact the sale of current output, enabling firms to cover their production costs (either by restoring their working capital or by repaying bank loans), and thus prompting an expansion of activity. The positive influence of this mechanism on the level of employment, and growth, is rather straightforward to infer in this case, so that the identifier 'benign inflation' should be definitively justified to characterise the topic of this subsection. To put it clearly, 'speculative' bank lending may be a cause of inflation since it affects the relationship between current output and money. But any inflationary gap elicited by an excess of bank credit is destined to be absorbed by a disequilibrium of the opposite algebraic sign when these excessive loans are reimbursed, that is, when bank deposits are reduced by loan repayment.[57] In a nutshell, benign inflation is not cumulative in time.

Yet, the reader attentive to the rhetoric of the argument may eventually wonder if there also exists a kind of 'malign inflation', whose wording sounds already much more threatening than its altogether beneficial compeer. We need therefore to turn our attention to this problem: the remainder of this book should indeed be regarded as an attempt to dig out a fundamentally unexplored ground in inflation analysis (monetarist as well as Keynesian).

Inflation: Is There Any Macroeconomic Harm?

So far, excessive money emission has been associated with the bank credit process supporting agents' exchanges of goods, services and financial assets. Each time a bank grants a credit *ex nihilo*, that is not based on past or actual production (as in the real bills doctrine), it might put monetary equilibrium at risk, inasmuch as the extra amount of deposits thus formed adds to the stock necessary and sufficient to circulate current output. Yet, as we have seen, the inflationary bias of this phenomenon is not cumulative in time and is quite restrained in space also. In fact, credit-led inflation calls forth its own absorption within the macroeconomy. So much so that focusing on the evolution of assets and commodity (aggregate) prices over time can provide no relevant insight into the analysis of the pathological, irremediable alteration of the money–output relationship.

To develop the latter analysis, therefore, neither 'the state of trade' ('*Py*') nor the amount of total monetary transactions ('*PT*') can be a fruitful object of investigation. Expressions *Py* and *PT* subsume indeed exchanges occurring between items which exist simultaneously in the personal endowments of the contracting parties.[58] Since any exchange is identically a sale and a purchase for both parties, no disequilibrium between supply and demand can logically be conceived of, either at the disaggregate or at the aggregate level, at any point in time. In so far as attention is focused on exchange, the very concept of excess demand that underlies the inflationary gap is therefore going to lie outside the explanatory power of economic theories. As we have observed earlier, in fact, the distribution of income – hence of output – both in space and time, can have no inflationary bias at all in the whole economy. This means that the conflict view of, and the accommodative approach to (potentially) inflationary phenomena need to be replaced, ultimately, by a macro-theoretical analysis of the process by which money income is formed. In a nutshell, in order to discover the origin of macroeconomic disequilibria in the money–output relationship, production rather than distribution ought to be the focus of analysis.

The above argument amounts to the proposition that there is no analytical bridge between either *Py* or *PT*, on one side, and *Y*, on the other side (see Schmitt, 1972, pp. 15–56, for a logical demonstration that income is not a price). Both *Py* and *PT* are of a microeconomic nature and are directly related to an exchange economy. They imply aggregating prices into a particular price index, *P* (see Part One for a critique of this method). As such, they include transfers of income or profits earned by entrepreneurs at the expense of consumers (Keynes, 1930/1971, p. 301). And it need not be recalled here that no aggregation of microeconomic magnitudes can be interpreted as a macroeconomic outcome. Per contra, *Y* is a macroeconomic magnitude from its very formation. It pertains to a monetary economy of production. More precisely, as noted earlier, it is the measure in terms of the wage bill of the output newly produced (see Gnos, 1998).

Now, whilst it is impossible to find a gap between total demand and total supply as they can be observed in the whole national economy (recall the previous exploration of Keynes's principle of effective demand), it is nevertheless possible to conceive of a macroeconomic disequilibrium within the action whose result is the fundamental identity of income and output. This claim might appear quite extraordinary at first. We need therefore to focus attentively on the very process by means of which income (and output) is formed. In other words, we have to investigate the realm of flows, as opposed to the analysis of stocks changing hands within the national economy, before taking up the inflation problem again. Indeed, to repeat it, the object of a macroeconomic analysis of inflationary pressures must be production, not circulation, for those interested in discovering where the origin of these pressures lies.

When we get right to the core of the analysis, we observe that the formation of income, that is, the creation of the relation between money and current output in the banks' bookkeeping, is essentially an exchange of flows.[59] In Chapter 4 we already noted that payments on the factor market are absolute exchanges: workers abandon their product in kind, to receive it in the monetary form issued by banks. Thus, money intervenes within the flow of production, and not only when output has already been formed and is exchanged on the goods market.[60] As pointed out by Schmitt, '[m]oney creation and production of commodities are one and the same action' (Schmitt, 1984, p. 450; our translation).[61] In fact, the measure of output as a whole (which is given by the total wage bill of the relevant period, let us emphasise it) is established by the substitution of the real flow of goods and services with the monetary flow of nominal wages, at the precise instant when the wage bill is paid. So, 'instead of producing real goods directly in their physical form, the economy produces real goods in the monetary form' (ibid., pp. 458–9; our translation).[62]

Now, provided we distinguish money from income, only a small analytical step is necessary to draw a first important conclusion (which in Chapter 4 had been left implicit on purpose). Income, or the power to purchase the output newly produced, is the result of the exchange taking place on the factor market between the monetary flow (money) and the corresponding real flow (production). It is because the payment of the wage bill does not necessitate a pre-existent income that it has a positive-sum result for the economy as a whole. The income newly generated is a macroeconomic magnitude in the exact meaning of the term, for the income earned by workers is lost by nobody else. It is true that firms obtain the newly produced output when paying out the current wage bill. But they match their increase in stocks (+) with an identically equivalent increase in their financial indebtedness (–), either to their own wages fund or to the banks. Ultimately, their gain is zero on the labour market.[63] Workers, on the other hand, are the exclusive owners of total current output at the very instant the wage bill is paid, and in fact their gain is positive for the entire 'working class' as well as for the whole economy. In the language of Schmitt, '[r]emunerations of factors of production are *negative* expenditures both for the firms and their employees' (Schmitt, 1996a, p. 137). In other words, negative expenditures are income-generating for the national economy as a whole.

According to this line of thought – which some authors have traced back to Keynes –[64] expenditures on the market for produced goods and services are then objectively positive for all economic agents. This implies that, 'irrespective of the observer, such expenditures are . . . *income destroying* . . . for the national economy and for the whole world' (ibid., p. 137). Therefore, considered from the point of view of society as a whole, the link between money and output established by the remuneration of production factors is definitively severed by income expenditure on the product market. In particular, in so far as the deposits formed in the payment of the wage bill are expended for the purchase of the corresponding output, firms can cover their factor costs by balancing the debt originated in the labour market with the deposit obtained on the market for produced goods (see Cencini, 1988, ch. 6). Income formation (that is, production) and income destruction (consumption) are taken indeed in a macroeconomic circuit by the circular flow depicted by effective demand, as we have already noted in Chapter 4.

Yet, at this stage, the reader may be somewhat puzzled, if not irritated, by the exclusion of profits from the preceding analysis. This exclusion is only apparent. Our previous investigation of income distribution and inflation should have provided a case where profits are explained by the circular flow of nominal wages between firms and workers, linking the factor and product markets. The macroeconomic analysis developed by the Schmitt school shows in fact that profits are subsumed under the production–consumption process described earlier in terms of the circuit of income (see Sadigh, 1988; Gnos and Schmitt, 1990). It may be useful to recall here that profits are an income that wage-earners, or, more generally, income holders transfer to firms on the product market (via the mark-up price mechanism). More precisely, the amount of bank deposits transferred from the buyer to the seller of newly produced goods and services that exceeds the corresponding factor costs is not destroyed in the economy. It persists in the banks' accounts and represents the firms' profit. Hence, firms always have the purchasing power necessary and sufficient to acquire the whole physical output defining the real content (that is, the substance) of their monetary profit.

Now, granted that income redistribution on the product market cannot alter the relationship between money and output, that is, monetary equilibrium, one has to consider what are the likely consequences if firms do not spend their profit on the market for produced goods and services. In fact, firms may well decide not to consume their profit, that is, they may want to invest it instead of distributing it to their shareholders. If so, then firms can invest their profit either (1) on the financial market or (2) in the production process. When the firms' profit is invested on the financial market, 'at the end of the chain' there will always be a seller of financial assets who consumes his earnings in the purchase of the output corresponding to the firms' profit. This case is therefore not interesting here, for logically no discrepancy between total supply and total demand can thus be detected in the whole economy. To be true, from a macroeconomic point of view the firms' investment of profit on the financial market is not an investment at all. It is consumption, since the substance of the firms' monetary profit is finally consumed by an unidentified seller of financial assets. This case is therefore similar, ultimately, to the consumption of redistributed profits by the firms' shareholders and entitled agents. We are thus left with the investment of profit on the factor market, an issue whose macroeconomic implications are far from simple to investigate and to deal with, as we shall see.

Let us try to set out the conceptual framework of our analysis, to be developed later.

It is well known that a firm's payment of current factor costs does not necessarily give rise to a proportional increase in the firm's debt to the banking sector. It can and is in fact much likely to be nourished (in part) with a pre-existent profit, that the firm invests on the labour market for a new production. 'But then the payment of wages becomes a twofold operation: monetisation of new production on one side, and expenditure of pre-existent income on the other' (Cencini, 1995, pp. 73–4). Such a twofold operation can be represented in terms of the macro-objective distinction between negative and positive expenditures described in Figure 5.1. As is shown in Figure 5.1, an income-generating expenditure may include an income-destroying expenditure. For instance, a payment of a wage bill equal to 100 pounds could be financed up to 10 per cent (say) by accumulated profits and 90 per cent by new bank loans.

Now, to focus on the issue of immediate interest, it is important to observe that the expenditure of a firm's profit on the factor market gives rise to an anomalous result. This anomalous result does not arise because of the immediate consequences of this operation on capital accumulation (which may be altogether beneficial to growth and employment). It arises because the actual recording of this expenditure in bank accounting leads to the emission of what one may define as 'extra-money' (De Vroey, 1984) or, more properly, as 'empty money' (Schmitt, 1984; Cencini, 1995; 1996; 1999). To the extent that it pays the current wage bill out of pre-existent income, the firm in fact purchases its workers' activity (hence its result also), 'so that workers are effectively credited with a sum of "empty" money' (Cencini, 1996, p. 53), that is, with an amount of deposits to which no new saleable output corresponds.

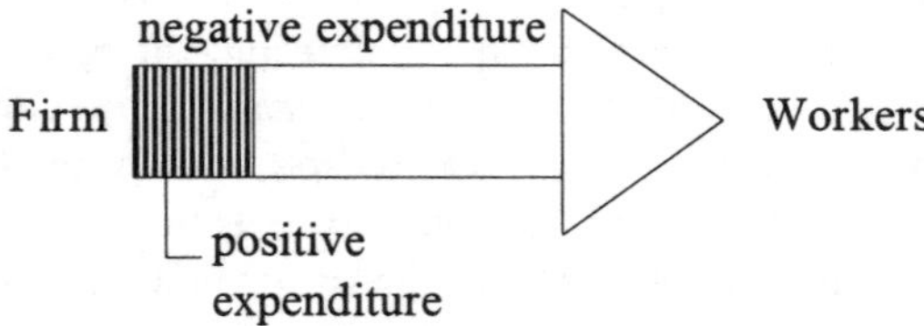

Figure 5.1 Inclusion of a positive expenditure into a negative expenditure

Let us consider a simple numerical example to try to illustrate the problem further. Suppose that in period 1 a firm makes a profit equal to 10 pounds, say by marking-up its products' retail prices. Were the firm to redistribute this profit (to its share or equity holders, or even to the general government sector in payment of taxes), the latter would ultimately be used up for the final consumption of period-1 yet unsold output. The fact that there exists an unsold output matching the newly formed profit cannot be overlooked.[65] If this profit is redistributed, no discrepancy between total supply and total demand could ever be detected in the economy, for such a gap would not really exist, as we hope to have established by now. It is therefore the firm's 'productive consumption' of (invested) profit that ought to be of interest to those aiming to study, and hopefully manage, actual inflationary pressures. So, let us focus on the new production set up by the firm's investment in period 2. By investing its profit on the factor market, the firm acquires a new capital good through the very same payment of its production costs (equal to 10 pounds in the example at hand). Assuming that the firm's production in period 2 gives rise to a total output measured by 100 money units (as resulting from the corresponding wage bill), 90 per cent of the latter units are deposits of 'full' money. Still more precisely, 90 money units out of 100 have the power necessary, and sufficient, to purchase the whole stock of goods and services newly produced in period 2 (a stock worth 90 pounds because of the firm's purchase (10) on the factor market). There is nevertheless a remaining 10 per cent of money units which, although created in the same income-generating finance process (to use Davidson's phrase), have no real object in terms of current saleable output. Investment of the firm's profit on the labour market removes in fact the corresponding output (10) from the newly formed deposits at the very instant workers obtain their remuneration, so that the measure of the new production remains numerically unchanged (100) but its actual object is reduced *ipso facto* (to 90). In Schmitt's own words, '[t]his withdrawal leaves *money* wages unaltered but decreases their purchasing power' (Schmitt, 1984, p. 208; our translation).[66]

In summary, as we shall see more in detail in Chapter 6, when a pre-existent income is consumed by an income-generating expenditure, the present payment structure of our monetary production economies brings about an anomalous, and paradoxical, outcome. Although total supply and total demand are identically equivalent as measured by the wage bill, total demand implies a sum of empty money that elicits a pathological disequilibrium between money and current output. With respect to the previous example, this paradox can be restated in numerical terms as follows (figures relate to period 2).

- Total supply and total demand are both equal to 100, since 100 is the amount of the wage bill paid out to workers for the new production, in strict adherence to the principle of effective demand described earlier. The newly produced goods and services elicit a wage bill of 100, which is their precise measure and defines at the same time an identical amount of wage-earners' bank deposits.
- Total supply and total demand are not equal, because, at the very instant of its formation, output is curtailed by the firm's purchase occurring on the factor market. Receiving a sum of bank deposits numerically equal to 100, wage-earners really obtain overall only 90 units of purchasing power – before any mechanism of income distribution may come into play on the product market.

Surprisingly enough, the disequilibrating exchange between the monetary flow and the real flow does not impinge on its actual outcome, that is, identical demand and supply in the economy as a whole. However, although total supply and total demand are equal in 'constant money' (that is, in terms of purchasing power) at any point in time, there is also an excess total demand in 'current money' (Schmitt, 1972, p. 156; Gnos and Schmitt, 1990,

p. 68; Bradley et al., 1996, p. 133). Indeed, the numerical value of total demand (100) differs from its real value (90) because of the investment of the firm's profit on the labour market, an operation that *ipso facto* reduces the purchasing power of income holders at the instant the latter income is formed. The paradox of a disequilibrium within an identity is thus explained when it is shown that '[a] part *p(r)* of output is sold *before any expenditure of national income [on the market for produced goods and services]*' (Schmitt, 1988, p. 192); income and output being the two identical terms of the macroeconomic relation resulting from the new production process, where an accumulated profit equal to *p(r)* is invested.

Some authors have rooted this approach in Keynes's *Treatise on Money*, and in particular in his analysis of 'profit inflation' (Keynes, 1930/1971, chs 10–11).[67] In the *Treatise*, in fact, Keynes seeks the explanation of inflation in the essence of capitalist economies, that is, in the investment of profit in the production process. More specifically, Keynes's message points out that 'profit inflation' originates in a new production of investment goods or, as he puts it, in a production of new investment goods (Keynes, 1930/1971, pp. 135–8). As a matter of fact, by '[f]inancing the production of investment goods with a pre-existing profit, the firms create an excess demand in real goods' (Bradley et al., 1996, p. 122). Restated in modern terminology, Keynes's path-breaking analysis indicates therefore that inflationary disequilibria do not arise simply because too much money chases too few goods, but fundamentally because a part of the newly produced output is definitively not for sale to income holders, although it is included in the measure of current national income.

Stated in its most troublesome terms, this conclusion amounts to the proposition that the result of the blending between income-generating and income-destroying expenditures on the factor market 'is that the goods corresponding to the net investment of profit are no longer in the economic possession of income holders' (Cencini, 1996, p. 54). As Schmitt pointed out, it is because investment goods become the definitive property of '*a "non-person", [that is] the set of the country's disembodied firms*' (Schmitt, 1984, p. 208; our translation),[68] that the emission of empty money leads to an irremediable monetary disequilibrium.[69] Were the new capital goods, that is, the goods produced via the investment of profit, entirely owned by 'embodied' firms (that is, their share and equity holders), the economic system would not suffer the malignant disorder elicited by the present recording of capital accumulation in the banks' bookkeeping. In particular, any income that wage-earners are at present deprived of on the factor market would be distributed to other categories of economic agents, without such a distribution being a possible inflationary phenomenon (as recalled many times already). So much so, that, at any point in time, shareholders and entitled agents would own the entire stock of accumulated capital,[70] for which a one-to-one relationship between its financial and material aspects would absolutely exist in the economy.

It is particularly to the attempt at working out a structural monetary framework capable of achieving such a correlation between the two aspects of real capital that the next chapter will be devoted, after a more in-depth analysis of the consequences brought about by the emission of empty money just sketched here.

NOTES

1. 'Post Keynesian economists maintain that the conventional method of analysis, what has been labelled the neo-Walrasian code, has only limited power to encompass the essential macroeconomic phenomena of money, uncertainty and time and thus has only limited ability in explaining macroeconomic problems as high unemployment, persistent inflation and severe financial crises. The Post Keynesian code is the alternative to the neo-Walrasian code' (Fontana, 1999, p. 174).
2. What is a unit of output? How is it to be established in economics? Clearly, one cannot abstract from money when trying to answer these questions (see Chapters 3 and 4).
3. The title of the *GT* was indeed meant to be *A Monetary Theory of Production*, a title Keynes chose for his contribution to the 1933 *Festschrift für Arthur Spiethoff* (Keynes, 1933/1973).
4. See also Wray (1999, p. 14), who remarks that the choice of units is of fundamental importance to discover essential properties and relations in the macroeconomy. As we shall see later, it is a pity that 'Keynes' proposal on measurement of labour has been ignored by all subsequent macroeconomic schools' (Desai, 1995a, p. 347).
5. This is the Sraffa (1961, p. 305) problem mentioned in Chapter 3 (see note 37). Theoretical measures require absolute precision, because any imperfection in them knocks down the whole theoretical basis.
6. Physical heterogeneity also concerns the physical measure of labour (that is, the measure of output in terms of labour-time). As we shall see later, Keynes (1936/1973, p. 41) noted that the physical measure of labour can be made homogeneous by reverting to its monetary measure, that is, the workers' remuneration. See note 9.
7. Carabelli (1992, p. 23) observes that Keynes does not explain why money is homogeneous. She thus puts forward a tentative explanation based on an analogy between the role of money in the economic process and the role of ordinary language in present-day societies. However, as pointed out by Bradford and Harcourt (1997, p. 129, n. 16), this analogy is forced and unnecessary. Since money as such is nothing but a number, issued by the banking system as an asset–liability, each unit of money is essentially identical to any other unit of money (existing at the same time), for their origin and nature are the same. £1 today is fundamentally identical to any other £1 existing at the same date, no matter of the support (material or immaterial). The exchange at par on the interbank market is further proof of the uniformity of money units existing at the same time.
8. Given the fundamental importance of this question, it is a pity that '[n]o economist – Keynesian, post-Keynesian, neoclassical or new classical – has paid any attention to Keynes' discussion in chapter 4 of the *General Theory* as to how to measure employment'

(Desai, 1995a, p. 353). As we shall argue, those rare economists who have considered Keynes's choice of units have done so on purely exegetic grounds, that is, within the rather orthodox boundaries of the *GT*. They have thus been trapped (an opportune word) within the confines of a basically neoclassical, exogeneity-of-money view.

9. 'For, in so far as different grades and kinds of labour and salaried assistance enjoy a more or less fixed relative remuneration, the quantity of employment can be sufficiently defined for our purpose by taking an hour's employment of ordinary labour as our unit and weighting an hour's employment of special labour in proportion to its remuneration; *i.e.* an hour of special labour remunerated at double ordinary rates will count as two units' (Keynes, 1936/1973, p. 41). On this point, Keynes seems to have gained analytical insight in the transition from the *Treatise* to the *GT*. In fact, when in 1930 he devised the 'earnings standard' as the measure of what he called 'the labour power of money', he noticed that '[t]he chief obstacle in the way of computing this standard is to be found in the difficulty of finding a common unit in which to compare different kinds of human effort' (Keynes, 1930/1971, p. 63). At that time he thus was probably looking for a kind of average wage index, built ultimately on the same conceptual grounds as those on which aggregate price indices were, and still are, established (see Keynes, 1909/1983, pp. 60–1). See also note 14.
10. 'In practice the best we can achieve – even if we can achieve that – is to take as our index of the labour power of money or earnings standard the average hourly money earnings of the whole body of workers of every grade' (Keynes, 1930, p. 63).
11. As Carabelli observes, '[a] complex object needs a complex theory. . . . The problem of the choice of the appropriate units of quantity and of measure [of output as a whole] is the link between these two aspects of theory, that is, object and method' (Carabelli, 1992, p. 19).
12. 'Finalement, le *nombre* des unités de salaires émises est la *mesure* du produit de l'économie' (Schmitt, 1984, p. 458).
13. Note that labour is the sole factor of production because only the remuneration of workers elicits wage-units, whose total amount defining the current wage bill is the economic measure of all produced goods and services (inclusive of profit goods). 'So stated, this result seems to be very similar to the classical (pre-classical in Keynes' own terms) theory of value. In fact, it differs from it on a small but very essential point: the monetary measure of labour. According to the classics, labour is measured in physical units, whereas Keynes' basic unit is a monetary one. Wages are then the objective link between money and product, a link that is the direct result of the process of creation called production. Two main difficulties never overcome by the classics are thereby avoided, namely the physical heterogeneity of labour and the integration of money into the real world' (Cencini, 1982, p. 134).
14. That this may be so can also be deduced from a short passage taken from Chapter 10 of the *Treatise*, where Keynes defines 'The fundamental equations for the value of money'. In so doing, he proposes to 'choose our units of quantities of goods in such a way that a unit of each has the same cost of production at the base date; and let *O* be the total output of goods in terms of these units in a unit of time' (Keynes, 1930/1971, p. 135). Stated more clearly and in the language of the *GT*, this may amount to saying that the wage-unit is the measure equal to one unit of the production costs of current national output. Indeed, the same claim can also be found at the beginning of Chapter 18 of the *GT*, where it is stressed that national income is measured in wage-units (Keynes, 1936/1973, p. 245).
15. In other words, the value of each good is determined by the corresponding wage bill. The same is of course true for services (that is, 'invisible goods').
16. Rogers notes that 'the principle of effective demand emerges as the key element in a monetary theory of production in the [Schumpeterian] tradition of Monetary Analysis' (Rogers, 1989, p. 178).
17. 'Effective demand is the point of intersection of two curves; it is thus as much a supply as a demand, indifferently one or the other, *identically*' (Schmitt, 1988, p. 183). See also Chick (1983, p. 65) and Lavoie (1985, pp. 135–7).

18. See Schmitt (1972) for an analysis of virtual magnitudes and of their importance for income determination.
19. This does not mean that full employment is always attained, or that this approach applies exclusively to a Say's Law, real-wage economy (in the traditional interpretation of this law), as maintained by Lavoie (1987, p. 87). Recent works by Schmitt (1984; 1996b) and Cencini (1995; 1996; 2001) concentrate on structural issues associated with capital accumulation and income distribution that show how unemployment situations can in reality arise out of a yet imperfect bookkeeping framework used by the banking system to keep track of monetary transactions. More on this later.
20. As we shall see later on, some critics of this framework have raised concern with the conception of the period of production adopted in this approach (Deprez, 1989, p. 203), based on the frequency used to pay out wages, as well as with the idea that output is saleable when the wage bill is paid out (Graziani, 1985, p. 139). This framework appears to them as being unable to supply a theoretical explanation of those cases where a good (for example a Boeing 777) needs several production periods, defined as above, in order to be manufactured and put on sale on the market for produced goods and services. These cases have been explored by Schmitt (1984, pp. 94–105), who explains how financial claims issued by firms substitute the corresponding fraction of produced output in any period where output has not yet been completed physically.
21. Of course, any physical object (say, a light bulb) produced in period 1 might generate a higher wage bill when produced in period 2, thus conveying the impression of the existence of an inflationary pressure in the latter period. Yet, this is just an illusion. As we shall see in the second section of this chapter, an inflationary disequilibrium can only come into being by an excessive number of money units associated with the same output (that is, output of one and the same period). This is perhaps the most fundamental criticism of traditional inflation analysis, based as it is on the rate of variation of the targeted price index with respect to some reference period.
22. It has been argued by Lord Desai that this approach to monetary phenomena 'is still an equilibrium one and leaves one very little room for disequilibrium dynamics' (Desai, 1988, p. xiii). This criticism is linked to the functional isolation of each production period from any other (Deprez, 1989, p. 204), since in this framework there is no functional link between periods. As a careful reading of Schmitt (1984) will show, however, the approach developed in this part is not dynamic but 'quantic' (see Realfonzo, 1999, p. 377); it is in fact based on quantum time, in contrast with either continuum or discrete-period analysis. See the Conclusion for more details.
23. 'Il est vrai sans doute que le progrès des équipements permet à l'économie nationale d'introduire de plus en plus de biens dans la forme-utilité; mais le produit prend la mesure de la forme et non inversement; il s'ensuit que le progrès technique et l'accumulation des moyens de production sont incapables de multiplier les *produits* en leur sens exact: une plus grande diversité et un plus grand nombre de biens sont compris dans un produit inchangé. . . . [L]e produit est mesuré en unités de salaires; or la multiplication et le perfectionnement des moyens de production sont des actions neutres quant à l'émission des salaires' (Schmitt, 1984, p. 495).
24. Let us refer to a Robinson Crusoe economy in an attempt to convince even the most doubtful reader. Suppose that the production of shirts (by W) represents the whole production of a given, very small, national economy, both in period 1 and in period 2. National income is therefore measured by 100 money units in either period, since the wage bill generated in either period is equal to 100. But so is national output too, because the production of the whole economy has given rise to a total output associated – through the payment of the wage bill – with 100 money units (which, needless to say, may be distributed in such a way that, ultimately, the wage-earner, that is, W, can purchase only part of total output, the rest being the firm's profit elicited by the marking-up of retail prices). The fact that the number of physical objects subsumed by the money wages is

greater when technological change is enhanced does not affect the fundamental conclusion of our analysis (though it affects, of course, the level of consumers' personal satisfaction).

25. This is not to say, of course, that prices are not going to vary over time. In fact, if in period 1 W's output (10 shirts) was sold at a retail price (x) that possibly covered – if not exceeded – factor costs (100 pounds), in period 2 the same worker's output (30 shirts) will probably be sold at a retail price (x', with x' > x) that also covers the increased production costs (110 pounds). Any price index analysis would thus be likely to conclude that an inflationary pressure exists in period 2, since the level of prices could be driven upward (on the *ceteris paribus* assumption) by the increased price of shirts. Note however that this is not sure yet. In fact, the shirt's production cost has decreased, from 10 to $3^2/_3$ pounds, which may induce an analogous decrease in its retail price. As Hicks observed, 'in a modern economy, what has normally to be expected is rising productivity; and rising productivity, combined with constant money wages, means falling prices' (Hicks, 1955, p. 395). This may also illustrate the well-known fact that profits can rise while prices go down, for prices can decrease less than the decrease in unitary costs. However, a macroeconomic analysis based on the choice of units to measure output as a whole would show that the increase in prices must not be confused with the birth of an inflationary gap between total supply and total demand. 'The variations of productivity as well as the variations of cost give rise to a price variation but with no consequence to the purchasing power of money because the public will always receive in the aggregate amount of income the power to purchase the entire product' (Bradley et al., 1996, p. 117).
26. This claim is however a matter of debate among CIA advocates. Dawson states that '[t]he conflict theory can be seen as combining demand pull and wage push factors, either one being capable of instigating the inflationary process (or price–wage spiral) but the interaction of both being required for its development' (Dawson, 1992, p. 26). By contrast, according to the author of *Foundations of Post-Keynesian Economic Analysis* (whose Chapter 7 provides a skilful discussion of conflict theory), '[i]nflation is not the result of an objective scarcity. . . . The influence of demand is only an indirect one. . . . Inflation is cost-led' (Lavoie, 1992, pp. 377–8). See also Burdekin and Burkett (1996, p. 33) and Smithin (1997, pp. 400–1).
27. When monetarism was still in vogue, Davidson used to claim that '[t]he distribution of income is both a cause and a consequence of inflationary processes' (Davidson, 1972/1978, p. 347).
28. 'Une modification de la répartition du revenu national ne met en œuvre que des mouvements à somme nulle: ce que gagnent les uns est perdu par les autres' (Bradley and Gnos, 1991, p. 177).
29. CIA literature often refers to this case as productivity-led wage increases, although the latter increases may also result from a rapid increase in the firms' profits or in the demand for skilled labour (Hicks, 1955, pp. 398–401; Kaldor and Trevithick, 1981, pp. 17–18; Lavoie, 1992, p. 415). It is indeed easier for trade unions to ask for wage increases in technological-improving industries. Note also that trade unions cannot ask for a reduction in retail prices, since the latter involve several elements apart from factor cost.
30. According to Rowthorn (1977, p. 215), were inflation (correctly) anticipated by all concerned agents, it would have no redistributive effect, for then everyone would take advance measures to allow for future price increases.
31. For the sake of brevity we abstract here from the general government sector.
32. Chick's monetary analysis is a noteworthy exception. See Chick (1982; 2000).
33. Morishima (1992) and Realfonzo (1998) analyse several examples of this neglect in twentieth-century economic theory.
34. See Howells (1999) and Howells and Hussein (1999).
35. Since in this numerical example prices are 25 per cent higher than production costs, a part of total output worth 96 (as measured by the corresponding wage bill) is sold at a price of 120. By selling it at a marked-up price, CC is therefore able to cover the relevant

production costs (96) and to gain a profit (24) on top of that.

36. See next chapter for an investigation of the link between income distribution and capital accumulation.
37. We borrow this felicitous expression from Desai (1989, p. 172; 1992, p. 120). It echoes the Monetary Analysis approach that Schumpeter (1954/1994, pp. 276–88) used to oppose to Real Analysis. A brilliant exposition of both approaches can be found in Rogers (1989).
38. The real bills doctrine has been traced back to Adam Smith's *Wealth of Nations*, where one can read that 'a real bill of exchange [is] drawn by a real creditor upon a real debtor, and . . . as soon as it becomes due, is really paid by that debtor' (Smith, 1776/1970, p. 402). As Green notes, 'echoes of the real bills doctrine reverberate in modern monetary theory' (Green, 1987, p. 101). This is essentially because money emission is traditionally understood as if it were an exchange between a bank's IOU and a non-bank 'bill', which may be backed by 'titles to real value or value in the process of creation' (ibid., p. 101), or it might not. See Sargent and Wallace (1982) and de Boyer (1998, pp. 65–7, 74–5).
39. See also Burdekin and Burkett (1996, p. 14).
40. See Screpanti (1997) for a recent attempt to work out a structural theory of endogenous money from a microeconomic point of view, where 'the core business of bank activity is identified in the transformation of generic risk' (ibid., p. 567).
41. 'Broadly speaking, liability management refers to the ability of banks to increase their lending activity by borrowing funds which appear on the liability side of their balance sheet, without having to dispose of their marketable assets – mainly treasury bills' (Lavoie, 1992, p. 212). See Moore (1989, pp. 13–20) and Goodhart (1989a, pp. 30–2) for a discussion on the importance of liability management in the evolution of modern banking.
42. See also Howells and Hussein (1998; 1999).
43. As Keynes already observed (partly quoted in Howells, 1999, p. 105), speculative transactions 'need not be, and are not, governed by the volume of current output. The pace at which a circle of financiers, speculators and investors hand round one to another particular pieces of wealth, or title to such, which they are neither producing nor consuming but merely exchanging, bears no definite relation to the rate of current production. The volume of such transactions is subject to very wide and incalculable fluctuations, easily double at one time what it is at another, depending on such factors as the state of speculative sentiment; and, whilst it is possibly stimulated by the activity and depressed by the inactivity of production, its fluctuations are quite different in degree from those of production' (Keynes, 1930/1971, pp. 47–8). See also Chick (1994).
44. Recall that when consumption occurs, income holders spend their deposits and thus extinguish the firm's debt, which was recorded either towards the bank or with respect to its own wages fund (working capital). In either case the firm is able in fact to cover on the product market the previously disbursed factor costs.
45. As Keynes (1930/1971, p. 42) remarked in *A Treatise on Money*, one ought to bear in mind that the amount of a customer's unused overdraft does not appear anywhere at all in a bank's statement of its assets and liabilities.
46. It is worth while to emphasise here that this subjective choice is necessarily subsequent to the deposit automatically formed at the very instant the payment is made.
47. Note that in both entries (3) and (4) client C might also be a firm, selling financial claims in order to purchase other firms' output. Within the time-dimensional sequence depicted by entries (2) and (3), we would therefore experience the case where 'households buy from households and lend to firms' (Howells, 1997, p. 431).
48. Several authors have studied the relationship between inflation and growth. See the survey paper by Driffill et al. (1990) and Barro (1996).
49. A similar point has been raised by De Vroey in connection with unsuccessful business ventures, when he maintained that the endogeneity of money is 'not a sufficient guarantee of the eventual correctness of private money creation decisions' (De Vroey, 1984, p. 388). See also Smithin (1997, pp. 397–8), who emphasises the role of bank credit for

consumption purposes (beyond the need for the firms' initial finance). On the concept of 'initial finance', and its link to 'final finance', see Lavoie (1987, p. 69) and Graziani (1990, pp. 14–16), who elaborate on Keynes's (1937) *Economic Journal* finance motive. See also Chick (1996, p. 14) for the importance to distinguish 'finance' from 'funding'.

50. See also Minsky (1975, pp. 121–4).
51. See Schmitt (1984, pp. 192–8).
52. This does not imply that the borrower is the original holder of the income used to reimburse the bank. It might well be the case that this income has to be borrowed from period-n income holders. In this case, the borrower once again anticipates a future (period $n+m$) income, so that there simply is a substitution of due dates, leaving the overall situation unaffected. In what follows, we assume therefore that the borrower can repay his debt in period n with no further commitment, since the opposite hypothesis is not germane to the present analysis.
53. This is the link that money provides between the present and the future, as noted by Keynes (1936/1973, p. 293). More recently, Minsky (1994, pp. 154–5) has reasserted the link that financial relations provide between the past, the present and the future, enabling deficit-spending units to consume today what they will earn in the future.
54. Recall that bank notes and coins are the material representation of a bank deposit, to wit, a deposit in central bank money.
55. See Arestis and Howells (1999, p. 118).
56. Theoretically, if all deposit banks acted together to grant, overall, excessive credit, then inflation would exist until the latter excess is absorbed by the borrowers' reimbursements. However, as we shall see in the remainder of this subsection, this highly hypothetical case is very unrealistic in modern banking.
57. Needless to say, this does not exclude that in reality a new inflationary gap might arise out of the new loans granted by the banking system at precisely the same time when the previously granted loans are reimbursed. It is this continuum of newly granted bank loans that makes it 'empirically' impossible to observe the absorption of benign inflation.
58. In this theoretical framework, an illustration of this phenomenon is the exchange between total output and the existing money stock on the market for produced goods and services. See Chapters 3 and 4 for a fundamental critique of this view.
59. By contrast, output circulation is an exchange of (pre-existent) stocks (see also previous note).
60. This is essentially a restatement of the most fundamental critique of the quantity-theoretic approach to monetary production economies, as discussed in Part Two.
61. 'La création de monnaie et la production de biens sont une seule et même action' (Schmitt, 1984, p. 450). In English, 'each monetary flow and the corresponding real flow are the two components of one and the same "motion"' (Schmitt, 1996b, p. 96).
62. '[A]u lieu de produire les biens réels directement sous leur forme physique, l'économie produit les biens réels dans la forme monétaire' (Schmitt, 1984, pp. 458–9).
63. In fact, the firms' profit is realised on the market for produced goods, as we have seen in the discussion of the conflict inflation approach (see previous section).
64. See Cencini (1988, ch. 4) and Gnos (1992a, Part Three).
65. This output can be viewed as the wage-earners' forced saving. In fact, workers have no alternative but not to consume the part of total output corresponding to the income that firms capture on the product market by the mark-up of prices.
66. 'Ce prélèvement laisse les salaires *monétaires* intacts; il ne diminue que le produit dans les salaires monétaires' (Schmitt, 1984, p. 208).
67. See Friboulet (1985a; 1985b; 1988), Schmitt (1988) and, more recently, Bradley et al. (1996).
68. '[U]ne "non-personne", l'ensemble désincarné des entreprises du pays' (Schmitt, 1984, p. 208).
69. If the investment 'pays off', the output newly produced with the capital goods resulting

from profit investment will be associated with new money units, as these units are issued in the new, periodic payment of factor costs. The 'initial' emission of empty money will thus never be absorbed, and the inflationary gap born in the investment of the firm's profit will be irremediably pathological indeed.

70. Notice that ownership does not imply location. Share and equity holders can own instrumental capital which is located with firms, and serves their production plans.

6. Inflation and Fixed Capital Accumulation

In Chapter 5 we observed that inflation is a macroeconomic disequilibrium, that is, it affects the relationship between money (total demand) and output (total supply). To acquire an understanding of the macroeconomic nature of inflationary pressures, we explored the production process, instead of focusing on the exchange of goods already produced. More precisely, we set off the investigation of profit investment on the factor market (that is, capital accumulation) as an alternative direction for monetary research into the inflation problem. This chapter seeks to forge ahead this line of investigation, first put to the fore by Schmitt (1984). In particular, it attempts to point out that the most serious consequences of the emission of empty money on macroeconomic equilibrium occur when the fixed capital accumulated in the whole economy is replaced within a monetary structure of payments not fully complying with the fundamental rules of non-inflationary bank money. This theoretical analysis is therefore not only fundamentally macroeconomic; it is also monetary, because it focuses on the financial capital invested in the means of production.

To introduce the reader to this macro-monetary analysis of inflation, let us say from the beginning that, in this framework, the problem of inflationary pressures is related to the process of accumulation in a capitalist economy, which in reality may occur in an orderly or in a disorderly way. To avoid any possible misunderstanding, let us stress that order and disorder refer to the manner in which the accumulation of fixed capital, that is, profit capitalisation, is recorded in the banks' bookkeeping. The agents' forms of behaviour are not at stake here.[1] In other words, it is not the behaviour of the different categories of economic agents that can account, ultimately, for the disequilibrium between money and output existing in a national economy. As Cencini states, 'the relationship between money and output can be pathologically modified by a simple accounting mechanism that does not pay sufficient attention to the banking nature of money and to its functional link with production and circulation' (Cencini, 1995, p. 70). In short, the accumulation of capital may take place in a bookkeeping structure of banks' accounts that mechanically respects the distinction between money, income and fixed capital (order), or in an accounting structure that does not (disorder).[2] An example of structural monetary disorder has been explored in Chapter 5, when we discussed the problem of an excess of bank credit (that is, benign inflation). Centred on output circulation, that example showed that inflation may result from a book-entry structure which does not enable banks to distinguish between money emission and financial intermediation.[3] Yet, a further, and more worrying, analytical case must be investigated, a case where the focus of analysis is on production rather than on exchange of commodities already produced. As Schmitt (1984) pointed out, (malign) inflation originates in the production process; in particular, in the production of amortisation goods destined to replace fixed capital. It is to this complex, and difficult, object of inquiry that we turn next, in an attempt to carry on the investigation of empty money started off in the last section of Chapter 5.

EMPTY MONEY AND INFLATION

As noted in Chapter 5, profit investment on the labour market elicits empty money. It is because the payment of the wage bill out of a pre-existent income entails a compensation of their amounts in banks' balance sheets that current period wage-earners are credited with a sum of empty money, that is, with nominal income deprived of purchasing power over current output. Reasserted in these terms, it should be clear that the emission of empty money cannot be imputed to any form of economic behaviour. In particular, the firms' investment of profit is not to blame, and the formation of the latter is indeed definitely legitimate. As has been stated by Cencini, '[t]he anomaly lies with a mechanism inappropriate to the nature of money, with a monetary structure still defective, and not with the decision to invest profit more or less productively' (Cencini, 1995, p. 89). Despite the very high banking standards existing in present-day payment systems, which aim to ensure both the efficiency and the stability of the whole financial system, there exists a yet unnoticed discrepancy between the actual working of the monetary structure of payments and the principles of modern money. More precisely, since the wage-earners' remuneration and the capitalisation of profits are recorded today in the same 'department' of the banks' bookkeeping, the pathological birth of empty money cannot be avoided in actual facts. As we shall see later, an improvement of the book-entry structure of bank accounting could eradicate the emission of empty money, leaving agents' forms of behaviour totally unaffected and completely free (subject to a set of moral values that any civilised society ought to have).

Yet, before putting forth some policy proposals aimed at improving the structural monetary framework of modern banking and payment systems, we need to refine the analysis of empty money. More precisely, we must further explore the link between empty money and inflation, which in Chapter 5 has just been proclaimed and not really treated yet.

Empty Money, Forced Saving and Fixed Capital

Let us start by recalling that profits are formed as consumers (that is, households) transfer to firms on the commodity market an income which exceeds the production costs of the goods and services purchased. In fact, whilst the households' expenditure on the market for produced goods and services is income-destroying for the whole economy to the extent that it enables firms to cover factor costs of the output sold, it merely conserves income for the amount exceeding the latter costs. Indeed, as the abundant post-Keynesian literature existing on this topic clearly shows, profits are elicited by the firms' mark-up of retail prices over factor costs. Now, it is a fact that any income captured on the commodity market entitles its holder to buy the corresponding goods (which define its objective substance), provided that the relevant production costs are entirely paid for. This is evident when profits are redistributed to, say, the firms' stockholders, who can thus consume what has not yet been purchased by original income holders (that is, wage-earners). To focus on the point at issue, it must indeed be kept in mind that the firms' profit is defined by, and corresponds to, what may be labelled the wage-earners' forced saving.[4] When retail prices are higher than the corresponding output's costs, the workers' income expenditure elicits a stock of wage goods which become in fact the firms' property. These goods literally are the substance of the wage-earners' forced saving of the current period. They define at one and the same time the real object of the monetary profit earned by firms on the product market. They thus represent the original form of capital, which can be invested in a new production process by 'productively consuming' the accumulated profit. As Schmitt puts it, '[c]apital goods, or investment goods, are not the primitive form of fixed capital; they are the secondary form, obtained by the "productive consumption" of the wage goods saved in the formation of the monetary profit' (Schmitt, 1984, p. 170; our translation).[5]

It is also possible to couch the same point in different terms, perhaps more familiar to the reader. By paying the wage bill out of pre-existent deposits (that is, accumulated profits), firms become the owners of the output produced through the investment of profit. As already noted at the end of Chapter 5, this output is purchased on the factor market at the moment it is formed. In fact, the corresponding wage bill is deprived of its real object (that is, the new investment goods) when it is paid out to wage-earners. The money units paid out to these wage-earners are literally and materially empty, because of the inclusion of an income-destroying expenditure into an income-generating expenditure (see Figure 5.1).

Yet, this complex operation is not inflationary in and by itself. In other words, the emission of empty money originating in the net investment of profit (on the labour market) does not give rise to a disequilibrium between total demand and total supply in the economy as a whole. In fact, as we have noticed, the formation of the firms' profit elicits an identically equivalent stock of goods, which are the wage-earners' forced saving. So much so that the monetary profit gained by firms on the product market has the power to purchase the goods yet unsold to wage-earners (or, more generally, to initial income holders). Hence, when the investment of profit occurs, the resulting sum of empty money has the purchasing power that corresponds to the wage goods accumulated when profit has been formed. Profit investment is, ultimately, the conversion of a stock of wage goods into a 'stock' of new capital goods (Schmitt, 1984, p. 166).[6] Deprived of the power to purchase the newly produced investment goods (because these goods are definitively acquired by firms on the factor market), the current period wage-earners thus have nonetheless the power necessary, and sufficient, to buy the accumulated stock of consumption goods which are the original form of retained profit. In Schmitt's own words, 'the money units issued in the investment of profit find ultimately a "body", that is, the wage goods saved within the process by which monetary profit is formed' (ibid., p. 190; our translation).[7]

Let us try to reconsider this process through a numerical example. In this analytical context, the period (1) when profit is formed may be distinguished from the period (2) when profit is invested and generates empty money. Suppose that the firms' mark-up pricing policy in period 1 allows them to earn a profit equal to 10 per cent of total households' current expenditure on the goods market. Accordingly, if original income holders spend an income of 100, the firms' profit is equal to 10. This means that households consume an output of 90 (because 90 per cent of their expenditure covers the production costs of sold output), and transfer an income of 10 to firms, which then have the power to purchase the equivalent output. Now, since profit is not consumed but invested, the latter output is not sold to period-1 income holders. It defines indeed period-1 forced saving, as we have already recalled. As a matter of fact, this profit is spent on the factor market, where it purchases labour and, consequently, its result. We need therefore to focus on a new production process, namely on the production of new capital or investment goods taking place, say, in period 2. When the latter production occurs, as we know, workers obtain a sum of empty money to the extent that the wage bill is paid out of pre-existent deposits. Remunerated with the firms' accumulated profit (equal to 10 in our stylised example), wage-earners literally obtain a non-income, or a sum of money units with no purchasing power over period-2 output. However, the stock of wage goods corresponding to the period-1 forced saving (necessarily equal to 10 in the case in point) is still available, for sale, in period 2. Hence, the amount of empty money generated by the firms' investment of profit acquires, ultimately, a real object. It has precisely the power to purchase the goods saved in the period when this profit has been formed. In a nutshell, '[p]aid by profits, workers obtain an empty income and, as a compensation, a claim over the wage goods saved by the previous transformation of wages in profits' (Schmitt, 1984, p. 215; our translation).[8]

On the whole, neither the formation of profit nor its 'productive consumption', that is, net investment, can affect monetary equilibrium. When profit is formed, total demand is identical to total supply, for no redistribution of income can impinge on the relationship between money and output (see Chapter 5). On the other hand, as we have seen earlier on, when profit is invested, the amount of empty money elicited by the remuneration of workers through an income-destroying expenditure on the factor market ultimately does not generate an inflationary gap in the economy either. To the extent that the wage goods accumulated when profit was formed take the place of the newly produced capital goods definitively acquired by firms, the current period wage-earners obtain in fact a money capital, that is, the primitive form of capitalised income. The monetary disorder called forth by empty money is thus not much worrying yet, because current period wage-earners automatically own a capital – in the form of the wage goods previously produced – in substitution of the income they were entitled to hold as a result of their remunerated activity in the investment goods sector. 'It remains true that period-2 production elicits empty money, but the latter is inoffensive because the capital goods instantaneously withdrawn from real wages . . . are exactly compensated by the wage goods [previously] saved' (Schmitt, 1984, pp. 205–6; our translation).[9]

Now, the presence of capital goods (for example machinery) in the economy requires their maintenance. Introduced by Keynes's 'Appendix on user cost' (Keynes, 1936/1973, pp. 66–73) – which the author of *The*

General Theory did not have the time to develop further – the macroeconomic investigation of fixed capital amortisation may be fundamental for the analysis of inflation. In so far as attention is focused on net investment, no disequilibrium between money and output can indeed be discovered in the whole economy, at any point in time (for, let us repeat it, the newly created empty money instantaneously acquires as its substance the wage goods saved when profit was formed). By contrast, as Cencini and Baranzini state, 'the production of amortisation goods plays a determinant role in explaining the possible discrepancy between total demand and total supply' (Cencini and Baranzini, 1996, p. 8). It is to the analysis of this production that we must now turn, in an attempt to explore the inflationary gap further and deeper. To be sure, the ultimate origin of (malign) inflation has yet to come to light. Our investigation has then to be carried on, if it aims to understand the efficient cause of the loss of money's purchasing power.

The Amortisation of Fixed Capital

As is well known, Keynes (1936/1973) defined by 'user cost', U, the cost incurred for the use of fixed capital and the production of replacement goods, that is, amortisation. To be true, as pointed out by Chick (1983, pp. 49–50, 91–2), Keynes's definition of user cost was broader than that, since it also included wear and tear of fixed capital not yet replaced and 'optimal maintenance', a forward-looking approach which we do not consider here. For the sake of argument we shall include in U only the production costs of replacement goods. In fact, this seems also to be the case for the bulk of existing literature.

Now, a quick look at the scarce literature on user cost shows that contemporary authors are not at ease with the macroeconomic dimension, and implications, of this difficult, and multifaceted, concept (see Torr, 1992, and the references therein). 'While it is rare to find a comprehensive discussion of user cost in the post-1936 macroeconomic literature, it seems fair to say that those expositions that have appeared have tended to concentrate on clarification of what Keynes meant by user cost rather than on development of the concept' (Torr, 1997, p. 144).[10] In particular, within the economics profession there seems to be unanimity for considering total output of an economic system net of aggregate user cost (see Keynes, 1936/1973, p. 67). To take only a recent, but important and authoritative, example, let us quote three significant passages from *A 'Second Edition' of The General Theory*, whose Chapter 8 is precisely on 'User cost'. Writing 'as J.M. Keynes', the author of the chapter states a generally undisputed point, namely that replacement goods (R) are nothing more than intermediate goods,[11] because they replace the fraction of fixed capital used up over the period under examination.

> User cost has one footing resting in microeconomics and the other in macroeconomics. . . . At the macro level, user cost must . . . be subtracted from total sales, since it is the cost of items used up in the production process and as such must not be included in the total of final consumption and investment goods (Torr, 1997, p. 133).

> User cost must always be incorporated in the analysis, at both the micro and macro levels. . . . [W]e take it into account at the macro level to ensure that our measure of total output does not include goods used up in the production process (ibid., p. 134).

> At the macro level we need to subtract user cost to arrive at a measure of the aggregate level of output and income. . . . If we do not do so, national income will include those goods used up in the production process.
>
> To arrive at the income for the whole economy, we need to take the total sales of all firms and subtract certain intermediate sales. User cost identifies which inter- and intra-firm transactions must be subtracted (ibid., p. 139).

In practice, if not in theory, most economists assert that the measure of output as a whole, hence national income determination, can be arrived at 'either by the method of subtraction ($Y = A - U$, where A is the sum of total sales of all firms and U is total user cost) or by the method of addition ($Y = C + I$)' (Torr, 1997, p. 140; brackets' content rendered explicit for the clarity of exposition). This statement is further reinforced by the allegation that '[t]he method of addition amounts to the same thing as the method of subtraction' (ibid., p. 134).

Now, 'the method of subtraction' does not pertain to macroeconomic thinking. In this framework, as we have noted in Chapter 5, no link can be conceived of between Y (production) and A (exchange): national income is smaller than A, for it includes only production costs (Schmitt, 1972, p. 109). In fact, the sum of total sales of all firms includes, by definition, the whole amount of profits, that is, that part of national income that firms can capture on the goods market by selling their products at a mark-up over factor costs. Further, since user cost has not to be mixed up with what Keynes (1936/1973, p. 53) defined as 'prime cost', U cannot be thought of as the analytical (or even merely arithmetical) difference between A and Y. We are thus left with 'the method of addition', if we really aim to avert any double counting. Yet, if all double counting must be disposed of, attention has also to be paid to counting everything. So, is it fundamentally correct to claim that the measure of national income, and hence of output as a whole, can be apprehended by the canonical expression $Y = C + I$? Still less enigmatically, from a macroeconomic vantage point would it not be necessary to write that $Y = C + I + U$, where U is the total value of replacement goods? As a matter of fact, to exist, amortisation goods have to be produced by current-period workers.[12] Ultimately, then, remuneration of the latter adds to the wage bill paid out by firms, thus counting for the determination of national income. As Schmitt points out,

> [i]n fact, the production of the goods which replace the fraction of fixed capital that is lost in the period yields goods that are *final* and not merely, as is generally thought, *intermediate*. . . . '[R]eplacement goods' exist in two distinct forms or definitions; this amounts to saying, curiously enough, that these goods belong simultaneously in the separate categories of intermediate and final goods (Schmitt, 1996b, p. 77).

As any economist or accountant knows, amortisation goods are intermediate goods, since they replace the fraction of fixed capital used up in the production process. This is also the empirical stance of entrepreneurs and, as such, it can be studied according to a microeconomic theory of the firm (see Davidson's 1987 dictionary article for references along that line). However, replacement goods are also final goods, since their production costs elicit a wage bill which logically enters into the macroeconomic measure of the output newly produced.[13] 'Replacement capital must be newly produced in each period; there is no difference in this respect between R-commodities [where R stands for replacement] and the other final goods, produced for consumption and investment' (Schmitt, 1996b, p. 95).

If this analysis is correct, then the value of replacement goods (U) has to be added to the value of C and I in national income determination, opening up a new avenue for both macroeconomic theory and research. More specifically, to focus on the problem of this book, the analysis of inflation takes on an entirely new dimension, since it has also to investigate the precise effect of fixed capital amortisation on the relationship between money and output. In this analytical framework, it may ultimately be possible to highlight the fundamental origin of inflation, which, as Schmitt maintains, '*is not a purely monetary disorder*; it is a pathology acting on money in its relationship with output: it thus affects both money and output' (Schmitt, 1984, p. 506; our translation).[14] In particular, the worrying pathology of (malign) inflation can be discovered by a macro-monetary analysis of the production of replacement goods, that is, the monetisation by banks of fixed capital amortisation. Certainly this is a topic which needs to be further investigated by our profession. Indeed, to the best of our knowledge, the monetary issues of fixed capital amortisation are still neglected in contemporary macroeconomic analysis. There thus seems to be a strong case for further research in this field.[15]

Without entering here into the technical details of the Schmitt analysis,[16] it must be emphasised that, according to the line of thought we adhere to, the inflation problem originates in a structural monetary disorder that up to now has framed the recording of fixed capital accumulation in the banks' bookkeeping. The macro-theoretical analysis developed by Schmitt (1984) and Cencini (1995; 1996) shows indeed that the production of amortisation goods gives rise to a set of book entries recorded in a still imperfect structure of bank accounting, that is, a monetary structure not yet fully in line with the fundamental requirements of bank money. It is because the amortisation of fixed capital is recorded in a yet too simple accounting structure of the banking system that a disequilibrium between total demand and total supply can occur in the economy as a whole. Eliciting a sum of empty money, in today's capitalist economies the production of replacement goods through the investment of profit increases total demand without identically increasing total supply. Whereas in the net investment of the firms' profit a pre-existent stock of commodities can ultimately 'fill the gap' – thus preserving the overall monetary equilibrium in the national economy – fixed capital amortisation is at present irremediably pathological, for total demand is definitively greater than total supply.[17] 'It is appropriate to say *irremediably* since, by contrast to the empty money elicited by net investment, the empty money obtained from the production of amortisation goods results in a sum of money units whose emptiness is not compensated at all; this time, no pre-existent wage goods are waiting to fill up the gap' (Schmitt, 1984, p. 223; our translation).[18]

In sum, the pathological nature of fixed capital amortisation is the concrete, and mechanical, result of a still partial discrepancy between the actual structure of the banks' bookkeeping and the essence of bank money, a discrepancy that elicits a sum of nominal income deprived of value, thus epitomising an excessive money supply. All in all, inflation does not occur because, as the famous phrase goes, too much money chases too few goods, but because the relationship between money and output established by the banks' monetisation of current production is instantaneously hampered by fixed capital amortisation. To be more precise, the actual monetary structure of payments is such that the production of replacement goods gives rise to an output instantaneously withdrawn from the set of saleable commodities, although the corresponding nominal wage bill adds to the sum total of newly formed income. To put it in the terms of Chapter 5, although total demand is identically equivalent to total supply in constant money, the former is greater than the latter in current money. There is an irreducible excess of demand on the product market because of fixed capital amortisation.

AN OUTLINE OF STRUCTURAL MONETARY REFORM

In this section, we shall attempt to polish up the solution of inflationary pressures put forth by Schmitt (1984; 1995–96) and Cencini (1996), who insist in particular on the necessity to spread monetary operations over three bank departments, functionally distinct in bookkeeping terms, to have an inflation-proof economy. In short, a structural reform of the bookkeeping framework within which banks operate is the sine qua non condition to make sure that any monetary transaction actually complies with the nature of modern money – independently of the agents' behaviour, let us stress it again. In other words, to avoid the generation of empty money, the working of the banking system must conform 'empirically' to the fundamental distinction existing between money, income and capital, so neatly articulated by Cencini (1995, pp. 70–4; 1999, pp. 139–42). For the sake of exposition it is worth treating the case of benign inflation first, so as to follow an order of increasing difficulty and to provide an explicit link with the subject matter of the last section of Chapter 5. The solution of malign inflation relies indeed on the same principles, and is ultimately a refinement, of the reform treated next.

On the Book-Entry Distinction between Money and Credit

Being the direct result of the banks' monetisation of the production process, excessive money supply (that is, empty money) might be thought of as depending on economic behaviour of the banking system as a whole. In Chapter 5 we observed indeed that bank credit may be granted beyond the level established by the relationship between money and current output. We also attempted to show, however, that credit-led inflation can never be so troublesome for the macroeconomy, since it entails a self-correcting process, namely credit reimbursement. Yet, to set the record straight, we may begin by addressing the issue of making sure that the emission of money is not confused, most importantly in practice, with a credit operation originating in banks. Still more precisely, since excessive bank loans originate in the 'empirical' mixing up of money and credit – a principal confusion also made in a number of theoretical approaches to money and banking, as shown elsewhere (see Rossi, 1998; 1999) – the solution consists in introducing a clear-cut, and operational, distinction between money emission and financial intermediation in the banks' bookkeeping.

As Ricardo clearly noted at the outset of his 1823 *Plan for the Establishment of a National Bank*, published in 1824 six months after his death, banks still perform two fundamentally distinct operations in the economy: they issue money and make loans to the non-bank public. Let us quote Ricardo.

> The Bank of England performs two operations of banking, which are quite distinct, and have no necessary connection with each other: it issues a paper currency as a substitute for a metallic one; and it advances money in the way of loan, to merchants and others.
>
> That these two operations of banking have no necessary connection, will appear obvious from this, – that they might be carried on by two separate bodies, without the slightest loss of advantage, either to the country, or to the merchants who receive accommodation from such loans (Ricardo, 1824/1951, p. 276).

Although applying his analysis to the central bank only, Ricardo correctly pointed out that the emission of money has neither conceptually nor in practice to be mixed up with the granting of credit by banks. As Keynes was also to distinguish in early drafts of his *Treatise on Money* (Moore, 1988, p. 195), the money-purveying function must be kept distinguished from the credit-purveying function, both in theory and practice. However, Ricardo certainly went too far when he claimed that these two functions bear 'no necessary connection with each other'. In fact, the creation of modern money requires that banks grant a credit to the economy. This complex operation, that is, a payment,[19] involves money's creation and bank lending in such a close relationship that the infelicitous expression 'credit-money' has often been used to stress that link. 'Yet, from an analytical point of view, these two operations are completely distinct: by creating money banks do not lend positive income to the public but a simple promise which becomes a net credit only when it is spent by its borrower' (Cencini, 1988, p. 65). In other words, as so often claimed by adherents to the so-called 'monetary circuit approach', the emission of money is the banks' spontaneous acknowledgement of debt to the economy. In this framework, Parguez and Seccareccia have recently noticed that 'money emerges *always* as a "debt" (or liability) issued by this third agent [that is, the bank] on itself' (Parguez and Seccareccia, 2000, p. 101). By this very action banks indeed do not lend anything, either real or nominal. They actually create money, that is, the numerical counter of any monetary transaction (as we have seen in Chapter 4). 'No creation is an intermediation. The reciprocal is also true: no intermediation is a creation. In fact, if banks lend an amount they borrow, they create nothing' (Schmitt, 1984, p. 303; our translation).[20] So, the book-entry distinction between money and credit is designed to put into banking practice the conceptual, and fundamental, distinction between money's emission and financial intermediation.[21]

Keeping within the limits of an outline, let us try to show how the creation of money and the granting of credit could be distinguished operationally in the banks' double-entry system of accounts. This distinction is not merely academic, as some practitioners might think at first, but has a direct, and important, implication on what, following Schmitt's (1984) work, we dubbed 'benign inflation', that is, the possibility for commercial banks to grant credit in excess of the existing deposits of the public.

To begin with, Table 6.1 is an attempt to illustrate the structure of the banks' bookkeeping that can avert credit-led inflation, although we noted in Chapter 5 that this kind of inflation does no irremediable harm, and may even be pretty useful to the economy in terms of growth and output sale.[22] Notice that the example at hand focuses on the payment of current production costs, to underline that any kind of loan implies an income – which is the result of economic activity, that is, production.[23]

Table 6.1 The bi-partition of the banks' bookkeeping[24]

Bank

Monetary department (I)

liabilities		assets	
(1) Department II	100	Firm	100

Financial department (II)

liabilities		assets	
(1') Workers	100	Department I	100

The first department, I, is in charge of money emission. The second department, II, records the newly formed income (which is in the form of a bank deposit).[25] Referring to the payment of the wage bill, department I must intervene to issue the monetary form of the transaction (say, 100 money units) – as asked by the payer (a firm in the case in point) –, once the credit-worthiness of the latter is considered acceptable by the bank's managers (entry (1)). Department II records instead the purchasing power generated by the monetisation of current production, which defines at one and the same time a new money income whose initial holders are workers, as recalled several times already (entry (1')). The accounting rule is universal, and its implementation mechanical.[26]

- For each payment, the payer is entered into the monetary department, for the bank issues a spontaneous acknowledgement of debt to 'count' the object of the monetary transaction.
- Simultaneously, the payee is entered into the financial department, since he holds a bank deposit, that is, an income saved in the form of a drawing right over current output.

Hence, monetary and financial operations always go together. They are in fact the two faces of the same reality, as we attempted to show in Chapters 4 and 5, and in much greater detail in Rossi (1998). The structural connection between the first and the second department in the banks' bookkeeping is therefore entirely in line with the nature of modern money. Without repeating the whole analysis elaborated in Chapters 4 and 5, let us merely recall here that wage-earners own an income (hence the qualifier income holders, IH) whose purchasing power is defined, exactly and objectively, by the newly produced output[27] (we abstract here from the pathological emission of empty money, which will be taken up again in the next subsection). Thus then, workers do not own a mere sum of money proper when they are remunerated for their labour services. The structural distinction between department I and II is in fact the translation in modern banking of the fundamental distinction between vehicular money and bank deposits (see, for instance, Figure 4.4). It is also the only operational way to distinguish a purely numerical form, issued by banks, from its real content, which must necessarily be provided by human effort (that is, production).[28]

So, let us now consider the time-dimensional sequence of bookkeeping entries epitomising the financial operations involved in the case of (say) a second-hand transaction in housing assets. This will enable us to provide an explicit link with the stylised example introduced while investigating credit-led inflation, in an attempt to show the fundamental difference when money emission and financial intermediation are kept separate in the bank's accounts (Table 6.2).

Table 6.2 Savings, the financial market and the two departments

Bank

Monetary department (I)

liabilities		assets	
(1) Department II	100	Firm	100
(2) Firm	100	Department II	100
(4) Department II	100	Borrower	100
(5) Borrower	100	Department II	100
(6) Department II	100	Seller	100
(7) Seller	100	Department II	100

Financial department (II)

liabilities		assets	
(1') Workers	100	Department I	100
(2') Department I	100	Firm	100
(3') Workers	100	Firm	100
(4') Seller	100	Department I	100
(5') Department I	100	Borrower	100
(6') Firm	100	Department I	100
(7') Department I	100	Seller	100
(8') Workers	100	Borrower	100

Entries (1) and (1') have already been explained above; they are simultaneous and epitomise the dual nature – monetary and financial – of any payment. Entries (2) and (2') define the transformation of the firm's monetary debt into a financial one by, say, the bank's end-of-day settlement protocol; they are recorded in the same instant, not necessarily contemporaneous with the first line of double entries.[29] 'Cancellation of first department entries derives from the purely vehicular nature of money, whose "mark" is financial and can be found in the bank's second department' (Cencini, 1995, p. 75). Entry (3') is the result of entries (1') and (2'): it shows that workers own an income (bank deposit) as a result of their remunerated activity by the firm, which has an identical debt for the financing of its newly produced stocks.[30]

Now, what happens if an agent whatsoever needs a bank loan to buy a second-hand item, say an housing asset?[31] At first thought, the bank is able to accommodate any loan request (upon provision, needless to say, of adequate credit-worthiness of the borrower), since up to now the only requirement for a bank to grant a loan has been to respect the 'golden rule' of double-entry bookkeeping: any entry on one side of the balance sheet has to be balanced by an equivalent, and simultaneous, entry on the other side (see Chapter 5).[32] It is here that the reformed structure of the banks' bookkeeping can avoid excessive credit to be granted, by separating the money-purveying function from the credit-purveying function. As pinpointed by Schmitt, 'without this separation, banks do not know the amount of savings deposited with them' (Schmitt, 1984, p. 311; our translation).[33] Indeed, as noted in Chapter 5, credit-led inflation is the result of an excess of bank loans with respect to the amount of savings. To repeat, any single bank can lend today an amount it literally creates *ex nihilo*, because of the lack of distinction between money and income (and, therefore, between money emission and financial intermediation) in our banking systems. The above structural bi-partition of the banks' bookkeeping is therefore necessary to make sure that the working of present-day monetary systems is consistent with the nature of modern money. 'The division of banks into two departments is thus very important to avert inflation. After the reform, each bank will know every day the exact amount it can lend, as is the case for a Savings and Loans fund. It will never be possible that the banking system as a whole can lend more than the savings it actually has' (Schmitt, 1995–96, vol. II, p. 33; our translation).[34]

In fact, only the income temporarily saved within the whole economy (which in the above example amounts to 100) may be lent to borrowers, if any anomalous alteration in the relationship between money and current output is to be prevented. So, to refer to the case at hand, if (and when) this loan is granted by the bank, the payment of the second-hand item gives rise to entries (4) and (4'):[35] entry (4) epitomises the fact that the payer has to be provided with the monetary form in which the payment is made; entry (4') records the purchasing power earned by the seller (of the house), who obtains a claim on a bank deposit in exchange for the housing asset he previously held. Entries (5) and (5') are then the transformation in the bank's bookkeeping of the borrower's monetary debt into a financial one. They depict the fact that, to obtain a loan from the bank, the borrower has to relinquish a financial claim (see Chapter 5), which is recorded on the assets side of the bank's financial department.

Now, supposing that the seller of the housing asset decides to spend his deposit – recorded in entry (4') – on the product market, entries (6)–(6') and (7)–(7') are recorded as soon as the consumption of current output (worth 100) takes place. Entry (6) defines the emission of the 'numerical counter'[36] of this operation, whose mark is financial and is recorded as entry (6'): the firm obtains a claim on a bank deposit (100) for the sale of its total output (at a price of 100) to the seller of the house. Entries (7) and (7') transform the monetary debt of the payer into a financial one, since, as explained above, any purchase of goods, services or financial assets involves also a purchasing power and not merely a sum of numerical units. A purchasing power (in the form of a bank deposit) of 100 is therefore literally destroyed in the purchase of the very output defining its physical object.[37] Indeed, we should not lose sight of the fact that all the income originally held by wage-earners is automatically lent to some other agents (a single borrower in the case in point), who ultimately spend it in place of its initial holders. As Keynes noted in his speech before the House of Lords on 18 May 1943, '[i]f an individual hoards his income, not in the shape of gold coins in his pockets or in his safe, but by keeping a bank deposit, this bank deposit is not withdrawn from circulation but provides his banker with the means of making loans to those who need them' (Keynes, 1980, p. 273).[38] It would in fact be naive to deny that '[b]anks are intermediaries in financial transactions that the depositors are not necessarily aware of' (Gnos, 1998, p. 46). Applied to the stylised example we are investigating, this amounts to saying that the original depositors (that is, workers), willingly or not, exchange their drawing right over current production (entry (3')) with an interest-bearing financial claim over an identically equivalent future production (entry (8')) – an issue we already drew attention to in Chapter 5. What the overall book-entry result (8') shows, in fact, is that original income holders have in the end a purchasing power defined by the financial assets relinquished by the borrower. In simple terms, this means that workers (that is, IH) have a financial capital as the form in which their savings exist until they decide to spend them. 'Income is thus transformed into capital, and it is as such that money can play the role of bridge between present and future so clearly enunciated by Keynes' (Cencini, 1995, p. 71).

To cut short the story, the structural bi-partition between the monetary and the financial department is necessary to avert an excess of demand on the market for current output. 'Before the reform of the banks' bookkeeping, that is, in present-day economies, the financial market can let (the sellers of bonds) obtain an income whose expenditure relates to another period's product; in this case, demand is excessive since pre-existent incomes are spent together with new income' (Schmitt, 1984, p. 312; our translation).[39] Let us try to illustrate this crucial point by referring to the numerical example made earlier on. In the present situation, that is, when banks do not (and cannot) distinguish money from income, an excess of credit leads to an excess of demand for current output, because (say) 110 units of money chases an output of 100 (as measured by the total wage bill its production did generate in the current period) (see Table 5.2). In other words, 10 units of money may be lent *ex nihilo* to the non-bank public, in what is ultimately an advance of a future income via the banking system (see Chapter 5). Here lies the problem indeed. Being a future income, its expenditure on the product market must be made to coincide with the final purchase (that is, consumption) of the very output it will define when the corresponding wage bill is paid out. This is not what happens today: as is the case in Table 5.2, a future income of (say) 10 – advanced via the banking system – is spent jointly with a current income of 100 for the acquisition of a current output worth 100, thus eliciting an excess of demand whose effect on prices is well known in modern capitalist economies. To wit, retail prices are made to rise to re-establish, in numerical terms, the macroeconomic equality between income and current output.[40] Now, '[t]he anomaly [that is, an excess of demand on the product market] cannot occur any more in a system with the two departments. According to the new rule of the game, each new product is sold necessarily by the expenditure of the corresponding income' (ibid., p. 312; our translation).[41] In a nutshell, any excess of bank credit (hence any credit-led excess of aggregate demand over current output) is averted by introducing in modern banking the structural bookkeeping distinction between money and credit. By this bi-partition no bank will be able to finance an excess of demand on the market for produced goods and services. The mechanical working of the reformed monetary structure of bank accounts excludes it.

Of course, if there were enough space to expand here, this bi-partition could be developed further, in an attempt to illustrate the whole dynamics of the reformed payment structure and its beneficial implications for the management of credit-led inflationary pressures. However, at this stage of the argument the reader's attention has to be drawn on the analytical principle rather than on its practical implementation in modern banking.[42] The operational, and clear-cut, distinction between the money-purveying and the credit-purveying department, and the accounting rules governing their relations, are sufficient to avert excessive bank credit to be granted.

On the Necessary Introduction of a Fixed Capital Department

So far, the Ricardian division of the banks' bookkeeping enables not only the banking system as a whole but also each bank individually to know exactly the amount of savings deposited by the public. Owing to the structural distinction between monetary and financial operations, no money creation can acquire the pathological status of a creation of credit any more. Thus then, each and every loan provided by any deposit bank originates in production, inasmuch as the sum total lent to banks' borrowers cannot exceed the exact amount of income deposited by saving units. To say it again, the clear-cut separation of department I from department II mechanically prevents a credit-led excess of demand for available output.

However, such a bookkeeping structure would yet be unable to prevent the birth of empty money in the production process, namely in the investment of the firms' profit. As a matter of fact, the bi-partition concisely explored in the previous subsection concerns output circulation, and can indeed avoid benign inflation as defined in Chapter 5. It is however on production that our structural monetary reform must ultimately focus, if it aims to get rid of malign inflation. As we have previously noted, the remuneration of wage-earners and the investment of profit in the production of fixed capital are recorded today in the same bank account (that is, department II). This is exactly the principal cause of empty money and, consequently, of the birth of an irreversible inflationary gap in present-day capitalist economies. The bi-partition introduced in the previous subsection is therefore a necessary, but not yet sufficient condition for solving the inflation problem. It resolves in fact benign inflation but cannot avoid malign inflation, which is certainly much more troublesome for the macroeconomy than the former can really be.[43]

As stated by Cencini, '[t]he problem within the actual structure of domestic payments is that the formation of fixed capital does not lead to the capitalisation of profits' (Cencini, 1996, p. 59). It is because invested profits are not withdrawn from 'financial circulation' (represented by department II, which is also the sole department in today's bank accounting) that they still form part of the 'loanable funds' (Schmitt, 1984, pp. 322–3). To repeat the crux of Schmitt's analysis, conflating the book-entry records for the investment of profit and the payment of the wage bill (in the capital goods sector) amounts to eliciting empty money, because the resulting deposit (recorded in the banks' financial department) has already been spent when the firms' profit was invested. 'Effectively, it is not the investment of profit that has to be questioned, but the way its entry is recorded in bank accounting' (Cencini, 1995, p. 74).

Let us try to clarify the main line of argument. If the income that firms invest on the labour market were kept within the banks' financial department, as is the case today, it would define at one and the same time an identical amount of savings at the disposal of any bank's borrower showing up with good credentials. Within the present structure of bank accounting, in fact, the expenditure of profit on the factor market (productively) consumes the profit, but not the corresponding bank deposits (Schmitt, 1995–96, vol. II, pp. 67–8). This means that the investment of profit in the production process does not simultaneously withdraw an equivalent amount of bank deposits from (financial) circulation, despite the fact that a macroeconomic capital is definitively absorbed in the investment goods newly produced. The income corresponding to the firms' invested profit can, and will, thus be lent by the banking system to some economic agents, and will be spent in the end on the product market. To this inference one then only needs to add that an income already spent on the factor market (when profit was invested) is spent again on the product market, to conclude that the second expenditure of the same income defines an inflationary gap for its whole amount.

Let us try to avoid a possible misunderstanding. We are not maintaining that profit investment is either anomalous or pathological per se: no monetary disequilibrium can be imputed to the decision of firms to invest their profit on the factor market, neither in theory nor in actual facts. As already noted, it is not the investment of profit in a new production activity that has to be blamed for generating inflationary pressures. It is the present, too simple structure of bank accounting that has to be improved. In particular, as Cencini puts it, 'since the deposits that correspond to invested profits have already been spent in the payment of wages, they ought not to be available to be spent on the product market any more' (Cencini, 1999, p. 143; our translation).[44] Today, these deposits are recorded as savings in the banking system, which can therefore lend the corresponding amount for consumption purposes.[45] This operation elicits an excess of demand on the product market, for it leads to the formation of an income void of any substance.[46] Since the corresponding goods and services newly produced have already been purchased by firms on the labour market, via the investment of profit, total saleable output is automatically diminished without at the same time identically diminishing the amount of money income nourishing total demand. The result is precisely the definition of an inflationary gap, irremediably confirmed by fixed capital amortisation (as seen above).

Now, since the emission of empty money in the investment of profits on the factor market is due to the direct imputation of the wage bill on firms' profits in the banks' bookkeeping, the solution of inflationary pressures depends on separating the workers' remuneration from the capitalisation of profits as recorded within the banking system. To be more precise, since the pathology of fixed capital amortisation originates in a still imperfect monetary structure of the banks' bookkeeping, the solution consists in reforming the latter so as to make sure that the macroeconomic capital invested in the new instruments of production is definitively withdrawn from the financial market, where at present it can be lent. In simple terms, to be effective, our anti-inflation policy must aim at guaranteeing that the whole amount of invested profits within the national economy does not add to the financial circulation of yet unspent incomes. Indeed, only in this situation would the production of replacement goods elicit a sum of 'full' money in the economy, that is, an income whose purchasing power is real and not merely nominal. Let us show briefly how this can be made to happen in the reformed structure of bank accounting.

Following Schmitt's (1984) analysis, a clear-cut and operational separation of profit capitalisation from workers' remuneration requires the institution of a third department in the banks' bookkeeping. In addition to the distinction, first pointed out by Ricardo, between the monetary and the financial department (as we have explored in the preceding subsection), a fixed capital department, III, has to be introduced in the payment structure of our domestic banking systems. The introduction of a department of fixed capital is specifically required to record in it any addition to the instrumental capital (that is, the means of production) of the whole economy, so as to impede the birth of empty money that leads, as we have seen above, to the generation of an inflationary disequilibrium between total demand and total supply. Let us concisely try to study the working of this new department with a simple numerical example, referring as much as we can to those raised earlier on (Table 6.3). Entries (1) and (2) concern the payment of the wage bill carried out by the bank on behalf of firms 1 and 2.[47]

Table 6.3 The working of the fixed capital department[48]

Bank

Financial department (II)

liabilities		assets	
(1) Workers 1	100	Firm 1	100
(2) Workers 2	100	Firm 2	100
(3) Firm 1	200	Workers 1 and 2	200
(4) Firm 1	100	Firm 2	100
(5) Department III	100	Firm 1	100
(6) Department III	100	Firm 2	100
(7) Workers 1	100	Firm 1	100
(8) Firm 2	100	Workers 1	100
(9) Department III	100	Firm 1	100

Fixed capital department (III)

liabilities		assets	
(5') Firm 1	100	Department II	100

As repeatedly noted earlier on, workers obtain an income (equal to, say, 200 units), formed as a bank deposit. Assuming, to simplify what fundamentally does not affect analysis, that no income redistribution occurs among households, entry (3) records the purchase of firm 1's output by the set of workers: income holders spend an income of 200 to acquire an output worth 100. By marking up the prices of its goods, firm 1 is able to capture an income of 100. It thus makes a profit corresponding to the financial debt incurred by firm 2 for the remuneration of its workers. Entry (4) is the net result of the first three entries. Now, since the profit gained by firm 1 is not redistributed (for example as a dividend to the firm's shareholders or to the government sector in payment of taxes) but spent for the production of fixed capital, it has to be withdrawn from the sum total of savings, because otherwise it will ultimately be spent again on the product market. Entry (5), and its alter ego entry (5'), are the necessary, and sufficient, accounting device to impede that banks can lend the savings which correspond to the sum of profits invested in the means of production (fixed capital). Clearly, firm 1 cannot suffer any loss from these accounting operations, which are purely internal to the banking system. Indeed, at this stage firm 1 still has a bank deposit of 100, recorded as in entry (5'). However, since this is a capitalisation (not a redistribution) of the firm's profit, the corresponding amount must not be available to finance a new wage bill, because otherwise, as we know by now, after compensation in department II it will give rise to empty money and, consequently, to an irreducible excess of demand on the product market. Hence, when a fixed capital department is introduced in the banks' bookkeeping structure of domestic payments, entry (6) is the result of the automatic transfer from department II to III of the sum total of profits capitalised in the current period. This entry between the bank's second and third departments makes sure that no income invested in the production process can still circulate within the financial sector of the economy. By this token, when firm 1 remunerates its workers for a new production of investment or capital goods (supposing a new wage bill equal to 100), the bank records the payment as in entry (7). So, the payment of the new wage bill (entry (7)) is not compensated with the firm's capitalised income (entry (5')) in the bank's accounts.

Since in the reformed structure of payments the remuneration of workers does not conflate with the investment of profit on the labour market, the monetisation of any new production cannot affect the relationship between money and output. No inflationary gap is therefore generated in the production of fixed capital. So much so that wage-earners in the investment goods sector are paid with 'full' money, that is, with an income whose purchasing power is real and not merely nominal. To put it slightly differently, '[s]ince F_1's debt and credit are not entered in the same department, they do not cancel out: profit no longer finances the payment of wages and the entire system works without leading to the anomalous emission of empty money' (Cencini, 1996, p. 59).[49] Since the payment of any new wage bill is entered in the banks' financial department, this operation does not affect the sum total of profits withdrawn from financial circulation and recorded within the department of fixed capital.

The final expenditure of a new income (of 100) on the product market confirms that in the new structure of bank accounting the investment of profit on the factor market leaves the relationship between money and output unaffected. The deposit workers in the capital goods sector are paid with (entry (7)) gives them in fact the power to acquire the still unsold stock of wage goods, which are the substance of the forced saving elicited by entry (3). As a matter of fact, entry (8) defines the consumption of the items stocked within firm 2, which thus covers its production costs brought forward from entry (2).[50] On the whole, the profit invested by firm 1 is capitalised (entry (5'))[51] without affecting the same firm's financial debt to the bank's second department for the payment of the new wage bill (entry (9)).[52] Thanks to the reformed structure of the banks' bookkeeping, the investment of profit on the labour market succeeds therefore in transforming the stock of wage goods (forced saving) into capital goods together with the transformation of the firm's monetary profit into a fixed capital. In this framework, the capitalisation of profits occurs by withdrawing the whole amount of invested profits from financial circulation, that is, from the banks' second department. Thus then, by averting any emission of empty money, the threefold separation of the banks' bookkeeping guarantees ultimately that any investment on the factor market, even merely for the maintenance of the fixed capital accumulated in the economy, leaves the money–output relationship (that is, monetary equilibrium) absolutely unaffected and perfectly sound.

Let us conclude this chapter by observing that the achievement of an entirely inflation-proof monetary structure of payments (consistent with the nature of modern money) has a strong link with the need to respect the twofold nature of Real Capital called forth by Sir John Hicks (1974), as the reader interested in the history of economic analysis may have noticed.[53] In particular, the threefold distinction of a monetary, a financial and a fixed capital department in the banks' bookkeeping could be the *clé de voûte* for the synthesis between the physical and the financial aspects of the macroeconomic capital existing in any non-inflationary capitalist system.

- Firstly, a clear-cut separation between the first two departments ensures that every deposit recorded in the bank's financial department has a substance, that is, a stock of consumption goods as its objective purchasing power. Impeding any excess of bank credit, this bi-partition makes sure that no deposit can ever be created by a mere stroke of a pen. To exist, any deposit has to represent a production of goods or services monetised by a bank, because bank deposits are the monetary form in which output exists until the latter is sold on the market for produced goods. The newly-produced income (recorded as a deposit in department II) is the monetary measure of the physical stock defining objectively the firm's debt for the payment of the wage bill. This measure, occurring on the factor market when the current wage bill is paid, cannot change in the circulation of the corresponding output (on either the product market or the financial market), for the bi-partition of departments I and II automatically prevents excess credit creation.

- Secondly, the introduction of a fixed capital department ensures that any profit invested in the production process is embodied (to use Hicks's own word) in the means of production newly produced. Being an income definitively saved in the form of capital goods, the sum total of invested profits does not have to be kept in the financial circulation, for otherwise – as is the case today – it would define a Fund with no saleable object associated with it. The definition of an excess of demand over total saleable output is precisely given by an inflation of total income with respect to the volume of goods and services really to be sold. In short, the inflationary gap is defined by an excess of Fund over an insufficient Matter, to put it in the phraseology of Hicks (1974).

All in all, the idea that inflation arises when 'too much money chases too few goods' is correct, though in need of analytical elaboration. If it is true that excess money (with respect to existing output) is the cause of inflation, analysis must explain how it is possible for this disequilibrium really to occur, a question that Friedman (1987, p. 17) singled out as the deepest issue in inflation analysis. Once the exogeneity-of-money view is rejected on logical grounds, as we have done in Part Two, advocates of the endogenous money approach need to elaborate a theory of inflationary disequilibria in strict adherence to the banking nature of modern money. When this is done along the analytical lines of the macro-theoretical paradigm adopted in this book, it can be seen that inflation arises out of the emission of what may be labelled empty money, that is, it originates in a mechanism allowing banks to create a sum of deposits with no real purchasing power attached to them. When creations of empty deposits occur for the circulation of output, no irremediable inflationary gap is generated in the economy. It is when they originate from the monetisation of a production process, namely with the production of capital goods, that these emissions of empty money elicit a pathological alteration of the relationship between money and output. The purpose of the structural reform of bank accounting proposed at the end of this chapter is to make sure that production of capital goods is financed by savings and not by the emission of empty money. Assuredly, the investment of profit in the production process is necessary for economic growth and development. But the way it has been entered up to now in the banks' bookkeeping does not yet respect the fundamental requirements of a monetary system fully complying with the book-entry nature of modern money. It is therefore towards a structural reform of the banks' bookkeeping that our efforts ought to aim, to make sure that the daily working of our payment systems cannot alter the relationship between money and output. In short, according to the analytical framework informing our macro-theoretical investigation, inflation owes its origin to a deficient, too simple structure of the bank accounting, and it is thus only a structural monetary reform that will be able to eradicate the problem.

NOTES

1. Contrast the explanation based on the possible different forms of savings behaviour across the various sectors of the economy, or between different categories of income holders, as put to the fore by Harris (1978) in his analysis of *Capital Accumulation and Income Distribution*. A classification of growth and distribution theories based on various savings assumptions and on the role of technical progress is provided by Baranzini (1991, pp. 45–8). See also Pasinetti (1993, pp. 82–104) for a macro-theoretical analysis of consumption, savings and inter-temporal distribution of income in a pure labour economy.
2. In other words, the monetary recording of the accumulation of capital in the banks' bookkeeping may be inflationary or not. See the last subsection on this point.
3. See the second section of this chapter for analytical elaboration.
4. See Chapter 5 (note 65).
5. 'Les biens-capitaux, ou biens d'investissement, ne sont pas la forme primitive du capital fixe mais sa forme seconde, obtenue par la "consommation productive" des biens-salaires épargnés dans la formation du profit monétaire' (Schmitt, 1984, p. 170).
6. We put the word 'stock' in inverted commas, because the newly produced capital goods are not for sale to income holders. The firm owns them since their very formation, because the latter results from the investment of profit (that is, its capitalisation). This does not exclude, however, both inter- and intra-industrial transactions (see Bradley and Gnos, 1991, pp. 185–6; Friboulet, 1991).
7. '[L]a monnaie émise dans l'investissement du profit trouve finalement un "corps", en l'espèce des biens-salaires épargnés dans l'acte de la formation du profit monétaire' (Schmitt, 1984, p. 190). Note that the sale of this stock of wage goods may, of course, give rise to a new profit for the seller. The point to underline here is that the emission of empty money in the investment of profit is not yet harmful for the economy, since the corresponding money units acquire a purchasing power over the stock of wage goods saved when profit has been formed. The actual distribution of this purchasing power (between firms and households) is not germane to the problem at stake, and will therefore be put aside here.
8. 'Payés au moyen des profits, les travailleurs obtiennent un revenu vide et, en compensation, un titre sur les biens-salaires épargnés par la captation antérieure de salaires en profits' (Schmitt, 1984, p. 215).
9. 'Il reste vrai que la production de p^+ comprend une émission vide, mais elle est inoffensive puisque les biens-capitaux instantanément retirés des salaires réels . . . sont exactement compensés par les biens-salaires épargnés' (Schmitt, 1984, pp. 205–6, translation fitted to match our numerical example).
10. For an illustration of recent attempts at clarification, see Davidson (1987) and Deprez (1993).

11. Conversely, consumption goods (*C*) and investment goods (*I*) are final goods.
12. As Schmitt observes, '[a situation] where the national income is equal to C + I, could only exist if a national economy produced goods without the help of any fixed capital, or, at least, if no user cost were incurred in a given period by an economy. Clearly, such an economy cannot be found in the world as anyone can observe it, unless the chosen period is unduly, not to say ludicrously, short' (Schmitt, 1996b, p. 79).
13. A phraseology that might be more convincing for at least some readers relies on a Marxian interpretation of fixed capital amortisation, a process Wray attempts to render along Keynesian lines in the following terms: 'constant capital used in production that is not replaced does not set any live labor in motion (to produce replacement means of production); in other words, it does not generate a wage bill (in the period it depreciates) in the means of production department ("investment" sector). Only *replaced* dead labor can lead to the realization of value by creating wages and spending on consumption goods' (Wray, 1999, p. 14).
14. '*[L'inflation] n'est pas un désordre purement monétaire*; elle est une pathologie définie sur la monnaie dans sa relation avec le produit: elle touche donc à la fois la monnaie et le produit' (Schmitt, 1984, p. 506).
15. As clearly noticed by Joan Robinson, the problem of fixed capital replacement is difficult to analyse, at least in macroeconomic terms, also because it is not straightforward to distinguish net investment from amortisation of existing capital goods. 'New investment is normally going on and at the same time the composition of output and techniques of production are changing. A worn-out plant is rarely replaced by an exact replica of its original self, and when the physical specification of the replacement, or its expected future life, is different, or the market conditions in which it will operate are different, there is no precise and unambiguous criterion by which to judge whether it is exactly equivalent to what it replaces. We cannot then draw a clear line between replacements and new investment, though firms must adopt accounting conventions to make the distinction between amortisation and profit' (Robinson, 1956, p. 42).
16. See Schmitt (1984, Part Two, especially pp. 189–233).
17. Note that the proposed solution is not to allow fixed capital to run down (to zero). It consists in a structural monetary reform, as we shall see later.
18. 'Il convient bien de dire *irrémédiablement* car, à la différence de l'émission vide définie par l'investissement net, l'émission vide induite de la production des biens d'amortissement aboutit à une monnaie dont la vacuité n'est nullement compensée; cette fois, aucune épargne de biens-salaires n'est en attente pour remplir le vide' (Schmitt, 1984, p. 223). As noted at the end of Chapter 5, since fixed capital is appropriated by the set of the country's 'disembodied' firms, its amortisation (that is, the production of replacement goods) does not elicit a stock of goods to be sold to 'embodied' agents.
19. As pointed out by Schmitt, '[m]oney and payments are one and the same thing. No money, if correctly defined, exists either before or after a given payment' (Schmitt, 1996b, p. 88).
20. 'Aucune création n'est une intermédiation. La réciproque est vraie aussi: aucune intermédiation n'est une création. En effet, si les banques prêtent une somme d'argent par elles empruntée, elles ne créent rien' (Schmitt, 1984, p. 303).
21. Vallageas (1988, p. 189) claims that this distinction is impossible on account of the variety of bank loans.
22. The choice to avert credit-led inflation might therefore be considered as an issue of economic policy. The decision of economic policy makers notwithstanding, from an analytical point of view this problem has however to be investigated on purely conceptual grounds.
23. In Table 6.1 we assume for the sake of simplicity that a single bank represents the banking system as a whole. It need not be emphasised that the proposed bookkeeping reform applies to any bank existing in the real world.
24. Notice here the similarity with the 1844 Bank Charter Act, which followed Ricardo's *Plan*

some twenty years after it was put forth and separated the business of the Bank of England into a 'Department of issue' and a 'Department of deposit and discount'. See Rotelli (1982, pp. 242–50) for more details on the 1844 Act.

25. Ricardo himself used to think in terms of departments in his *Plan* (Ricardo, 1824/1951, p. 291).
26. As put by Schmitt, '[a] computer program can be devised and established whose theoretical goal and practical effect is, when applied by the banking system of the nation, to eradicate all positive creations of purely nominal incomes' (Schmitt, 1996b, p. 105). Applied to the practical distinction between money emission and financial intermediation, the required structural monetary reform is therefore a matter of mechanically preventing the mixing-up of two kinds of fundamentally distinct operations.
27. Remember that this does not mean that wage-earners can obtain the whole output newly produced when they spend their income. In fact, firms may mark-up retail prices, so as to capture on the product market a share of national income (formed on the factor market, when workers are paid).
28. Today's bank accounting does not distinguish the numerical means of payment from the very object of the latter, that is, income in the form of bank deposits. See Rossi (1998, pp. 35–43) for an attempt to introduce this distinction in the present structure of banks' bookkeeping.
29. One might admit that the second line of book entries has to be recorded by the end of a bank's business day, when interest charges are computed in practice. However, from a theoretical viewpoint the first and the second double-entry lines can be made to coincide in chronological time, so that entry (3') would be the immediate result of any payment (where workers (income holders) and the firm stand, respectively, for the payee and the payer). Today, only entry (3') is recorded in bank accounting, since the latter does not (yet) distinguish between monetary and financial operations.
30. Since we focus here on the macroeconomic result of current production, we abstract from any pre-existent deposit the firm might have. See the next subsection for analytical elaboration.
31. Note that if this unspecified agent were to ask for a consumption loan to purchase the goods newly produced and stocked within the firm, the bookkeeping entries would be simpler than in the case at hand. To wit, entry (4') would be replaced by entry (6'), and entries (6), (7) and (7') would not exist, leaving the overall result unchanged, as in entry (8').
32. In *A Treatise on Money*, Keynes noticed that there is no limit to the amount of bank lending if banks '*move forward in step*' (Keynes, 1930/1971, p. 26). Indeed, this unlimited growth of bank loans is the theoretical result of the accounting equivalence of assets and liabilities of any individual bank. Any credit granted *ex nihilo* by a bank is in fact always matched by an equivalent, and simultaneous, deposit, made by the recipient of the payment the bank makes on behalf of its client (the borrower). Today, it is only by the clearing mechanism that each bank can know its financial situation in the interbank market, that is, if its loans have been greater, equal to, or less than the savings deposited in it over the business day just closed. This is *ex post* information, as opposed to *ex ante* knowledge of the exact amount of savings.
33. '[À] défaut de cette séparation, les banques ne connaissent pas le montant des épargnes constituées chez elles' (Schmitt, 1984, p. 311).
34. 'La division des banques en deux départements a donc une grande importance au titre des remèdes de l'inflation. Après la réforme, chaque banque connaîtra chaque jour les sommes exactes qu'elle peut prêter, comme c'est le cas pour une Caisse d'épargne. Il ne pourra plus arriver que la somme des banques prête au-delà de ses ressources' (Schmitt, 1995–96, vol. II, p. 33).
35. Recall that unused overdraft and credit lines do not appear in the bank's balance sheet.
36. The redundancy (numerical counter) is deliberate.

37. This action closes the current period; a new production is necessary to open next period and to form new income. Note again that the retail price paid on the product market by, say, the seller of the housing asset may include the firm's mark-up over factor costs. In this case, an income of 100 is only partially destroyed, to wit, for an amount equal to the firm's production costs of the output sold. Indeed, entries (6') and (7') testify that an income expenditure of 100 enables the firm to reimburse its initial debt (recorded as in entries (1) and (2')) either to the bank or to its own wages fund.
38. No income holder can spend his income at the very instant when the latter is formed. Each income holder thus saves his income up to the instant (of his choice) when he spends it on the product market. The act of saving of the newly formed income by its original holder implies, therefore, that this amount is lent by the bank where it is recorded as a deposit. 'The association between money and output elicits an income [in the form of] a bank deposit. And it is precisely because it is formed as a bank deposit that income is immediately lent. Through the financial intermediation of banks, savings are instantaneously lent by their initial owners and spent by their borrowers' (Cencini, 1995, p. 71). In *The General Theory*, Keynes clearly observed in fact that monetary transactions are of a bilateral character. He explained that 'regarding an individual depositor's relation to his bank as being a one-sided transaction, instead of seeing it as the two-sided transaction which it actually is', is 'an optical illusion' (Keynes, 1936/1973, p. 81).
39. 'Avant réforme de la comptabilité des banques, donc dans l'économie actuelle, le marché financier peut faire parvenir (aux vendeurs de titres) des revenus dont la dépense est rapportée au produit d'une autre période; dans ce cas, la demande est excédentaire parce que des revenus anciens sont dépensés en concours avec les revenus nouveaux' (Schmitt, 1984, p. 312).
40. Note in passing that this rise in prices is probably captured (at least in part) by the targeted price index, although analysis of an increase in the latter cannot explain its cause (see Parts One and Two).
41. 'L'anomalie ne peut plus se produire dans le régime des deux départements. Selon la nouvelle règle du jeu, tout nouveau produit est nécessairement écoulé par la dépense des revenus correspondants' (Schmitt, 1984, p. 312).
42. As noted by Schmitt in his 'Introduction' to the Italian edition of Ricardo's monetary writings, from a theoretical point of view the reform brought about by the Peel Act in 1844 is less interesting than the underlying analytical principle, that is, the separation of money's emission from financial intermediation (Schmitt, in Ricardo, 1985, p. 82).
43. Let us recall that the distinction between benign and malign inflation consists in the fact that the former is not cumulative in time, since its effect on monetary equilibrium is destined to be compensated by loan repayment. Malign inflation, by contrast, elicits an irretrievable inflationary disequilibrium between total demand and total supply, as we shall see more clearly in what follows.
44. '[I] depositi corrispondenti ai profitti investiti essendo già stati spesi nel pagamento dei salari, non devono più poter essere spesi sul mercato dei prodotti' (Cencini, 1999, p. 143).
45. We leave speculation aside here, since, as we have seen, 'at the end' of any purely speculative chain of transactions there always is an output consumption. The case made in the present context is therefore general, despite the simplicity of the argument. See also Chapter 5.
46. To state the obvious, the nominal income thus created takes on per osmosis purchasing power from the existing real incomes, diluting value among an increased number of money units. 'As a consequence of inflation, the content of money, unchanged in real terms, acquires a new numerical expression. A greater quantity of money is needed, therefore, to purchase the same product' (Cencini, 1995, p. 59).
47. Let us emphasise once again that these entries are recorded in any case, that is, even in the much likely situation when firms have pre-existent deposits. This should become clear as the explanation of this general example proceeds. Impatient readers may be reminded that,

analytically, the formation of profit has to be explained before tackling the expenditure of profit on the factor market. Both in theory and practice, the formation of national income always precedes its expenditure logically (though not necessarily chronologically).

48. For the sake of brevity we omit here department I, which must therefore be considered as implicit in this context, since, let us repeat, any transaction requires the emission of its monetary instrument. Also, the bank here represents the national banking system as a whole.
49. F_1 corresponds to firm 1 in our example. The firm's debt is recorded in entry (7); its credit in entry (5').
50. The retail price at which the output of firm 2 is sold does not matter for the present discussion. If these goods (worth 100) are sold at a mark-up over factor costs, the firm makes a profit which, if not redistributed, will be recorded in department III. Analysis in this case will merely replicate the situation of firm 1 in the example considered here, adding no further theoretical issues.
51. Were the firm's profit – recorded as in entry (5') – successively redistributed or directly spent by the firm on the product market (instead of being invested on the labour market), the corresponding deposit would be transferred back again to department II, were it would be literally destroyed in the funding of the production costs of the items bought.
52. Entry (9) is the net result of entries (6) to (8) in Table 6.3.
53. 'If it is capital in the volume sense that is being measured, capital is physical goods; but in the value sense capital is not physical goods. It is a sum of values which may conveniently be described as a Fund. A Fund that may be embodied in physical goods in different ways. There are these two senses of Real Capital which need to be distinguished. I do of course borrow the term Fund from the history, and to the history I now turn. I am going to maintain that the distinction is quite ancient; it divides economists, ancient and modern, into two camps. There are some for whom Real Capital is a Fund – I shall call them Fundists; and there are some for whom it consists of physical goods. It is tempting to call the latter Realists; but since one wants to emphasize that both concepts are *real*, this is not satisfactory. I shall venture in this paper to call them Materialists' (Hicks, 1974, p. 309).

Conclusion

The objective of this book has been to investigate inflation from a macro-theoretical point of view. This ambitious research programme has taken us in an extended journey into the political economy of inflation, with attention focused on the main conceptual and analytical issues of present-day theory, research and policy. We surely leave behind a number of points that need further clarification, as well as a list of important questions that remain to be addressed. No attempt has been made to provide definitive answers to all the problems raised. Rather, our efforts have focused on clarifying, and forging ahead, the principal line of argument for an alternative, policy-oriented theory of inflation, integrating it with a conceptual appraisal of conventional wisdom. Time has now come to review and assess the criticisms raised in the interpretation of our theoretical framework. We shall conclude this book with some perspectives for further research, since we are well aware that our analysis was situated at a very high level of abstraction and that it could just hint at a few issues where a much more refined research work has yet to be done.

ON THE DEFINITION OF MONEY

Firstly, there is the basic question of the new analytical conception of money, defined as a numerical form, or as an immaterial vehicle, of which physical output is its real content, or load. The first (to our knowledge) published critical review of the Schmitt school – by a supporter outside it – noted that in this framework 'money is distinct from its purchasing power "as blood is distinct from its oxygen"' (Devillebichot, 1969, p. 693; our translation).[1] More recently, a reviewer of Cencini's 1995 book positively stated that the Schmitt–Cencini theory offers 'powerful insights into (theoretical) monetary issues via an analysis of money in a world of banking, where money is essentially a book entry' (Cohen, 1996, p. 1134). As was expected by Lord Desai in his 'Foreword' to Cencini (1984), this analysis has 'puzzle[d], stimulate[d], infuriate[d], or annoy[ed] many readers' (Desai, 1984, p. xi). Essentially, these reactions can be ascribed to the transcendent definition of money put forward by this new school,[2] that is to say, to an analytical conception of money transcending the agents' perception of the instrument they use to accomplish their monetary transactions. In particular, Schmitt's theory of money appears to some critics as being 'nothing more than the fact that when a bank creates money it simultaneously creates an asset and a liability' (Watkins, 1985, p. 596). Certainly the asset–liability nature of bank money challenges a number of monetary analyses. So much so, that it has elicited an analysis in terms of circular flows where the numerical form of any monetary transaction is created and destroyed in the same instant, that is, when a payment is made.[3] This has puzzled those critics who question 'why the value of something (or some action) which is, by [the Schmitt school] description, evanescent, or destroyed almost as soon as it is created, should be of interest' (Chick, 2000, p. 129). An attempt at clarification has been provided at the end of Chapter 4. In fact, a subsidiary aim of this work has been to clarify (of course, within the limited scope and boundaries of the present book) the theoretical approach used in it, couching the Schmitt–Cencini framework in simple, or more familiar, language. Surely, further intellectual efforts are required to build a bridge with other schools of monetary thought where this possibility might exist, although this bridge-building cannot come from an individual's effort alone.[4]

ON THE RELATIONSHIP BETWEEN MONEY AND PRODUCTION

Secondly, and closely related to the preceding point, there is the fundamental link between money and production, which may require further elaboration. In his book review of Cencini (1988), Deprez has claimed that '[t]he [Cencini] discussion of the emission and circuits of money and income is based around a classical conception of the period of production, which is implied to be uniform and synchronised for all production in the economy' (Deprez, 1989, p. 203). A similar point had in fact already been raised by Graziani (1985, p. 139), who questioned on practical grounds the idea that output is saleable at the precise instant when wages are paid out. There seems to exist here a problem in the case of those goods (say, a Boeing 777) which require several production periods – as defined by the periodic payment of wages – in order to be completed and put on sale on the product market.[5] An analogous, and perhaps more challenging, problem seems also to exist with those goods and services which cannot be sold directly to the holders of bank deposits (recall Keynes's famous example of wage-earners digging holes in the ground),[6] and with those goods which have been produced but for which there actually is no market demand (for instance, those out-of-fashion items piled up in the firms because no consumer wants to buy them). Given the importance of these issues, let us very briefly indicate how they have been addressed by Schmitt's school.[7]

The case of those goods and services which cannot be sold directly to income holders may be illustrated referring to public sector production. It is indeed a well-known fact that many public goods and services are not sold directly to income holders, who cannot buy (say) the protective services of the armed forces as they buy a chocolate bar at a shop. The nature of public sector output is such that, as a general rule, the general government sector cannot sell its products on the market. Therefore, being unable to cover all its production costs in the usual manner (on the product market), the state uses taxation for the 'selling' of its output. In fact, as far as the relation between money and production is concerned, production by the general government sector does not differ from private sector production.[8] 'Whether it is a matter of weapons, welfare services or mere holes, public enterprise output is an integral part of national product and plays a part in the determination of global supply in the same way as wages paid out by public firms do in the determination of global demand' (Cencini, 1995, p. 65). This does not mean, of course, that the physical characteristics of the general government output is of no importance. For both individual and social welfare it is surely more important to produce (say) national health services than nuclear weapons. Needless to say, similar alternatives exist also in the private sector economy. This important subject matter lies however far beyond the scope of this book.

The case of unsaleable goods can be dealt with in a similar way. If a firm has produced a stock of unwanted goods and cannot find a single consumer wanting to buy them, it encounters a loss (or a decrease in its profit) since it cannot cover the corresponding production costs on the product market. The problem can be analysed following two alternative approaches. If one measures income at the time of sale, the existence of unwanted goods piled up in a firm implies that this very firm has to buy them, for it must cover their costs of production. This is done by a decrease in this firm's profit, a decrease which may be of such an amount to give rise to a net loss in the firm's cash flow statement. The firm's future production plans are thus much likely to be revised – and perhaps to such an extent that the firm will cut back on the employment it offers – in order to avert the further heaping-up of unwanted goods. The same conclusions are reached if one defines income at the time of production (that is, when the wage bill is paid), although this approach is different from the previous one.[9] In this framework, income exists in the form of a bank deposit as soon as wages are paid out to workers. Even if these workers' output is destined to be unsold to income holders, its production generates the exact amount of income necessary and sufficient to cover the corresponding factor costs. Now, since income is in the form of a bank deposit, banks will lend the corresponding amount which is not spent by income holders. This implies that those goods which are not bought by consumers are bought by the firm itself, because, let us repeat it, firms must sell unwanted output to cover its costs of production. By lending to firms, banks therefore guarantee the identity between total demand and total supply of current output at any point in time – which is another proof of the necessity to search for the causes of inflation beyond the analysis of consumers' or producers' forms of behaviour (see Part Three).

ON THE FUNCTIONAL LINK BETWEEN PERIODS

A third set of critical remarks concern the fact that the Schmitt–Cencini view 'results in the production periods being isolated from each other' (Deprez, 1989, p. 204), an isolation that accounts for the unitary value of the multiplier.[10] This probably is the most recurrent critique raised in the literature published up to now. It has been pointed out twice by Lord Desai (1984, pp. xi–xiv; 1988, p. xiii) and results from the 'refusal [by the new school] to recognise that income earned in one period is spent in the next and, through being spent, generates new income in a still later period' (Hennings, 1985, p. 621). To put it differently, this criticism amounts to claiming that 'the role of investment goods, the saving propensity of workers, and the consumption of capitalists or rentiers is not explored [by the Schmitt–Cencini analysis]' (Deprez, 1989, p. 204). In this framework, according to Chick, 'investment is not singled out for special treatment: it does not matter whether production takes place in the consumption goods industries or the capital goods industries' (Chick, 2000, p. 129). It is in this connection that Lord Desai pointed out that 'the Dijon School's theory is still an equilibrium one and leaves one very little room for disequilibrium dynamics' (Desai, 1988, p. xiii). As he had already stated back in 1984, '[t]he multiplier process is a disequilibrium dynamic one whereby output changes from one level to another' (Desai, 1984, p. xii). This amounts to saying that the Schmitt school has no disequilibrium dynamic theory.

As a perusal of Schmitt (1984, pp. 39–74) will show, his theory is however neither static nor dynamic, because it is 'quantic' (see Realfonzo, 1999, p. 377). The idea of 'quantum time' is indeed at the core of this theory (see for example Schmitt, 1982), for which any production process is an emission of a quantum of time (that is, a finite and indivisible period of time taken as a whole) as soon as it is monetised by banks. 'We have a quantum theory of production because the act of producing is a *wave*, which quantizes production time' (Schmitt, 1986, p. 127). The production period is precisely defined by the periodic payment of wages. For example, if the latter are paid on a fortnightly basis, the former has a duration of two weeks (fifteen days); if the latter are paid once a month, the former has a duration of four weeks (thirty days), and so on, independently of the number of working days (or hours) necessary for manufacturing output physically (Schmitt, 1984, pp. 437–48). In this framework, production and consumption are two actions whose result is, respectively, the creation and the destruction of current income via two emissions of the same quantum of time (for instance two weeks). According to this theory, '[t]he final expenditure of income is, in fact, an emission, and therefore as such it also defines a finite and indivisible period of time. Moreover, creation and destruction being related to the same income, this second emission defines the same quantum of time defined by the first emission' (Cencini, 1984, p. 191). In this framework there is therefore no functional link between production periods, because expenditures are defined in quantum time and depict a circular flow representing a production–consumption (that is, a creation–destruction) of the same money income (ibid., pp. 94–162). Hence, there is no 'earning through spending' causal mechanism, in so far as expenditures on the market for produced goods and services cover the production costs of sold output. There is nevertheless a sort of link between periods, since a firm's loss in, say, period 1 (due to a failure to sell all its output on the product market – see above) is much likely to lead this firm to reduce its level of activity (hence to cut back on the employment it offers) in the following period(s), according to the principle of effective demand explored in Chapter 5.

ON ECONOMIC CRISES

An important corollary of the latter critique has raised concern with the exclusion of economic cycles from the Schmitt–Cencini view. This has led a few critics to claim that this theory applies to a Say's Law (real-wage) economy,[11] and that it maintains that crises are outside the field of economic analysis (Lavoie, 1987, p. 87).[12] A slightly different version of this criticism maintains in fact that the monetary analysis of the new school has no place for unemployment (dis)equilibria, so that it would be a theory of a dream-world or, at least, an explanation of an ideal (utopian?) state of the world. Certainly the unemployment problem cannot be neglected by any economic theory whose adherents claim to have something to say about the real world. Yet, it would be unfair, if not an a priori conjecture, to address this critique to the Schmitt–Cencini view, as a perusal of Schmitt (1984; 1996b) and Cencini (1995; 1996; 2001) will show, although nobody denies the need for further contributions in order to construct a fully-articulated, and policy-oriented, theory of unemployment within that framework.

It is particularly on the relationship between inflation and unemployment that future research seems to be much needed, along the lines informing the macro-theoretical analysis attempted in this book. In our highly capitalised economies the accumulation of fixed capital may reach such an extent that its remuneration becomes more and more difficult. On account of the decrease in the rate of profit in respect of the interest rate paid on the financial market, firms may decide to stop investing in the production of capital goods and to invest their profits for the production of consumption goods. 'By so doing, however, they would provoke an increase in the supply of these goods without matching it with an equivalent increase in demand. The subsequent deflation would force them to reduce their activity, and, with it, the level of employment' (Cencini, 1995, p. 90). No-one doubts that this is an extremely important topic on which further research is needed. As Cencini and Baranzini have in fact pointed out in their 'Introduction' to a recent co-edited book on inflation and unemployment, 'the coexistence of two apparently complementary disequilibria such as inflation and deflation is still a mystery, and very little progress has been made towards explaining the nature of their relationship' (Cencini and Baranzini, 1996, p. 1).

NOTES

1. '[L]a monnaie est distincte de son pouvoir d'achat "comme le sang de son oxygène"' (Devillebichot, 1969, p. 693). This analogy is intended to point out that blood (money) is the vehicle of oxygen (money's worth, that is, physical output). Notice here the similarity with the idea of 'the great wheel of [output] circulation' put to the fore by Smith (1776/1970).
2. See Chick (2000, p. 130), who complains that the Schmitt–Cencini definition of money does not conform to the statistical definition used by central banks and international organisations.
3. See Chapter 4.
4. This book has made a first step towards bridge-building in respect of the problem of excess bank credit and its link with inflationary pressures (see Part Three).

5. See Chapter 5 (note 20).
6. See Keynes (1936/1973, p. 220).
7. See particularly Schmitt (1984, pp. 94–123).
8. Chick has recently argued that the Schmitt school puts to the fore a 'production theory of money' (in contrast to Keynes's 'monetary theory of production'), because Schmitt's theory is founded on 'the generative power of labour to create income and the role of this activity to give value (purchasing power) to "money"' (Chick, 2000, p. 129).
9. Besides measuring income at market prices, national accountants also measure income at factor costs.
10. In his recent account of the French circuit school, Deleplace (1999, p. 475) notes that neither production nor income distribution creates a link between periods, so that the multiplier is necessarily equal to one.
11. On the distinction between a real-wage economy and a monetary economy of production, particularly in connection with Say's Law, see Rotheim (1981, pp. 575–84). Now, the monetary interpretation of Say's Law shows that the latter is in fact a sales–purchases identity (see Schmitt, 1975): for every economic agent the total (outgoing) flow of expenditures is always identically equal to the total (incoming) flow of earnings over any given period of time, because there can never exist either a net purchase or a net sale for any agent in the whole economy. An agent's net purchase on the market for produced goods is inevitably funded by a net sale of financial assets (for the same agent), because any cession of a bank deposit – either owned or borrowed – in exchange for a commodity defines the cession of a financial claim over domestic output. See Rossi (1998, p. 34, n. 27) for analytical elaboration.
12. In connection with the explanation of 'crises' by the French–Swiss school, Realfonzo has noted that 'Schmitt puts forward a new interpretation of Say's Law' (Realfonzo, 1999, p. 377). It is a pity that Realfonzo could not expand on this crucial point his entry on the French circuit school in the recently published *Encyclopedia of Political Economy*. Had he done it, he would have noted that it is possible to observe a 'Say's Law economy' affected by unemployment. Recall the previous explanation of unsaleable goods on the product market: those goods not bought by consumers are bought by producers, for the latter must cover their costs of production. Thus then, although the consumers' aggregate demand can differ from aggregate supply, total demand is always identical to total supply.

Bibliography

Abraham, K.G., J.S. Greenlees and B.R. Moulton (1998), 'Working to improve the consumer price index', *Journal of Economic Perspectives*, **12** (1), 27–36.

Advisory Commission to Study the Consumer Price Index (1996), *Toward a More Accurate Measure of the Cost of Living: Final Report to the Senate Finance Committee*, Washington (DC): Government Printing Office ('Boskin Report').

Alchian, A.A. and B. Klein (1973), 'On a correct measure of inflation', *Journal of Money, Credit, and Banking*, **5** (1), 173–91.

Allais, M. (1966), 'A restatement of the quantity theory of money', *American Economic Review*, **56** (5), 1123–57.

Allen, R.G.D. (1975), *Index Numbers in Theory and Practice*, London and Basingstoke: Macmillan.

Allen, W.A. (1997), 'Inflation measurement and inflation targets: the UK experience', *Federal Reserve Bank of St. Louis Review*, **79** (3), 179–85.

Anderson, R.G., B.E. Jones and T.D. Nesmith (1997), 'Monetary aggregation theory and statistical index numbers', *Federal Reserve Bank of St. Louis Review*, **79** (1), 31–51.

Arestis, P. (1997), *Money, Pricing, Distribution and Economic Integration*, London and New York: Macmillan and St. Martin's Press.

Arestis, P. and P. Howells (1996), 'Theoretical reflections on endogenous money: the problem with "convenience lending"', *Cambridge Journal of Economics*, **20** (5), 539–51.

Arestis, P. and P. Howells (1999), 'The supply of credit money and the demand for deposits: a reply', *Cambridge Journal of Economics*, **23** (1), 115–19.

Armknecht, P.A., W.F. Lane and K.J. Stewart (1997), 'New products and the U.S. consumer price index', in T.F. Bresnahan and R.J. Gordon (eds), *The Economics of New Goods*, ('Studies in Income and Wealth', 58), Chicago and London: University of Chicago Press (for the National Bureau of Economic Research), 375–96.

Armknecht, P.A. and D. Weyback (1989), 'Adjustments for quality change in the U.S. consumer price index', *Journal of Official Statistics*, **5** (2), 107–23.

Asimakopulos, A. (1975), 'A Kaleckian theory of income distribution', *Canadian Journal of Economics*, **8** (3), 313–33.

Balasko, Y. and K. Shell (1981), 'The overlapping-generations model. II: The case of pure exchange with money', *Journal of Economic Theory*, **24** (1), 112–42.

Balk, B.M. (1980), 'A method for constructing price indices for seasonal commodities', *Journal of the Royal Statistical Society*, **143** (1), 68–75.

Ball, R.J. (1964), *Inflation and the Theory of Money*, ('Minerva Series of Students' Handbooks', 12), London: George Allen & Unwin.

Bank of England (1996), *Inflation Report*, London: Bank of England, November.

Baranzini, M. (ed.) (1982), *Advances in Economic Theory*, Oxford and New York: Basil Blackwell and St. Martin's Press.

Baranzini, M. (1991), *A Theory of Wealth Distribution and Accumulation*, Oxford: Clarendon Press.

Barnett, W.A. (1987), 'The microeconomic theory of monetary aggregation', in W.A. Barnett and K.J. Singleton (eds), *New Approaches to Monetary Economics*, ('International Symposia in Economic Theory and Econometrics', 1), Cambridge: Cambridge University Press, 115–68.

Barro, R.J. (1976), 'Rational expectations and the role of monetary policy', *Journal of Monetary Economics*, **2** (1), 1–32.

Barro, R.J. (1996), 'Inflation and growth', *Federal Reserve Bank of St. Louis Review*, **78** (3), 153–69.

Beaton, R. and P.G. Fisher (1995), 'The construction of RPIY', *Bank of England Working Paper*, 28.

Berndt, E.R., I.M. Cockburn, D.L. Cocks, A. Epstein and Z. Griliches (1997), 'Is price inflation different for the elderly? An empirical analysis of prescription drugs', *NBER Working Paper*, 6182.

Berndt, E.R. and Z. Griliches (1993), 'Price indexes for microcomputers: an exploratory study', in M.F. Foss, M.E. Manser and A.H. Young (eds), *Price Measurements and Their Uses*, ('Studies in Income and Wealth', 57), Chicago and London: University of Chicago Press (for the National Bureau of Economic Research), 63–93.

Bernhardt, D. and M. Engineer (1994), 'Rivalrous money supply among overlapping generations', *Canadian Journal of Economics*, **27** (2), 494–504.

Bertocchi, G. and Y. Wang (1995), 'The real value of money under endogenous beliefs', *Journal of Economic Theory*, **67** (1), 205–22.

Black, S. (1987), 'Seigniorage', in J. Eatwell, M. Milgate and P. Newman (eds), *The New Palgrave: A Dictionary of Economics*, London and Basingstoke: Macmillan, vol. IV, 287.

Blinder, A.S. (1980), 'The consumer price index and the measurement of recent inflation', *Brookings Papers on Economic Activity*, **11** (2), 539–65.

Blow, L. and I. Crawford (1999a), 'A nonparametric bound on substitution bias in the UK retail prices index', *The Institute for Fiscal Studies Working Paper*, W99/15.

Blow, L. and I. Crawford (1999b), *Cost-of-Living Indices and Revealed Preference*, London: The Institute for Fiscal Studies.

Boland, L.A. (1982), *The Foundations of Economic Method*, London: George Allen & Unwin.

Bordo, M.D. (1987), 'Equation of exchange', in J. Eatwell, M. Milgate and P. Newman (eds), *The New Palgrave: A Dictionary of Economics*, London and Basingstoke: Macmillan, vol. II, 175–7.

Bortis, H. (1997), *Institutions, Behaviour and Economic Theory: A Contribution to Classical–Keynesian Political Economy*, Cambridge: Cambridge University Press.

Boskin, M.J. (1996), 'Prisoners of faulty statistics', *The Wall Street Journal Europe*, 6–7 December, in Deutsche Bundesbank (ed.), *Auszüge aus Presseartikeln*, Frankfurt am Main: Deutsche Bundesbank, (77), 22–3.

Boskin, M.J., E.R. Dulberger, R.J. Gordon, Z. Griliches and D.W. Jorgenson (1998), 'Consumer prices, the consumer price index, and the cost of living', *Journal of Economic Perspectives*, **12** (1), 3–26.

Boskin, M.J. and M.D. Hurd (1985), 'Indexing social security benefits: a separate price index for the elderly?', *Public Finance Quarterly*, **13** (4), 436–49.

Bouvet, P. (1996), 'Les théoriciens contemporains de la monnaie endogène: consensus et désaccords', *L'Actualité économique*, **72** (4), 451–70.

Bowley, A.L. (1928), 'Notes on index numbers', *Economic Journal*, **38** (150), 216–37.

Bradford, W. and G.C. Harcourt (1997), 'Units and definitions', in G.C. Harcourt and P.A. Riach (eds), *A 'Second Edition' of The General Theory*, London and New York: Routledge, vol. I, 107–31.

Bradley, X., J.-J. Friboulet and C. Gnos (1996), 'From Keynes's to the modern analysis of inflation', in A. Cencini and M. Baranzini (eds), *Inflation and Unemployment: Contributions to a New Macroeconomic Approach*, ('Routledge Studies in the Modern World Economy', 4), London and New York: Routledge, 107–34.

Bradley, X. and C. Gnos (1991), 'Définition de l'inflation: actualité de la problématique keynésienne des unités de salaire', *Économies et Sociétés*, ('Série Monnaie et Production', 8), **25** (11–12), 173–89.

Braithwait, S.D. (1980), 'The substitution bias of the Laspeyres price index: an analysis using estimated cost-of-living indexes', *American Economic Review*, **70** (1), 64–77.

Bronfenbrenner, M. and F.D. Holzman (1963), 'Survey of inflation theory', *American Economic Review*, **53** (4), 593–661.

Brunner, K. (1968), 'The role of money and monetary policy', *Federal Reserve Bank of St. Louis Review*, **50** (7), 9–24. Reprinted in K.A. Chrystal (ed.) (1990), *Monetarism*, ('Schools of Thought in Economics', 11), Aldershot and Brookfield: Edward Elgar Publishing Ltd, vol. II, 391–406.

Brunner, K. (1970), 'The "monetarist revolution" in monetary theory', *Weltwirtschaftliches Archiv*, **105** (1), 1–30.

Brunner, K. and A.H. Meltzer (1971), 'The uses of money: money in the theory of an exchange economy', *American Economic Review*, **61** (3), 784–805.

Brunner, K. and A.H. Meltzer (1976), 'Monetarism: the principal issues, areas of agreement and the work remaining', in J.L. Stein (ed.), *Monetarism*, ('Studies in Monetary Economics', 1), Amsterdam: North-Holland Publishing Company, 150–82.

Bryan, M.F. and S.G. Cecchetti (1994), 'Measuring core inflation', in N.G. Mankiw (ed.), *Monetary Policy*, ('Studies in Business Cycles', 29), Chicago and London: University of Chicago Press (for the National Bureau of Economic Research), 195–219.

Burdekin, R.C.K. and P. Burkett (1996), *Distributional Conflict and Inflation: Theoretical and Historical Perspectives*, London and New York: Macmillan and St. Martin's Press.

Bureau of Labor Statistics (1988), *An Analysis of the Rates of Inflation Affecting Older Americans Based on an Experimental Reweighted Consumer Price Index*, U.S. Department of Labor, mimeo.

Bureau of Labor Statistics (1997), 'Measurement issues in the consumer price index', paper prepared in response to a letter from Jim Saxton, Chairman of the Joint Economic Committee. Online. Available HTTP: http://stats.bls.gov/cpigm697.html (7 June 1999).

Caballero, R.J. (1992), 'A fallacy of composition', *American Economic Review*, **82** (5), 1279–92.

Cagan, P. (1987), 'Monetarism', in J. Eatwell, M. Milgate and P. Newman (eds), *The New Palgrave: A Dictionary of Economics*, London and

Basingstoke: Macmillan, vol. III, 492–7.

Carabelli, A. (1992), 'Organic interdependence and Keynes's choice of units in the *General Theory*', in B. Gerrard and J. Hillard (eds), *The Philosophy and Economics of J.M. Keynes*, Aldershot and Brookfield: Edward Elgar Publishing Ltd, 3–31.

Carruthers, A.G., D.J. Sellwood and P.W. Ward (1980), 'Recent developments in the retail prices index', *The Statistician*, **29** (1), 1–32.

Cecchetti, S.G. (1996), 'Measuring short-run inflation for central bankers', *NBER Working Paper*, 5786.

Cencini, A. (1982), 'The logical indeterminacy of relative prices', in M. Baranzini (ed.), *Advances in Economic Theory*, Oxford and New York: Basil Blackwell and St. Martin's Press, 126–36.

Cencini, A. (1984), *Time and the Macroeconomic Analysis of Income*, London and New York: Pinter Publishers.

Cencini, A. (1988), *Money, Income and Time: A Quantum-Theoretical Approach*, London and New York: Pinter Publishers.

Cencini, A. (1995), *Monetary Theory, National and International*, London and New York: Routledge.

Cencini, A. (1996), 'Inflation and deflation: the two faces of the same reality', in A. Cencini and M. Baranzini (eds), *Inflation and Unemployment: Contributions to a New Macroeconomic Approach*, ('Routledge Studies in the Modern World Economy', 4), London and New York: Routledge, 17–60.

Cencini, A. (1999), 'Inflazione', in *Capitoli di teoria monetaria*, ('Research Laboratory of Monetary Economics', 1), Lugano and Bellinzona: Centre for Banking Studies and Meta-Edizioni, 113–47.

Cencini, A. (2001), *Monetary Macroeconomics: A New Approach*, ('Routledge International Studies in Money and Banking', 15), London and New York: Routledge.

Cencini, A. and M. Baranzini (1996), 'Introduction', in A. Cencini and M. Baranzini (eds), *Inflation and Unemployment: Contributions to a New Macroeconomic Approach*, ('Routledge Studies in the Modern World Economy', 4), London and New York: Routledge, 1–14.

Chick, V. (1978), 'Keynes's theory, Keynesian policy and the postwar inflation', *British Review of Economic Issues*, **1** (3), 1–24. Reprinted as 'Inflation from a longer-run perspective', in P. Arestis and S.C. Dow (eds) (1992), *On Money, Method and Keynes: Selected Essays of Victoria Chick*, London and New York: Macmillan and St. Martin's Press, 31–54.

Chick, V. (1982), 'A comment on "*IS–LM*: an explanation"', *Journal of Post Keynesian Economics*, **4** (3), 439–44. Reprinted in P. Arestis and S.C.

Dow (eds) (1992), *On Money, Method and Keynes: Selected Essays of Victoria Chick*, London and New York: Macmillan and St. Martin's Press, 95–100.

Chick, V. (1983), *Macroeconomics After Keynes: A Reconsideration of the General Theory*, Oxford: Philip Allan.

Chick, V. (1986), 'The evolution of the banking system and the theory of saving, investment and interest', *Économies et Sociétés*, ('Série Monnaie et Production', 3), **20** (8–9), 111–26. Reprinted in P. Arestis and S.C. Dow (eds) (1992), *On Money, Method and Keynes: Selected Essays of Victoria Chick*, London and New York: Macmillan and St. Martin's Press, 193–205.

Chick, V. (1994), 'Speculation', in P. Arestis and M. Sawyer (eds), *The Elgar Companion to Radical Political Economy*, Aldershot and Brookfield: Edward Elgar Publishing Ltd, 380–4.

Chick, V. (1996), 'The monetary theory of Keynes and the Post Keynesians', *Discussion Papers in Economics*, University College London, 96-09.

Chick, V. (1998), 'On knowing one's place: the role of formalism in economics', *Economic Journal*, **108** (451), 1859–69.

Chick, V. (2000), 'Money and effective demand', in J. Smithin (ed.), *What is Money?*, ('Routledge International Studies in Money and Banking', 6), London and New York: Routledge, 124–38.

Chowdhury, A. (1983), 'The decentralized labor market and the nonmarket consideration of wage change', *Journal of Post Keynesian Economics*, **5** (4), 648–63.

Clower, R.W. (1967), 'A reconsideration of the microfoundations of monetary theory', *Western Economic Journal*, **6** (1), 1–8.

Clower, R.W. (1969), 'Introduction', in R.W. Clower (ed.), *Monetary Theory: Selected Readings*, ('Penguin Modern Economics Readings'), Harmondsworth: Penguin Education, 7–21.

Clower, R.W. (1977), 'The anatomy of monetary theory', *American Economic Review*, **67** (1), 206–12.

Cohen, I.K. (1996), 'Book review of A. Cencini (1995), *Monetary Theory, National and International*', *Economic Journal*, **106** (437), 1134–5.

Colander, D. (1996), 'Overview', in D. Colander (ed.), *Beyond Microfoundations: Post Walrasian Macroeconomics*, Cambridge: Cambridge University Press, 1–17.

Congdon, T. (1978), *Monetarism: An Essay in Definition*, London: Centre for Policy Studies.

Craven, B.M. and R. Gausden (1991), 'How best to measure inflation? The UK and Europe', *The Royal Bank of Scotland Review*, (170), 26–37.

Cubadda, G. and R. Sabbatini (1997), 'The seasonality of the italian cost-of-living index', *Temi di discussione*, Roma: Banca d'Italia, 313.

Cunningham, A.W.F. (1996), 'Measurement bias in price indices: an application to the UK's RPI', *Bank of England Working Paper*, 47.

Dalziel, P.C. (1990), 'Market power, inflation, and incomes policies', *Journal of Post Keynesian Economics*, **12** (3), 424–38.

Davidson, P. (1978), *Money and the Real World*, London and Basingstoke: Macmillan (first published 1972).

Davidson, P. (1987), 'User cost', in J. Eatwell, M. Milgate and P. Newman (eds), *The New Palgrave: A Dictionary of Economics*, London and Basingstoke: Macmillan, vol. IV, 766–7.

Davidson, P. (1988), 'Endogenous money, the production process, and inflation analysis', *Économie appliquée*, **41** (1), 151–69.

Davidson, P. (1991), 'Three views on inflation: monetarist, neoclassical Keynesian and Post Keynesian', in *Controversies in Post Keynesian Economics*, Aldershot and Brookfield: Edward Elgar Publishing Ltd, 83–110.

Davidson, P. (1998), 'Setting the record straight', in R.J. Rotheim (ed.), *New Keynesian Economics/Post Keynesian Alternatives*, ('Routledge Frontiers of Political Economy', 9), London and New York: Routledge, 15–38.

Davidson, P. and S. Weintraub (1973), 'Money as cause and effect', *Economic Journal*, **83** (332), 1117–32.

Dawson, G. (1992), *Inflation and Unemployment: Causes, Consequences and Cures*, Aldershot and Brookfield: Edward Elgar Publishing Ltd.

de Boyer, J. (1998), 'Endogenous money and shareholders' funds in the classical theory of banking', *European Journal of the History of Economic Thought*, **5** (1), 60–84.

De Vroey, M. (1984), 'Inflation: a non-monetarist monetary interpretation', *Cambridge Journal of Economics*, **8** (4), 381–99.

Dean, E. (ed.) (1965), *The Controversy over the Quantity Theory of Money*, Boston: D.C. Heath & Co.

Deaton, A. (1998), 'Getting prices right: what should be done?', *Journal of Economic Perspectives*, **12** (1), 37–46.

Deaton, A. and J. Muellbauer (1980), *Economics and Consumer Behavior*, Cambridge: Cambridge University Press.

Debreu, G. (1959), *Theory of Value: An Axiomatic Analysis of Economic Equilibrium*, ('Cowles Foundation Monograph', 17), New York: John Wiley.

Deleplace, G. (1999), 'Des hétérodoxies diverses', in *Histoire de la pensée économique: du 'royaume agricole' de Quesnay au 'monde à la Arrow–*

Debreu', Paris: Dunod, 433–79.

Deleplace, G. and E.J. Nell (eds) (1996), *Money in Motion: The Post Keynesian and Circulation Approaches*, London and New York: Macmillan and St. Martin's Press.

Deprez, J. (1989), 'Book review of A. Cencini (1988), *Money, Income and Time: A Quantum-Theoretical Approach*', *Economic Journal*, **99** (394), 203–4.

Deprez, J. (1993), 'Fixed capital and inflation: an analysis applying Keynes' notion of user cost', *Review of Radical Political Economics*, **25** (3), 34–42.

Desai, M. (1981), *Testing Monetarism*, London: Pinter Publishers.

Desai, M. (1984), 'Foreword', in A. Cencini, *Time and the Macroeconomic Analysis of Income*, London and New York: Pinter Publishers, xi–xiv.

Desai, M. (1987), 'Endogenous and exogenous money', in J. Eatwell, M. Milgate and P. Newman (eds), *The New Palgrave: A Dictionary of Economics*, London and Basingstoke: Macmillan, vol. II, 136–7. Reprinted in M. Desai (1995), *The Selected Essays of Meghnad Desai* (vol. I *Macroeconomics and Monetary Theory*), Aldershot and Brookfield: Edward Elgar Publishing Ltd, 250–4.

Desai, M. (1988), 'Foreword', in A. Cencini, *Money, Income and Time: A Quantum-Theoretical Approach*, London and New York: Pinter Publishers, xi–xiv.

Desai, M. (1989), 'The scourge of the monetarists: Kaldor on monetarism and on money', *Cambridge Journal of Economics*, **13** (1), 171–82.

Desai, M. (1992), 'A Keynesian model for a post-monetarist open economy', in H. Brink (ed.), *Themes in Modern Macroeconomics*, London and Basingstoke: Macmillan, 115–39. Reprinted in M. Desai (1995), *The Selected Essays of Meghnad Desai* (vol. I *Macroeconomics and Monetary Theory*), Aldershot and Brookfield: Edward Elgar Publishing Ltd, 208–32.

Desai, M. (1995a), 'The natural rate of unemployment: a fundamentalist Keynesian view', in R. Cross (ed.), *The Natural Rate of Unemployment: Reflections on 25 Years of the Hypothesis*, Cambridge: Cambridge University Press, 346–61.

Desai, M. (1995b), *The Selected Essays of Meghnad Desai* (vol. I *Macroeconomics and Monetary Theory*), Aldershot and Brookfield: Edward Elgar Publishing Ltd.

Desai, M. (1996), 'A monetary theory for a monetary economy', *The Federico Caffè Memorial Lectures*, Rome and London: Università degli studi di Roma and London School of Economics.

Deutsche Bundesbank (1998), 'Problems of inflation measurement', *Monthly*

Report, **50** (5), 51–64.

Deutsche Bundesbank (2000), 'Core inflation rates as a tool of price analysis', *Monthly Report*, **52** (4), 45–58.

Devillebichot, G. (1969), 'Note sur les travaux de Bernard Schmitt', *Revue d'économie politique*, **79** (3), 693–702.

Diewert, W.E. (1976), 'Exact and superlative index numbers', *Journal of Econometrics*, **4** (2), 115–45.

Diewert, W.E. (1987), 'Index numbers', in J. Eatwell, M. Milgate and P. Newman (eds), *The New Palgrave: A Dictionary of Economics*, London and Basingstoke: Macmillan, vol. II, 767–80.

Diewert, W.E. (1990), 'The theory of the cost-of-living index and the measurement of welfare change', in W.E. Diewert (ed.), *Price Level Measurement*, ('Contributions to Economic Analysis', 196), Amsterdam: Elsevier Science Publishers B.V. (North-Holland), 79–147.

Diewert, W.E. (1997), 'Comment', in T.F. Bresnahan and R.J. Gordon (eds), *The Economics of New Goods*, ('Studies in Income and Wealth', 58), Chicago and London: University of Chicago Press (for the National Bureau of Economic Research), 423–36.

Diewert, W.E. (1998), 'Index number issues in the consumer price index', *Journal of Economic Perspectives*, **12** (1), 47–58.

Divisia, F. (1925), 'L'indice monétaire et la théorie de la monnaie', *Revue d'économie politique*, **39** (4), 842–64; **39** (5), 980–1008; **39** (6), 1121–51.

Divisia, F. (1926), 'L'indice monétaire et la théorie de la monnaie', *Revue d'économie politique*, **40** (1), 49–81.

Dostaler, G. (1998), 'Friedman and Keynes: divergences and convergences', *European Journal of the History of Economic Thought*, **5** (2), 317–47.

Dow, A.C. and S.C. Dow (1989), 'Endogenous money creation and idle balances', in J. Pheby (ed.), *New Directions in Post-Keynesian Economics*, Aldershot and Brookfield: Edward Elgar Publishing Ltd, 147–64.

Dow, S.C. (1996), 'Horizontalism: a critique', *Cambridge Journal of Economics*, **20** (4), 497–508.

Dow, S.C. (1997), 'Endogenous money', in G.C. Harcourt and P.A. Riach (eds), *A 'Second Edition' of The General Theory*, London and New York: Routledge, vol. II, 61–78.

Dow, S.C. and J. Smithin (1999), 'The structure of financial markets and the "first principles" of monetary economics', *Scottish Journal of Political Economy*, **46** (1), 72–90.

Driffill, J., G.E. Mizon and A. Ulph (1990), 'Costs of inflation', in B.M. Friedman and F.H. Hahn (eds), *Handbook of Monetary Economics*, ('Handbooks in Economics', 8), Amsterdam: Elsevier Science B.V., vol.

II, 1013–66.

Duck, N.W. (1993), 'Some international evidence on the quantity theory of money', *Journal of Money, Credit, and Banking*, **25** (1), 1–12.

Duffy, J. (1994), 'On learning and the nonuniqueness of equilibrium in an overlapping generations model with fiat money', *Journal of Economic Theory*, **64** (2), 541–53.

Duisenberg, W. (1998), 'Introductory statement by the President of the European Central Bank at the press conference held in Frankfurt on 13 October 1998', *Bank for International Settlements Review*, (82), 1–7.

Dutt, A.K. (1992), 'Conflict inflation, distribution, cyclical accumulation and crises', *European Journal of Political Economy*, **8** (4), 579–97.

Dutt, A.K. (1998), 'Representing the representative agent', *Journal of Economic Methodology*, **5** (2), 310–17.

Economist, The (2000), 'Fighting America's inflation flab', *The Economist*, 7 October 2000, 111–12.

Edgeworth, F.Y. (1925), 'The plurality of index-numbers', *Economic Journal*, **35** (139), 379–88.

Eichner, A.S. (1991), 'Money and credit', in *The Macrodynamics of Advanced Market Economies*, New York: M.E. Sharpe, 803–63.

Eichner, A.S. and J.A. Kregel (1975), 'An essay on Post-Keynesian theory: a new paradigm in economics', *Journal of Economic Literature*, **13** (4), 1293–314.

Eshag, E. (1963), *From Marshall to Keynes: An Essay on the Monetary Theory of the Cambridge School*, Oxford: Basil Blackwell.

European Central Bank (1999), 'The stability-oriented monetary policy strategy of the Eurosystem', *Monthly Bulletin*, **1** (1), 39–50.

European Monetary Institute (1997), *The Single Monetary Policy in Stage Three: Specification of the Operational Framework*, Frankfurt am Main: European Monetary Institute.

Eurostat (1997), 'Big step on consumer price indices: harmonizing the way EU measures inflation', *News Release*, Luxembourg: Office for Official Publications of the European Communities, 21.

Evans, A.W. (1989), 'Housing costs and the retail price index', *National Westminster Bank Quarterly Review*, 39–55.

Fama, E.F. (1980), 'Banking in the theory of finance', *Journal of Monetary Economics*, **6** (1), 39–57.

Felderer, B. and S. Homburg (1992), *Macroeconomics and New Macroeconomics*, Berlin and Heidelberg: Springer Verlag, second edition (first published 1987).

Fischer, S. (1980), 'On activist monetary policy with rational expectations', in S. Fischer (ed.), *Rational Expectations and Economic Policy*, Chicago and London: University of Chicago Press (for the National Bureau of Economic Research), 211–47.

Fischer, S. (1983), 'A framework for monetary and banking analysis', *Economic Journal*, **93**, Association of University Teachers of Economics (1982) Conference Supplement, 1–16.

Fischer, S. (1987), 'New classical macroeconomics', in J. Eatwell, M. Milgate and P. Newman (eds), *The New Palgrave: A Dictionary of Economics*, London and Basingstoke: Macmillan, vol. III, 647–51.

Fisher, D. (1989), *Money Demand and Monetary Policy*, Hemel Hempstead: Harvester Wheatsheaf.

Fisher, F.M. and Z. Griliches (1995), 'Aggregate price indices, new goods, and generics', *Quarterly Journal of Economics*, **110** (1), 229–44.

Fisher, F.M. and K. Shell (1972), *The Economic Theory of Price Indices: Two Essays on the Effects of Taste, Quality, and Technological Change*, New York and London: Academic Press.

Fisher, I. (1911/1931), *The Purchasing Power of Money: Its Determination and Relation to Credit Interest and Crises*, New York: Macmillan.

Fisher, I. (1922), *The Making of Index Numbers*, Boston: Houghton, Mifflin & Co.

Fontana, G. (1999), *Essays on Money, Uncertainty and Time in the Post Keynesian Tradition*, unpublished PhD dissertation, University of Leeds.

Fortin, P. (1990), 'Do we measure inflation correctly?', in R.G. Lipsey (ed.), *Zero Inflation: the Goal of Price Stability*, ('Policy Study', 8), Toronto and Calgary: C.D. Howe Institute, 109–30.

Foss, M.F. (1993), 'Does government regulation inhibit the reporting of transactions prices by business?', in M.F. Foss, M.E. Manser and A.H. Young (eds), *Price Measurements and Their Uses*, ('Studies in Income and Wealth', 57), Chicago and London: University of Chicago Press (for the National Bureau of Economic Research), 275–301.

Foss, M.F., M.E. Manser and A.H. Young (eds) (1993), *Price Measurements and Their Uses*, ('Studies in Income and Wealth', 57), Chicago and London: University of Chicago Press (for the National Bureau of Economic Research).

Friboulet, J.-J. (1985a), 'Une conception hétérodoxe des volumes: l'analyse de Keynes dans le *Traité sur la monnaie*', *Cahier de la Revue d'économie politique*, ('Production et monnaie', special issue), 31–9.

Friboulet, J.-J. (1985b), 'Le *Traité de la monnaie* et l'inflation d'équilibre', in F. Poulon (ed.), *Les écrits de Keynes*, Paris: Dunod, 111–30.

Friboulet, J.-J. (1988), *Profit, investissement et inflation: Essai sur le Traité de la monnaie*, ('Publications Universitaires Européennes: Série 5', 936), Berne and Paris: Peter Lang.

Friboulet, J.-J. (1991), 'Inflation de demande et coût d'usage', *Économies et Sociétés*, ('Série Monnaie et Production', 8), **25** (11–12), 127–53.

Friedman, M. (1959), 'Statement on monetary theory and policy', in *Employment, Growth and Price Levels* (Hearings before the Joint Economic Committee, 86th Congress, 1st session, 25–28 May 1959), Washington (DC): Government Printing Office, 605–12. Reprinted in R.J. Ball and P. Doyle (eds) (1969), *Inflation: Selected Readings*, ('Penguin Modern Economics Readings'), Harmondsworth: Penguin Education, 136–45.

Friedman, M. (1968), 'The role of monetary policy', *American Economic Review*, **58** (1), 1–17.

Friedman, M. (1969), *The Optimum Quantity of Money and Other Essays*, Chicago: Aldine Publishing.

Friedman, M. (1970), 'The counter-revolution in monetary theory', First Wincott Memorial Lecture, University of London, 16 September 1970, *Institute of Economic Affairs Occasional Paper*, 33. Reprinted in M. Friedman (1991), *Monetarist Economics*, ('IEA Masters of Modern Economics'), Oxford: Basil Blackwell, 1–20.

Friedman, M. (1971), 'A monetary theory of nominal income', *Journal of Political Economy*, **79** (2), 323–37.

Friedman, M. (1974), 'A theoretical framework for monetary analysis', in R.J. Gordon (ed.), *Milton Friedman's Monetary Framework: A Debate with His Critics*, Chicago and London: University of Chicago Press, 1–62.

Friedman, M. (1977), 'Nobel lecture: inflation and unemployment', *Journal of Political Economy*, **85** (3), 451–72.

Friedman, M. (1987), 'Quantity theory of money', in J. Eatwell, M. Milgate and P. Newman (eds), *The New Palgrave: A Dictionary of Economics*, London and Basingstoke: Macmillan, vol. IV, 3–20.

Frisch, H. (1977), 'Inflation theory 1963–1975: a "second generation" survey', *Journal of Economic Literature*, **15** (4), 1289–317.

Frisch, H. (1983), *Theories of Inflation*, ('Cambridge Surveys of Economic Literature'), Cambridge: Cambridge University Press.

Fuerst, T.S. (1994), 'Optimal monetary policy in a cash-in advance economy', *Economic Inquiry*, **32** (4), 582–96.

Gale, W.A. (1981a), 'Introduction', in W.A. Gale (ed.), *Inflation: Causes, Consequents, and Control*, Cambridge (Massachusetts): Oelgeschlager, Gunn & Hain, 1–11.

Gale, W.A. (1981b), 'How well can we measure price changes?', in W.A.

Gale (ed.), *Inflation: Causes, Consequents, and Control*, Cambridge (Massachusetts): Oelgeschlager, Gunn & Hain, 51–114.

Geanakoplos, J. (1987), 'Overlapping generations model of general equilibrium', in J. Eatwell, M. Milgate and P. Newman (eds), *The New Palgrave: A Dictionary of Economics*, London and Basingstoke: Macmillan, vol. III, 767–79.

George, E.A.J. (1998), 'Britain in Europe: speech by the Governor of the Bank of England at the financial forum of West Flandres in Bruges on 21 October 1998', *Bank for International Settlements Review*, (88), 1–7.

Gnos, C. (1992a), *Production, répartition et monnaie*, ('Publications de l'Université de Bourgogne', 72), Dijon: Editions Universitaires de Dijon.

Gnos, C. (1992b), 'La transition vers l'union économique et monétaire: les vertus négligées de la monnaie commune', *Revue du Marché commun et de l'Union européenne*, (360), 621–6.

Gnos, C. (1998), 'The Keynesian identity of income and output', in P. Fontaine and A. Jolink (eds), *Historical Perspectives on Macroeconomics: Sixty Years After the General Theory*, ('Routledge Studies in the History of Economics', 22), London and New York: Routledge, 40–8.

Gnos, C. and B. Schmitt (1990), 'Le circuit, réalité exhaustive', *Économies et Sociétés*, ('Série Monnaie et Production', 6), **24** (2), 63–74.

Godley, W. (1999), 'Money and credit in a Keynesian model of income determination', *Cambridge Journal of Economics*, **23** (4), 393–411.

Goodhart, C.A.E. (1989a), 'Has Moore become too horizontal?', *Journal of Post Keynesian Economics*, **12** (1), 29–34.

Goodhart, C.A.E. (1989b), *Money, Information and Uncertainty*, London and Basingstoke: Macmillan, second edition (first published 1975).

Goodhart, C.A.E. (1997), 'Two concepts of money, and the future of Europe', London School of Economics, *Financial Markets Group Special Paper*, 96.

Gordon, R.J. (1971), 'Measurement bias in price indexes for capital goods', *Review of Income and Wealth*, **17** (2), 121–74.

Gordon, R.J. (1981), 'The consumer price index: measuring inflation and causing it', *The Public Interest*, (63), 112–34.

Gordon, R.J. (1990), *The Measurement of Durable Goods Prices*, Chicago and London: University of Chicago Press (for the National Bureau of Economic Research).

Gordon, R.J. (1992), 'Measuring the aggregate price level: implications for economic performance and policy', *NBER Working Paper*, 3969.

Gordon, R.J. (1996), 'The time-varying NAIRU and its implications for economic policy', *NBER Working Paper*, 5735.

Gottardi, P. (1996), 'Stationary monetary equilibria in overlapping generations models with incomplete markets', *Journal of Economic Theory*, **71** (1), 75–89.

Grandmont, J.-M. (1983), *Money and Value: A Reconsideration of Classical and Neoclassical Monetary Theory*, ('Econometric Society Monographs in Pure Theory', 5), Cambridge and Paris: Cambridge University Press and Editions de la Maison des Sciences de l'Homme.

Grandmont, J.-M. and Y. Younès (1972), 'On the role of money and the existence of a monetary equilibrium', *Review of Economic Studies*, **39** (3), 355–72.

Graziani, A. (1985), 'Commento ad Alvaro Cencini', *Studi economici*, **40** (25), 131–42.

Graziani, A. (1990), 'The theory of the monetary circuit', *Économies et Sociétés*, ('Série Monnaie et Production', 7), **24** (6), 7–36.

Graziani, A. (1994a), 'Monetary circuits', in P. Arestis and M. Sawyer (eds), *The Elgar Companion to Radical Political Economy*, Aldershot and Brookfield: Edward Elgar Publishing Ltd, 274–8.

Graziani, A. (1994b), *La teoria monetaria della produzione*, ('Studi e Ricerche', 7), Arezzo: Banca Popolare dell'Etruria e del Lazio.

Green, R. (1987), 'Real bills doctrine', in J. Eatwell, M. Milgate and P. Newman (eds), *The New Palgrave: A Dictionary of Economics*, London and Basingstoke: Macmillan, vol. IV, 101–2.

Greenlees, J.S. (1997), 'A Bureau of Labor Statistics perspective on bias in the consumer price index', *Federal Reserve Bank of St. Louis Review*, **79** (3), 175–8.

Greenlees, J.S. and C.C. Mason (1996), 'Overview of the 1998 revision of the consumer price index', *Monthly Labor Review*, **119** (12), 3–9.

Greenspan, A. (1997a), 'Testimony before the Committee on finance of the US Senate on 30 January 1997', *Bank for International Settlements Review*, (10), 1–5.

Greenspan, A. (1997b), 'Problems of price measurement: remarks by the Chairman of the Board of Governors of the Federal Reserve System at the Center for financial studies, in Frankfurt, on 7 November 1997', in Deutsche Bundesbank (ed.), *Auszüge aus Presseartikeln*, Frankfurt am Main: Deutsche Bundesbank, (66), 1–4.

Greenspan, A. (1998), 'Problems of price measurement: remarks by Chairman of the Board of the US Federal Reserve System at the annual Meeting of the American Economic Association and the American Finance Association, in Chicago, on 3 January 1998', *Bank for International Settlements Review*, (1), 1–7.

Greenstein, S.M. (1997), 'From superminis to supercomputers: estimating surplus in the computing market', in T.F. Bresnahan and R.J. Gordon (eds), *The Economics of New Goods*, ('Studies in Income and Wealth', 58), Chicago and London: University of Chicago Press (for the National Bureau of Economic Research), 329–71.

Griliches, Z. (1971), 'Introduction: hedonic price indexes revisited', in Z. Griliches (ed.), *Price Indexes and Quality Change: Studies in New Methods of Measurement*, Cambridge (Massachusetts): Harvard University Press, 3–15.

Griliches, Z. (1990), 'Hedonic price indexes and the measurement of capital and productivity: some historical reflections', in E.R. Berndt and J.E. Triplett (eds), *Fifty Years of Economic Measurement: The Jubilee of the Conference on Research in Income and Wealth*, ('Studies in Income and Wealth', 54), Chicago and London: University of Chicago Press (for the National Bureau of Economic Research), 185–202.

Griliches, Z. (1997), 'Commentary', *Federal Reserve Bank of St. Louis Review*, **79** (3), 169–73.

Gurley, J.G. and E.S. Shaw (1960), *Money in a Theory of Finance*, Washington (DC): The Brookings Institution.

Hagemann, R.P. (1982), 'The variability of inflation rates across household types', *Journal of Money, Credit, and Banking*, **14** (4), 494–510.

Hahn, F.H. (1973), 'On the foundations of monetary theory', in M. Parkin and A.R. Nobay (eds), *Essays in Modern Economics*, London: Longman, 230–42.

Hahn, F.H. (1982), *Money and Inflation*, ('Mitsui Lectures in Economics'), Oxford: Basil Blackwell.

Hahn, F.H. (1987), 'The foundations of monetary theory', in M. de Cecco and J.-P. Fitoussi (eds), *Monetary Theory and Economic Institutions*, London and Basingstoke: Macmillan, 21–43.

Haliassos, M. and J. Tobin (1990), 'The macroeconomics of government finance', in B.M. Friedman and F.H. Hahn (eds), *Handbook of Monetary Economics*, ('Handbooks in Economics', 8), Amsterdam: Elsevier Science B.V., vol. II, 889–959.

Hamilton, K. and G. Atkinson (1996), 'Air pollution and green accounts', *Energy Policy*, **24** (7), 675–84.

Handa, J. (2000), *Monetary Economics*, London and New York: Routledge.

Harris, D.J. (1978), *Capital Accumulation and Income Distribution*, Stanford (California): Stanford University Press.

Harrod, R. (1969), *Money*, London: Macmillan.

Hartley, J.E. (1997), *The Representative Agent in Macroeconomics*,

('Routledge Frontiers of Political Economy', 10), London and New York: Routledge.

Hausman, J.A. (1994), 'Valuation of new goods under perfect and imperfect competition', *NBER Working Paper*, 4970.

Hayek, F.A. (1978), 'Denationalisation of money: the argument refined', *Institute of Economic Affairs Hobart Paper Special*, 70, second edition (first published 1976).

Hegeland, H. (1951), *The Quantity Theory of Money: A Critical Study of its Historical Development and Interpretation and a Restatement*, Göteborg: Elanders Boktryckeri Aktiebolag.

Hennings, K.H. (1985), 'Book review of A. Cencini (1984), *Time and the Macroeconomic Analysis of Income*', *Kyklos*, **38** (4), 620–2.

Herman, J. (1984), 'Monetarism: a paradoxical counter-revolution', *History of Political Economy*, **16** (4), 583–90.

Heymann, D. and A. Leijonhufvud (1995), *High Inflation*, Oxford: Clarendon Press.

Hicks, J.R. (1935), 'A suggestion for simplifying the theory of money', *Economica*, **2** (5), 1–19. Reprinted in J.R. Hicks (1967), *Critical Essays in Monetary Theory*, Oxford: Clarendon Press, 61–82.

Hicks, J.R. (1940), 'The valuation of the social income', *Economica*, **7** (26), 105–24.

Hicks, J.R. (1946), *Value and Capital: An Inquiry into Some Fundamental Principles of Economic Theory*, Oxford: Oxford University Press, second edition (first published 1939).

Hicks, J.R. (1955), 'Economic foundations of wage policy', *Economic Journal*, **65** (259), 389–404.

Hicks, J.R. (1966), 'Foundations of monetary theory', Lecture given at the London School of Economics in January 1966. Reprinted as 'The two triads – Lecture 1' in J.R. Hicks (1967), *Critical Essays in Monetary Theory*, Oxford: Clarendon Press, 1–16.

Hicks, J.R. (1967), *Critical Essays in Monetary Theory*, Oxford: Clarendon Press.

Hicks, J.R. (1974), 'Capital controversies: ancient and modern', *American Economic Review*, **64** (2), 307–16. Reprinted in J.R. Hicks (1977), *Economic Perspectives: Further Essays on Money and Growth*, Oxford: Clarendon Press, 149–65.

Hicks, J.R. (1989), *A Market Theory of Money*, Oxford: Oxford University Press.

Hoffmann, J. (1998), 'Probleme der Inflationsmessung in Deutschland', *Diskussionspapier der Volkswirtschaftlichen Forschungsgruppe der*

Deutschen Bundesbank, 1/98.

House of Commons (1988), 'The measurement of inflation', *House of Commons Background Paper*, London: House of Commons Library Research Division, 214.

Howells, P.G.A. (1995), 'The demand for endogenous money', *Journal of Post Keynesian Economics*, **18** (1), 89–106.

Howells, P.G.A. (1996), 'Endogenous money and the "state of trade"', in P. Arestis (ed.), *Keynes, Money and the Open Economy: Essays in Honour of Paul Davidson*, Cheltenham and Brookfield: Edward Elgar Publishing Ltd, vol. I, 105–22.

Howells, P.G.A. (1997), 'The demand for endogenous money: a rejoinder', *Journal of Post Keynesian Economics*, **19** (3), 429–35.

Howells, P.G.A. (1999), 'The source of endogenous money', *Economic Issues*, **4** (1), 101–12.

Howells, P.G.A. and K. Hussein (1998), 'The endogeneity of money: evidence from the G7', *Scottish Journal of Political Economy*, **45** (3), 329–40.

Howells, P.G.A. and K. Hussein (1999), 'The demand for bank loans and the "state of trade"', *Journal of Post Keynesian Economics*, **21** (3), 441–54.

Howitt, P.W. (1974), 'Stability and the quantity theory', *Journal of Political Economy*, **82** (1), 133–51.

Hudson, J. (1982), *Inflation: A Theoretical Survey and Synthesis*, London: George Allen & Unwin.

Hulten, C.R. (1973), 'Divisia index numbers', *Econometrica*, **41** (6), 1017–25.

Hulten, C.R. (1987), 'Divisia index', in J. Eatwell, M. Milgate and P. Newman (eds), *The New Palgrave: A Dictionary of Economics*, London and Basingstoke: Macmillan, vol. I, 899–901.

Hulten, C.R. (1997), 'Quality change in the CPI', *Federal Reserve Bank of St. Louis Review*, **79** (3), 87–100.

Hume, D. (1752/1955), 'Of money', in E. Rotwein (ed.), *David Hume: Writings on Economics*, Edinburgh: Thomas Nelson and Sons, 33–46.

Humphrey, T.M. (1999), 'Mercantilists and classicals: insights from doctrinal history', *Federal Reserve Bank of Richmond Economic Quarterly*, **85** (2), 55–82.

Huo, T.-M. (1995), 'Stationary sunspot equilibrium in a cash-in-advance economy', *Journal of Economic Dynamics and Control*, **19** (4), 831–43.

Ingham, G. (1996), 'Money is a social relation', *Review of Social Economy*, **54** (4), 507–29.

Janssen, M.C.W. (1993), *Microfoundations: A Critical Inquiry*, London and

New York: Routledge.

Kaldor, N. (1970), 'The new monetarism', *Lloyds Bank Review*, (97), 1–18.

Kaldor, N. and J. Trevithick (1981), 'A Keynesian perspective on money', *Lloyds Bank Review*, (139), 1–19.

Kalecki, M. (1971), 'Class struggle and the distribution of national income', *Kyklos*, **24** (1), 1–11. Reprinted in M. Kalecki (1971), *Selected Essays on the Dynamics of the Capitalist Economy, 1933–1970*, Cambridge: Cambridge University Press, 156–64.

Keynes, J.M. (1909/1983), 'The method of index numbers with special reference to the measurement of general exchange value', in *The Collected Writings of John Maynard Keynes* (vol. XI *Economic Articles and Correspondence: Academic*), London and Basingstoke: Macmillan, 49–173.

Keynes, J.M. (1923/1971), *A Tract on Monetary Reform*, in *The Collected Writings of John Maynard Keynes* (vol. IV *A Tract on Monetary Reform*), London and Basingstoke: Macmillan.

Keynes, J.M. (1930/1971), *A Treatise on Money* (vol. I *The Pure Theory of Money*), London: Macmillan. Reprinted in *The Collected Writings of John Maynard Keynes* (vol. V *A Treatise on Money: The Pure Theory of Money*), London and Basingstoke: Macmillan.

Keynes, J.M. (1933/1973), 'A monetary theory of production' in *The Collected Writings of John Maynard Keynes* (vol. XIII *The General Theory and After: Preparation*), London and Basingstoke: Macmillan, 408–11.

Keynes, J.M. (1936/1973), *The General Theory of Employment, Interest and Money*, London: Macmillan. Reprinted in *The Collected Writings of John Maynard Keynes* (vol. VII *The General Theory of Employment, Interest and Money*), London and Basingstoke: Macmillan.

Keynes, J.M. (1980), *The Collected Writings of John Maynard Keynes* (vol. XXV *Activities 1940–1944. Shaping the Post-War World: the Clearing Union*), London and Basingstoke: Macmillan.

King, M. (1997), 'The inflation target five years on', Lecture delivered at the London School of Economics on 29 October 1997, to commemorate the 10th anniversary of the Financial Markets Group and the 5th anniversary of the Bank of England *Inflation Report*.

King, R.G. and C.I. Plosser (1984), 'Money, credit, and prices in a real business cycle', *American Economic Review*, **74** (3), 363–80.

Kirman, A.P. (1992), 'Whom or what does the representative individual represent?', *Journal of Economic Perspectives*, **6** (2), 117–36.

Klein, L.R. (1946), 'Remarks on the theory of aggregation', *Econometrica*,

14 (4), 303–12.

Knapp, G.F. (1924), 'Payment, money and metal', in *The State Theory of Money*, abridged edition translated by H.M. Lucas and J. Bonar, London: Macmillan, 1–92 (first German edition 1905).

Kocherlakota, N.R. (1998a), 'The technological role of fiat money', *Federal Reserve Bank of Minneapolis Quarterly Review*, **22** (3), 2–10.

Kocherlakota, N.R. (1998b), 'Money is memory', *Journal of Economic Theory*, **81** (2), 232–51.

Kocherlakota, N.R. and N. Wallace (1998), 'Incomplete record-keeping and optimal payment arrangements', *Journal of Economic Theory*, **81** (2), 272–89.

König, S. (1995), *Estimation de la variance de l'indice suisse des prix à la consommation à l'aide de techniques empiriques, sous l'hypothèse d'échantillons aléatoires*, Neuchâtel: Imprimerie de l'Evole (PhD dissertation, University of Neuchâtel).

Konüs, A.A. (1939), 'The problem of the true index of the cost of living', *Econometrica*, **7** (1), 10–29.

Koopmans, T.C. (1947), 'Measurement without theory', *The Review of Economic Statistics*, **29** (3), 161–72.

Laidler, D. (1969), 'The definition of money: theoretical and empirical problems', *Journal of Money, Credit, and Banking*, **1** (3), 508–25.

Laidler, D. (1981), 'Monetarism: an interpretation and an assessment', *Economic Journal*, **91** (361), 1–28.

Laidler, D. (1988), 'Taking money seriously', *Canadian Journal of Economics*, **21** (4), 687–713.

Laidler, D. (1991), *The Golden Age of the Quantity Theory: The Development of Neoclassical Monetary Economics 1870–1914*, Hemel Hempstead: Philip Allan.

Laidler, D. (1993), 'Monetarism, microfoundations and the theory of monetary policy', in S.F. Frowen (ed.), *Monetary Theory and Monetary Policy: New Tracks for the 1990s*, Basingstoke and New York: Macmillan and St. Martin's Press, 21–42.

Laidler, D. (ed.) (1999), *The Foundations of Monetary Economics*, Cheltenham and Northampton: Edward Elgar Publishing Ltd, 3 vols.

Laidler, D. and M. Parkin (1975), 'Inflation: a survey', *Economic Journal*, **85** (340), 741–809.

Lancaster, K.J. (1971), *Consumer Demand: A New Approach*, ('Columbia Studies in Economics', 5), New York and London: Columbia University Press.

Lancaster, K.J. (1991), *Modern Consumer Theory*, Aldershot and Brookfield:

Edward Elgar Publishing Ltd.

Landau, B. (2000), 'Kerninflationsraten: ein Methodenvergleich auf der Basis westdeutscher Daten', *Diskussionspapier der Volkswirtschaftlichen Forschungsgruppe der Deutschen Bundesbank*, 4/00.

Laspeyres, E. (1871), 'Die Berechnung einer mittleren Waarenpreissteigerung', *Jahrbücher für Nationalökonomie und Statistik*, **16**, 296–314.

Lavoie, M. (1984), 'The endogenous flow of credit and the Post Keynesian theory of money', *Journal of Economic Issues*, **18** (3), 771–97.

Lavoie, M. (1985), 'La *Théorie générale* et l'inflation de sous-emploi', in F. Poulon (ed.), *Les écrits de Keynes*, Paris: Dunod, 131–52.

Lavoie, M. (1987), 'Monnaie et production: une synthèse de la théorie du circuit', *Économies et Sociétés*, ('Série Monnaie et Production', 4), **21** (9), 65–101.

Lavoie, M. (1992), *Foundations of Post-Keynesian Economic Analysis*, ('New Directions in Modern Economics'), Aldershot and Brookfield: Edward Elgar Publishing Ltd.

Lavoie, M. (1999), 'The credit-led supply of deposits and the demand for money: Kaldor's reflux mechanism as previously endorsed by Joan Robinson', *Cambridge Journal of Economics*, **23** (1), 103–13.

Lerner, A.P. (1947), 'Money as a creature of the state', *American Economic Review*, **37** (2), 312–17.

Lewbel, A. (1989), 'Exact aggregation and a representative consumer', *Quarterly Journal of Economics*, **104** (3), 621–33.

Liegey, P.R., Jr. (1993), 'Adjusting apparel indexes in the consumer price index for quality differences', in M.F. Foss, M.E. Manser and A.H. Young (eds), *Price Measurements and Their Uses*, ('Studies in Income and Wealth', 57), Chicago and London: University of Chicago Press (for the National Bureau of Economic Research), 209–26.

Lucas, R.E., Jr. (1972), 'Expectations and the neutrality of money', *Journal of Economic Theory*, **4** (1), 103–24.

Lucas, R.E., Jr. (1980), 'Equilibrium in a pure currency economy', in J.H. Kareken and N. Wallace (eds), *Models of Monetary Economies*, Minneapolis: Federal Reserve Bank of Minneapolis, 131–45.

Lucas, R.E., Jr. and N.L. Stokey (1983), 'Optimal fiscal and monetary policy in an economy without capital', *Journal of Monetary Economics*, **12** (1), 55–93.

Luxton, M. (1997), 'The UN, women, and household labour: measuring and valuing unpaid work', *Women's Studies International Forum*, **20** (3), 431–9.

Macesich, G. (1983), *Monetarism: Theory and Policy*, ('Praeger Studies in International Monetary Economics and Finance'), New York: Praeger.

Manser, M.E. and R.J. McDonald (1988), 'An analysis of substitution bias in measuring inflation, 1959–85', *Econometrica*, **56** (4), 909–30.

Marshall, A. (1887), 'Remedies for fluctuations of general prices', *The Contemporary Review*, **51**, 355–75.

Marshall, A. (1923), 'The total value of the currency needed by a country', in *Money, Credit and Commerce*, London: Macmillan, 38–50.

Martel, R.J. (1996), 'Heterogeneity, aggregation, and a meaningful macroeconomics', in D. Colander (ed.), *Beyond Microfoundations: Post Walrasian Macroeconomics*, Cambridge: Cambridge University Press, 127–44.

Marty, A.L. (1994), 'What is the neutrality of money?', *Economics Letters*, **44**, 407–9.

Mason, C.C. and C. Butler (1987), 'New basket of goods and services being priced in revised CPI', *Monthly Labor Review*, **110** (1), 3–22.

Mayer, T., M. Bronfenbrenner, K. Brunner, P. Cagan, B. Friedman, H. Frisch, H.G. Johnson, D. Laidler and A. Meltzer (1978), *The Structure of Monetarism*, New York and London: W.W. Norton & Co.

McCallum, B.T. (1980), 'Rational expectations and macroeconomic stabilization policy: an overview', *Journal of Money, Credit, and Banking*, **12** (4), 716–46.

McCallum, B.T. (1987), 'The optimal inflation rate in an overlapping-generations economy with land', in W.A. Barnett and K.J. Singleton (eds), *New Approaches to Monetary Economics*, ('International Symposia in Economic Theory and Econometrics', 1), Cambridge: Cambridge University Press, 325–39.

McCallum, B.T. (1990), 'Inflation: theory and evidence', in B.M. Friedman and F.H. Hahn (eds), *Handbook of Monetary Economics*, ('Handbooks in Economics', 8), Amsterdam: Elsevier Science B.V., vol. II, 963–1012.

Mehrling, P. (1998), 'Minsky, the banking school, and modern finance', paper delivered at an international conference on 'The Legacy of Hyman P. Minsky', University of Bergamo, 11–12 December 1998, mimeo.

Menger, K. (1892), 'On the origin of money', *Economic Journal*, **2** (6), 239–55.

Michael, R.T. (1979), 'Variation across households in the rate of inflation', *Journal of Money, Credit, and Banking*, **11** (1), 32–46.

Milgate, M. (1987), 'Quantity equations: early history', in J. Eatwell, M. Milgate and P. Newman (eds), *The New Palgrave: A Dictionary of Economics*, London and Basingstoke: Macmillan, vol. IV, 3.

Minsky, H.P. (1975), *John Maynard Keynes*, London and Basingstoke: Macmillan for the Columbia University Press.

Minsky, H.P. (1994), 'Financial instability hypothesis', in P. Arestis and M. Sawyer (eds), *The Elgar Companion to Radical Political Economy*, Aldershot and Brookfield: Edward Elgar Publishing Ltd, 153–8.

Moore, B.J. (1979), 'The endogenous money stock', *Journal of Post Keynesian Economics*, **2** (1), 49–70.

Moore, B.J. (1983), 'Unpacking the Post Keynesian black box: bank lending and the money supply', *Journal of Post Keynesian Economics*, **5** (4), 537–56.

Moore, B.J. (1988), *Horizontalists and Verticalists: The Macroeconomics of Credit Money*, Cambridge: Cambridge University Press.

Moore, B.J. (1989), 'A simple model of bank intermediation', *Journal of Post Keynesian Economics*, **12** (1), 10–28.

Moore, P.G. (1990), 'The skills challenge of the Nineties', *Journal of the Royal Statistical Society*, **153** (3), 265–85.

Morishima, M. (1992), *Capital and Credit: A New Formulation of General Equilibrium Theory*, Cambridge: Cambridge University Press.

Moulton, B.R. (1996), 'Bias in the consumer price index: what is the evidence?', *Journal of Economic Perspectives*, **10** (4), 159–77.

Myrdal, G. (1939), *Monetary Equilibrium*, London: William Hodge & Co.

National Bureau of Economic Research (1961), *The Price Statistics of the Federal Government: Review, Appraisal, and Recommendations*, ('General Series', 73), Washington (DC): National Bureau of Economic Research ('Stigler Report').

Nicholson, J.L. (1975), 'Whose cost of living?', *Journal of the Royal Statistical Society*, **138** (4), 540–2.

Niehans, J. (1978), *The Theory of Money*, Baltimore and London: Johns Hopkins University Press.

Nordhaus, W.D. (1997), 'Do real-output and real-wage measures capture reality? The history of lighting suggests not', in T.F. Bresnahan and R.J. Gordon (eds), *The Economics of New Goods*, ('Studies in Income and Wealth', 58), Chicago and London: University of Chicago Press (for the National Bureau of Economic Research), 29–70.

Nordhaus, W.D. (1998), 'Quality change in price indexes', *Journal of Economic Perspectives*, **12** (1), 59–68.

Office fédéral de la statistique (1993), *Révision de l'indice suisse des prix à la consommation: Conception du nouvel indice suisse des prix à la consommation*, ('Statistique de la Suisse', 5), Berne: Office fédéral de la statistique.

Office fédéral de la statistique (1999a), *Expertise sur la pertinence du "rapport Boskin" pour l'indice suisse des prix à la consommation*, ('Actualités OFS', 5), Berne: Office fédéral de la statistique.

Office fédéral de la statistique (1999b), *Révision de l'indice suisse des prix à la consommation 2000: Conception détaillée*, Berne: Office fédéral de la statistique.

Ohta, M. and Z. Griliches (1976), 'Automobile prices revisited: extensions of the hedonic hypothesis', in N.E. Terleckyj (ed.), *Household Production and Consumption*, ('Studies in Income and Wealth', 40), New York and London: Columbia University Press (for the National Bureau of Economic Research), 325–90.

Ormerod, P. (1994), *The Death of Economics*, London: Faber and Faber.

Paasche, H. (1874), 'Ueber die Preisentwicklung der letzten Jahre nach den Hamburger Börsennotirungen', *Jahrbücher für Nationalökonomie und Statistik*, **23**, 168–78.

Palley, T.I. (1996), *Post Keynesian Economics: Debt, Distribution and the Macro Economy*, London and New York: Macmillan and St. Martin's Press.

Parguez, A. (1999), 'The expected failure of the European economic and monetary union: a false money against the real economy', *Eastern Economic Journal*, **25** (1), 63–76.

Parguez, A. and M. Seccareccia (2000), 'The credit theory of money: the monetary circuit approach', in J. Smithin (ed.), *What is Money?*, ('Routledge International Studies in Money and Banking', 6), London and New York: Routledge, 101–23.

Parkin, M. (1987), 'Inflation', in J. Eatwell, M. Milgate and P. Newman (eds), *The New Palgrave: A Dictionary of Economics*, London and Basingstoke: Macmillan, vol. II, 832–7.

Pasinetti, L.L. (1981), *Structural Change and Economic Growth: A Theoretical Essay on the Dynamics of the Wealth of Nations*, Cambridge: Cambridge University Press.

Pasinetti, L.L. (1986), 'Theory of value – A source of alternative paradigms in economic analysis', in M. Baranzini and R. Scazzieri (eds), *Foundations of Economics: Structures of Inquiry and Economic Theory*, Oxford and New York: Basil Blackwell and St. Martin's Press, 409–31.

Pasinetti, L.L. (1993), *Structural Economic Dynamics: A Theory of the Economic Consequences of Human Learning*, Cambridge: Cambridge University Press.

Patinkin, D. (1956), *Money, Interest, and Prices: An Integration of Monetary and Value Theory*, Evanston (Illinois): Row, Peterson & Co.

Patinkin, D. (1969), 'The Chicago tradition, the quantity theory, and Friedman', *Journal of Money, Credit, and Banking*, **1** (1), 46–70.

Patinkin, D. (1972), *Studies in Monetary Economics*, New York: Harper & Row.

Patinkin, D. (1987), 'Neutrality of money', in J. Eatwell, M. Milgate and P. Newman (eds), *The New Palgrave: A Dictionary of Economics*, London and Basingstoke: Macmillan, vol. III, 639–45.

Patinkin, D. and O. Steiger (1989), 'In search of the "veil of money" and the "neutrality of money": a note on the origin of terms', *Scandinavian Journal of Economics*, **91** (1), 131–46.

Pearce, D., K. Hamilton and G. Atkinson (1996), 'Measuring sustainable development: progress on indicators', *Environment and Development Economics*, **1** (1), 85–101.

Phillips, A.W. (1958), 'The relation between unemployment and the rate of change of money wage rates in the United Kingdom, 1861–1957', *Economica*, **25** (100), 283–99.

Piffaretti, N. (2000), *Monnaie électronique, monnaie et intermédiation bancaire*, unpublished PhD dissertation, University of Fribourg.

Pigou, A.C. (1917), 'The value of money', *Quarterly Journal of Economics*, **32** (1), 38–65.

Pigou, A.C. (1920), *The Economics of Welfare*, London: Macmillan.

Pigou, A.C. (1949), *The Veil of Money*, London: Macmillan.

Pollak, R.A. (1989), *The Theory of the Cost-of-Living Index*, Oxford and New York: Oxford University Press.

Pollak, R.A. (1998), 'The consumer price index: a research agenda and three proposals', *Journal of Economic Perspectives*, **12** (1), 69–78.

Poterba, J.M. and J.J. Rotemberg (1987), 'Money in the utility function: an empirical implementation', in W.A. Barnett and K.J. Singleton (eds), *New Approaches to Monetary Economics*, ('International Symposia in Economic Theory and Econometrics', 1), Cambridge: Cambridge University Press, 219–40.

Prais, S.J. (1959), 'Whose cost of living?', *Review of Economic Studies*, **26** (170), 126–34.

Quah, D. and S.P. Vahey (1995), 'Measuring core inflation', *Economic Journal*, **105** (432), 1130–44.

Raff, D.M.G. and M. Trajtenberg (1997), 'Quality-adjusted prices for the American automobile industry: 1906–1940', in T.F. Bresnahan and R.J. Gordon (eds), *The Economics of New Goods*, ('Studies in Income and Wealth', 58), Chicago and London: University of Chicago Press (for the National Bureau of Economic Research), 71–107.

Randolph, W.C. (1988), 'Housing depreciation and aging bias in the consumer price index', *Journal of Business and Economic Statistics*, **6** (3), 359–71.

Realfonzo, R. (1998), *Money and Banking: Theory and Debate (1900–1940)*, Cheltenham and Northampton: Edward Elgar Publishing Ltd.

Realfonzo, R. (1999), 'French circuit school', in P.A. O'Hara (ed.), *Encyclopedia of Political Economy*, London and New York: Routledge, vol. I, 375–8.

Reinsdorf, M. (1993), 'The effect of outlet price differentials on the U.S. consumer price index', in M.F. Foss, M.E. Manser and A.H. Young (eds), *Price Measurements and Their Uses*, ('Studies in Income and Wealth', 57), Chicago and London: University of Chicago Press (for the National Bureau of Economic Research), 227–54.

Reserve Bank of New Zealand (1997), *Recommendations to the 1997 CPI Revision Advisory Committee*, Wellington: Reserve Bank of New Zealand.

Ricardo, D. (1810/1951), *The High Price of Bullion, A Proof of the Depreciation of Bank Notes*, London: John Murray. Reprinted in P. Sraffa and M. Dobb (eds), *The Works and Correspondence of David Ricardo* (vol. III *Pamphlets and Papers 1809–1811*), Cambridge: Cambridge University Press, 47–127.

Ricardo, D. (1824/1951), *Plan for the Establishment of a National Bank*, London: John Murray. Reprinted in P. Sraffa and M. Dobb (eds), *The Works and Correspondence of David Ricardo* (vol. IV *Pamphlets and Papers 1815–1823*), Cambridge: Cambridge University Press, 271–300.

Ricardo, D. (1985), *Scritti monetari*, ('Bibliotheca Biographica'), Roma: Istituto della Enciclopedia Italiana.

Richter, M.K. (1966), 'Invariance axioms and economic indexes', *Econometrica*, **34** (4), 739–55.

Robertson, D.H. (1922/1937), *Money*, ('Cambridge Economic Handbooks', 2), Cambridge: Cambridge University Press.

Robinson, J. (1933), 'The theory of money and the analysis of output', *Review of Economic Studies*, **1** (1), 22–6.

Robinson, J. (1956), *The Accumulation of Capital*, London: Macmillan.

Rochon, L.-P. (1999a), *Credit, Money and Production: An Alternative Post-Keynesian Approach*, Cheltenham and Northampton: Edward Elgar Publishing Ltd.

Rochon, L.-P. (1999b), 'The creation and circulation of endogenous money: a circuit dynamique approach', *Journal of Economic Issues*, **33** (1), 1–21.

Rogers, C. (1989), *Money, Interest and Capital: A Study in the Foundations of Monetary Theory*, ('Modern Cambridge Economics'), Cambridge:

Cambridge University Press.
Rogers, C. and T.K. Rymes (1997), 'Keynes's monetary theory of value and modern banking', in G.C. Harcourt and P.A. Riach (eds), *A 'Second Edition' of The General Theory*, London and New York: Routledge, vol. I, 304–23.
Rossi, S. (1996), *La moneta europea: utopia o realtà? L'emissione dell'ecu nel rispetto delle sovranità nazionali*, ('Prospettive internazionali', 3), Bellinzona and Lausanne: Meta-Edizioni.
Rossi, S. (1997), *Modalités d'institution et de fonctionnement d'une banque centrale supranationale. Le cas de la Banque Centrale Européenne*, ('Publications Universitaires Européennes: Série 5', 2013), Berne and Paris: Peter Lang.
Rossi, S. (1998), 'Endogenous money and banking activity: some notes on the workings of modern payment systems', *Studi economici*, **53** (66), 23–56.
Rossi, S. (1999), 'Money, value, and effective demand: a circular flow analysis', *Working Papers*, University of Fribourg (Faculty of Economic and Social Sciences), 322.
Rossi, S. and B. Dafflon (1996), 'La logique des critères budgétaires du *Traité sur l'Union Européenne*: premiers éléments d'analyse critique', *Working Papers*, University of Fribourg (Faculty of Economic and Social Sciences), 272.
Rossi, S. and B. Dafflon (1999), 'Public accounting fudges towards EMU: a first empirical survey and some public choice considerations', *Public Choice*, **101** (1–2), 59–84.
Rotelli, C. (1982), *Le origini della controversia monetaria (1797–1844)*, ('Saggi', 236), Bologna: Il Mulino.
Rotheim, R.J. (1981), 'Keynes' monetary theory of value (1933)', *Journal of Post Keynesian Economics*, **3** (4), 568–85.
Rowthorn, R.E. (1977), 'Conflict, inflation and money', *Cambridge Journal of Economics*, **1** (3), 215–39. Reprinted in R.E. Rowthorn (1980), *Capitalism, Conflict and Inflation: Essays in Political Economy*, London: Lawrence and Wishart, 148–81.
Sadigh, É. (1988), 'La spesa del profitto e le disfunzioni del sistema economico', in A. Graziani and M. Messori (eds), *Moneta e produzione*, ('Nuova Biblioteca Scientifica Einaudi', 81), Torino: Einaudi, 45–56.
Samuelson, P.A. and S. Swamy (1974), 'Invariant economic index numbers and canonical duality: survey and synthesis', *American Economic Review*, **64** (4), 566–93.
Sandilands Committee (1975), *Inflation Accounting: Report of the Inflation*

Accounting Committee, London: HMSO (Cmnd 6225).

Sargent, T.J. (1996), 'Expectations and the nonneutrality of Lucas', *Journal of Monetary Economics*, **37** (3), 535–48.

Sargent, T.J. and N. Wallace (1975), '"Rational" expectations, the optimal monetary instrument, and the optimal money supply rule', *Journal of Political Economy*, **83** (2), 241–54.

Sargent, T.J. and N. Wallace (1982), 'The real-bills doctrine versus the quantity theory: a reconsideration', *Journal of Political Economy*, **90** (6), 1212–36.

Schlicht, E. (1985), *Isolation and Aggregation in Economics*, Berlin and Heidelberg: Springer Verlag.

Schmitt, B. (1959), 'L'équilibre de la monnaie', *Revue d'économie politique*, **69** (5), 921–50.

Schmitt, B. (1966), *Monnaie, salaires et profits*, Paris: Presses Universitaires de France (also Albeuve: Castella, 1975).

Schmitt, B. (1972), *Macroeconomic Theory: A Fundamental Revision*, Albeuve: Castella.

Schmitt, B. (1975), *Théorie unitaire de la monnaie, nationale et internationale*, Albeuve: Castella.

Schmitt, B. (1982), 'Time as quantum', in M. Baranzini (ed.), *Advances in Economic Theory*, Oxford and New York: Basil Blackwell and St. Martin's Press, 115–25.

Schmitt, B. (1984), *Inflation, chômage et malformations du capital*, Paris and Albeuve: Economica and Castella.

Schmitt, B. (1986), 'The process of formation of economics in relation to other sciences', in M. Baranzini and R. Scazzieri (eds), *Foundations of Economics: Structures of Inquiry and Economic Theory*, Oxford and New York: Basil Blackwell and St. Martin's Press, 103–32.

Schmitt, B. (1988), 'The identity of aggregate supply and demand in time', in A. Barrère (ed.), *The Foundations of Keynesian Analysis*, London and Basingstoke: Macmillan, 169–93.

Schmitt, B. (1993), 'Les unités de salaires et le concept de valeur dans la *Théorie générale*', Lecture delivered at the University of Bourgogne, unpublished.

Schmitt, B. (1995–96), *Cours de théorie monétaire*, University of Fribourg, 2 vols, unpublished typescript.

Schmitt, B. (1996a), 'A new paradigm for the determination of money prices', in G. Deleplace and E.J. Nell (eds), *Money in Motion: The Post Keynesian and Circulation Approaches*, London and New York: Macmillan and St. Martin's Press, 104–38.

Schmitt, B. (1996b), 'Unemployment: is there a principal cause?', in A. Cencini and M. Baranzini (eds), *Inflation and Unemployment: Contributions to a New Macroeconomic Approach*, ('Routledge Studies in the Modern World Economy', 4), London and New York: Routledge, 75–105.

Schmitt, B. and A. Cencini (1982), 'Wages and profits in a theory of emissions', in M. Baranzini (ed.), *Advances in Economic Theory*, Oxford and New York: Basil Blackwell and St. Martin's Press, 137–46.

Schumpeter, J.A. (1954/1994), *History of Economic Analysis*, London: Routledge.

Screpanti, E. (1997), 'Banks, increasing risk, and the endogenous money supply', *Monte dei Paschi di Siena Economic Notes*, **26** (3), 567–87.

Shapiro, M.D. and D.W. Wilcox (1996), 'Mismeasurement in the consumer price index: an evaluation', *NBER Working Paper*, 5590.

Shapiro, M.D. and D.W. Wilcox (1997), 'Alternative strategies for aggregating prices in the CPI', *Federal Reserve Bank of St. Louis Review*, **79** (3), 113–25.

Shubik, M. (1987), 'Fiat money', in J. Eatwell, M. Milgate and P. Newman (eds), *The New Palgrave: A Dictionary of Economics*, London and Basingstoke: Macmillan, vol. II, 316–17.

Sidrauski, M. (1967), 'Inflation and economic growth', *Journal of Political Economy*, **75** (6), 796–810.

Siesto, V. (1987), 'Macroeconomic statistics and the submerged economy', *Review of Economic Conditions in Italy*, **1** (1), 21–47.

Silver, M. and C. Ioannidis (1994), 'The measurement of inflation; untimely weights and alternative formulae: European evidence', *The Statistician*, **43** (4), 551–62.

Skott, P. (1989), *Conflict and Effective Demand in Economic Growth*, Cambridge: Cambridge University Press.

Smith, A. (1776/1970), *The Wealth of Nations*, Harmondsworth: Penguin.

Smithin, J. (1997), 'An alternative monetary model of inflation and growth', *Review of Political Economy*, **9** (4), 395–409.

Smithin, J. (ed.) (2000), *What is Money?*, ('Routledge International Studies in Money and Banking', 6), London and New York: Routledge.

Spindt, P.A. (1985), 'Money is what money does: monetary aggregation and the equation of exchange', *Journal of Political Economy*, **93** (1), 175–204.

Sraffa, P. (1961), 'Comment', in F.A. Lutz and D.C. Hague (eds), *The Theory of Capital: Proceedings of a Conference held by the International Economic Association*, London and New York: Macmillan and St. Martin's Press, 305–6.

Starr, R.M. (1980), 'General equilibrium approaches to the study of monetary economies: comments on recent developments', in J.H. Kareken and N. Wallace (eds), *Models of Monetary Economies*, Minneapolis: Federal Reserve Bank of Minneapolis, 261–3.

Starr, R.M. (1989), 'Money in formal general equilibrium analysis', in R.M. Starr (ed.), *General Equilibrium Models of Monetary Economies: Studies in the Static Foundations of Monetary Theory*, ('Economic Theory, Econometrics, and Mathematical Economics'), San Diego: Academic Press, 3–6.

Stein, J.L. (1976), 'A Keynesian can be a monetarist', in J.L. Stein (ed.), *Monetarism*, ('Studies in Monetary Economics', 1), Amsterdam: North-Holland Publishing Company, 253–71.

Steindel, C. (1997), 'Are there good alternatives to the CPI?', *Federal Reserve Bank of New York Current Issues in Economics and Finance*, **3** (6), 1–6.

Stoker, T.M. (1993), 'Empirical approaches to the problem of aggregation over individuals', *Journal of Economic Literature*, **31** (4), 1827–74.

Tavlas, G.S. (1997), 'Chicago, Harvard, and the doctrinal foundations of monetary economics', *Journal of Political Economy*, **105** (1), 153–77.

Tavlas, G.S. (1998), 'Was the monetarist tradition invented?', *Journal of Economic Perspectives*, **12** (4), 211–22.

Taylor, J.B. (1985), 'Rational expectations models in macroeconomics', in K.J. Arrow and S. Honkapohja (eds), *Frontiers of Economics*, Oxford and New York: Basil Blackwell.

Taylor, J.B. (1997), 'How should monetary policy respond to shocks while maintaining long-run price stability? – Conceptual issues', paper delivered at the Annual meeting of the Swiss Society of Statistics and Economics, Lucerne, 20–21 March 1997, mimeo.

Tobin, J. (1980), 'Discussion', in J.H. Kareken and N. Wallace (eds), *Models of Monetary Economies*, Minneapolis: Federal Reserve Bank of Minneapolis, 83–90.

Tobin, J. (1981), 'The monetarist counter-revolution today: an appraisal', *Economic Journal*, **91** (361), 29–42.

Tobin, J. (1987), 'Commercial banks as creators of "money"', in *Essays in Economics* (vol. I *Macroeconomics*), Cambridge (Massachussetts): MIT Press (originally published by North-Holland Publishing Company), 272–82.

Törnqvist, L. (1936), 'The Bank of Finland's consumption price index', *Bank of Finland Monthly Bulletin*, **16** (10), 27–34.

Torr, C. (1992), 'The dual role of user cost in the derivation of Keynes's aggregate supply function', *Review of Political Economy*, **4** (1), 1–17.

Torr, C. (1997), 'User cost', in G.C. Harcourt and P.A. Riach (eds), *A 'Second Edition' of The General Theory*, London and New York: Routledge, vol. I, 132–44.

Trajtenberg, M. (1990), 'Product innovations, price indices and the (mis)measurement of economic performance', *NBER Working Paper*, 3261.

Triplett, J.E. (1969), 'Automobiles and hedonic quality measurement', *Journal of Political Economy*, **77** (3), 408–17.

Triplett, J.E. (1975), 'The measurement of inflation: a survey of research on the accuracy of price indexes', in P.H. Earl (ed.), *Analysis of Inflation*, Lexington: Lexington Books, 19–82.

Triplett, J.E. (1980), 'Comment to A.S. Blinder's "The consumer price index and the measurement of recent inflation"', *Brookings Papers on Economic Activity*, **11** (2), 567–72.

Triplett, J.E. (1987), 'Hedonic functions and hedonic indexes', in J. Eatwell, M. Milgate and P. Newman (eds), *The New Palgrave: A Dictionary of Economics*, London and Basingstoke: Macmillan, vol. II, 630–4.

Triplett, J.E. (1990), 'Hedonic methods in statistical agency environments: an intellectual biopsy', in E.R. Berndt and J.E. Triplett (eds), *Fifty Years of Economic Measurement: The Jubilee of the Conference on Research in Income and Wealth*, ('Studies in Income and Wealth', 54), Chicago and London: University of Chicago Press (for the National Bureau of Economic Research), 207–37.

Triplett, J.E. (1993), 'Comment', in M.F. Foss, M.E. Manser and A.H. Young (eds), *Price Measurements and Their Uses*, ('Studies in Income and Wealth', 57), Chicago and London: University of Chicago Press (for the National Bureau of Economic Research), 197–206.

Turvey, R. (ed.) (1989), *Consumer Price Indices: An ILO Manual*, Geneva: International Labour Organisation.

Ufficio federale di statistica (1993), *Il nuovo indice nazionale dei prezzi al consumo: maggio 1993 = 100*, ('Attualità UST', 5), Berna: Ufficio federale di statistica.

Vallageas, B. (1988), 'Le lancinant problème de Bernard Schmitt', *Économies et Sociétés*, ('Série Monnaie et Production', 5), **22** (9), 189–90.

Van Daal, J. and A.H.Q.M. Merkies (1984), *Aggregation in Economic Research: From Individual to Macro Relations*, Dordrecht: Reidel & Co.

Vane, H.R. and J.L. Thompson (1979), *Monetarism: Theory, Evidence and Policy*, Oxford: Martin Robertson.

Vercelli, A. (1991), *Methodological Foundations of Macroeconomics:*

Keynes and Lucas, Cambridge: Cambridge University Press.

Vercelli, A. (1998), 'Minsky, Keynes, and the structural instability of a monetary economy', paper delivered at an international conference on 'The Legacy of Hyman P. Minsky', University of Bergamo, 11–12 December 1998, mimeo.

Verdon, M. (1996), *Keynes and the 'Classics': A Study in Language, Epistemology and Mistaken Identities*, ('Routledge Studies in the History of Economics', 7), London and New York: Routledge.

Wallace, N. (1980), 'The overlapping generations model of fiat money', in J.H. Kareken and N. Wallace (eds), *Models of Monetary Economies*, Minneapolis: Federal Reserve Bank of Minneapolis, 49–82.

Wallace, N. (1988), 'A suggestion for oversimplifying the theory of money', *Economic Journal*, **98**, Association of University Teachers of Economics (1987) Conference Supplement, 25–36.

Wallace, N. (1998), 'Introduction to modeling money and studying monetary policy', *Journal of Economic Theory*, **81** (2), 223–31.

Walliser, B. and C. Prou (1988), 'Micro-économie et macro-économie', in *La science économique*, ('Économie et Société'), Paris: Seuil, 107–23.

Walras, L. (1954), *Elements of Pure Economics or the Theory of Social Wealth*, translated by W. Jaffé, London: George Allen & Unwin (first French edition 1874).

Watkins, T. (1985), 'Book review of A. Cencini (1984), *Time and the Macroeconomic Analysis of Income*', *Southern Economic Journal*, **52** (2), 596–7.

Weintraub, S. (1978), *Capitalism's Inflation and Unemployment Crisis*, Reading (Massachussetts): Addison Wesley.

White, D. (1999), 'Outlook good, but inflation a worry', *Financial Times*, 10 September 1999, in Deutsche Bundesbank (ed.), *Auszüge aus Presseartikeln*, (61), 3.

White, L.H. (1999), 'Hayek's monetary theory and policy: a critical reconstruction', *Journal of Money, Credit, and Banking*, **31** (1), 109–20.

Whittington, G. (1983), *Inflation Accounting: An Introduction to the Debate*, Cambridge: Cambridge University Press.

Winnett, A. (1992), 'Some semantics of endogeneity', in P. Arestis and V. Chick (eds), *Recent Developments in Post-Keynesian Economics*, Aldershot and Brookfield: Edward Elgar Publishing Ltd, 47–63.

Woodford, M. (1987), 'Credit policy and the price level in a cash-in-advance economy', in W.A. Barnett and K.J. Singleton (eds), *New Approaches to Monetary Economics*, ('International Symposia in Economic Theory and Econometrics', 1), Cambridge: Cambridge University Press, 52–66.

Woodford, M. (1990), 'The optimum quantity of money', in B.M. Friedman and F.H. Hahn (eds), *Handbook of Monetary Economics*, ('Handbooks in Economics', 8), Amsterdam: Elsevier Science B.V., vol. II, 1067–152.

Woodford, M. (1997), 'Doing without money: controlling inflation in a post-monetary world', *NBER Working Paper*, 6188.

Wray, L.R. (1990), *Money and Credit in Capitalist Economies: The Endogenous Money Approach*, Aldershot and Brookfield: Edward Elgar Publishing Ltd.

Wray, L.R. (1998a), 'Modern money', *The Jerome Levy Economics Institute Working Papers*, 252.

Wray, L.R. (1998b), *Understanding Modern Money: The Key to Full Employment and Price Stability*, Cheltenham and Northampton: Edward Elgar Publishing Ltd.

Wray, L.R. (1999), 'Theories of value and the monetary theory of production', *The Jerome Levy Economics Institute Working Papers*, 261.

Wray, L.R. (2000), 'Modern money', in J. Smithin (ed.), *What is Money?*, ('Routledge International Studies in Money and Banking', 6), London and New York: Routledge, 42–66.

Wynne, M.A. (1999), 'Core inflation: a review of some conceptual issues', *European Central Bank Working Paper*, 5.

Wynne, M.A. and F.D. Sigalla (1996), 'A survey of measurement biases in price indexes', *Journal of Economic Surveys*, **10** (1), 55–89.

Name Index

Subject Index